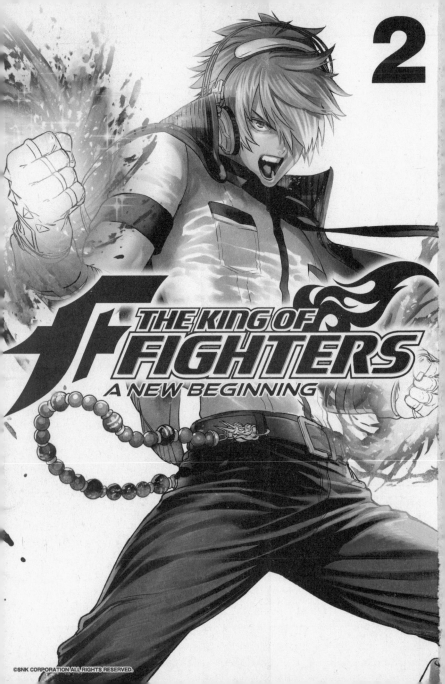

THE KING OF FIGHTERS

FIGHTERS

A NEW BEGINNING

2

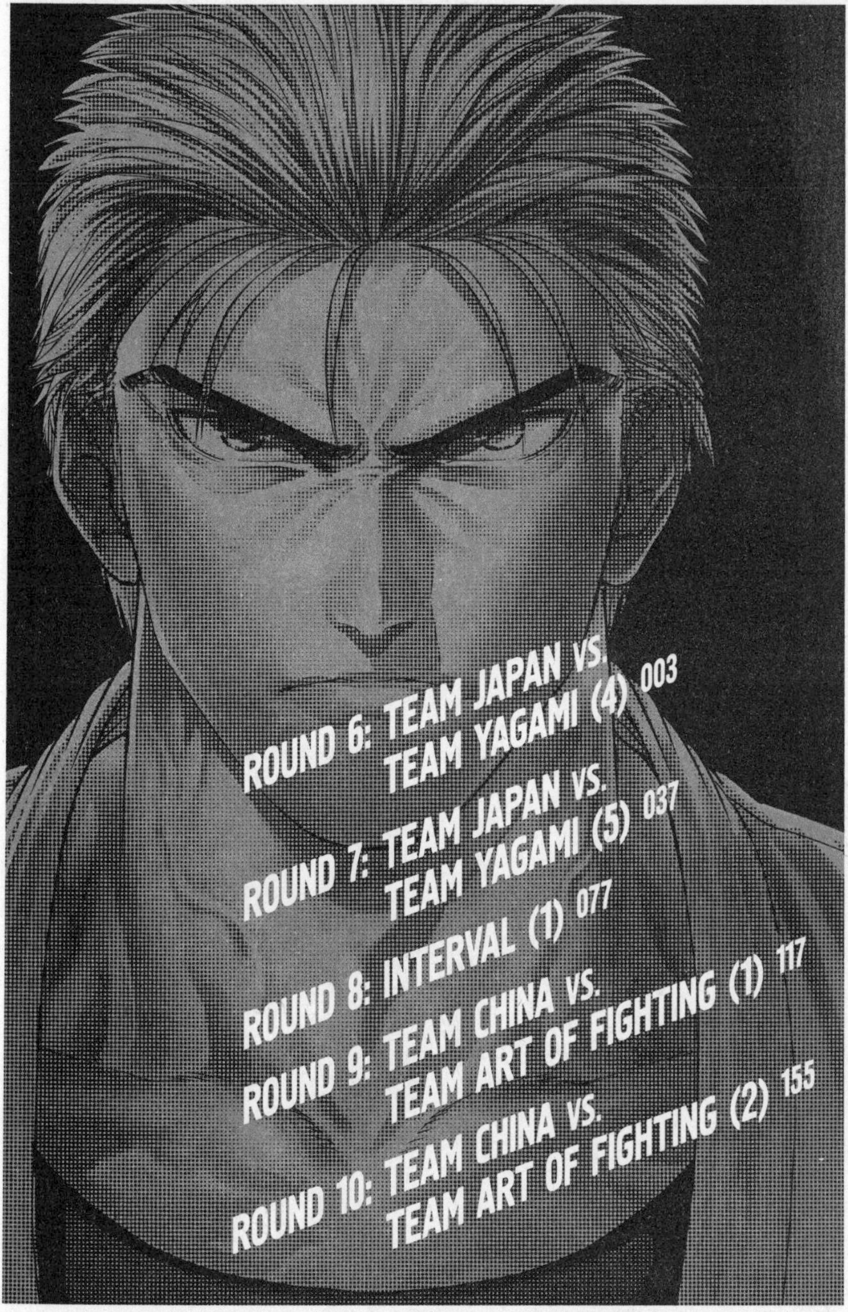

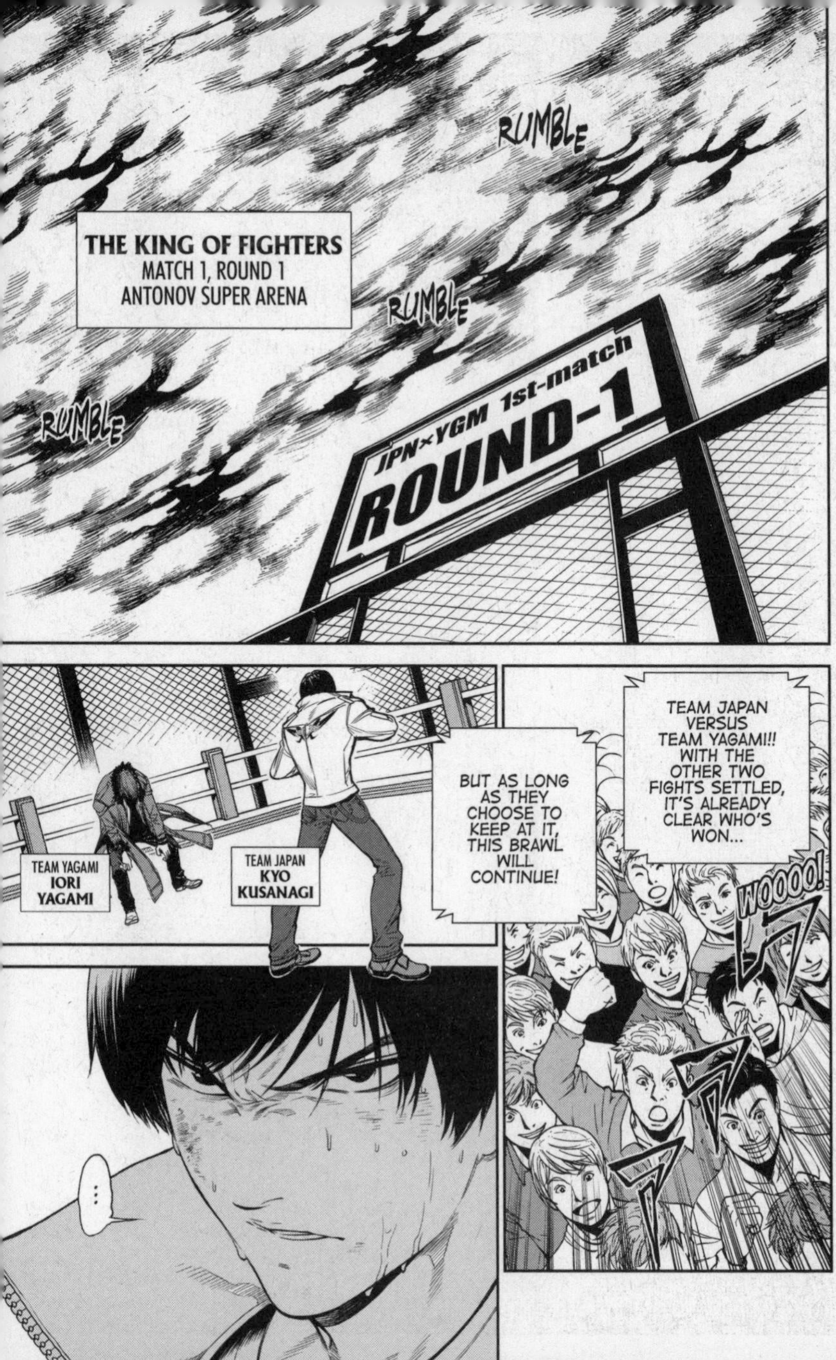
RUMBLE
RUMBLE
RUMBLE
THE KING OF FIGHTERS
MATCH 1, ROUND 1
ANTONOV SUPER ARENA
JPN×YGM 1st-match
ROUND-1
TEAM JAPAN VERSUS TEAM YAGAMI!! WITH THE OTHER TWO FIGHTS SETTLED, IT'S ALREADY CLEAR WHO'S WON...
BUT AS LONG AS THEY CHOOSE TO KEEP AT IT, THIS BRAWL WILL CONTINUE!
WOOOO!
TEAM JAPAN KYO KUSANAGI
TEAM YAGAMI IORI YAGAMI
...

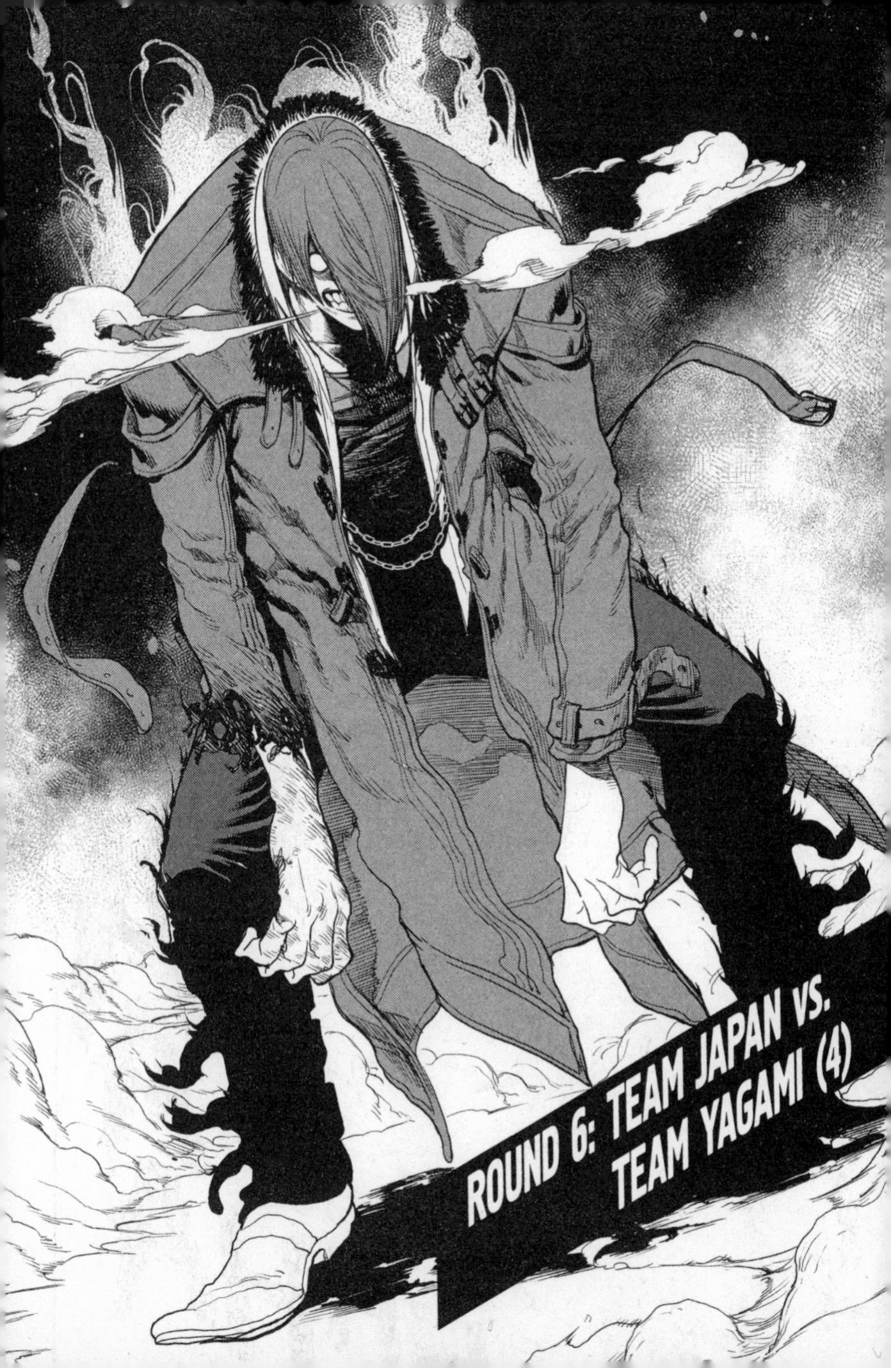
ROUND 6: TEAM JAPAN VS.
TEAM YAGAMI (4)

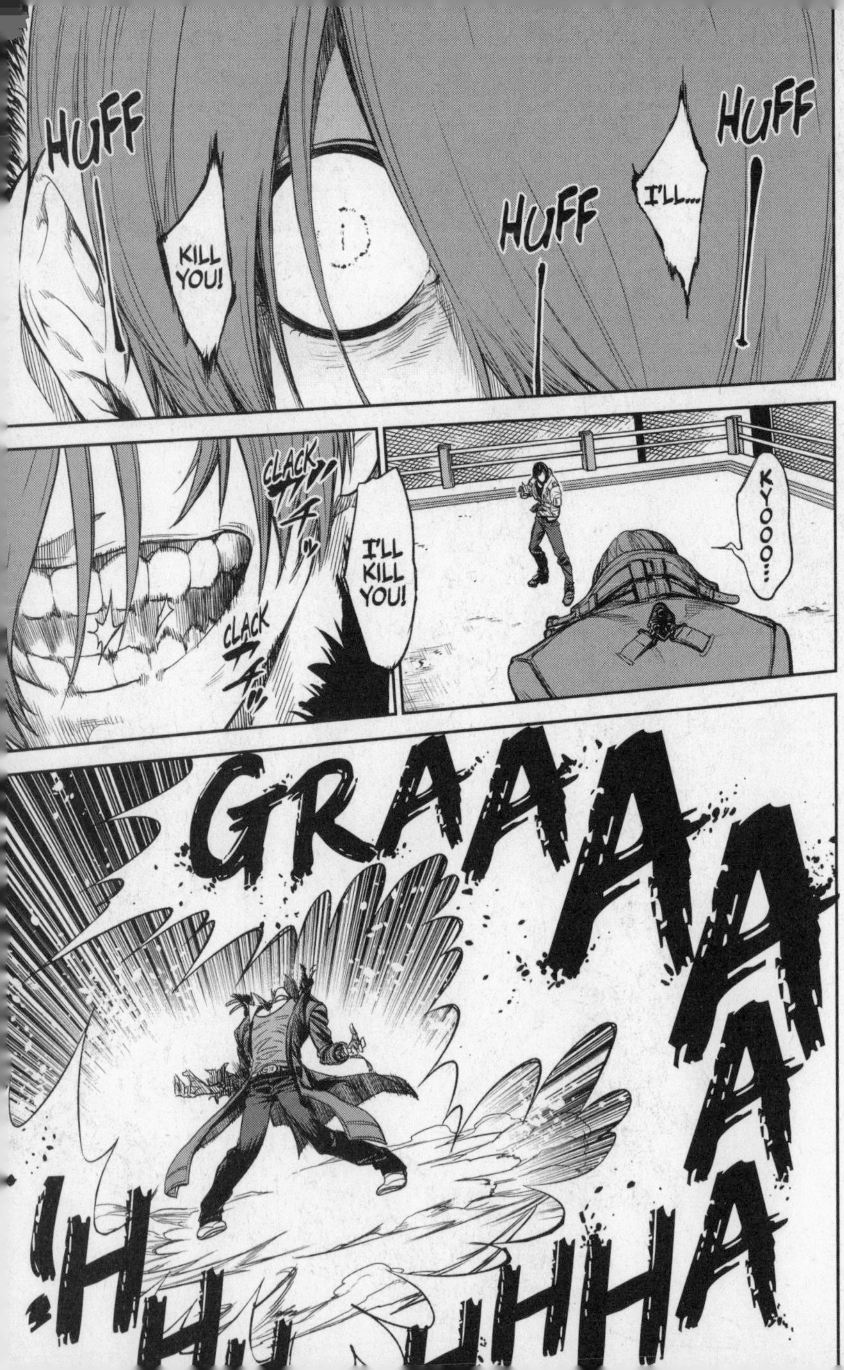

HUFF
I'LL...
HUFF
KILL YOU!
HUFF
KYOOO...
I'LL KILL YOU!
CLACK
CLACK
GRAAAAAAAHHHH!

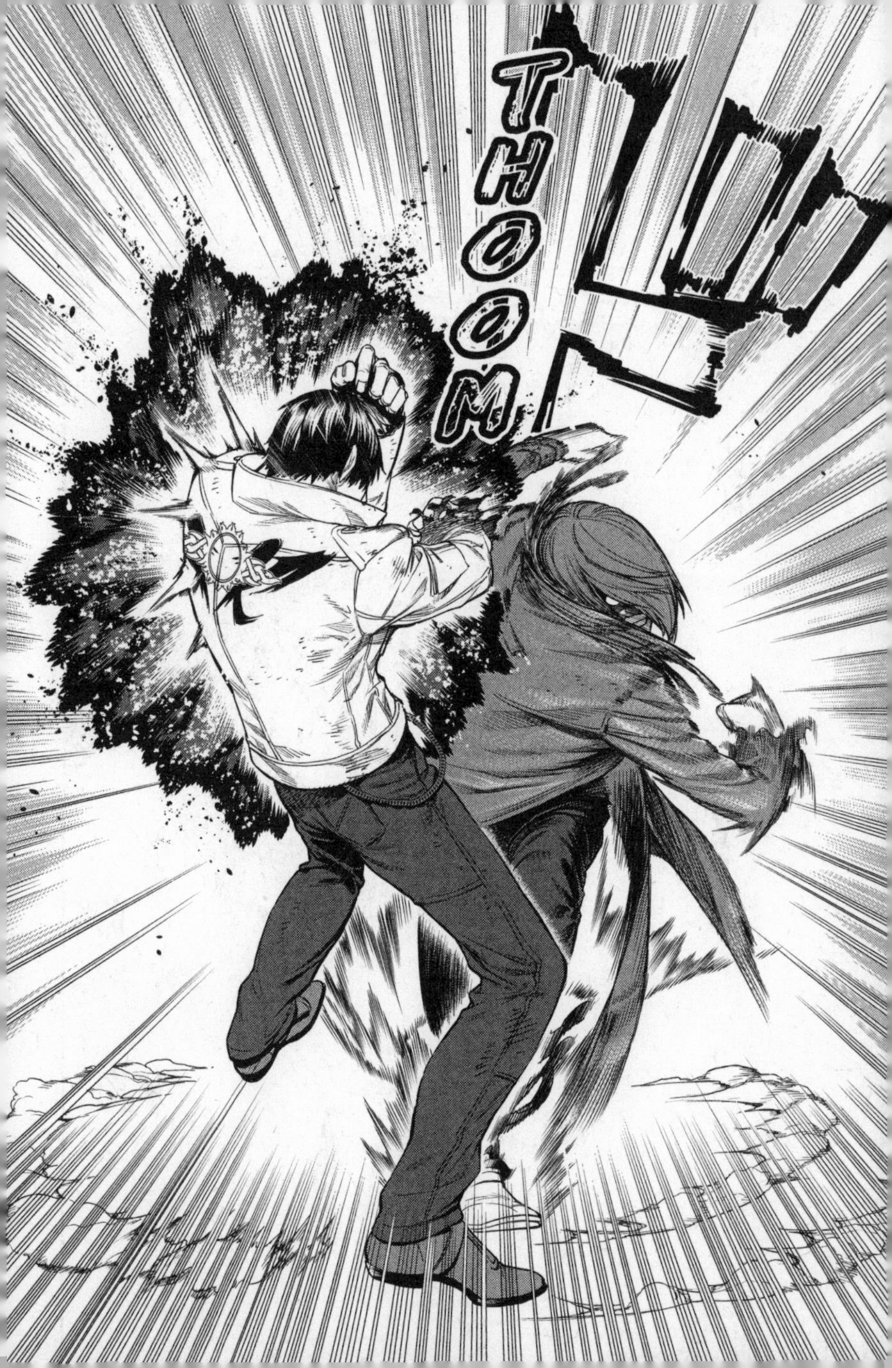
THOOM

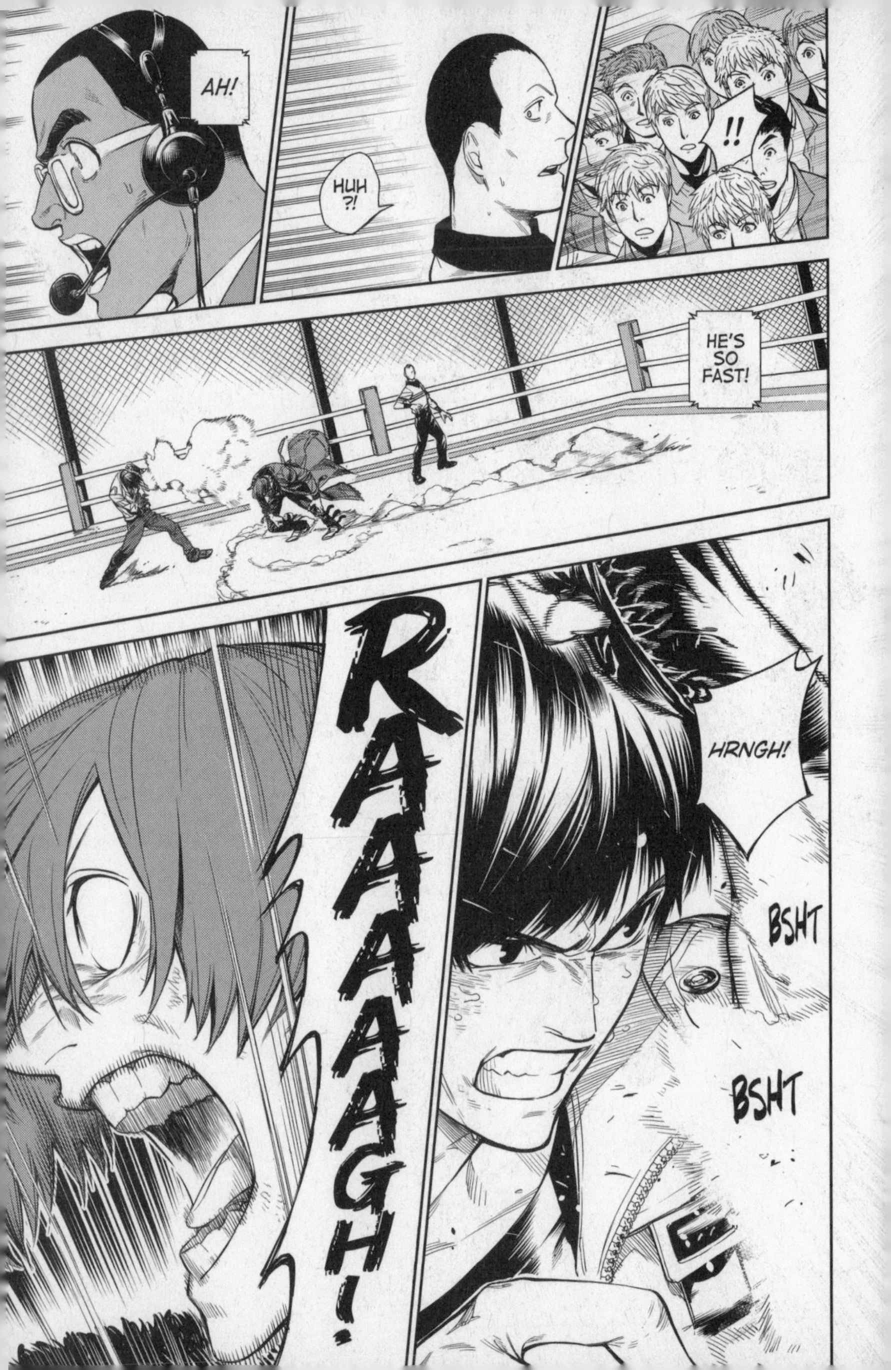
!!
HUH ?!
AH!
HE'S SO FAST!
HRNGH!
BSHT
BSHT
RAAAAAGH!

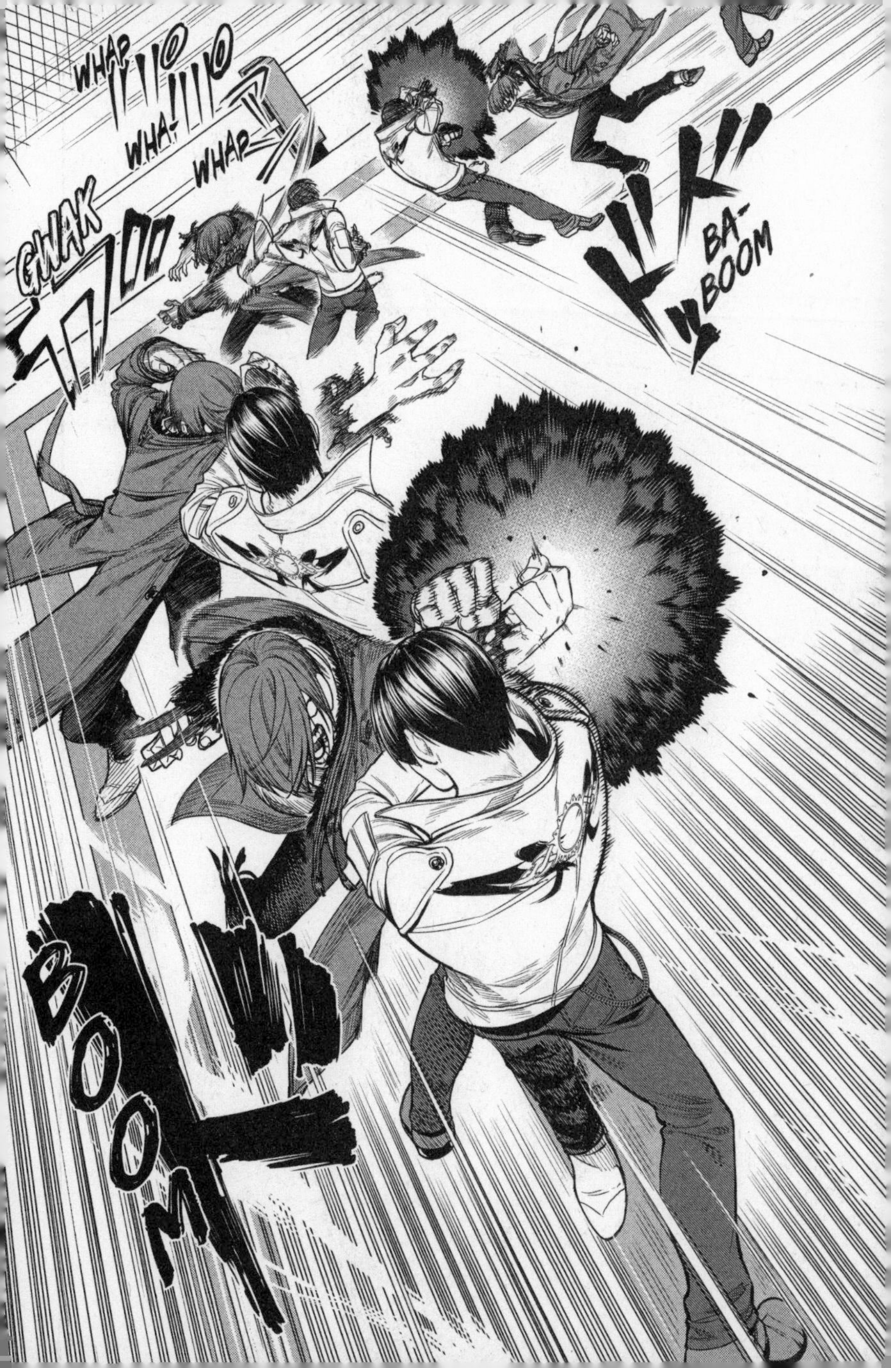
BA-BOOM
WHAP
WHA
WHAP
GWAK
BOOM

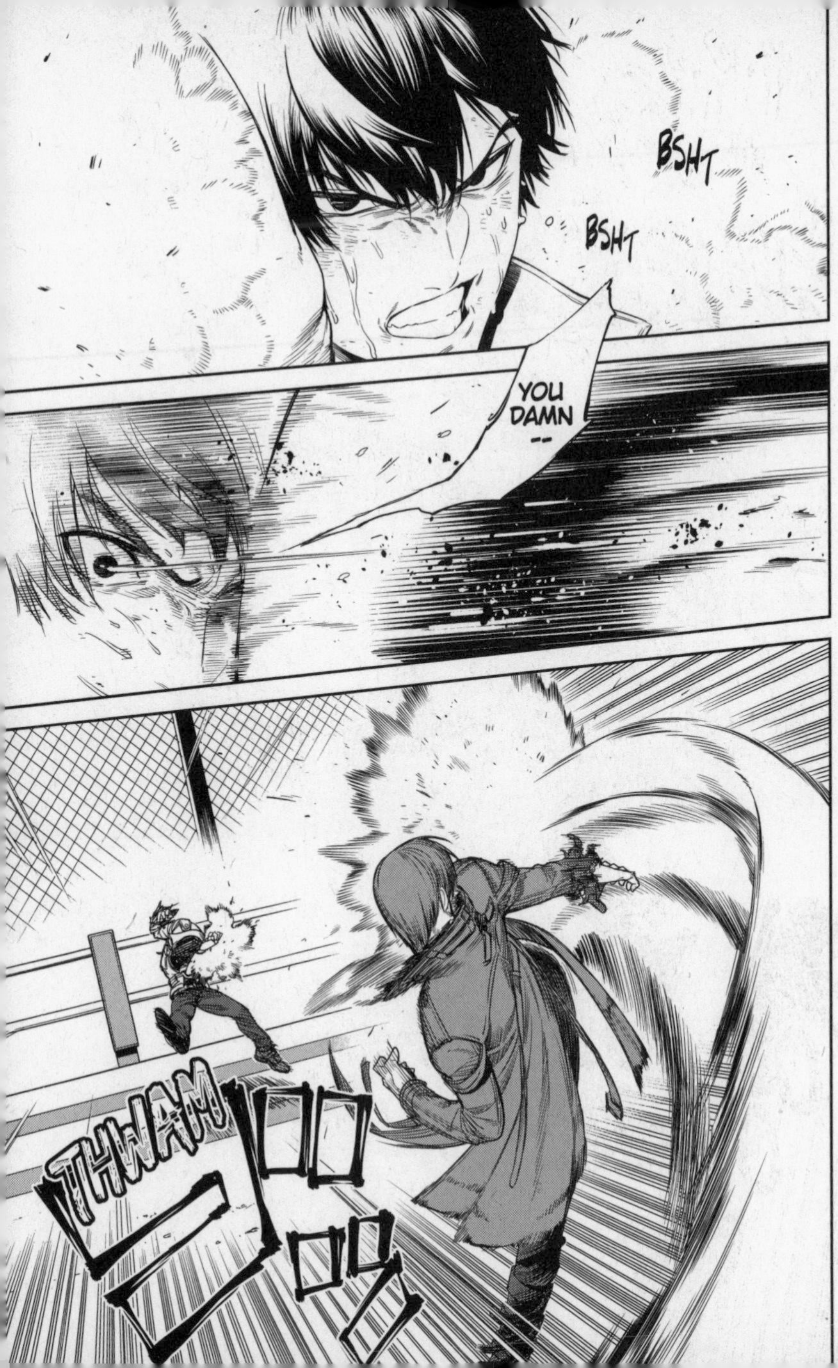
BSHT
BSHT
YOU DAMN --
THWAM

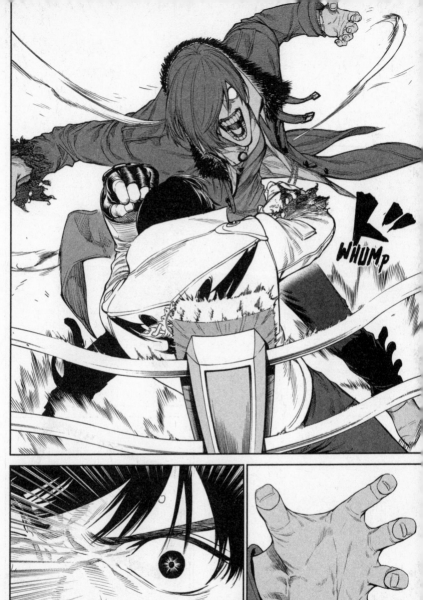

WHUMP

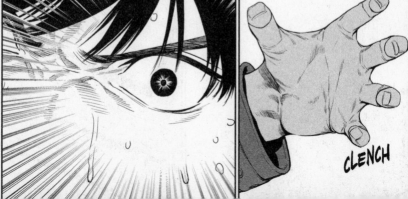

CLENCH

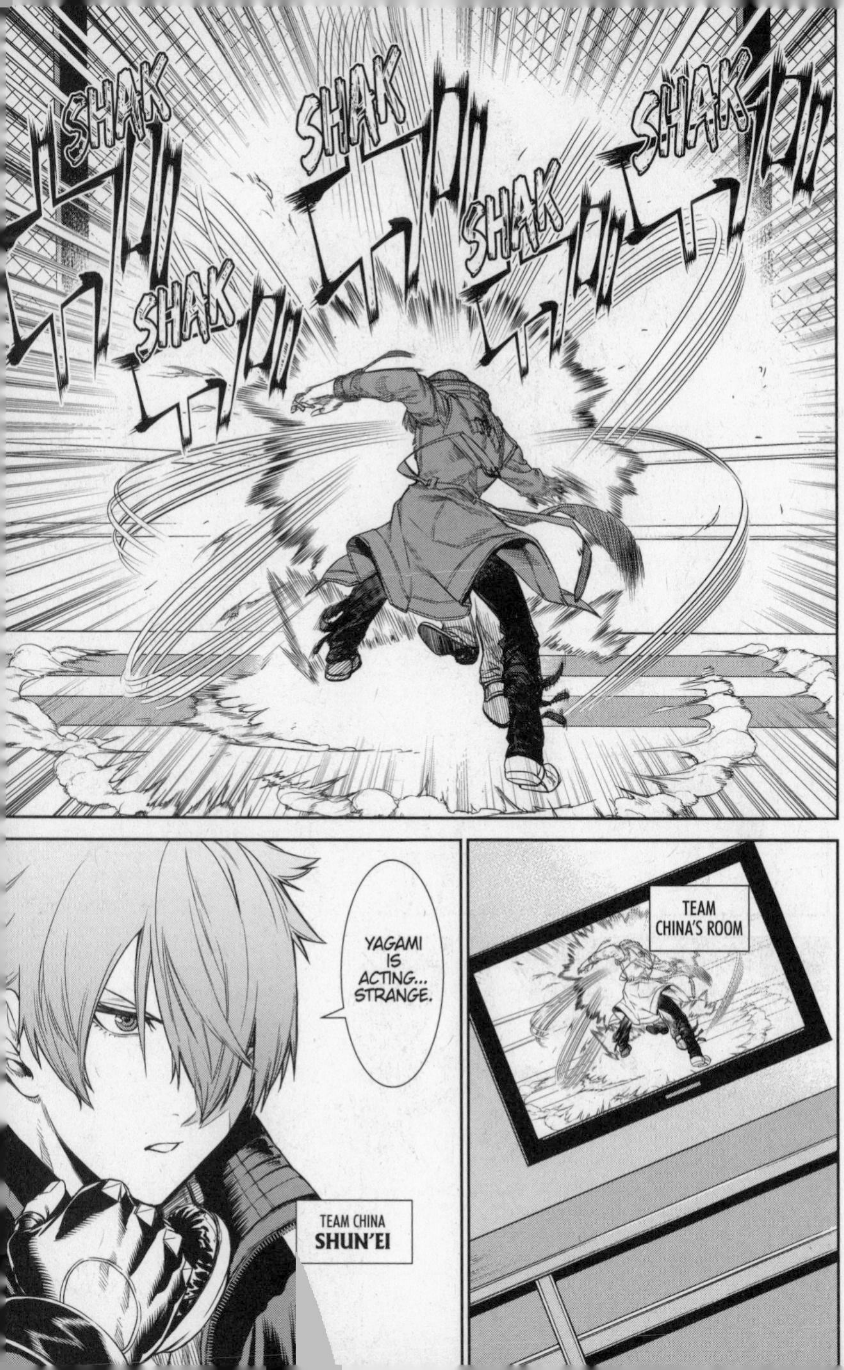
SHAK
SHAK
SHAK
SHAK
SHAK
TEAM CHINA'S ROOM
YAGAMI IS ACTING... STRANGE.
TEAM CHINA
SHUN'EI

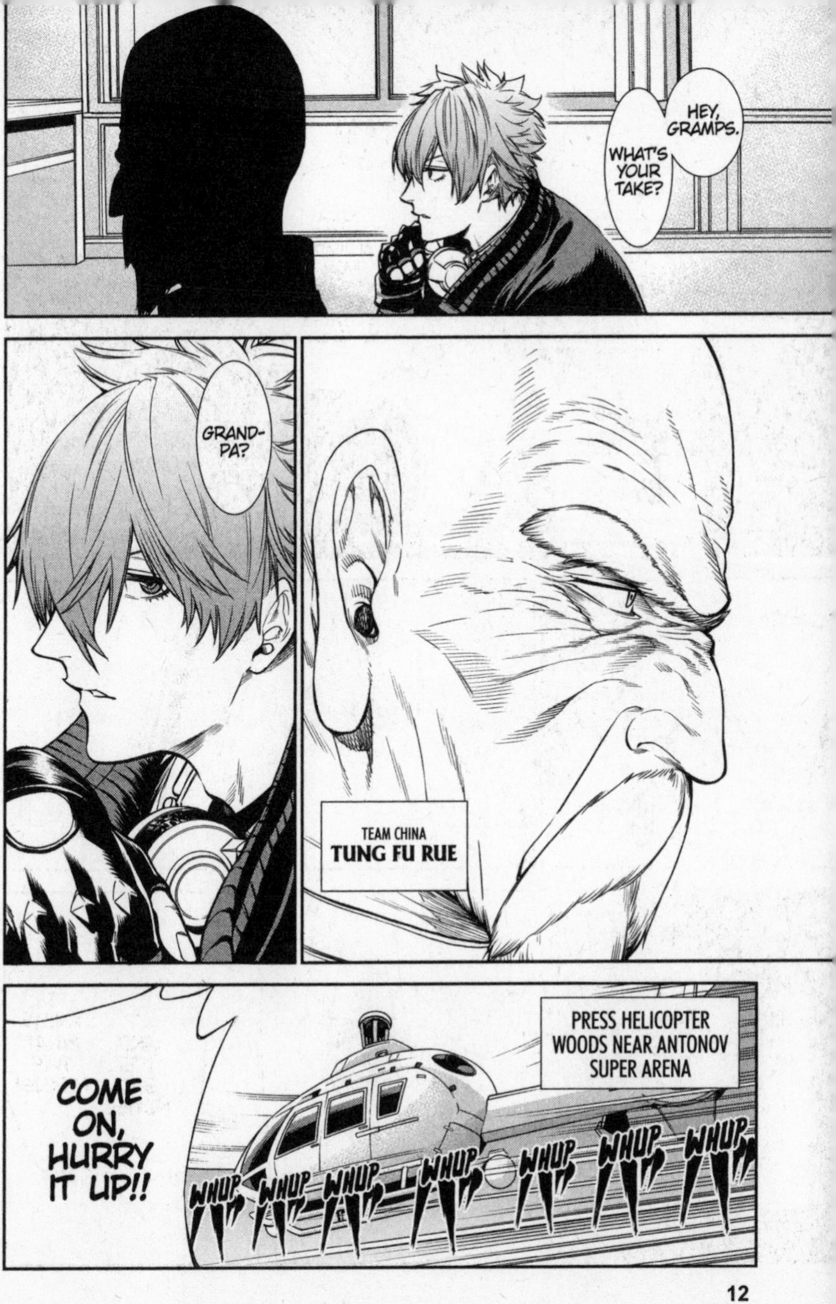
HEY, GRAMPS.
WHAT'S YOUR TAKE?
TEAM CHINA TUNG FU RUE
GRAND-PA?
PRESS HELICOPTER WOODS NEAR ANTONOV SUPER ARENA
COME ON, HURRY IT UP!!
WHUP WHUP WHUP WHUP WHUP WHUP WHUP WHUP

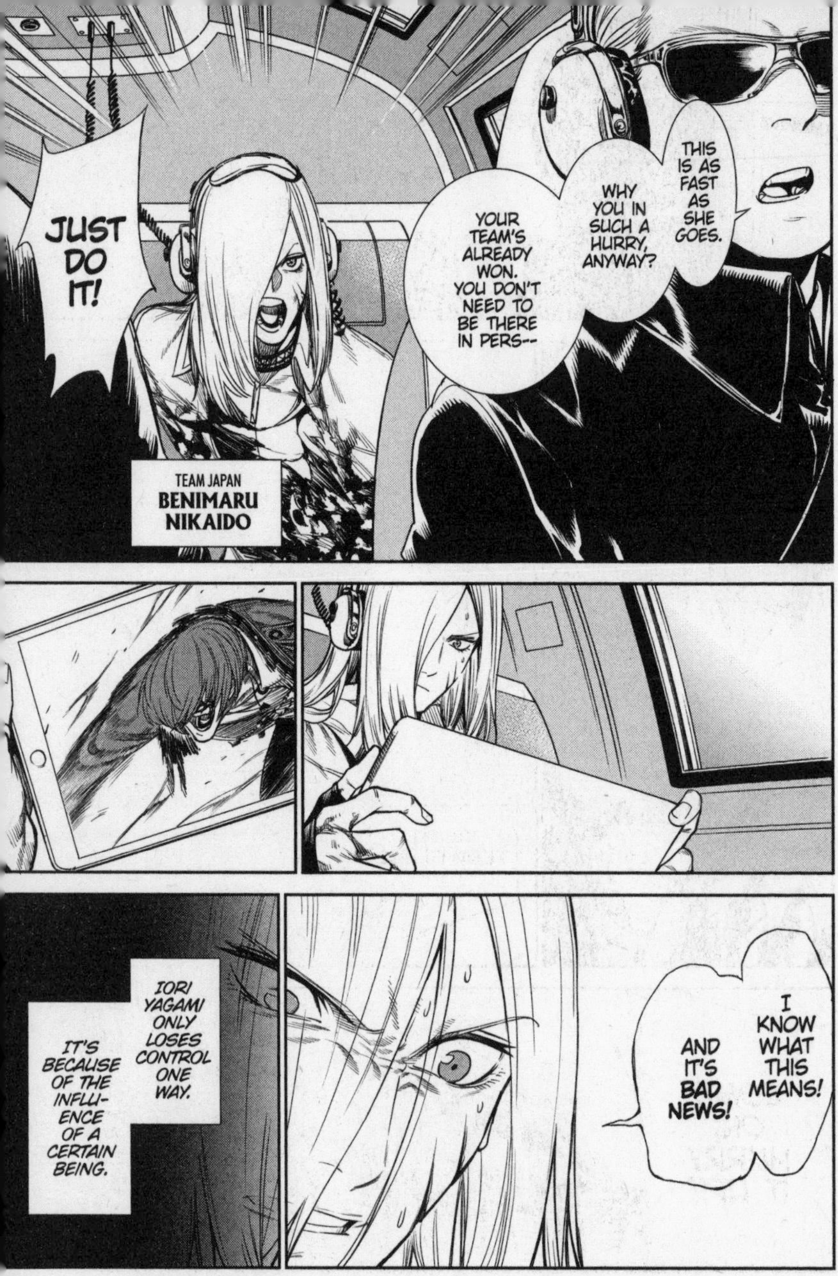
THIS IS AS FAST AS SHE GOES.
WHY YOU IN SUCH A HURRY, ANYWAY?
YOUR TEAM'S ALREADY WON. YOU DON'T NEED TO BE THERE IN PERS--
JUST DO IT!
TEAM JAPAN BENIMARU NIKAIDO
I KNOW WHAT THIS MEANS!
AND IT'S BAD NEWS!
IORI YAGAMI ONLY LOSES CONTROL ONE WAY.
IT'S BECAUSE OF THE INFLUENCE OF A CERTAIN BEING.

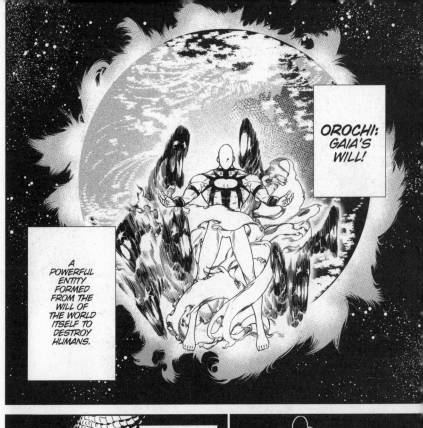

OROCHI: GAIA'S WILL!

A POWERFUL ENTITY FORMED FROM THE WILL OF THE WORLD ITSELF TO DESTROY HUMANS.

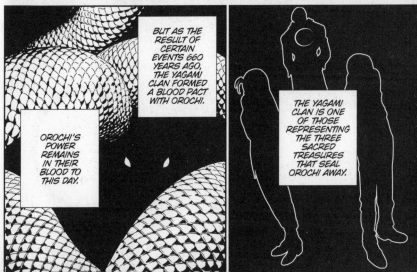

BUT AS THE RESULT OF CERTAIN EVENTS 660 YEARS AGO, THE YAGAMI CLAN FORMED A BLOOD PACT WITH OROCHI.

OROCHI'S POWER REMAINS IN THEIR BLOOD TO THIS DAY.

THE YAGAMI CLAN IS ONE OF THOSE REPRESENTING THE THREE SACRED TREASURES THAT SEAL OROCHI AWAY.

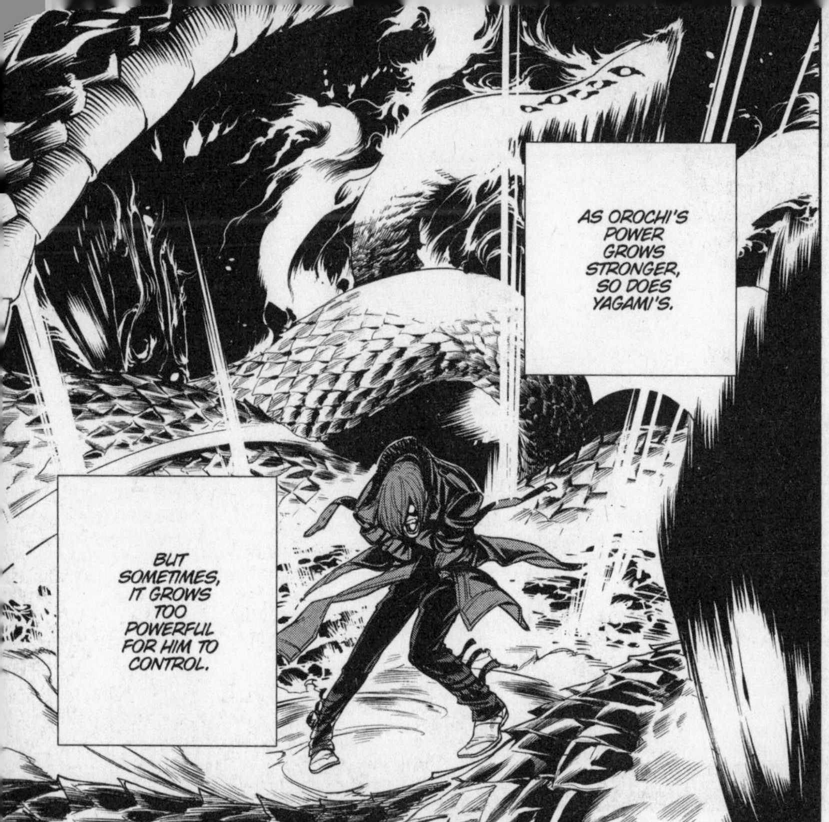
AS OROCHI'S POWER GROWS STRONGER, SO DOES YAGAMI'S.
BUT SOMETIMES, IT GROWS TOO POWERFUL FOR HIM TO CONTROL.
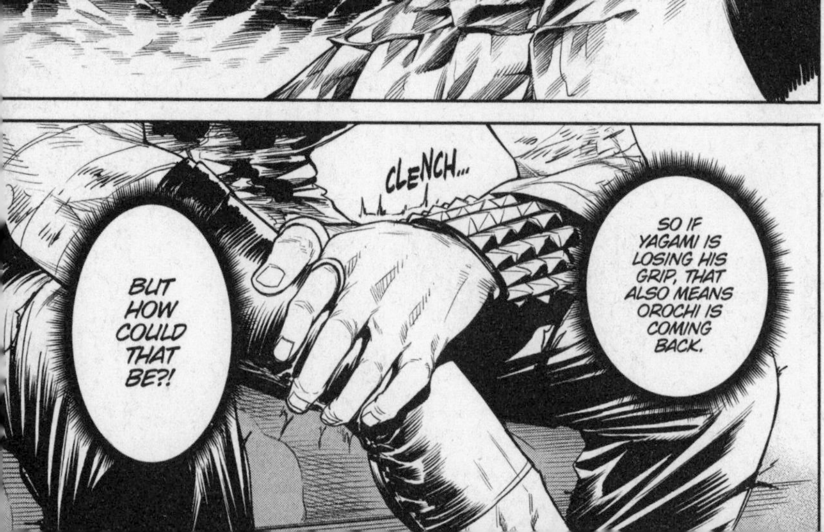
SO IF YAGAMI IS LOSING HIS GRIP, THAT ALSO MEANS OROCHI IS COMING BACK.
CLENCH...
BUT HOW COULD THAT BE?!

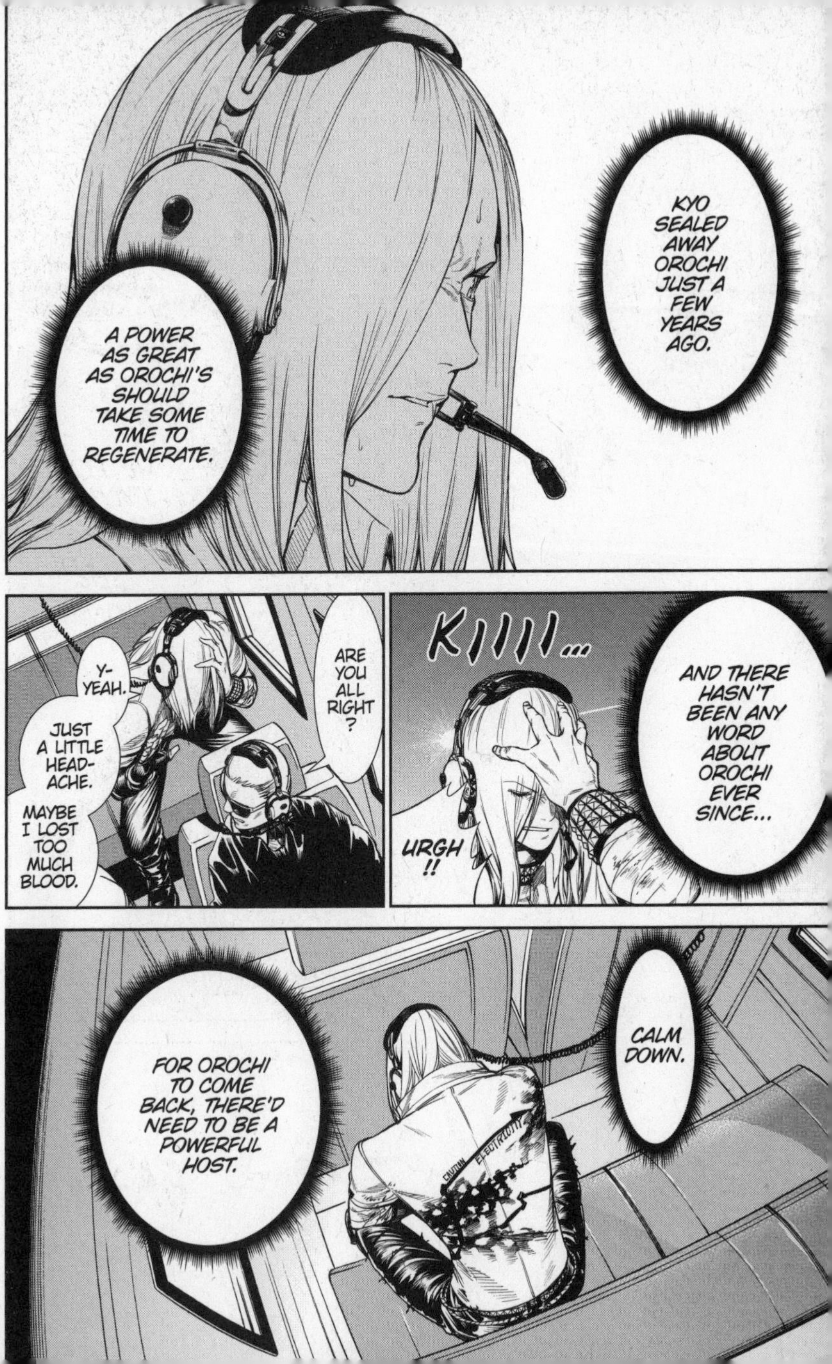
KYO SEALED AWAY OROCHI JUST A FEW YEARS AGO.
A POWER AS GREAT AS OROCHI'S SHOULD TAKE SOME TIME TO REGENERATE.
AND THERE HASN'T BEEN ANY WORD ABOUT OROCHI EVER SINCE...
KIIII...
URGH!!
ARE YOU ALL RIGHT?
Y-YEAH.
JUST A LITTLE HEAD-ACHE.
MAYBE I LOST TOO MUCH BLOOD.
CALM DOWN.
FOR OROCHI TO COME BACK, THERE'D NEED TO BE A POWERFUL HOST.

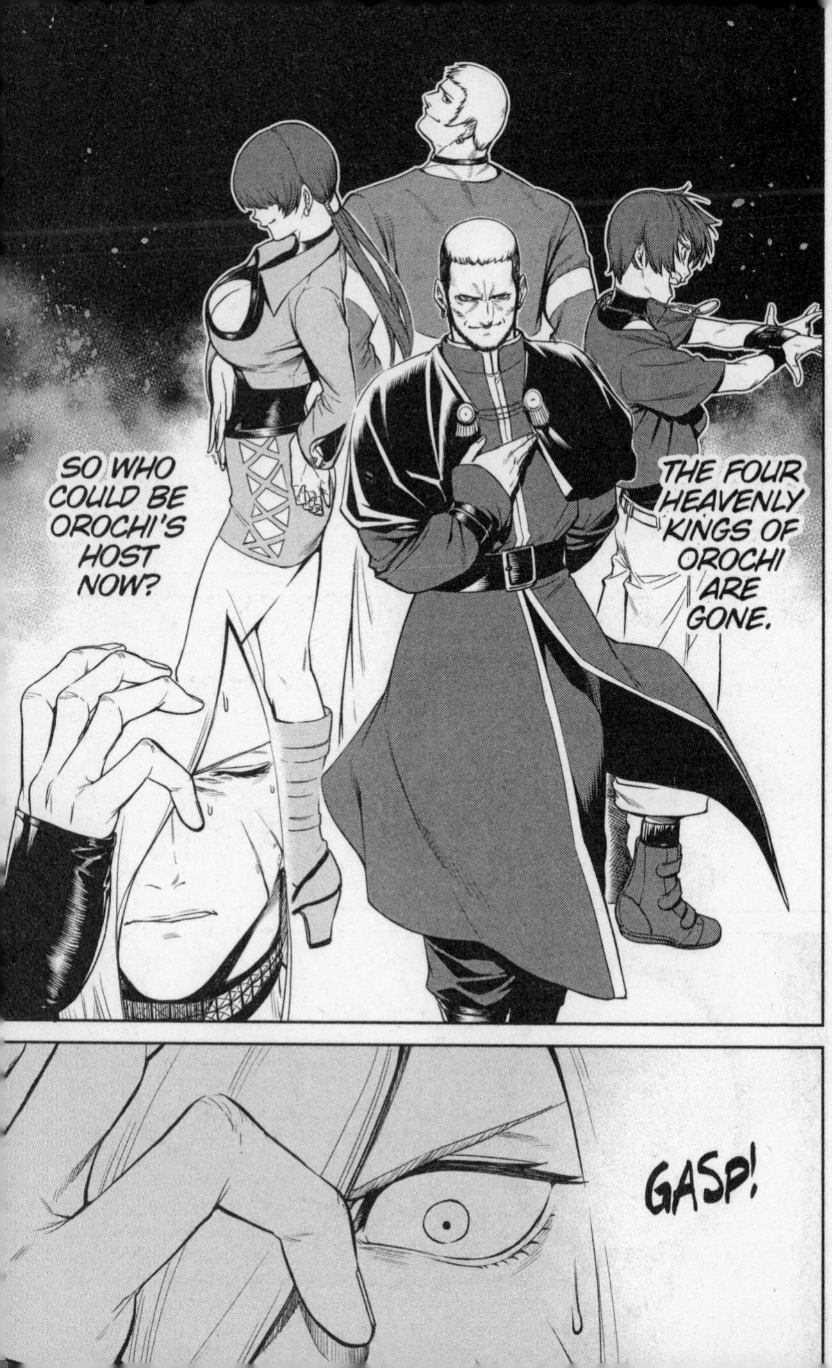
THE FOUR HEAVENLY KINGS OF OROCHI ARE GONE.
SO WHO COULD BE OROCHI'S HOST NOW?
GASP!

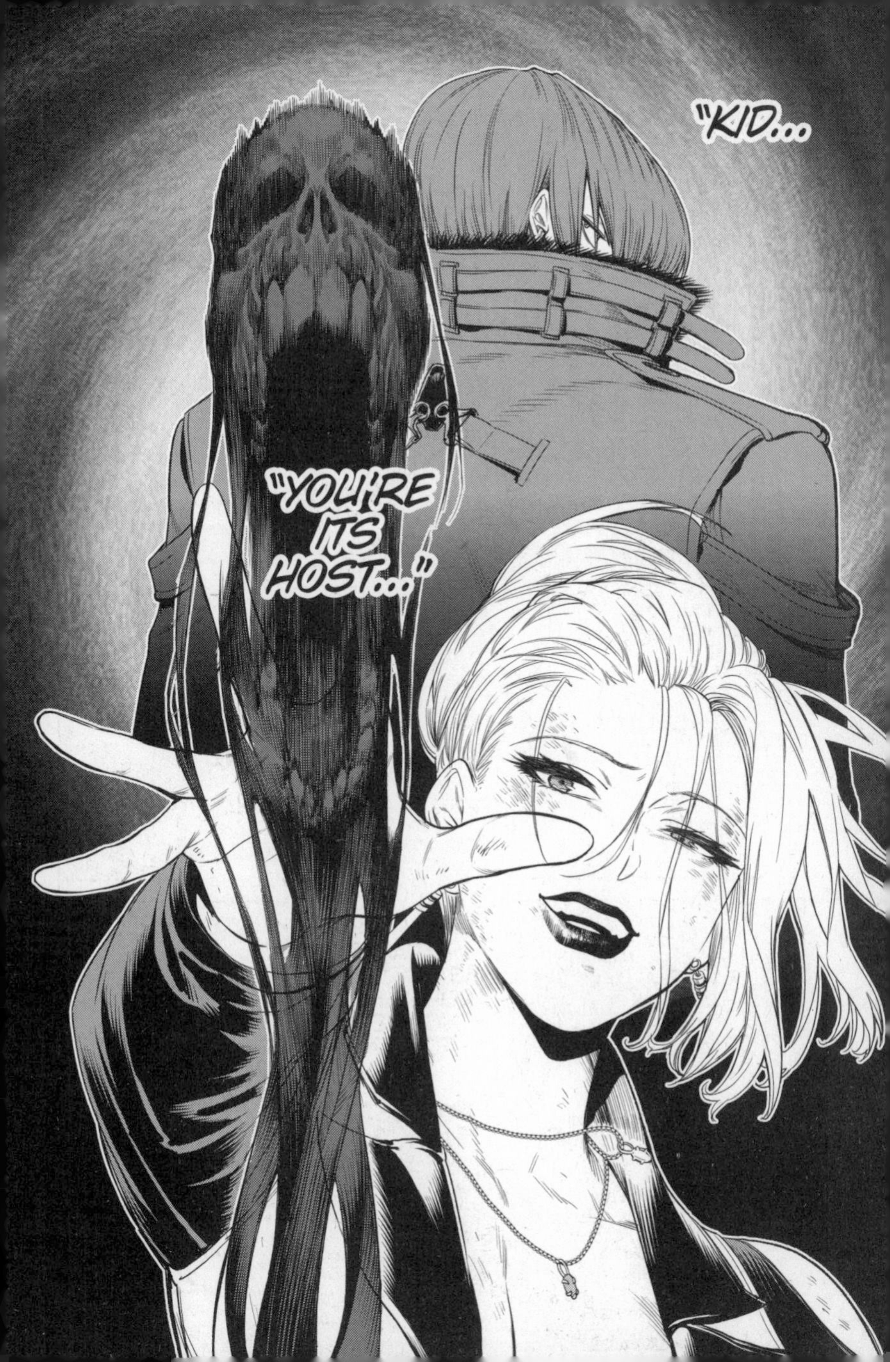
"KID...
"YOU'RE ITS HOST..."

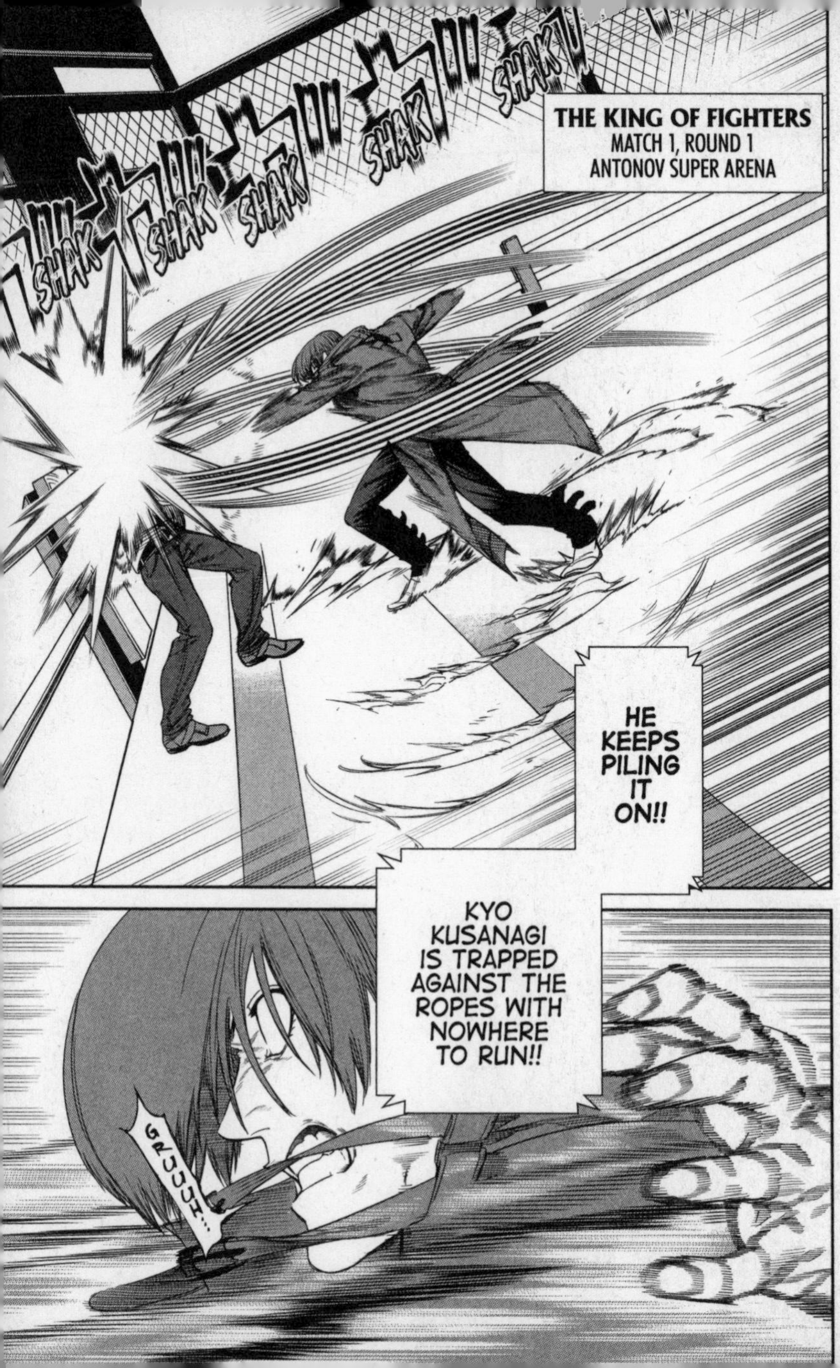
THE KING OF FIGHTERS
MATCH 1, ROUND 1
ANTONOV SUPER ARENA
SHAK
SHAK
SHAK
SHAK
SHAK
SHAK
HE KEEPS PILING IT ON!!
KYO KUSANAGI IS TRAPPED AGAINST THE ROPES WITH NOWHERE TO RUN!!
GRUUUH...

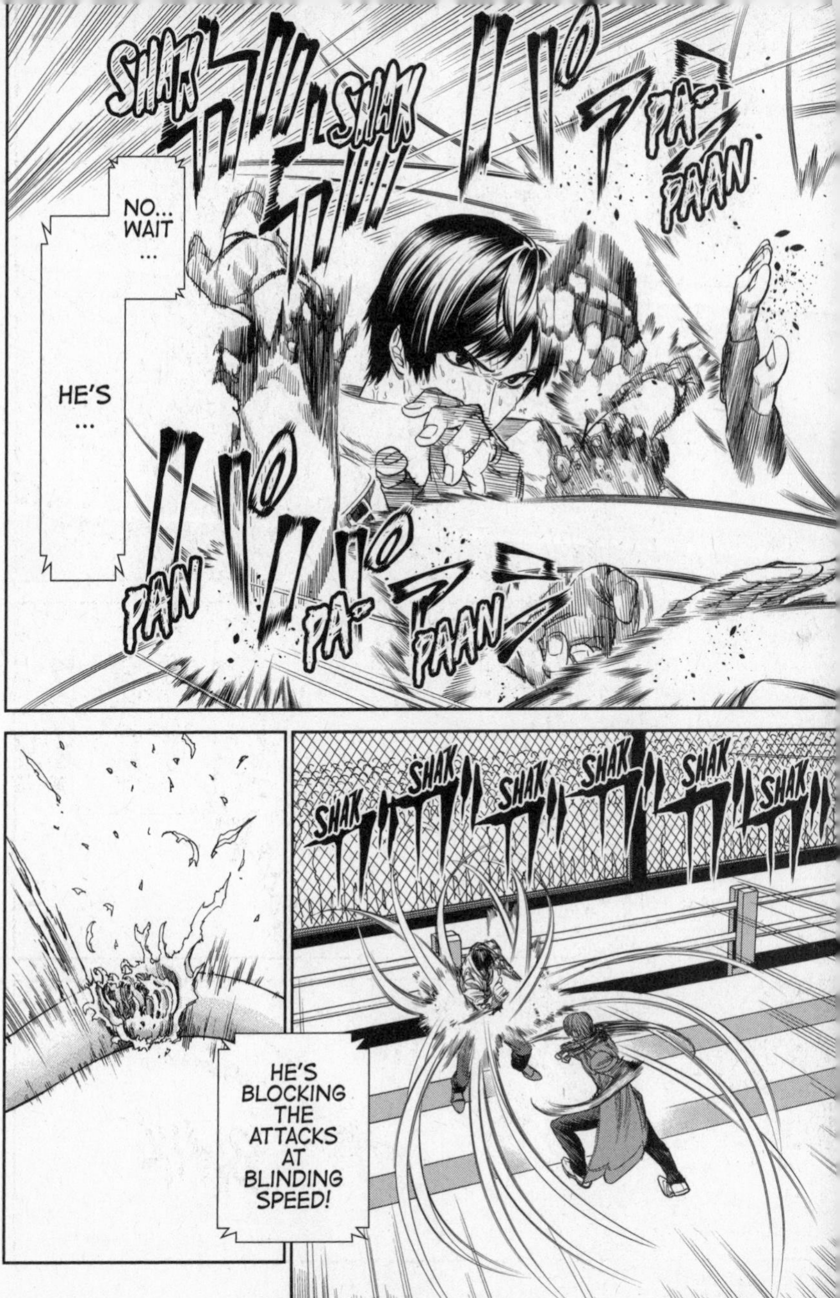
PA-PAAN
SHAK
SHAK
NO... WAIT ...
HE'S ...
PA-PAAN
PAN
SHAK SHAK SHAK SHAK SHAK SHAK
HE'S BLOCKING THE ATTACKS AT BLINDING SPEED!

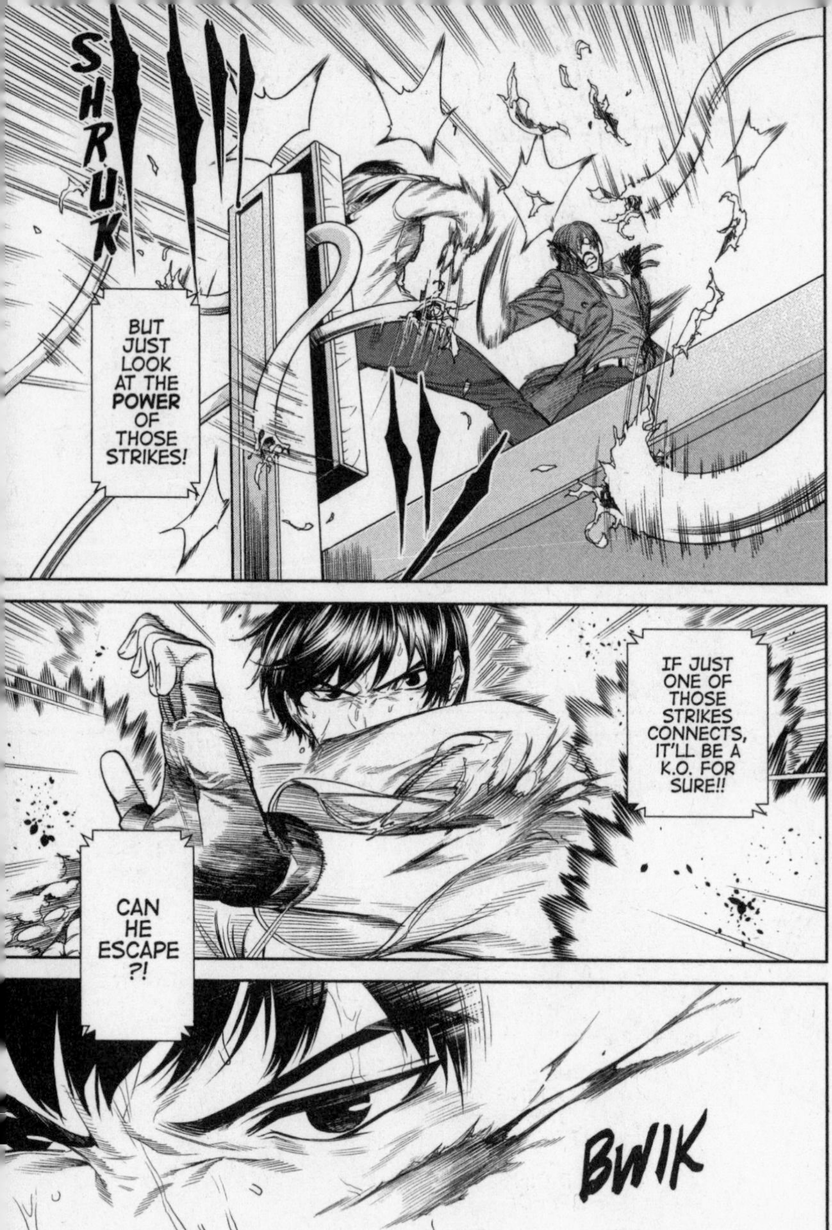
SHRUK
BUT JUST LOOK AT THE POWER OF THOSE STRIKES!
IF JUST ONE OF THOSE STRIKES CONNECTS, IT'LL BE A K.O. FOR SURE!!
CAN HE ESCAPE?!
BWIK

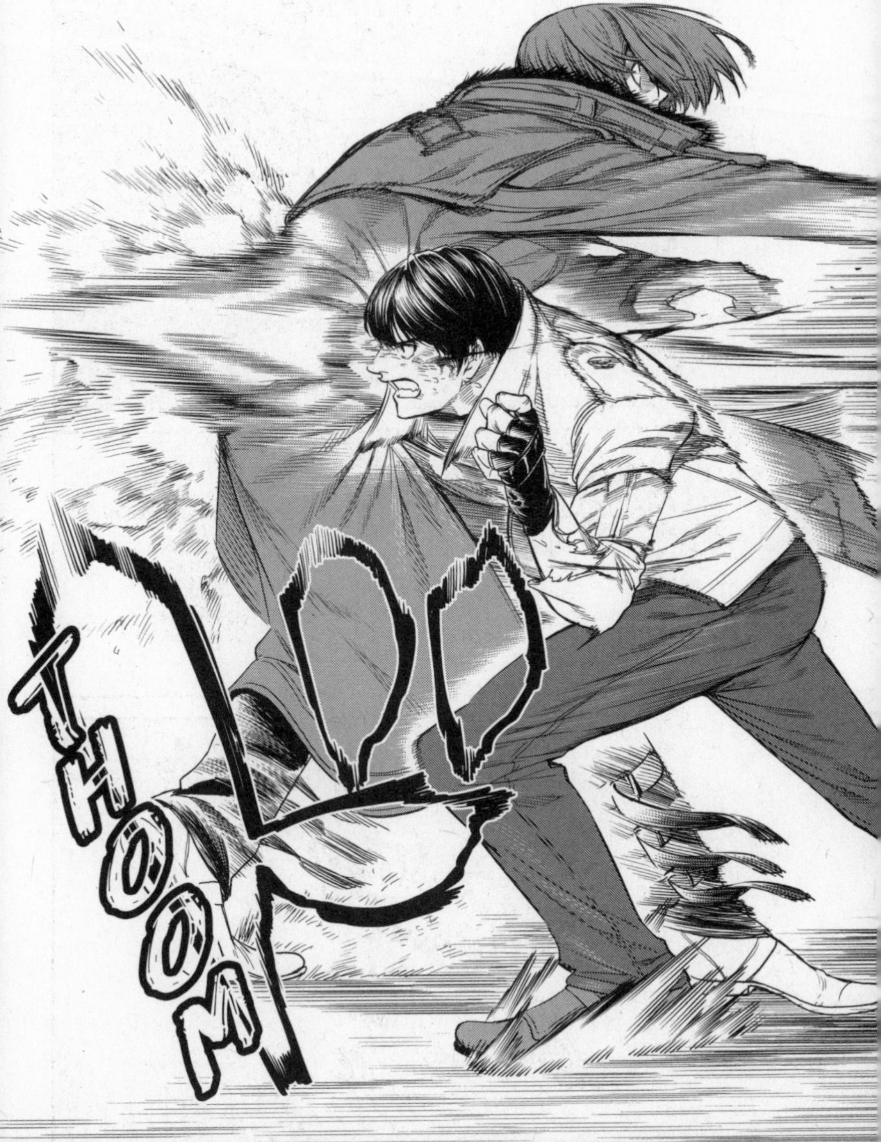
THOOM

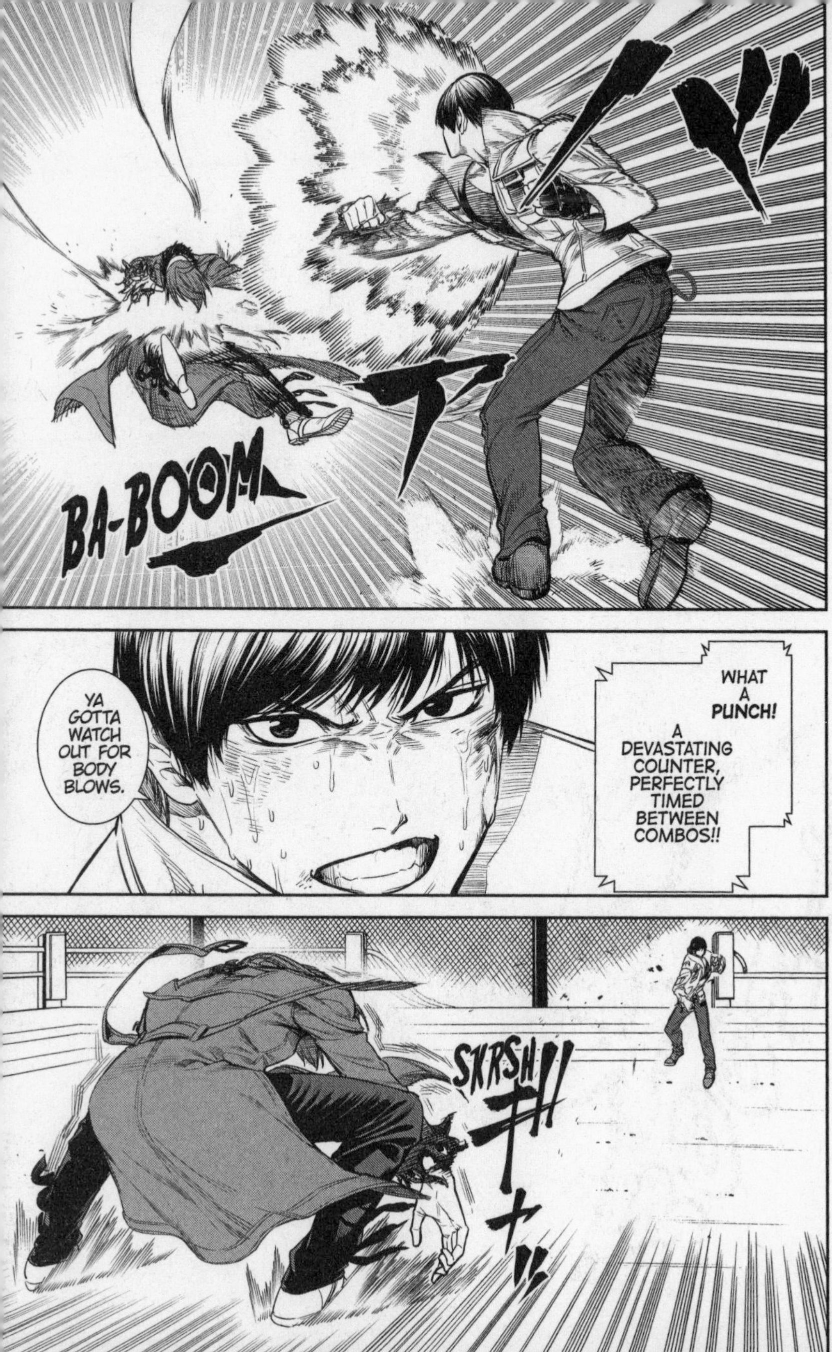
BA-BOOM
WHAT A PUNCH! A DEVASTATING COUNTER, PERFECTLY TIMED BETWEEN COMBOS!!
YA GOTTA WATCH OUT FOR BODY BLOWS.
SKRSH!!

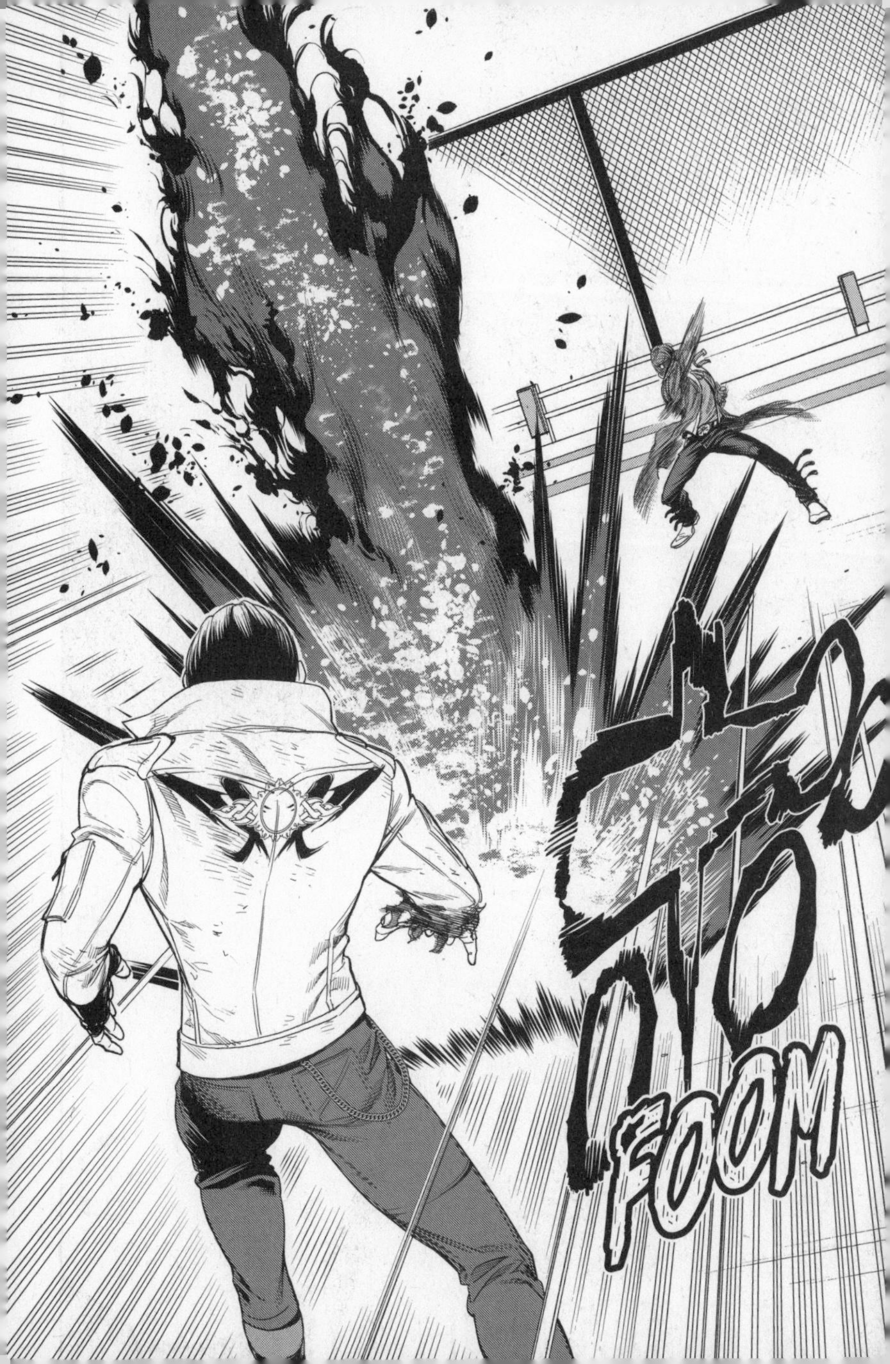
FOOM

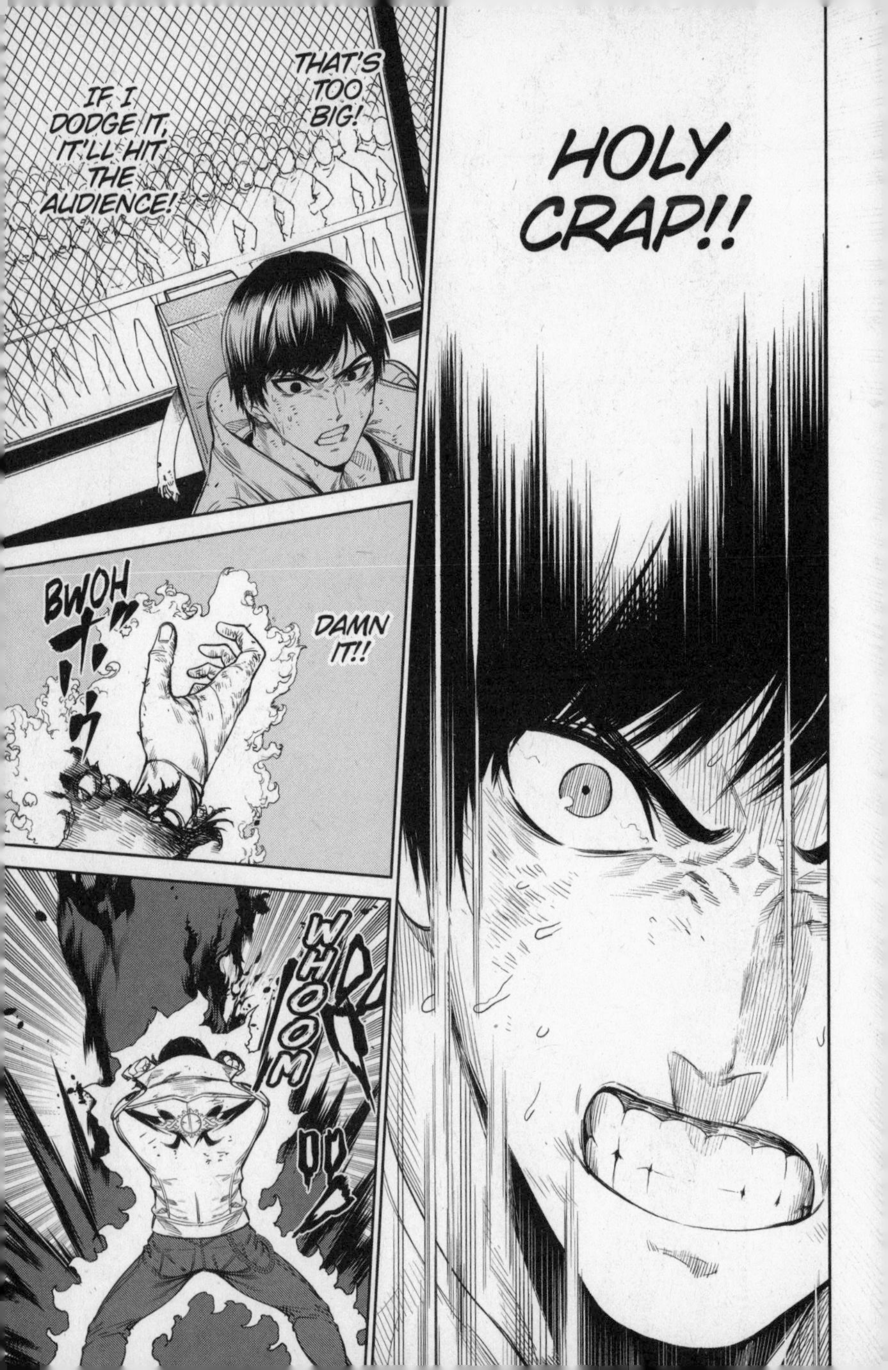
HOLY CRAP!!
THAT'S TOO BIG!
IF I DODGE IT, IT'LL HIT THE AUDIENCE!
DAMN IT!!
BWOH
WHOOOM

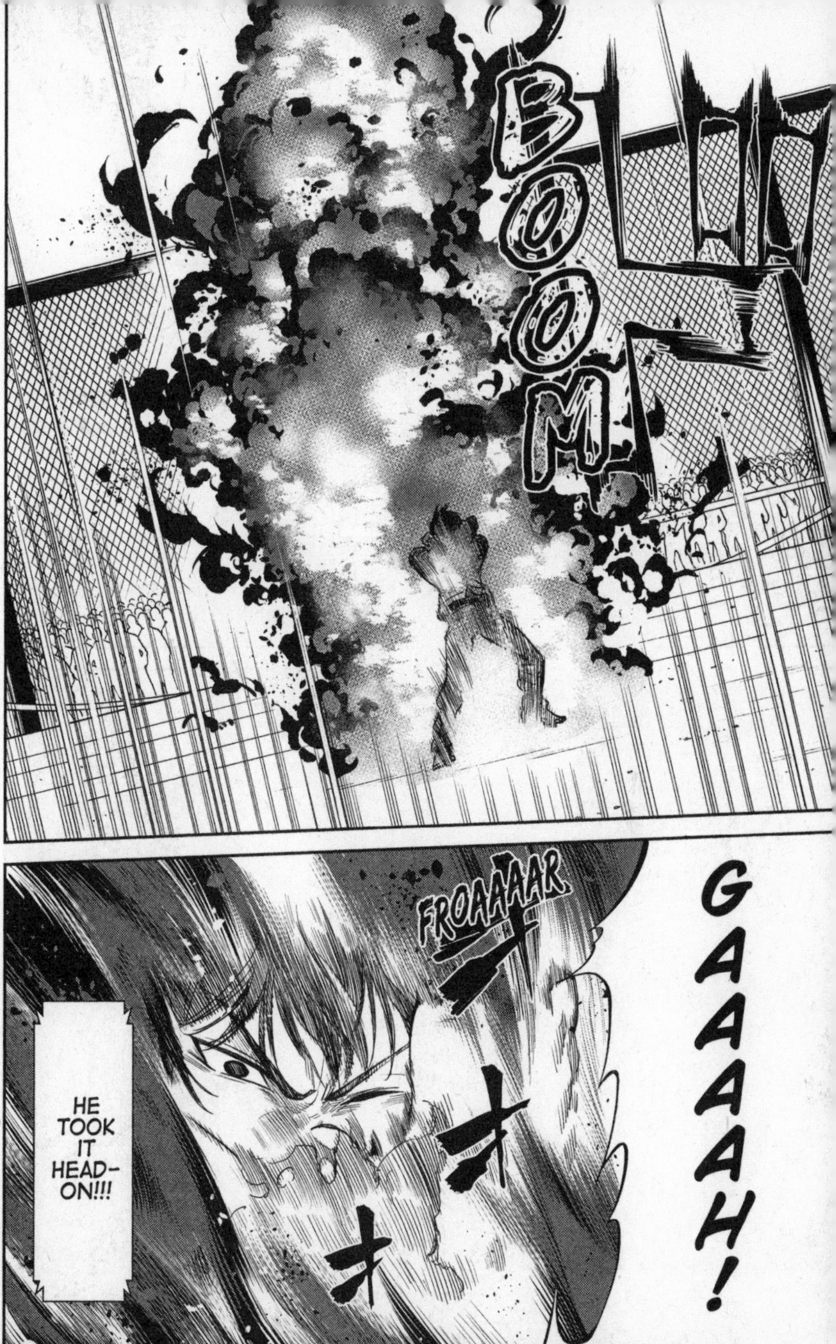
BOOOM
GAAAAH!
FROAAAAR
オ
オ
HE TOOK IT HEAD-ON!!!

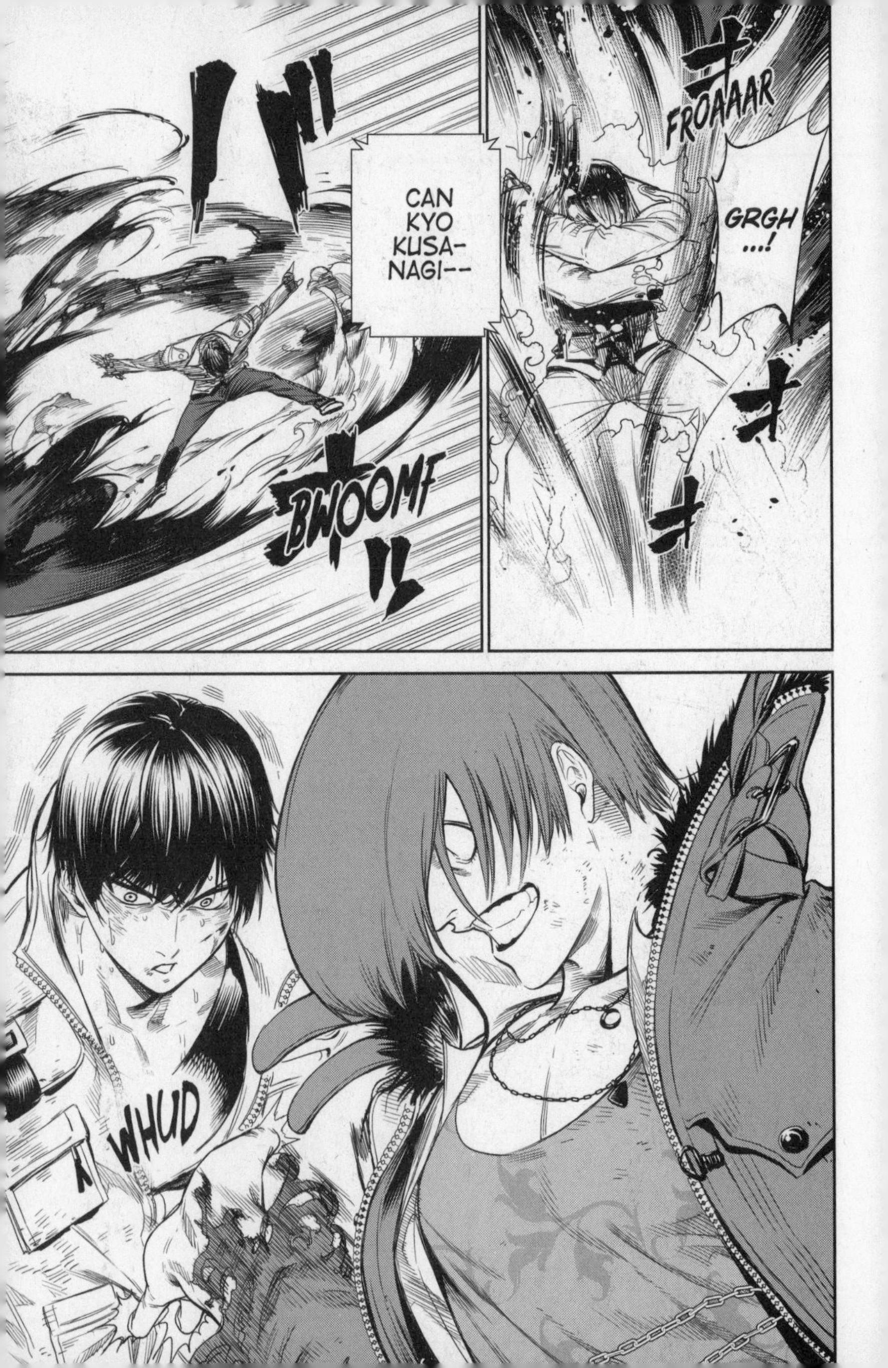
FROAAAR
GRGH ...!
CAN KYO KUSA-NAGI--
BWOOMF
WHUD

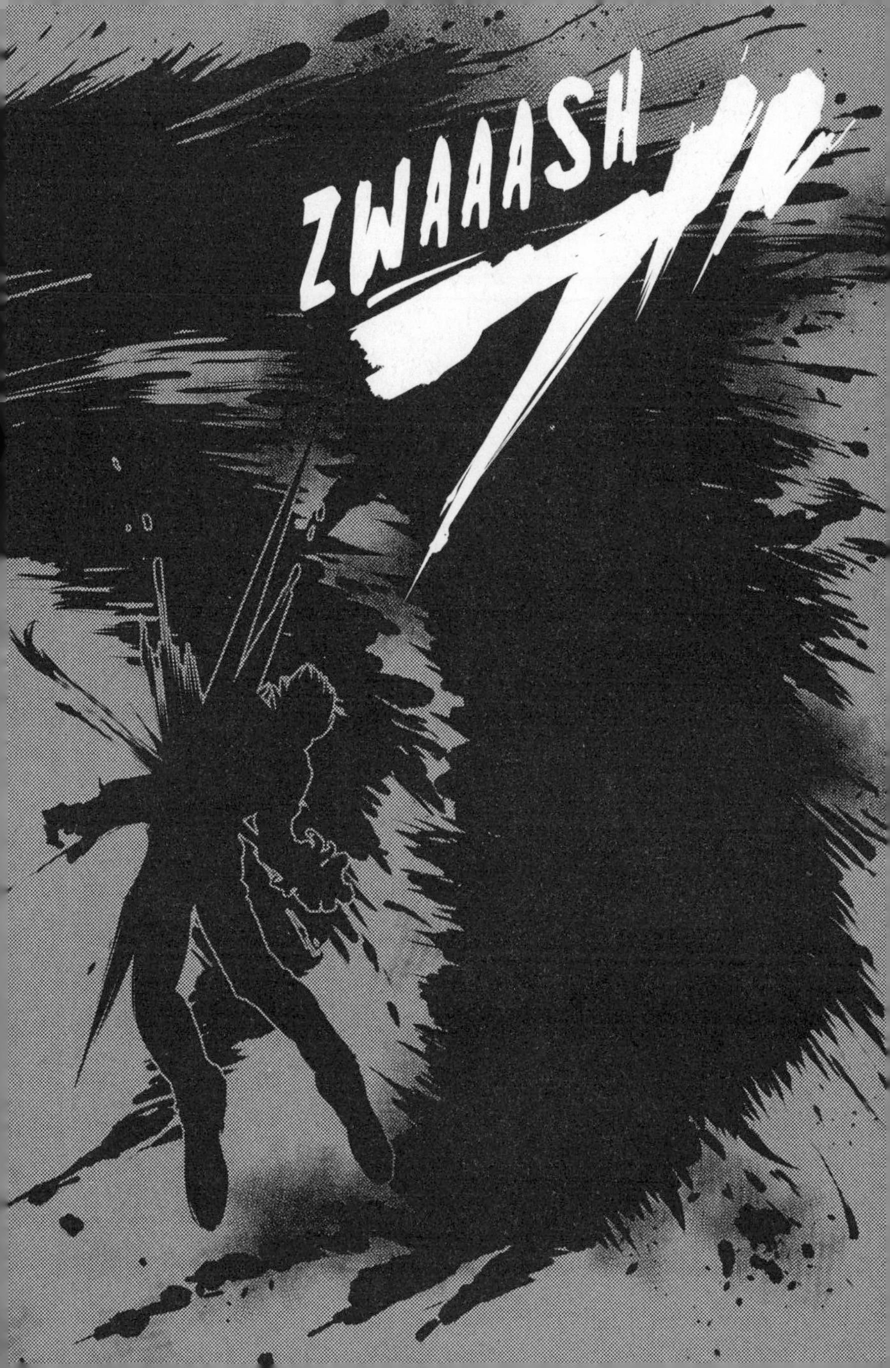
ZWAAASH

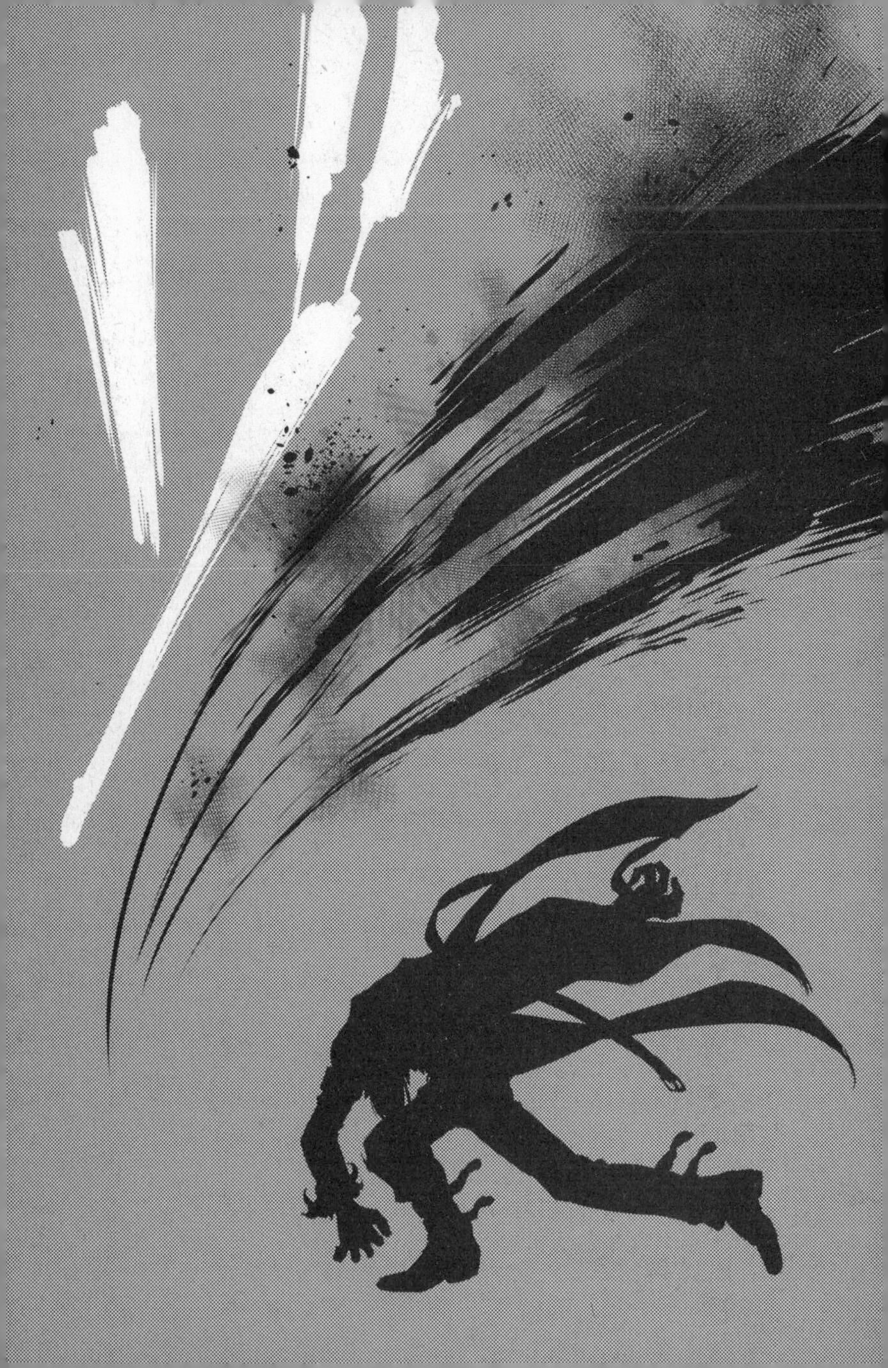

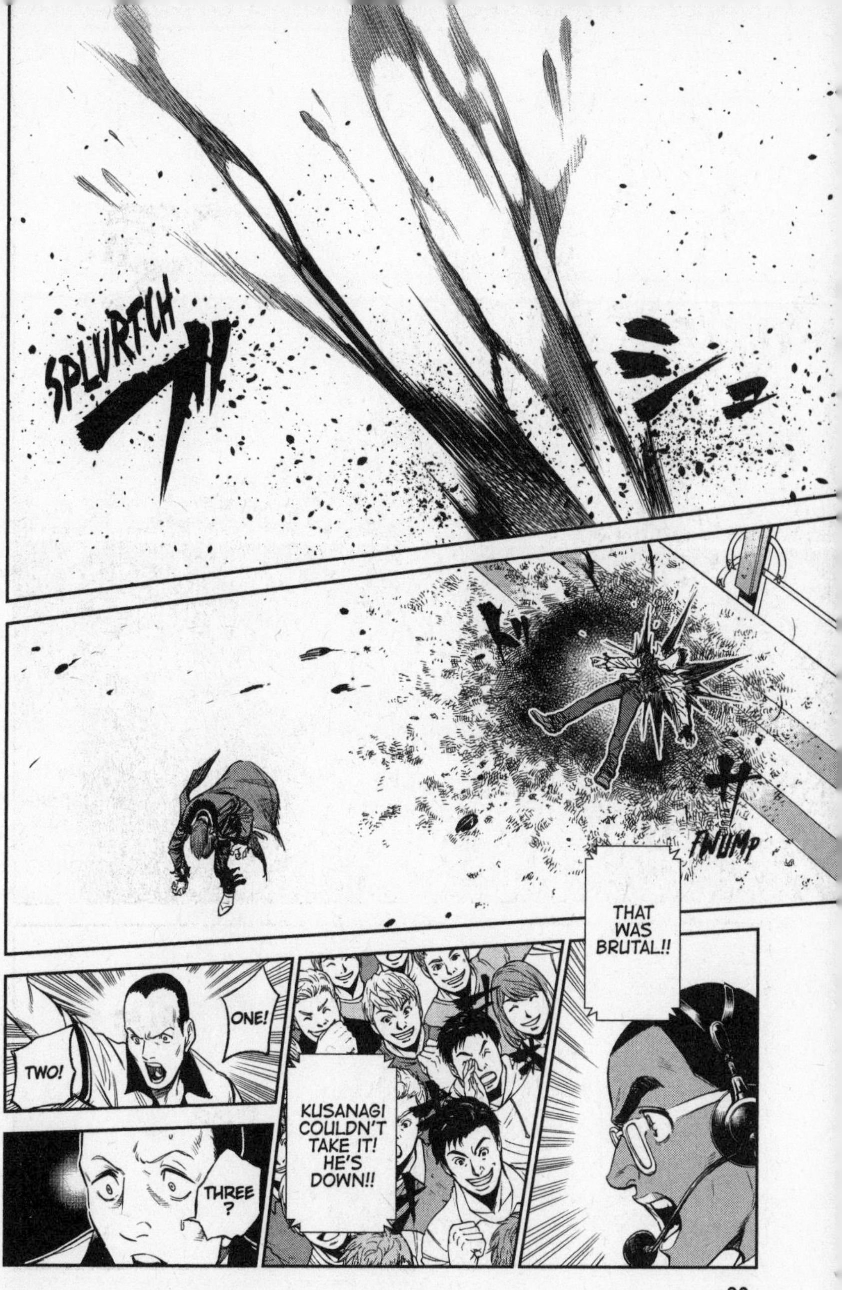
SPLURTCH
FWUMP
THAT WAS BRUTAL!!
KUSANAGI COULDN'T TAKE IT! HE'S DOWN!!
ONE!
TWO!
THREE ?

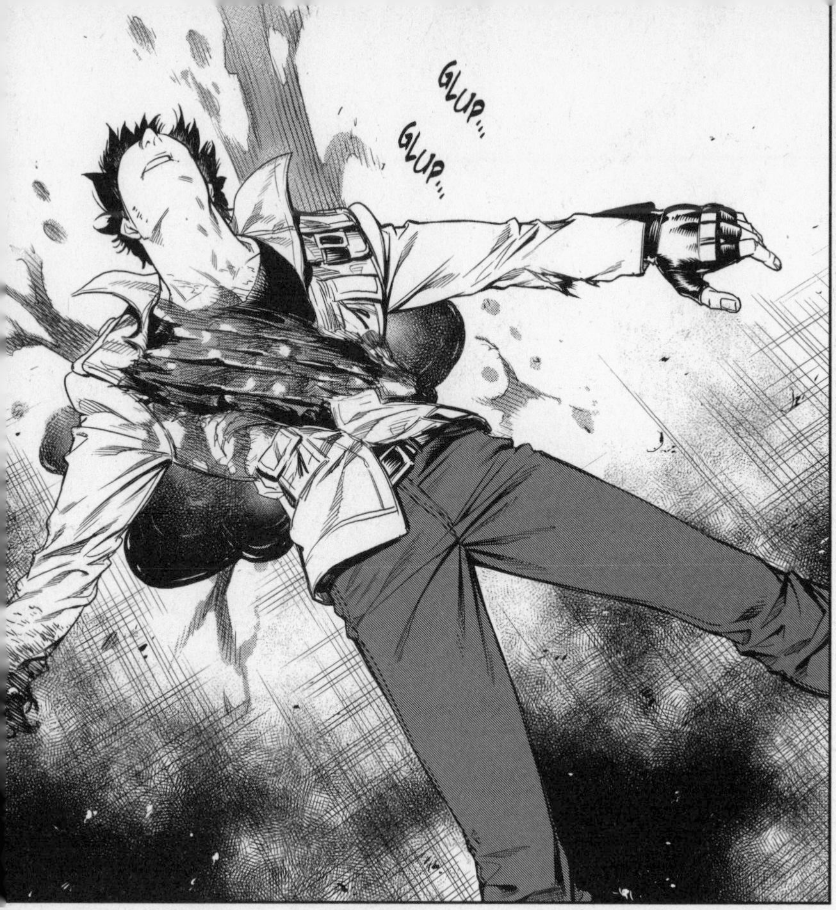
GLUP...
GLUP...

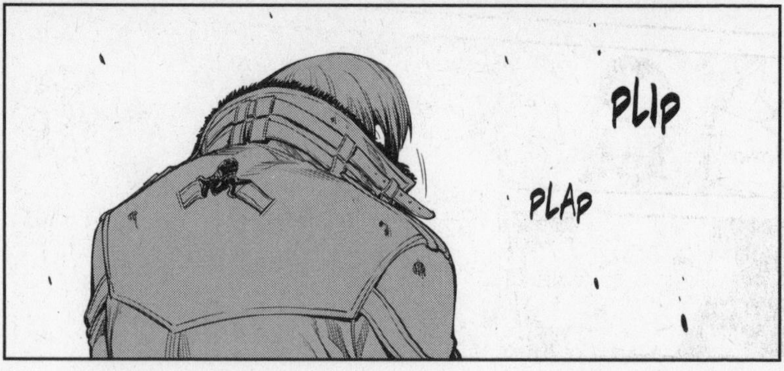
PLIP
PLAP

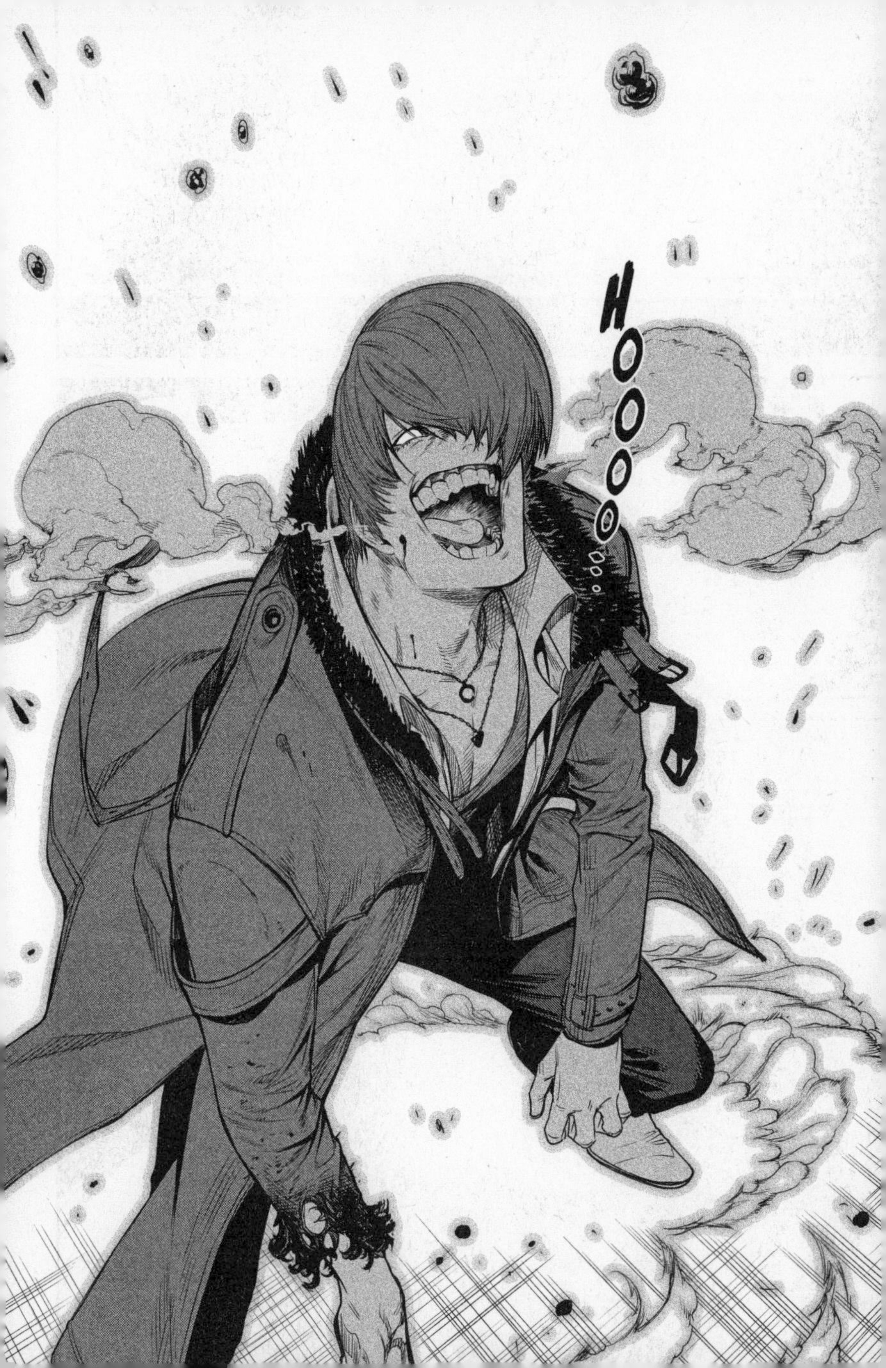
HOOOO

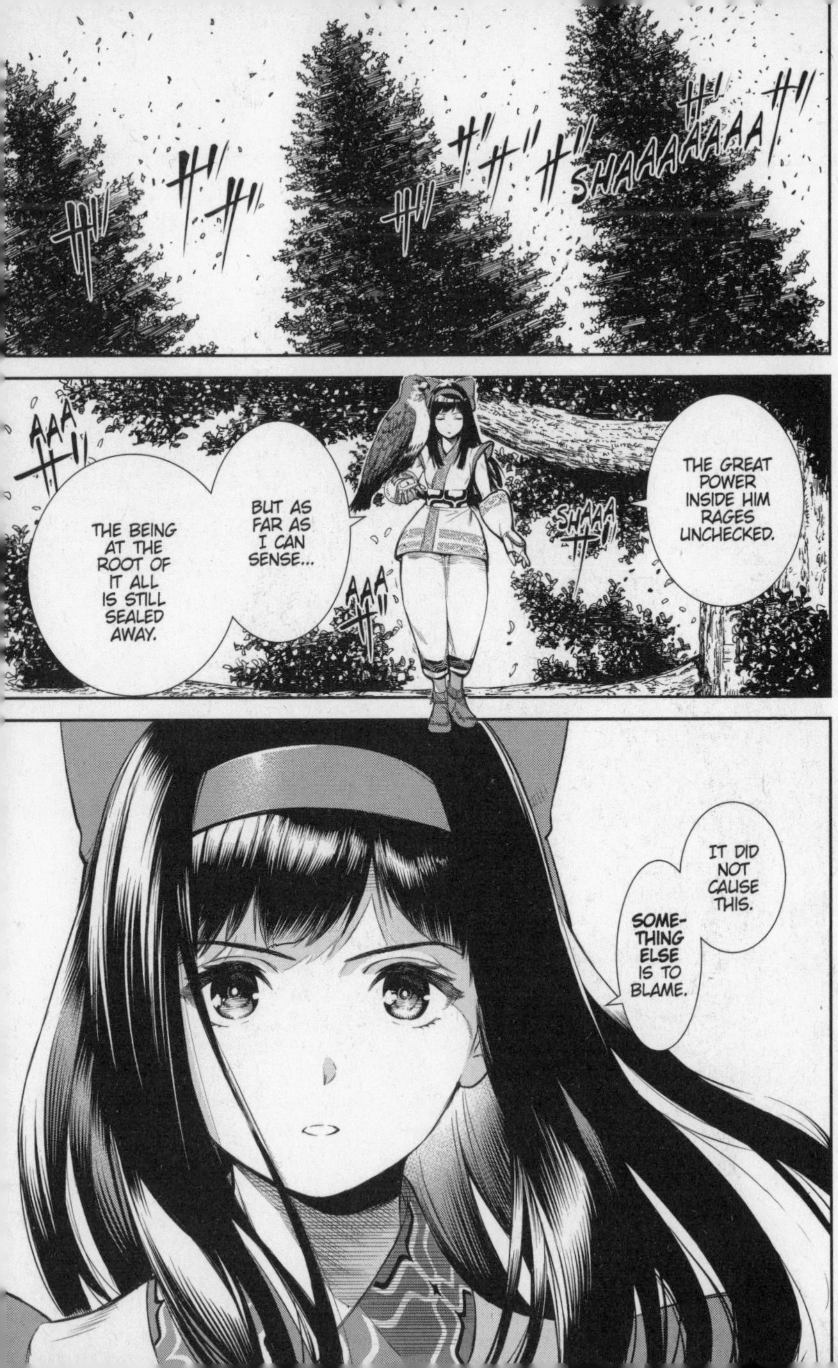
SHAAAAAAA
THE GREAT POWER INSIDE HIM RAGES UNCHECKED.
SHAAA
AAA
BUT AS FAR AS I CAN SENSE...
THE BEING AT THE ROOT OF IT ALL IS STILL SEALED AWAY.
AAA
IT DID NOT CAUSE THIS.
SOMETHING ELSE IS TO BLAME.

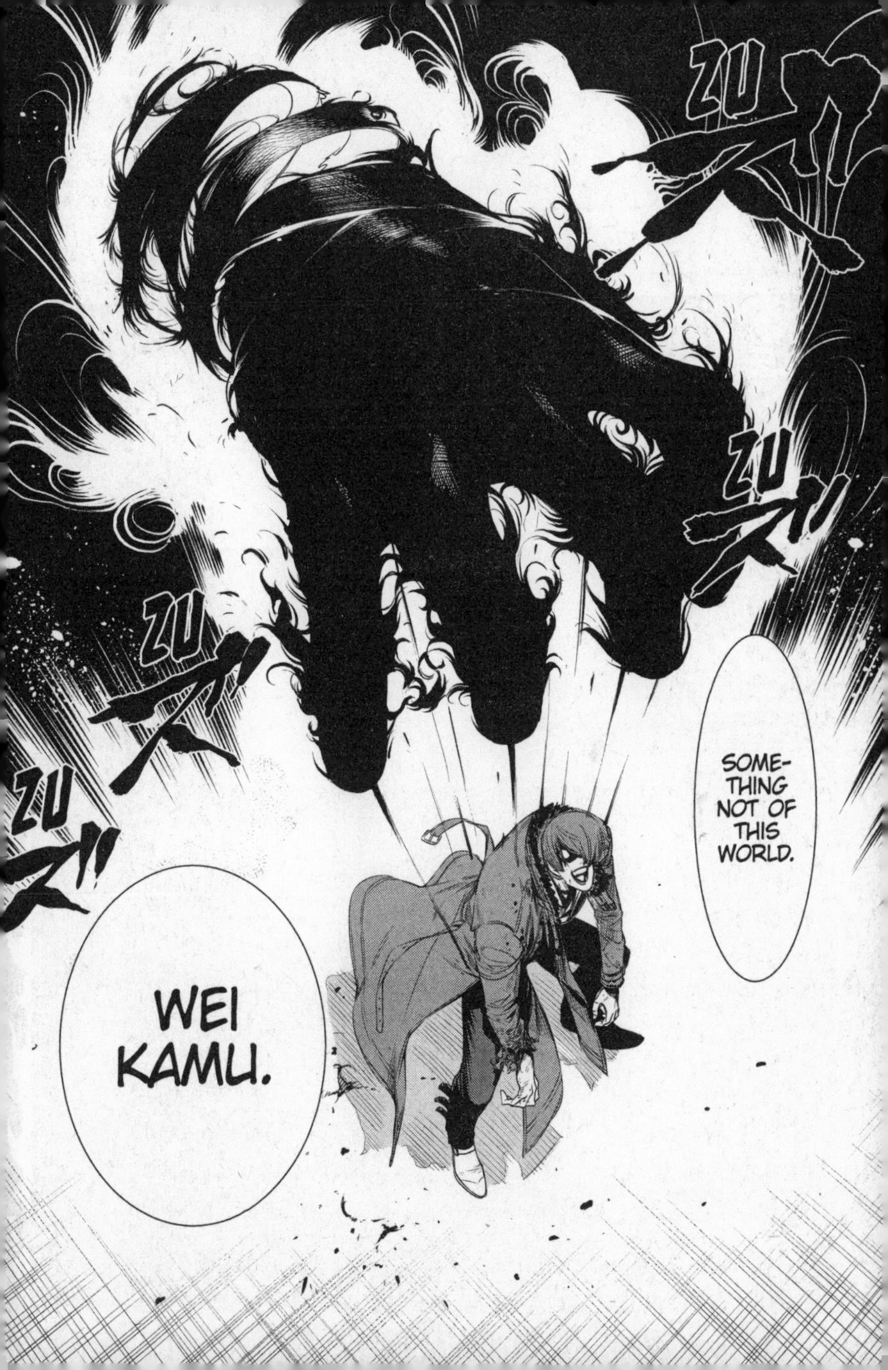
ZU
ZU
SOME-THING NOT OF THIS WORLD.
ZU
ZU
WEI KAMU.

MOVE LIST

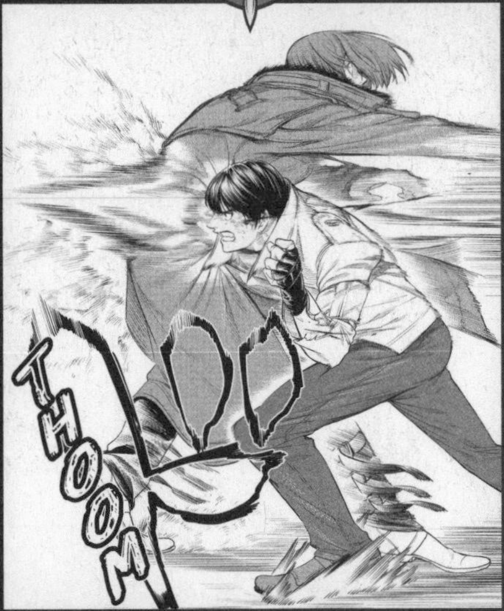
THOOOM

114 Shiki • Aragami

A close-range attack in which Kyo lets loose a flaming hook, along with a warning to watch out for body blows. A key Kyo move that can chain into a number of combos.

User: Kyo Kusanagi

Command:

↓↘→ + LP

MOVE 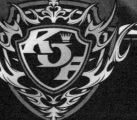 LIST

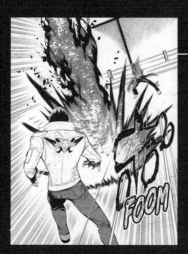

Ura 108 Shiki • Yasakazuki

A projectile move that releases a column of purple fire, immobilizing the opponent. Named after the "eight sake cups" that put Yamata no Orochi to sleep in the Susanoo myth.

User: Iori Yagami

Command:
↓↙←↙↓↘→ + LP or HP

(Seen in games such as *KOF '98*, *KOF 2003*, *NeoGeo Battle Coliseum*, *SNK vs. Capcom: The Match of the Millennium*, and *Capcom vs. SNK*)

Kin 1218 Shiki • Yatagarasu

A berserker's move that slashes the opponent up with claws using the power of Orochi. Named after the "eight-span crow," a mythical three-legged bird.

User: Iori Yagami

Command:
↓↘→↓↘→ + LK + HK

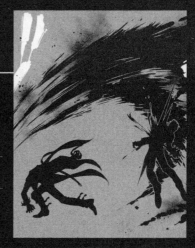

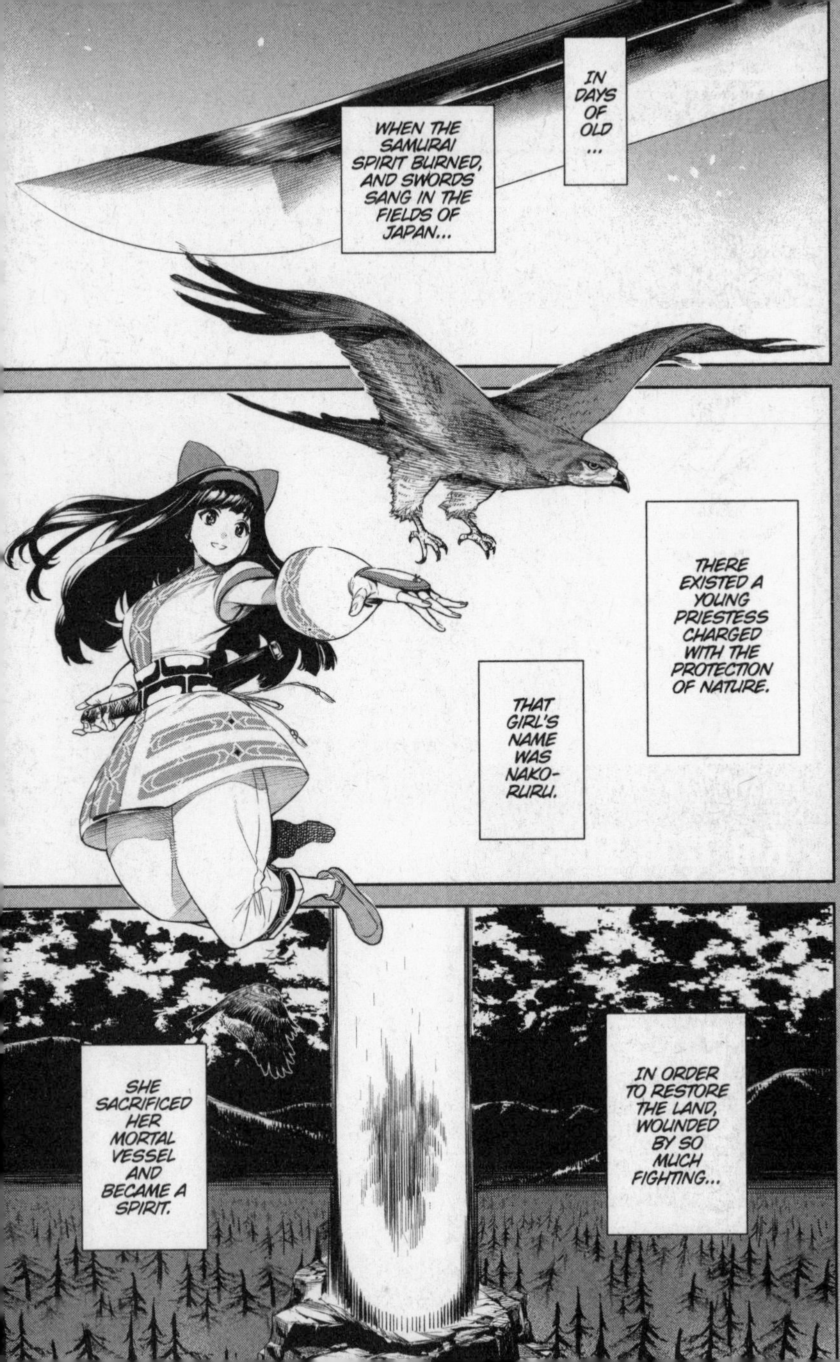
IN DAYS OF OLD ...
WHEN THE SAMURAI SPIRIT BURNED, AND SWORDS SANG IN THE FIELDS OF JAPAN...
THERE EXISTED A YOUNG PRIESTESS CHARGED WITH THE PROTECTION OF NATURE.
THAT GIRL'S NAME WAS NAKO-RURU.
IN ORDER TO RESTORE THE LAND, WOUNDED BY SO MUCH FIGHTING...
SHE SACRIFICED HER MORTAL VESSEL AND BECAME A SPIRIT.

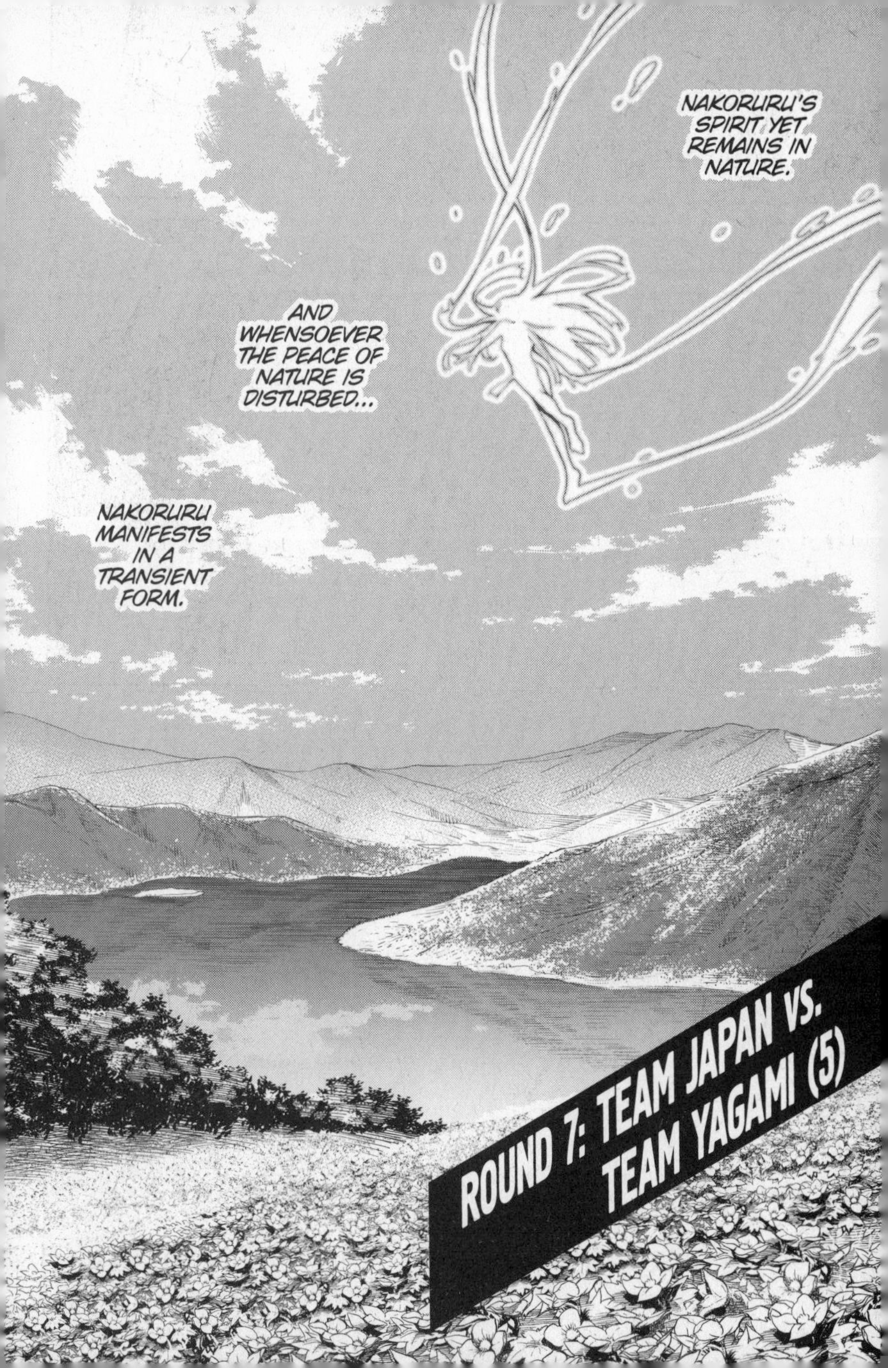
NAKORURU'S SPIRIT YET REMAINS IN NATURE.
AND WHENSOEVER THE PEACE OF NATURE IS DISTURBED...
NAKORURU MANIFESTS IN A TRANSIENT FORM.
ROUND 7: TEAM JAPAN VS. TEAM YAGAMI (5)

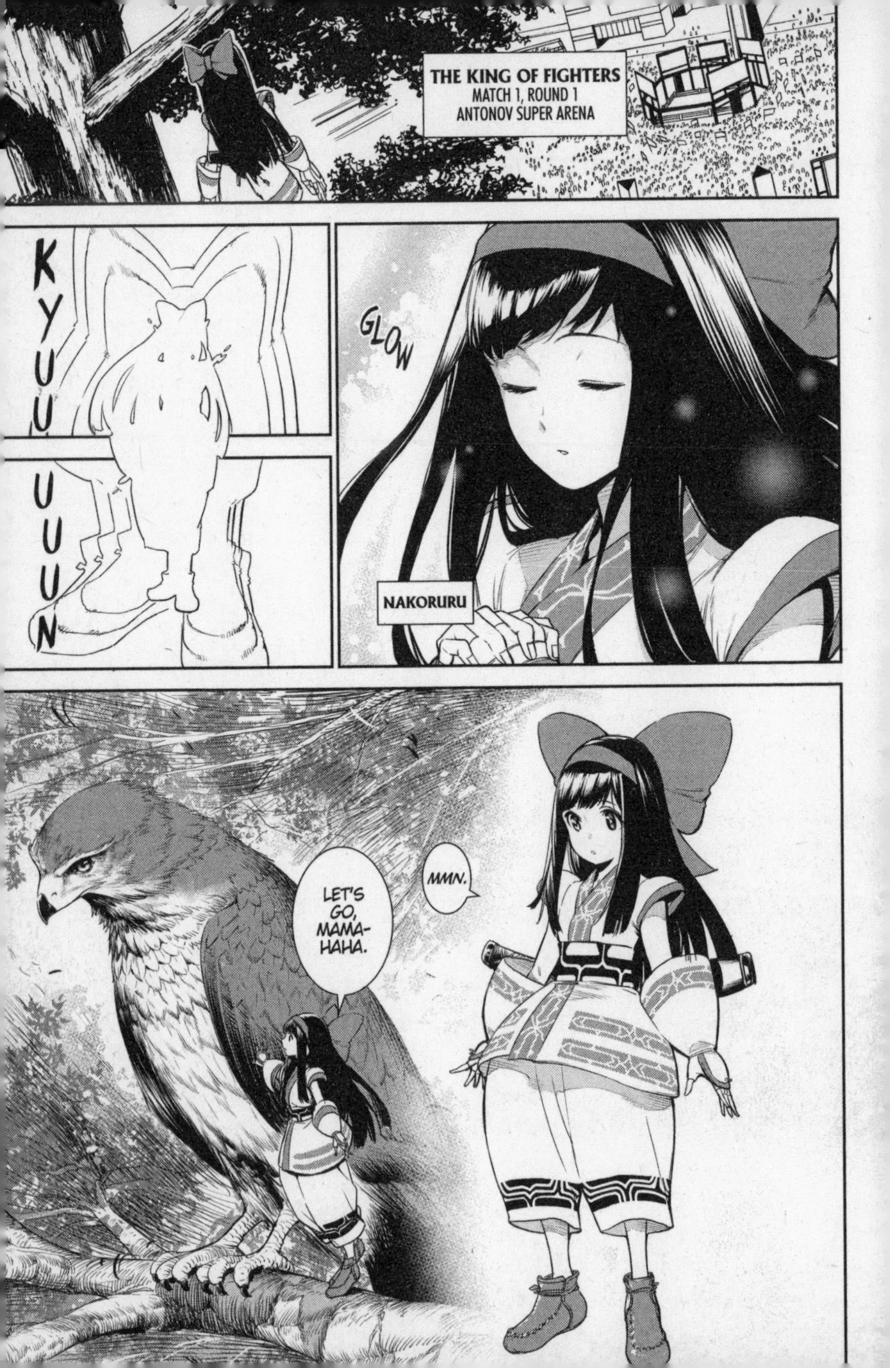
THE KING OF FIGHTERS
MATCH 1, ROUND 1
ANTONOV SUPER ARENA
GLOW
NAKORURU
KYUUUUUUN
MMN.
LET'S GO, MAMA-HAHA.

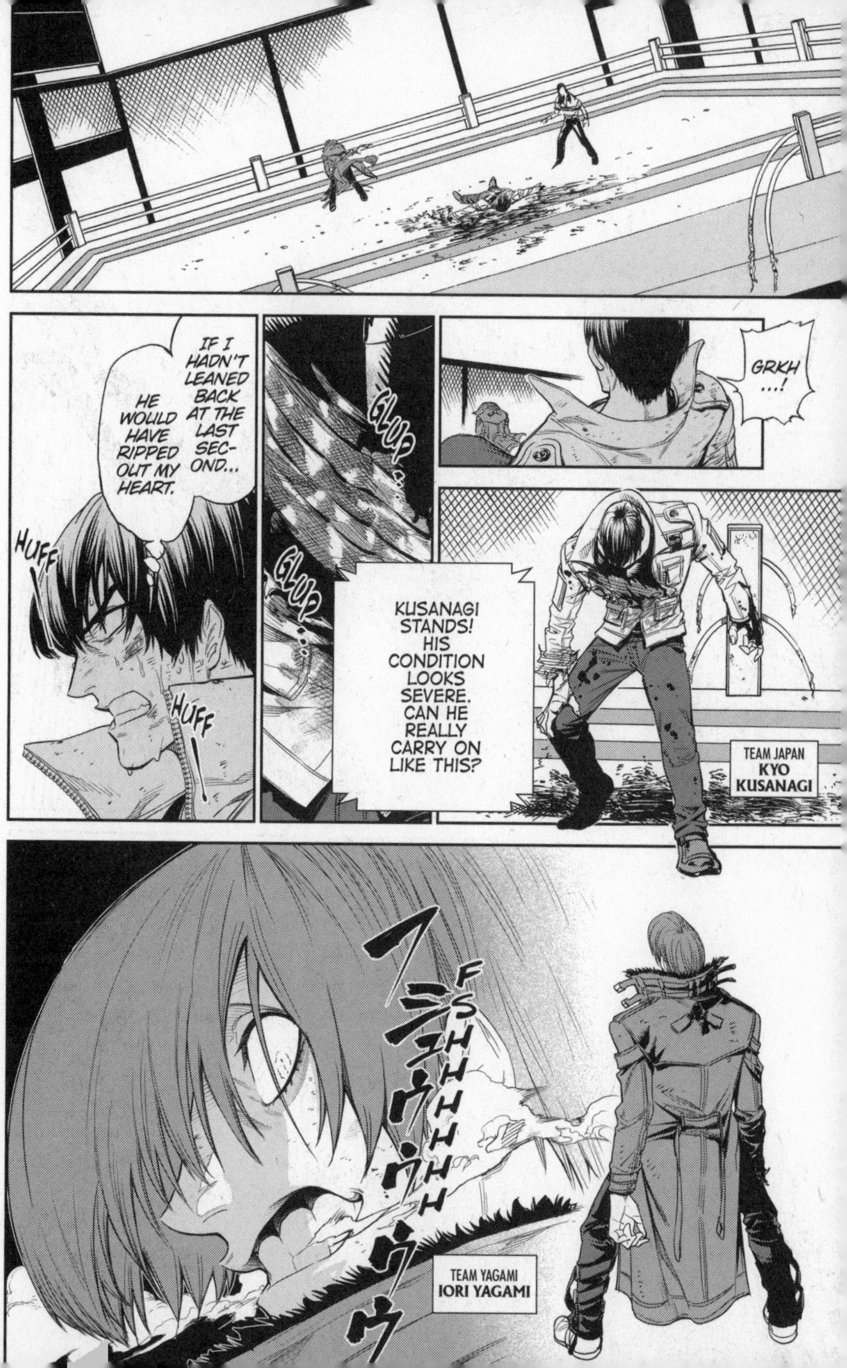
GRKH ...!
KUSANAGI STANDS! HIS CONDITION LOOKS SEVERE. CAN HE REALLY CARRY ON LIKE THIS?
TEAM JAPAN KYO KUSANAGI
GLUP
GLUP
IF I HADN'T LEANED BACK AT THE LAST SEC-OND...
HE WOULD HAVE RIPPED OUT MY HEART.
HUFF
HUFF
FSHHHHHHH
TEAM YAGAMI IORI YAGAMI

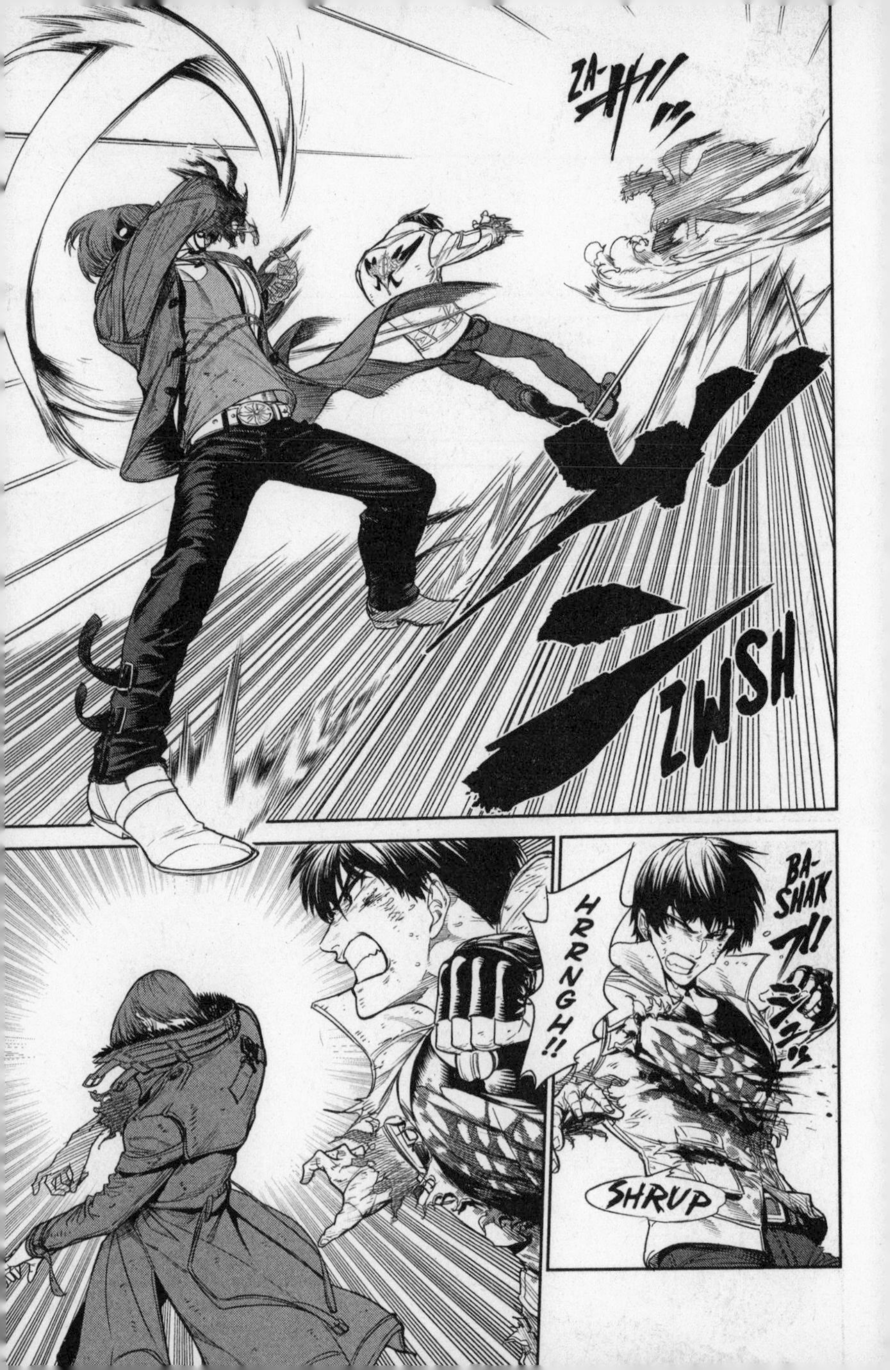
ZA-
ZWSH
BA-SHAK
SHRUP
HRRNGH!!

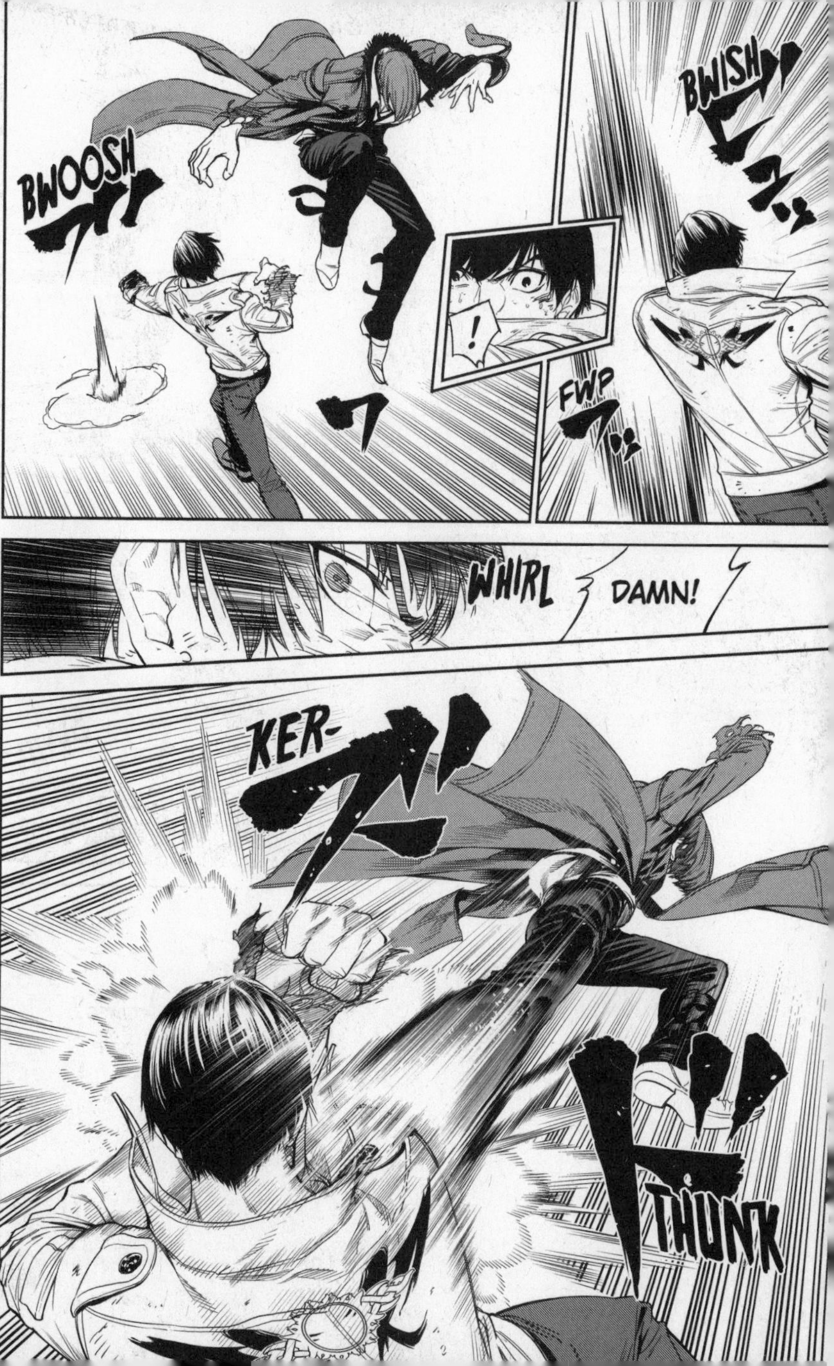
BWISH
!
FWP
BWOOSH
WHIRL
DAMN!
KER-
THUNK

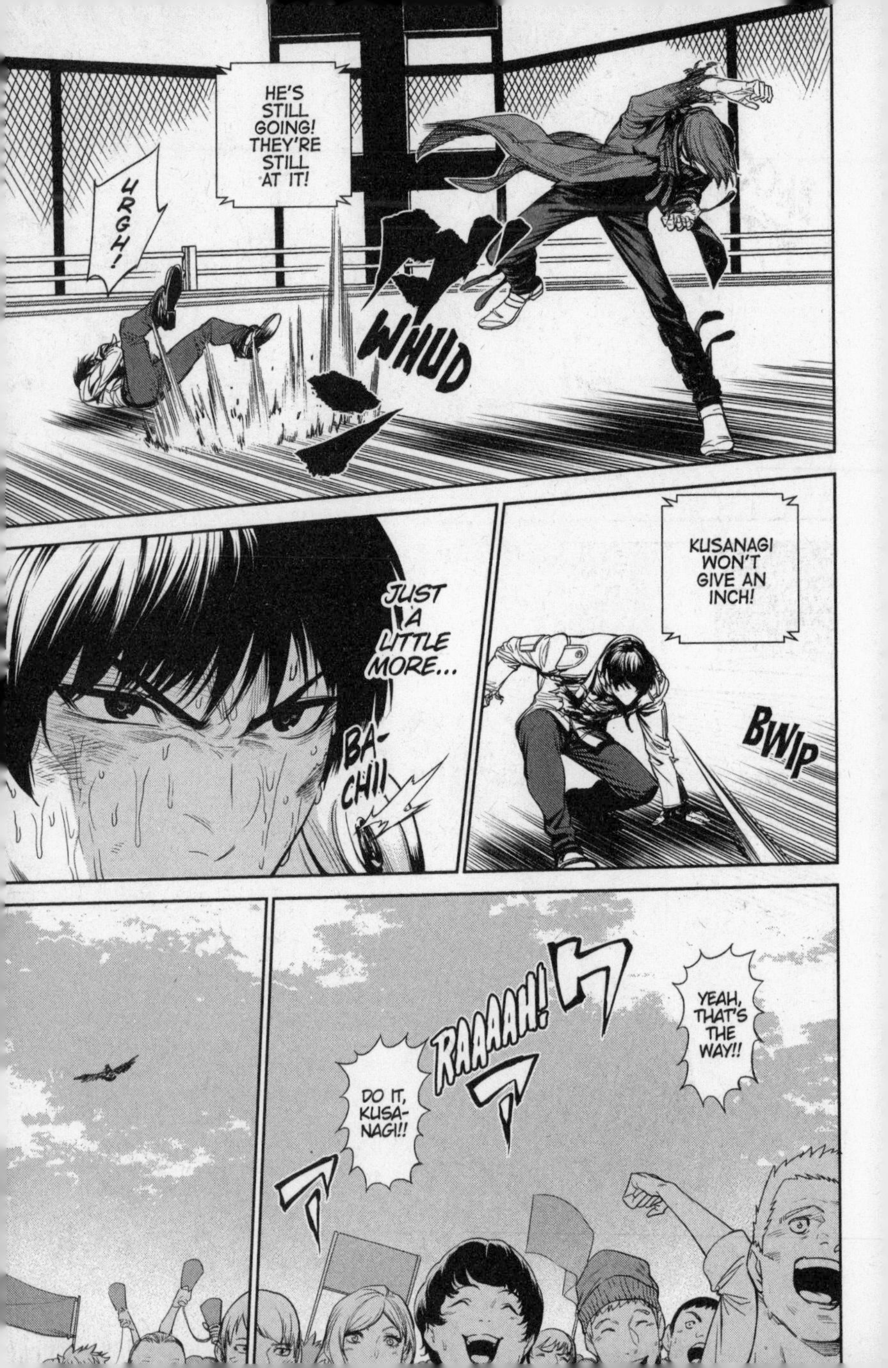

HE'S STILL GOING! THEY'RE STILL AT IT!
URGH!
WHUD
KUSANAGI WON'T GIVE AN INCH!
BWIP
JUST A LITTLE MORE...
BA-CHI!
YEAH, THAT'S THE WAY!!
RAAAAH!
DO IT, KUSA-NAGI!!

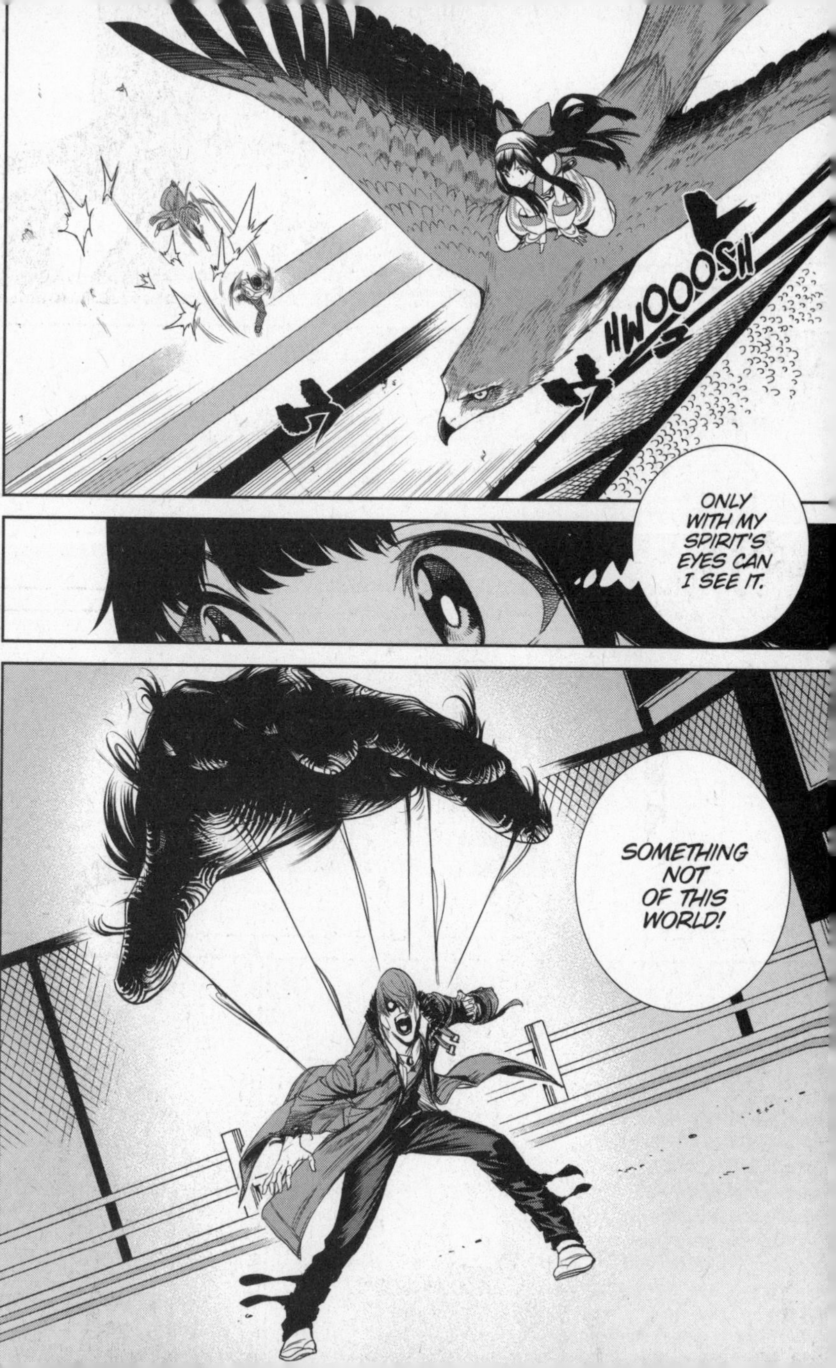
HWOOOSH
ONLY WITH MY SPIRIT'S EYES CAN I SEE IT.
SOMETHING NOT OF THIS WORLD!

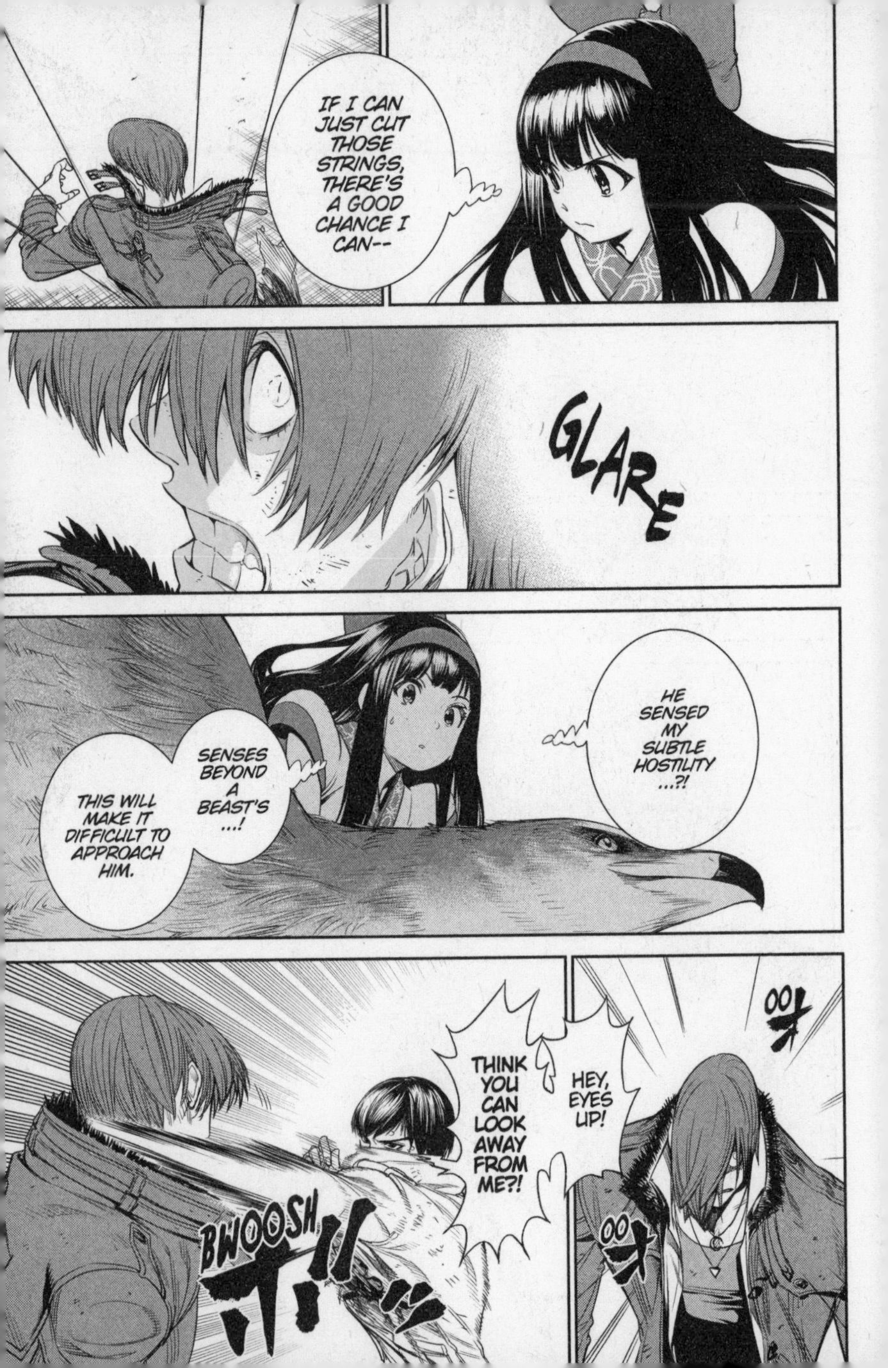
IF I CAN JUST CUT THOSE STRINGS, THERE'S A GOOD CHANCE I CAN--
GLARE
HE SENSED MY SUBTLE HOSTILITY ...?!
SENSES BEYOND A BEAST'S ...!
THIS WILL MAKE IT DIFFICULT TO APPROACH HIM.
OOF
HEY, EYES UP!
OOF
THINK YOU CAN LOOK AWAY FROM ME?!
BWOOSH

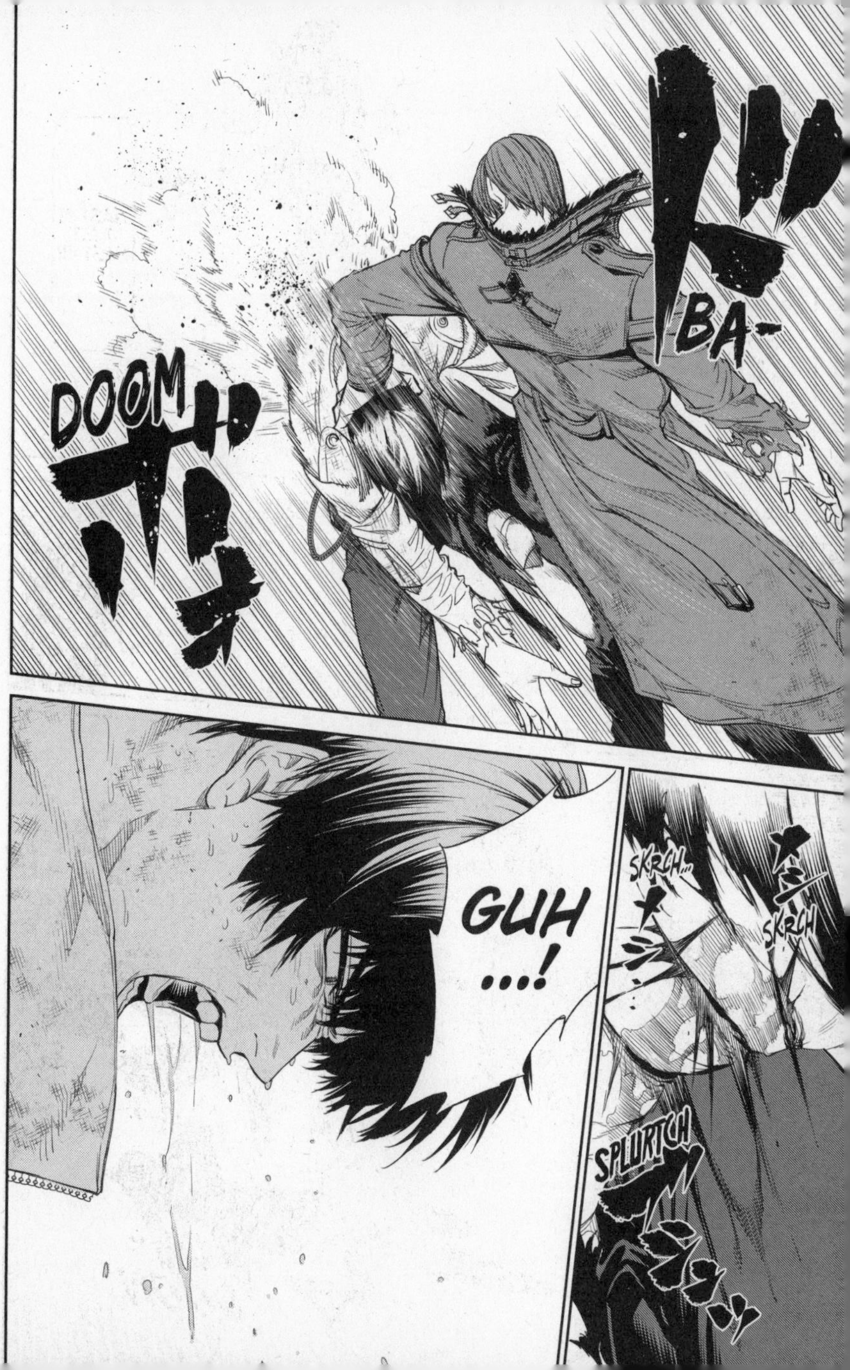
BA-
DOOM
SKRCH...
SKRCH
SPLURTCH
GUH ...!

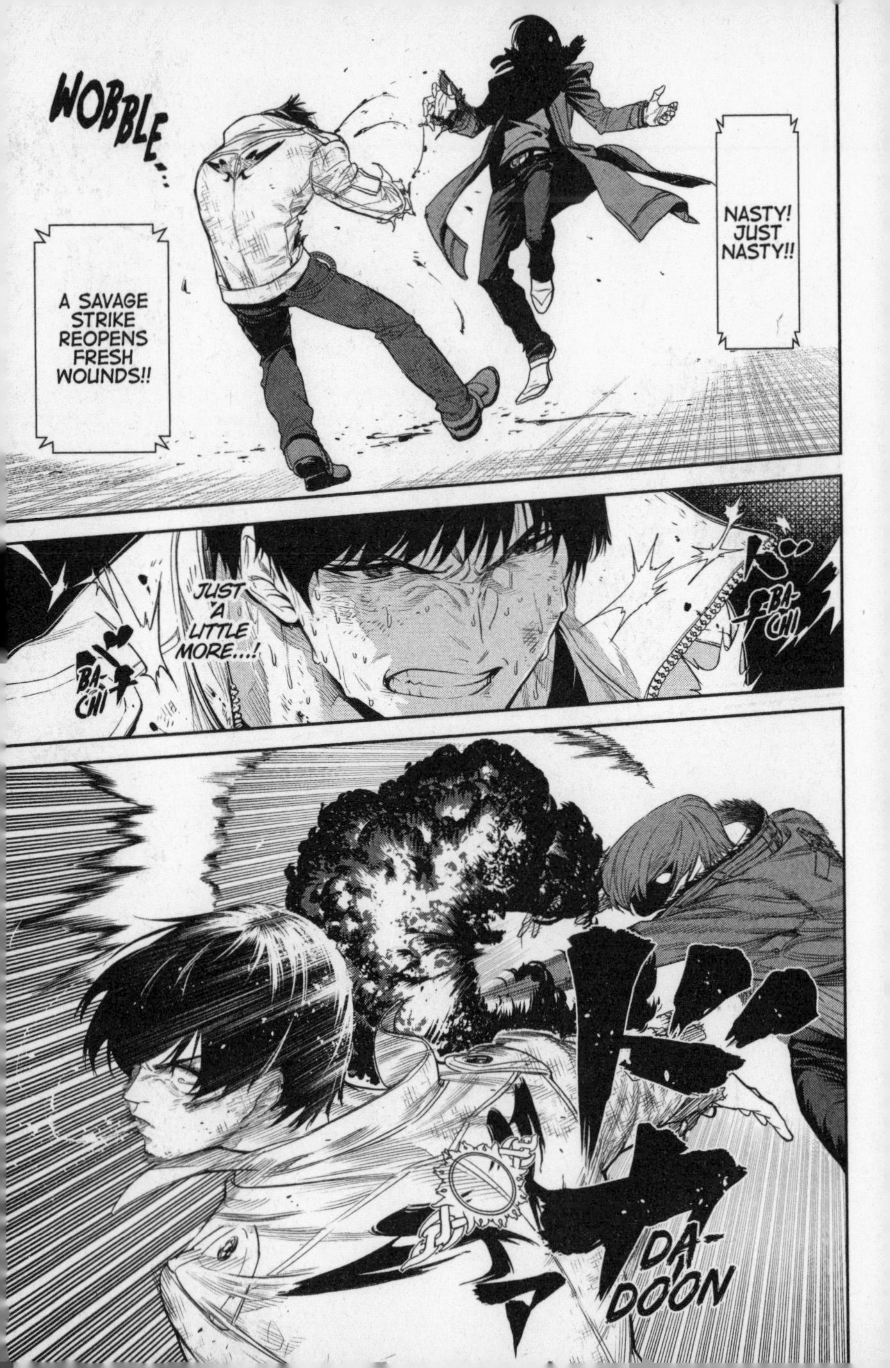
NASTY! JUST NASTY!!
WOBBLE...
A SAVAGE STRIKE REOPENS FRESH WOUNDS!!
BA-CHI
JUST A LITTLE MORE...!
BA-CHI
DA-DOON

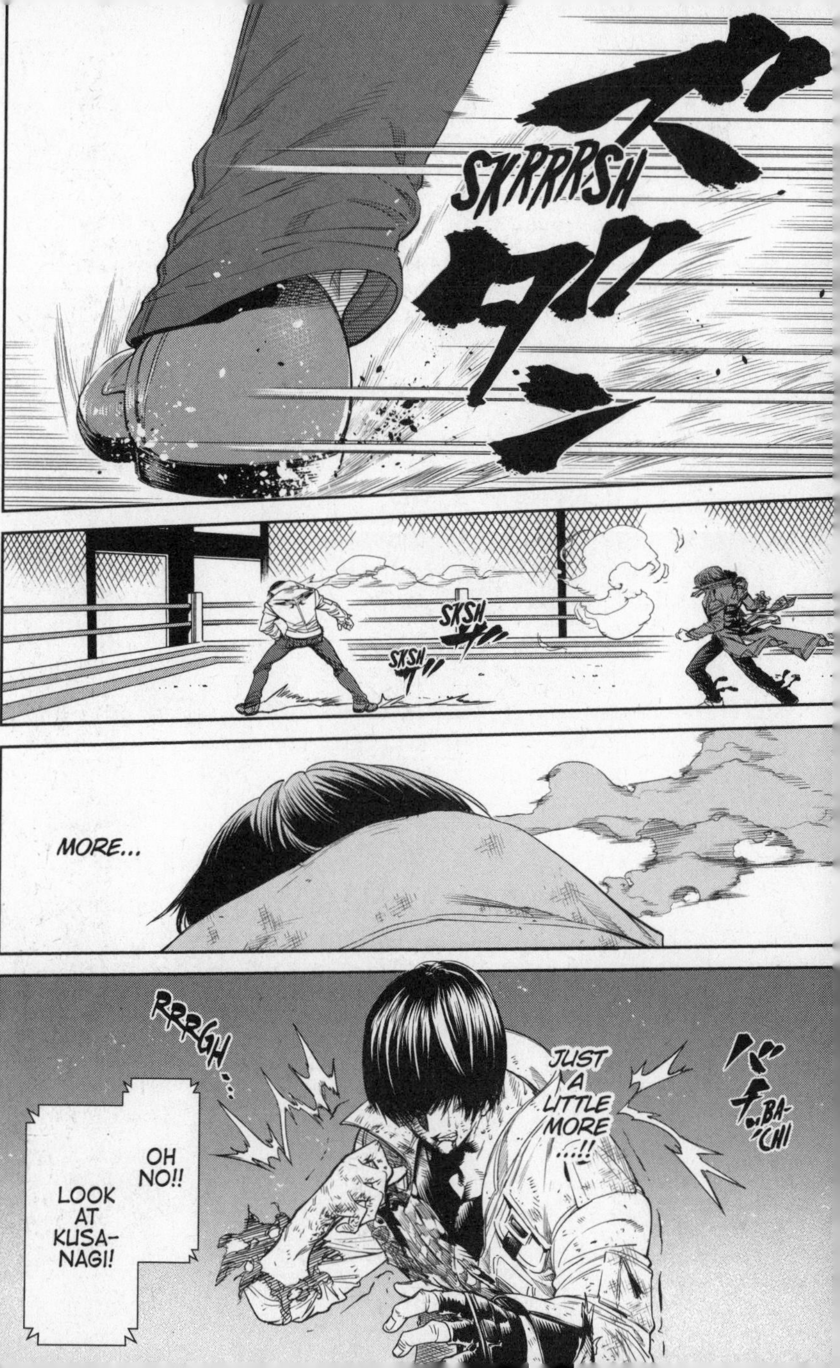

SKRRRSH
SKSH
SKSH
MORE...
BA-CHI
JUST A LITTLE MORE...!!
RRRGH...
OH NO!! LOOK AT KUSA-NAGI!

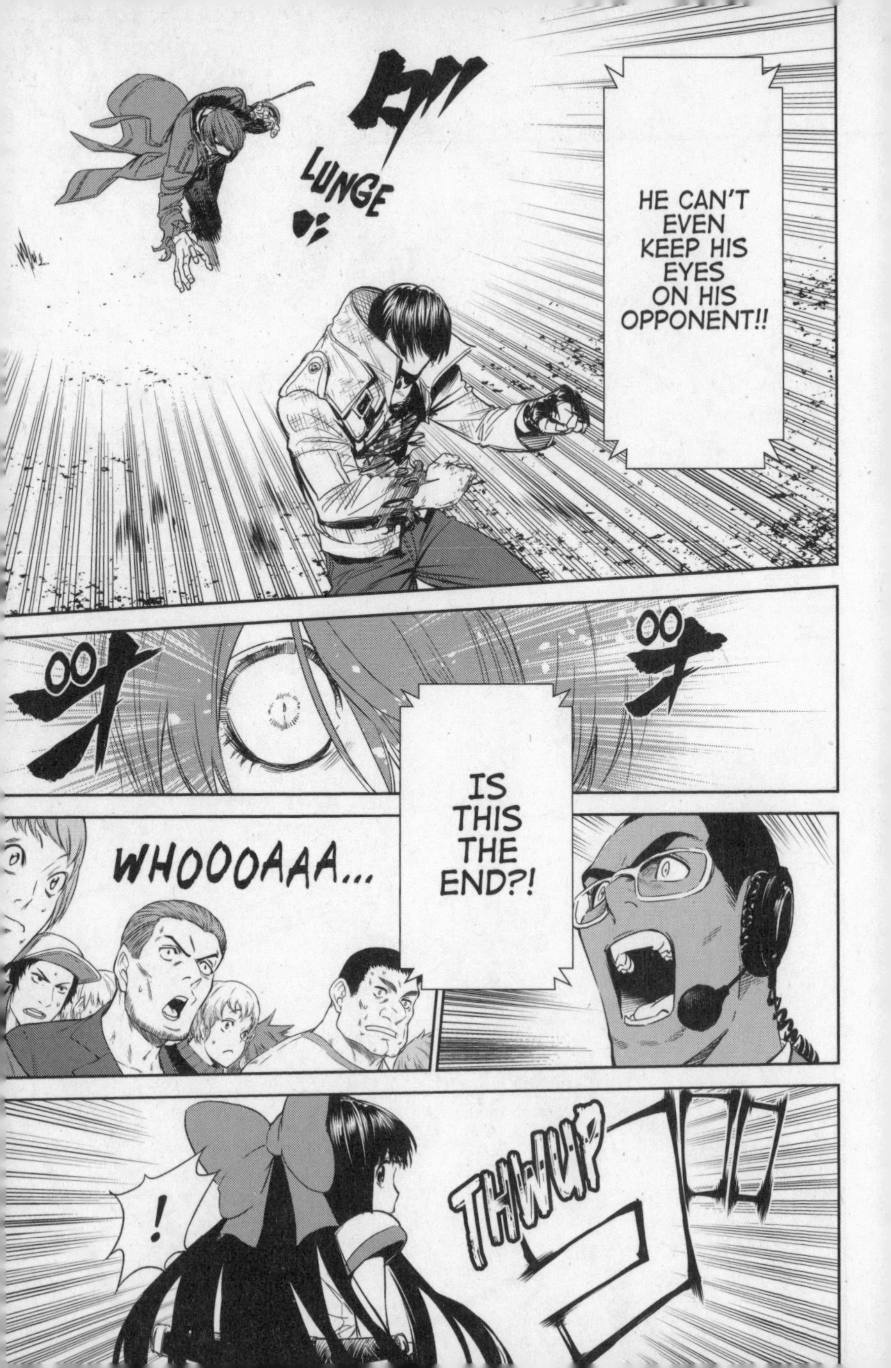
HE CAN'T EVEN KEEP HIS EYES ON HIS OPPONENT!!
LUNGE
IS THIS THE END?!
WHOOOAAA...
THWUP
!

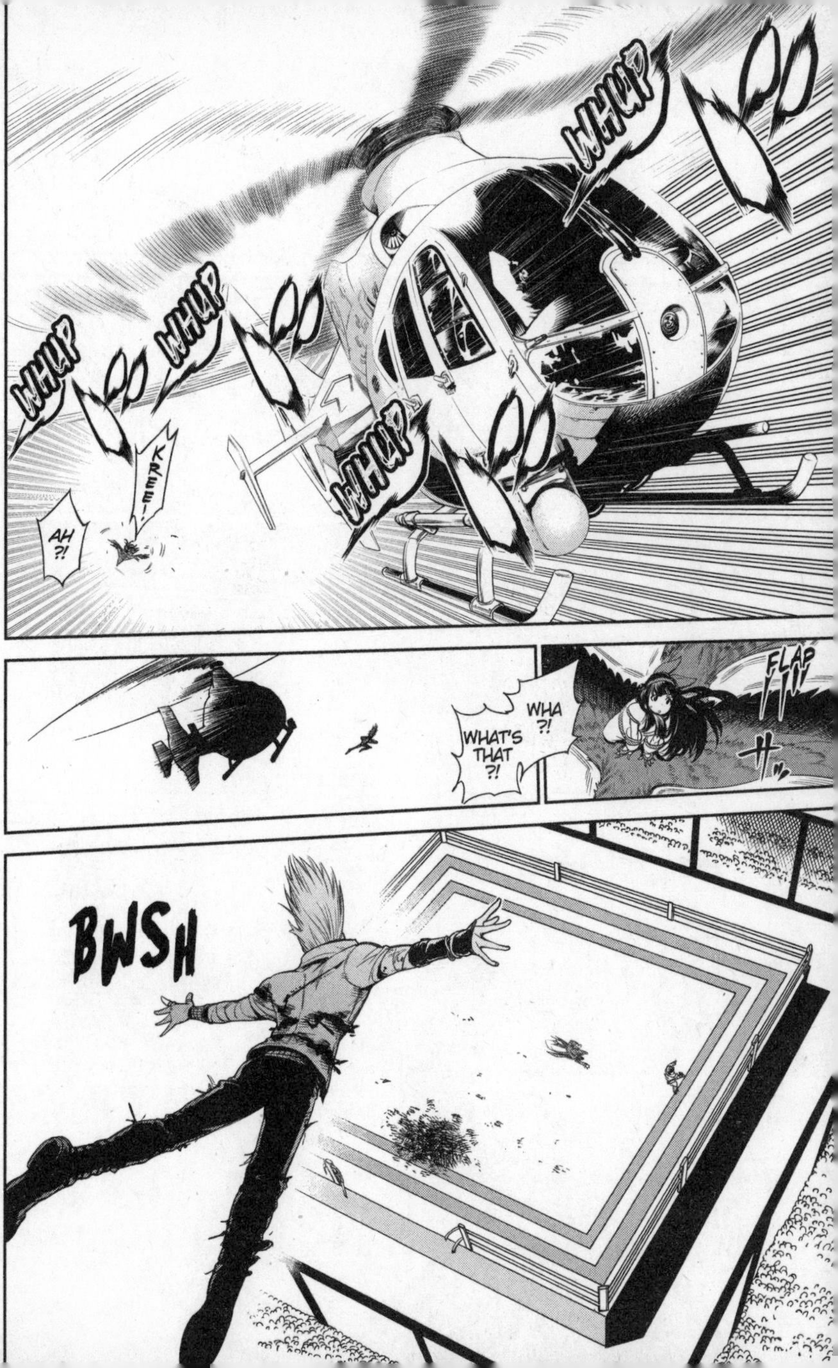
WHUP
WHUP
WHUP
WHUP
KREEE!
AH?!
WHA?!
WHAT'S THAT?!
FLAP
BWSH

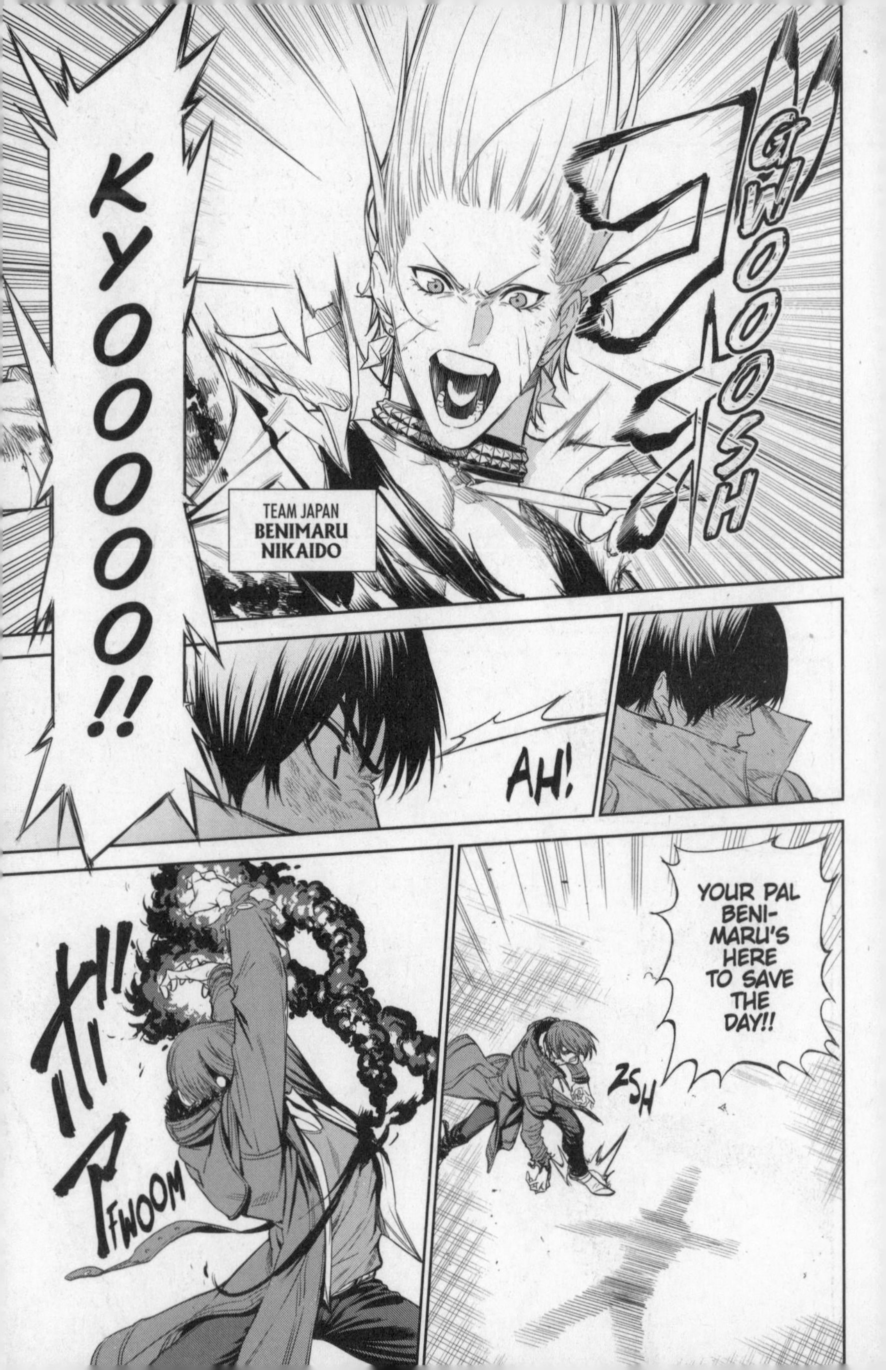
GWOOOOSH
KYOOOOO!!
TEAM JAPAN
BENIMARU NIKAIDO
AH!
YOUR PAL BENI-MARU'S HERE TO SAVE THE DAY!!
ZSH
FWOOM

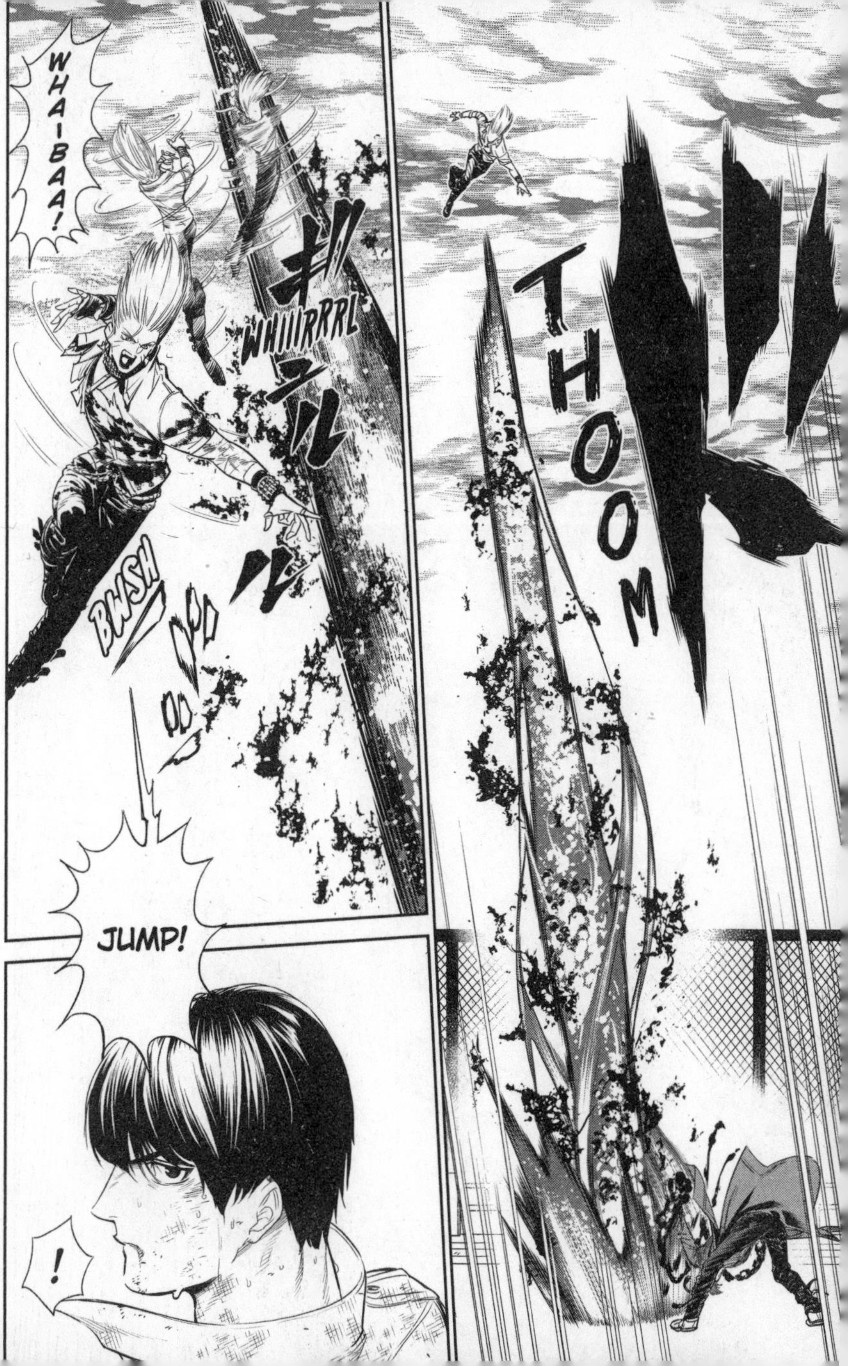
THOOM
WHAIBAAA!
WHIIIRRRL
BWSH
JUMP!
!

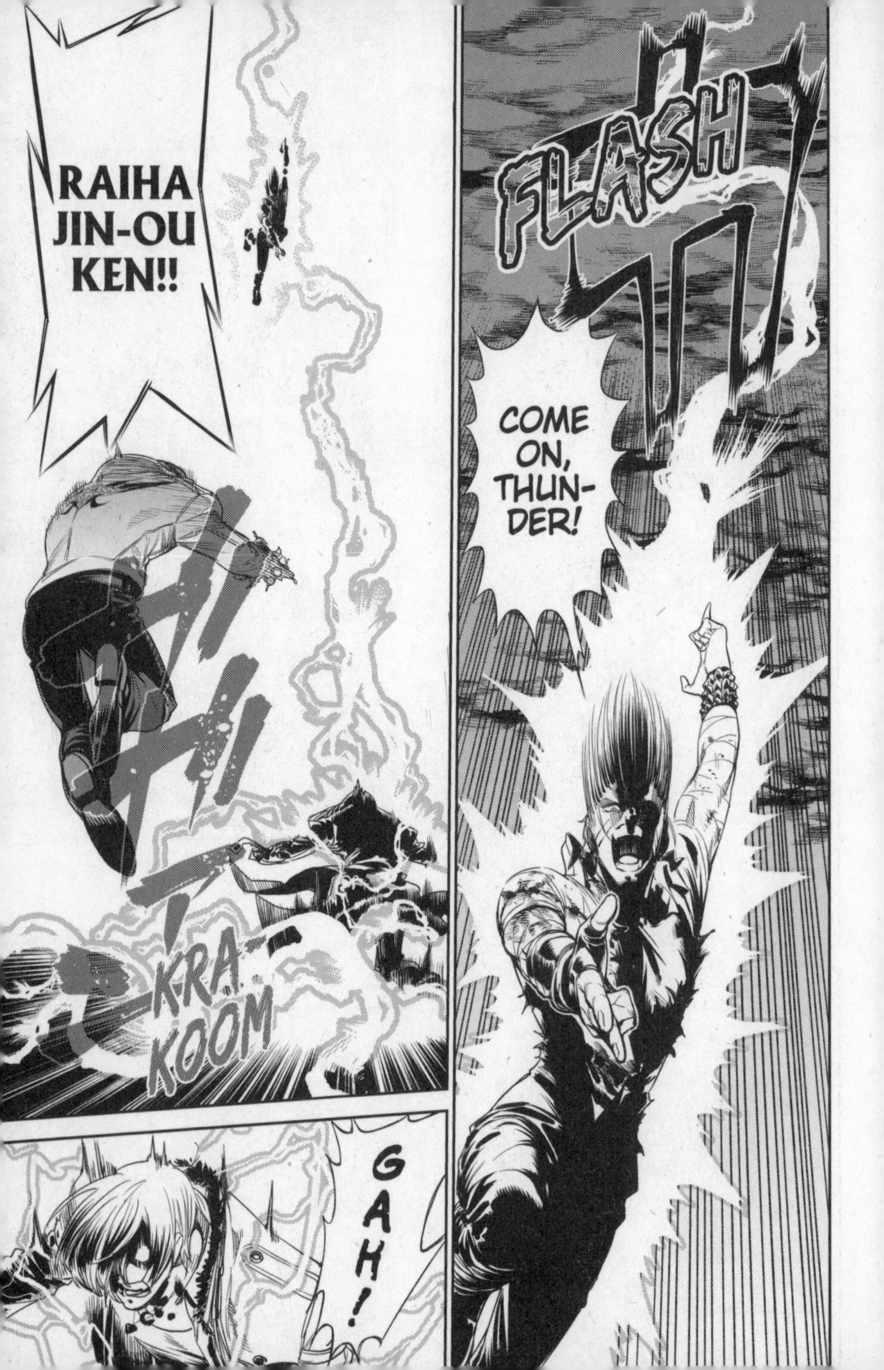
FLASH
COME ON, THUNDER!
RAIHA JIN-OU KEN!!
KRA-KOOM
GAH!

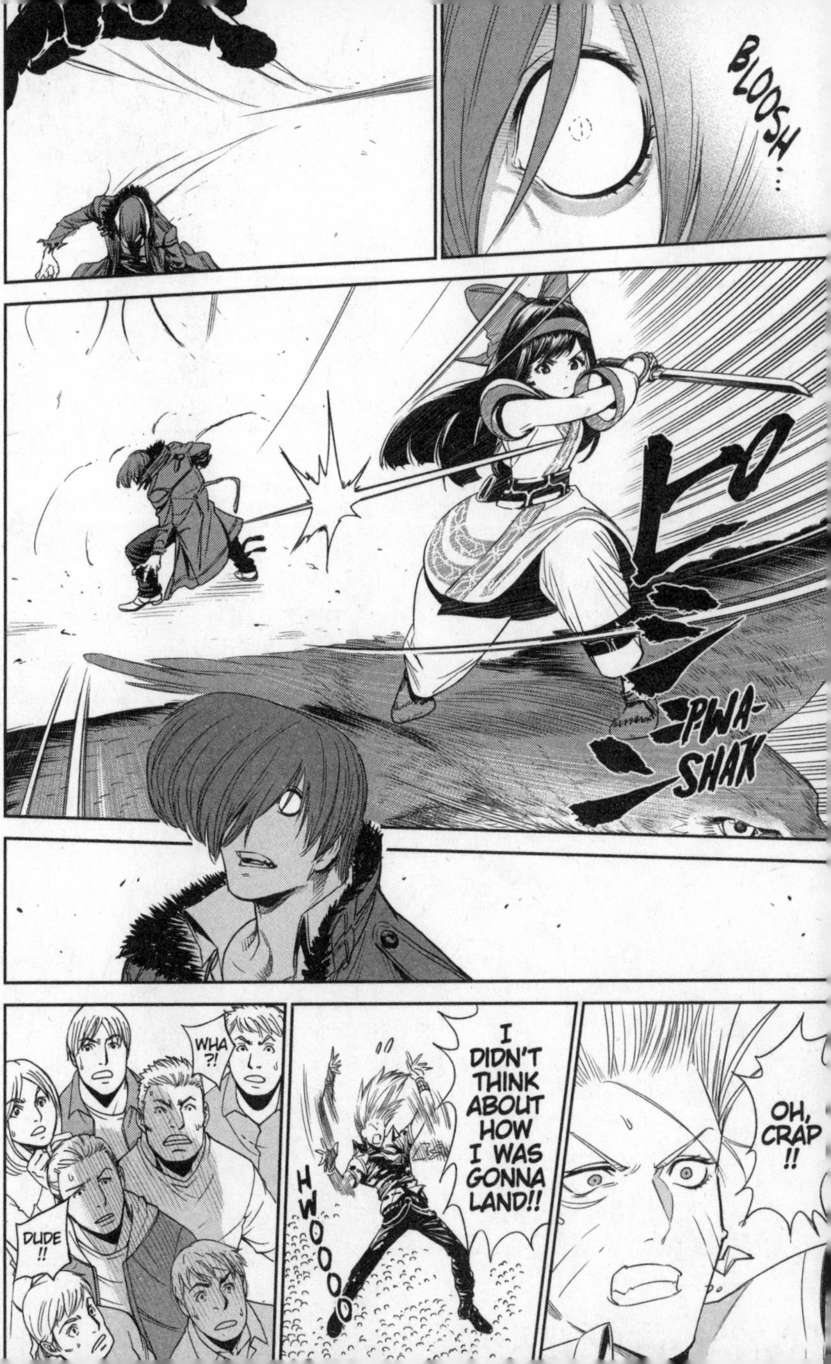
BLOOSH...
PWA-SHAK
OH, CRAP!!
I DIDN'T THINK ABOUT HOW I WAS GONNA LAND!!
HWOOOOO
WHA?!
DUDE!!

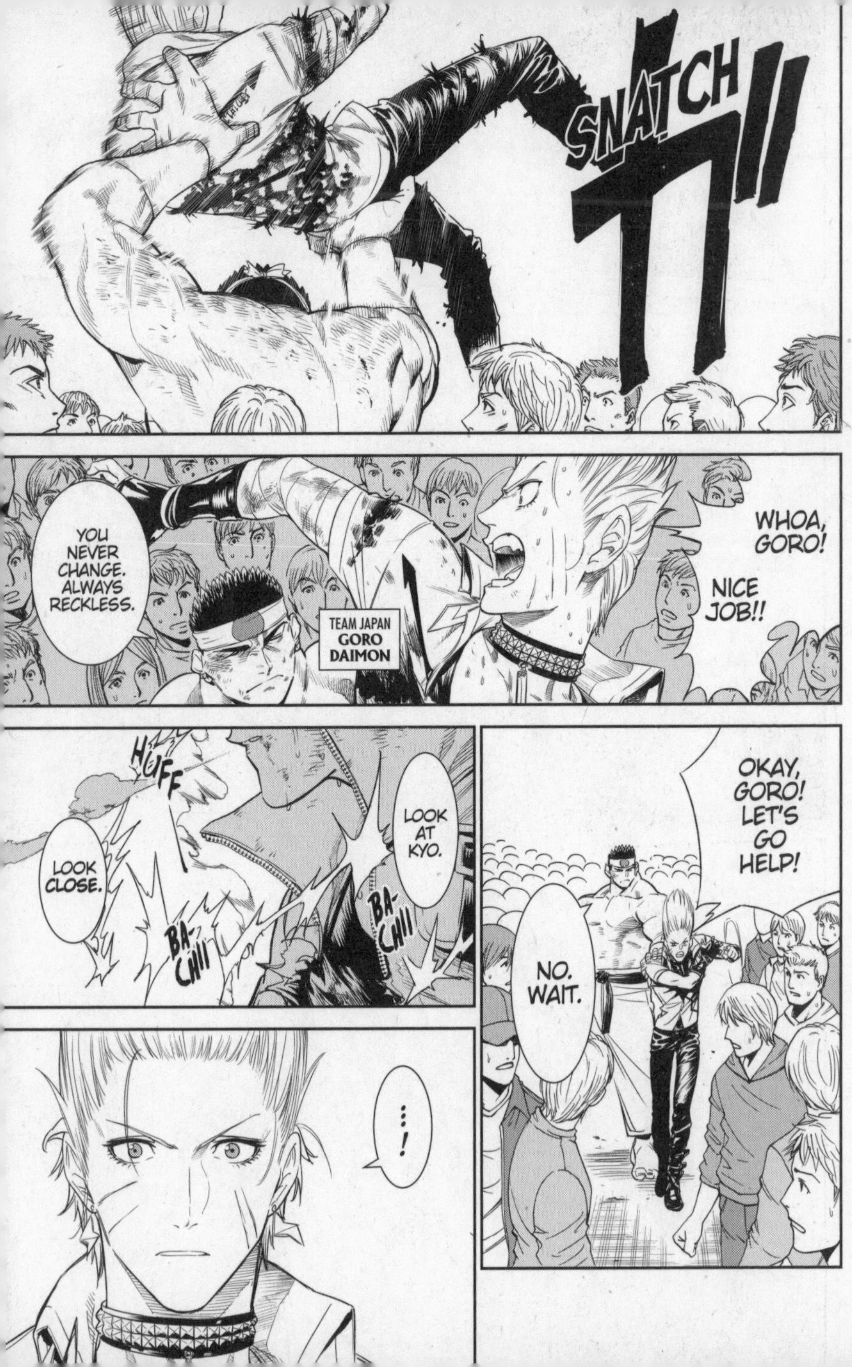
SNATCH
WHOA, GORO!
NICE JOB!!
TEAM JAPAN GORO DAIMON
YOU NEVER CHANGE. ALWAYS RECKLESS.
OKAY, GORO! LET'S GO HELP!
NO. WAIT.
LOOK AT KYO.
BA-CHII
HUFF
LOOK CLOSE.
BA-CHII
...!

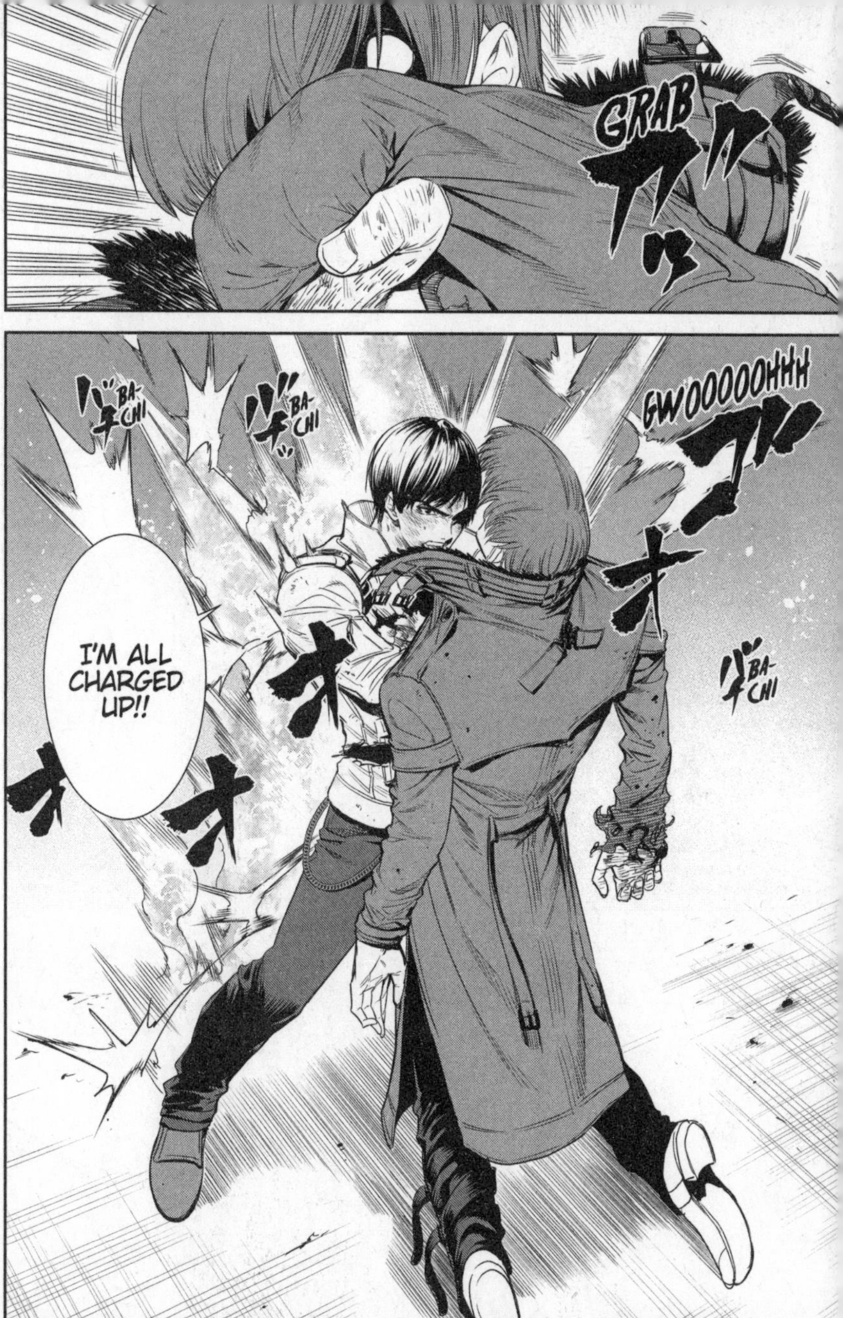
GRAB
GWOOOOOHHH
BA-CHI
BA-CHI
BA-CHI
I'M ALL CHARGED UP!!

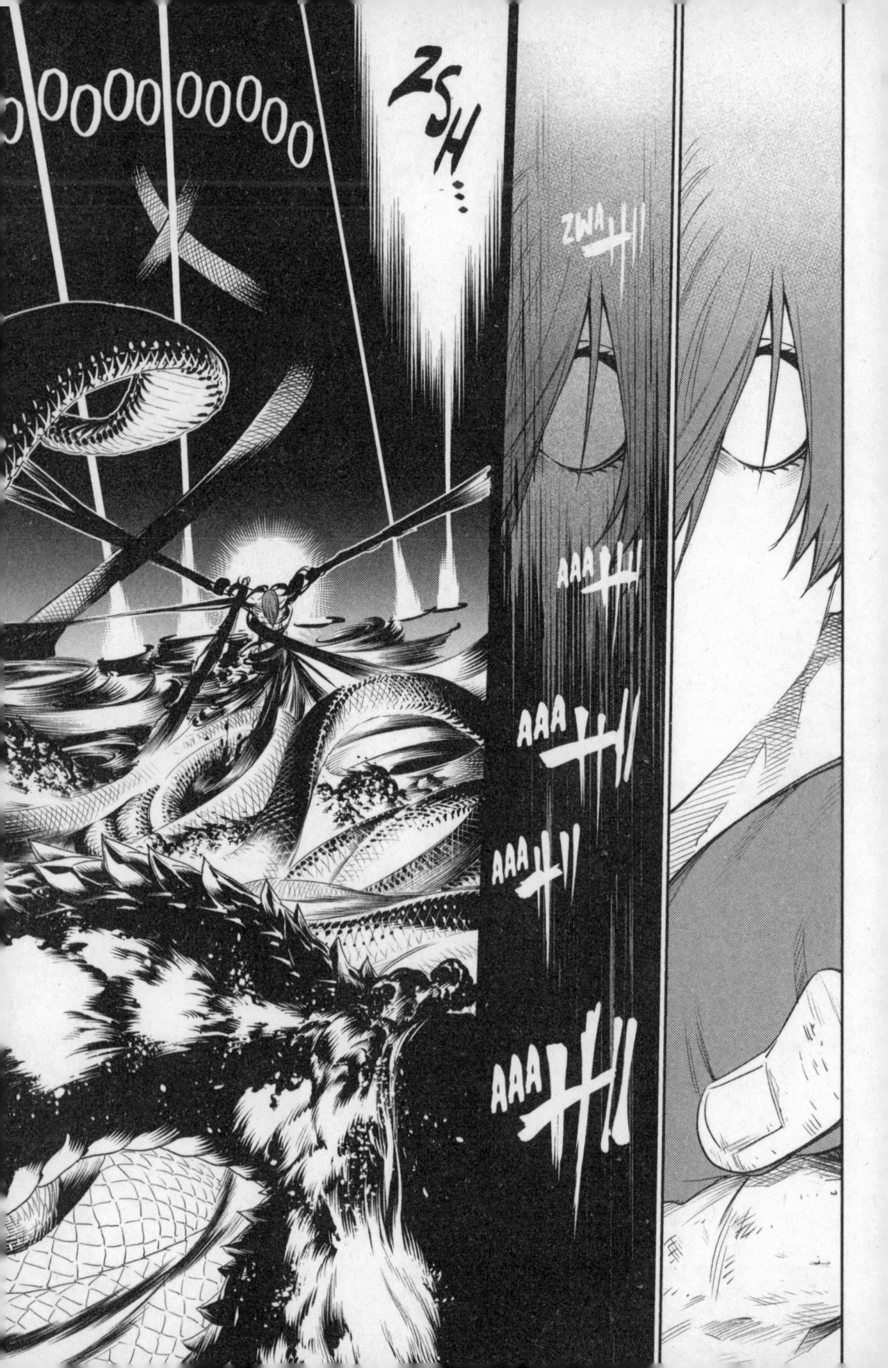
ZWA
AAA
AAA
AAA
AAA
ZSH...
OOOOOOOOOOOO

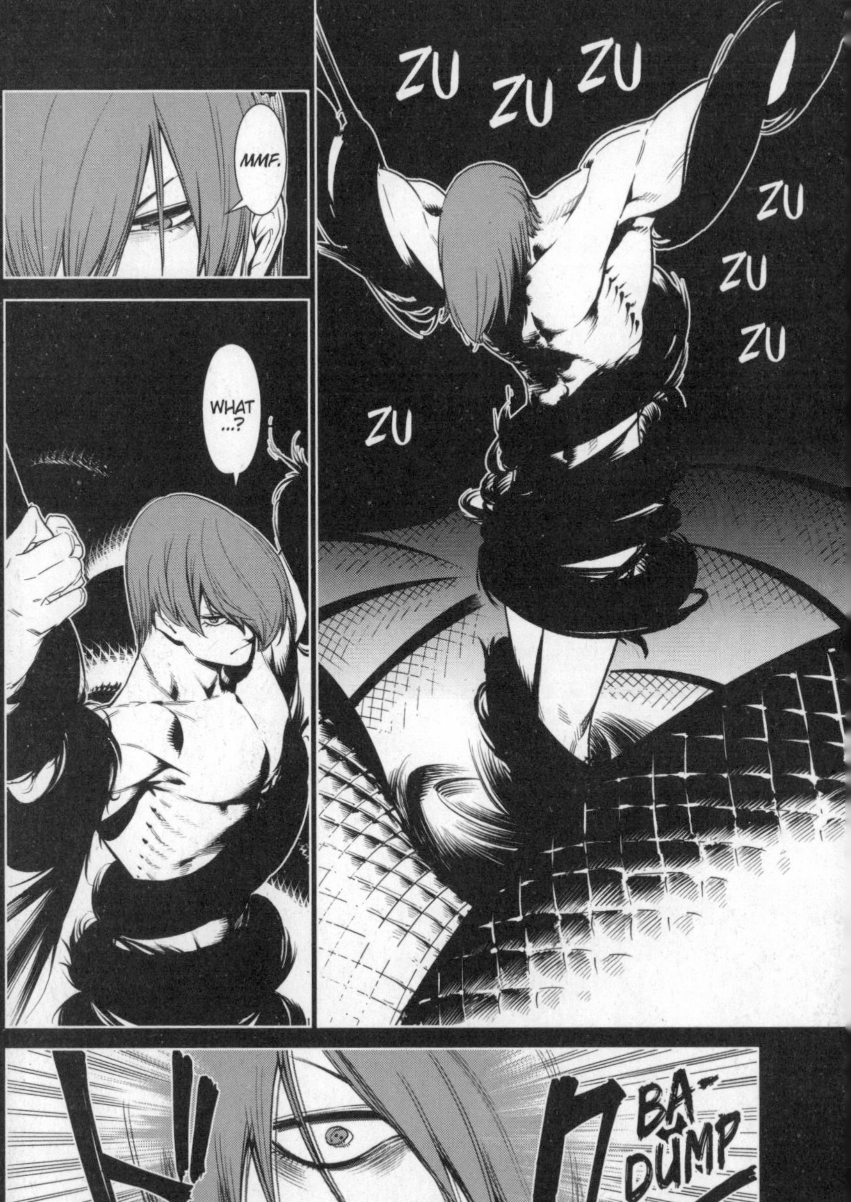
ZU ZU ZU
ZU ZU ZU
ZU
MMF.
WHAT ...?
BA-DUMP

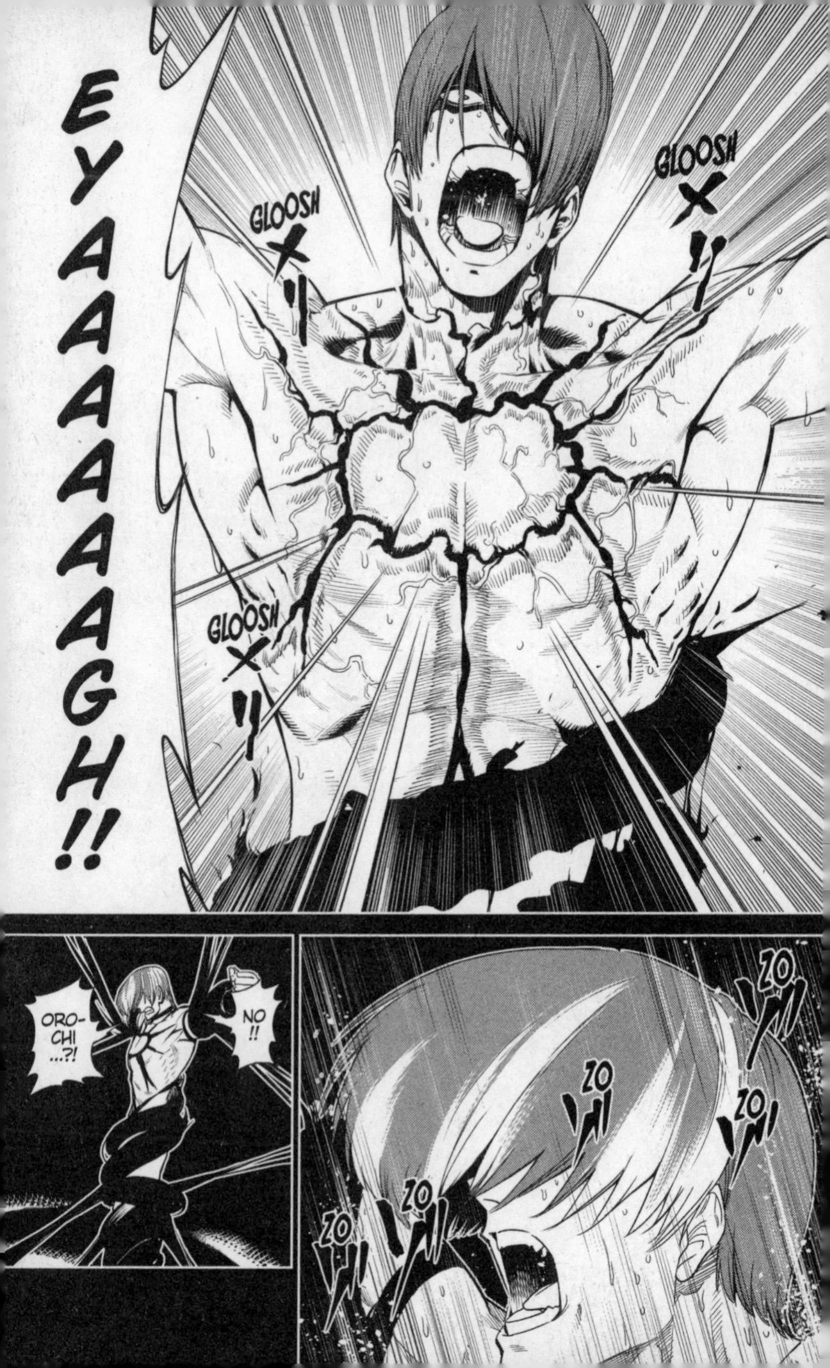
GLOOSH
GLOOSH
GLOOSH
EYAAAAAAGH!!
ZO
ZO
ZO
ZO
ZO
NO!!
ORO-CHI ...?!

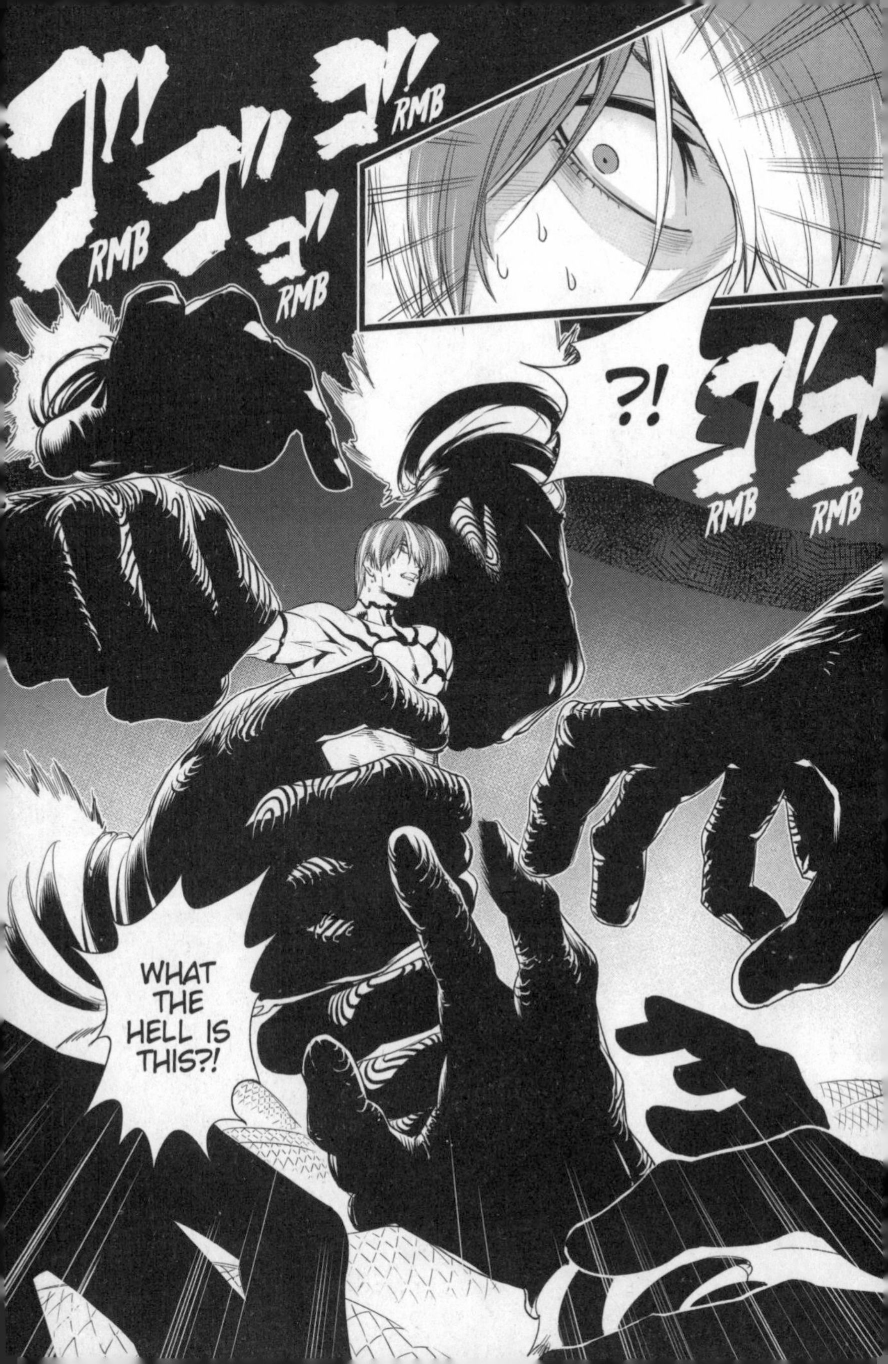

?!
RMB
RMB
RMB
RMB
RMB
WHAT THE HELL IS THIS?!

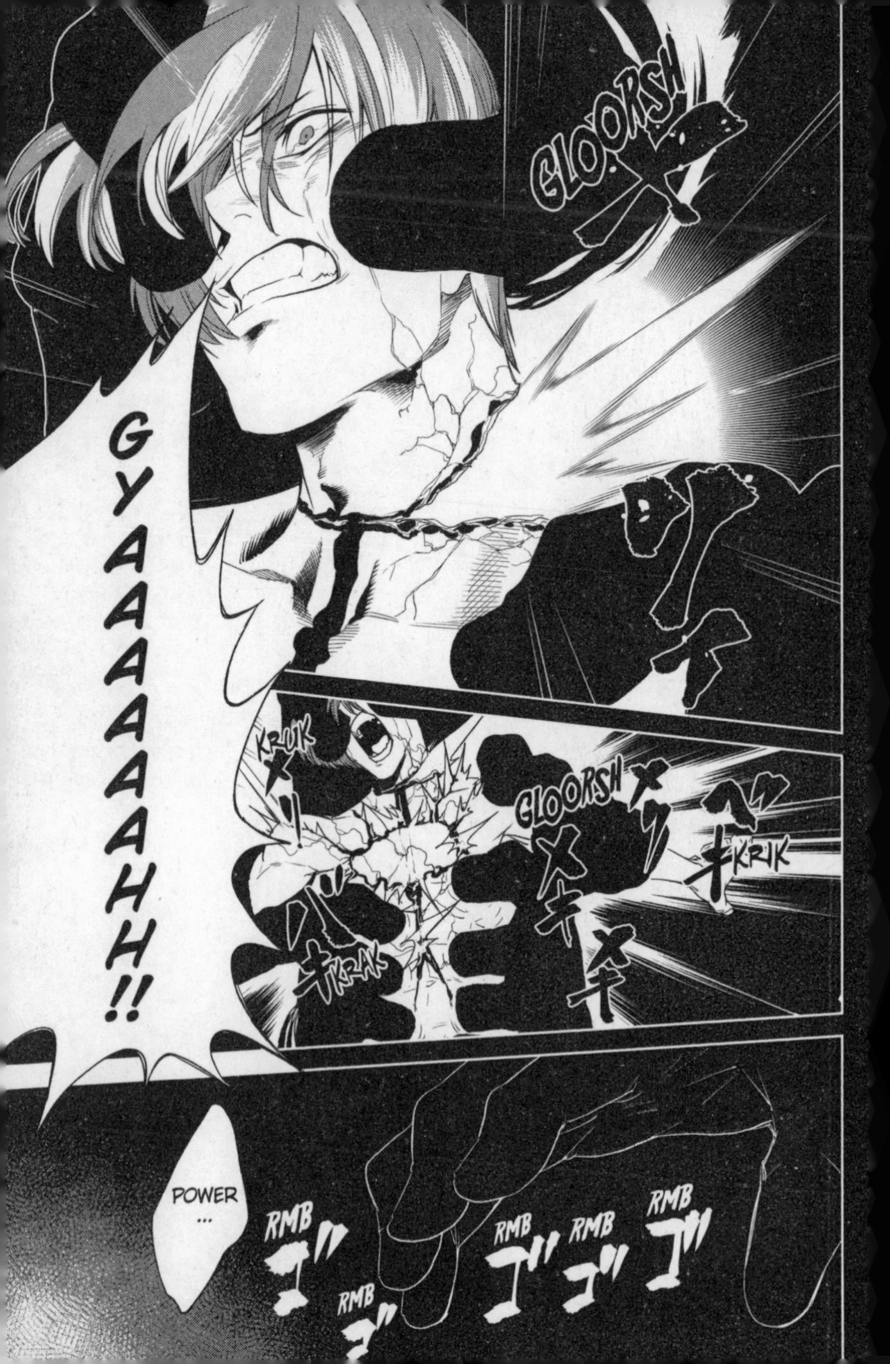
GLOORSH
GYAAAAAAAHH!!
GLOORSH
KRIK
KRUK
KRAK
POWER
...
RMB
RMB
RMB
RMB
RMB

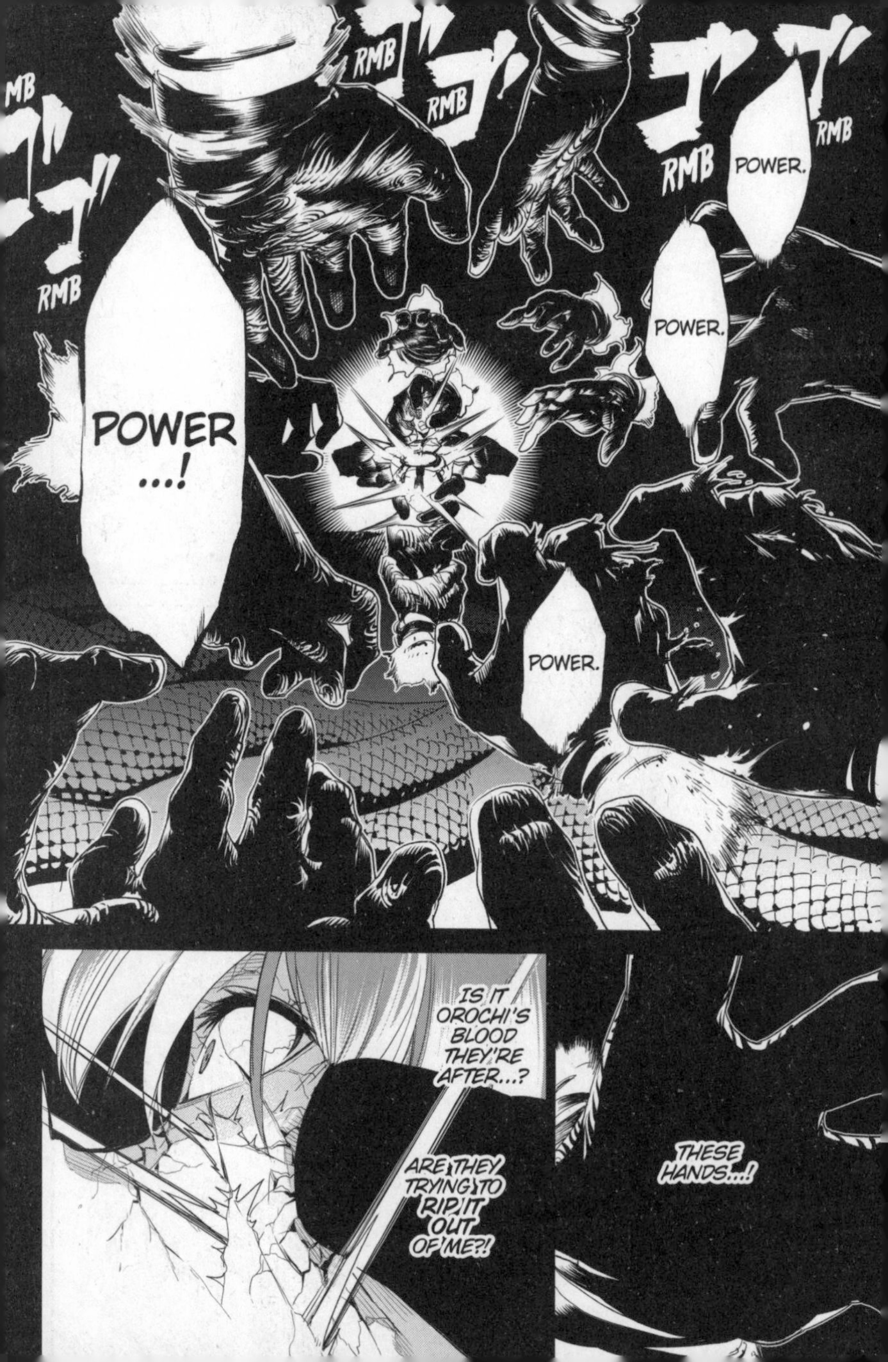
RMB
RMB
RMB
RMB
RMB
POWER.
POWER.
POWER.
POWER ...!
THESE HANDS...!
IS IT OROCHI'S BLOOD THEY'RE AFTER...?
ARE THEY TRYING TO RIP IT OUT OF ME?!

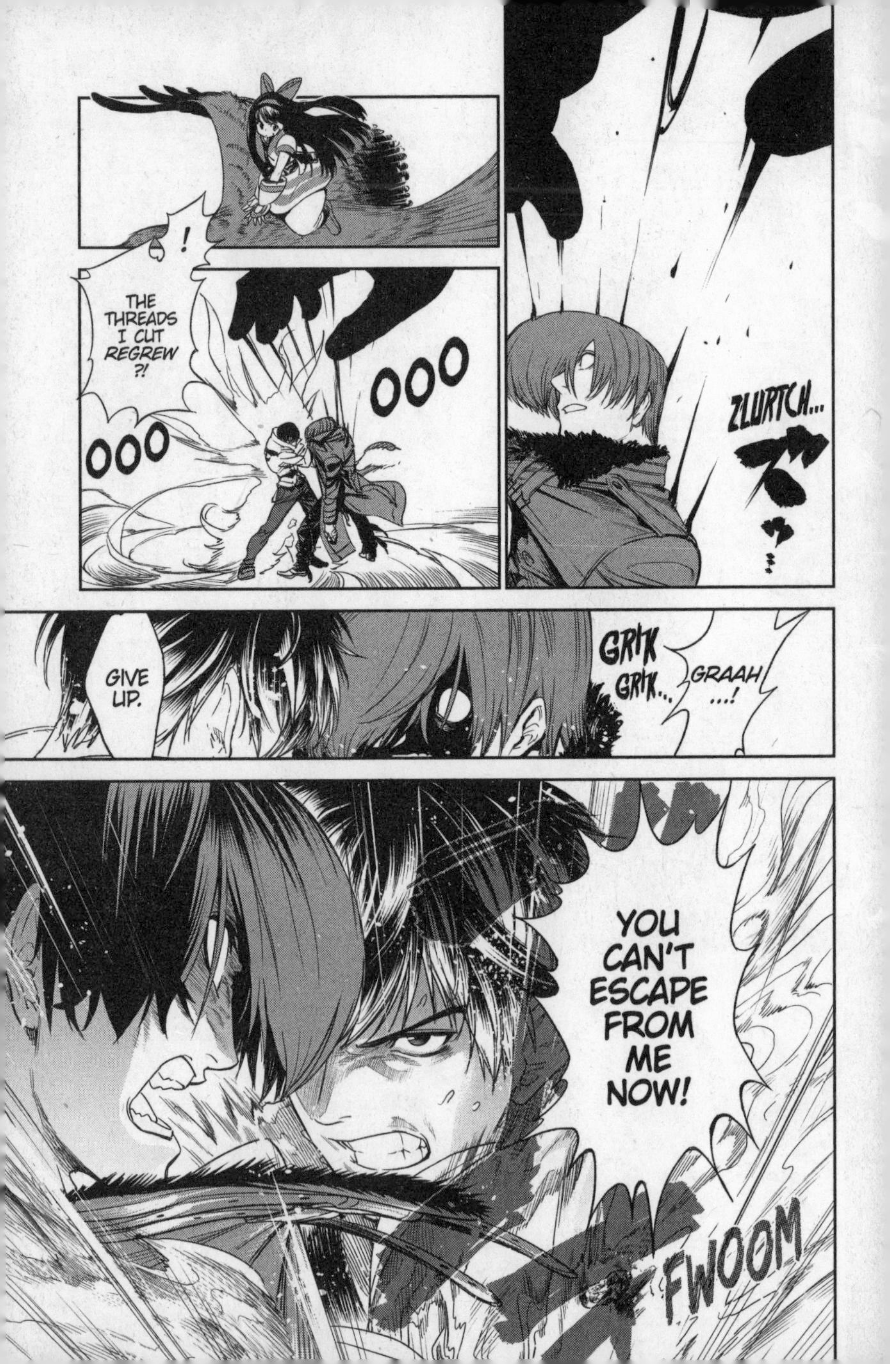
ZLURTCH...
!
THE THREADS I CUT REGREW ?!
OOO
OOO
GRIK GRIK...
GRAAH ...!
GIVE UP.
YOU CAN'T ESCAPE FROM ME NOW!
FWOOM

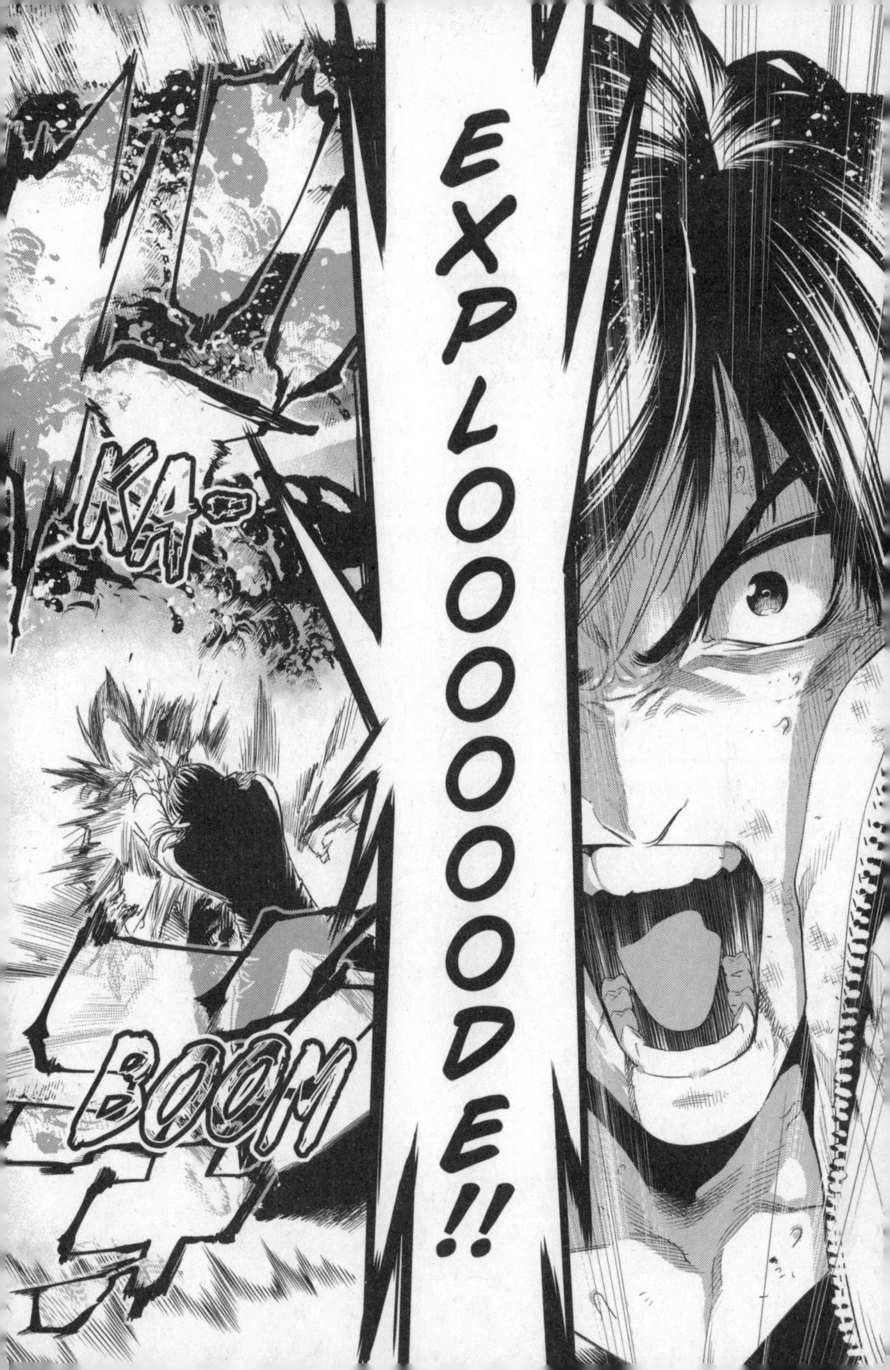
EXPLOOOOOODE!!
KA-
BOOM

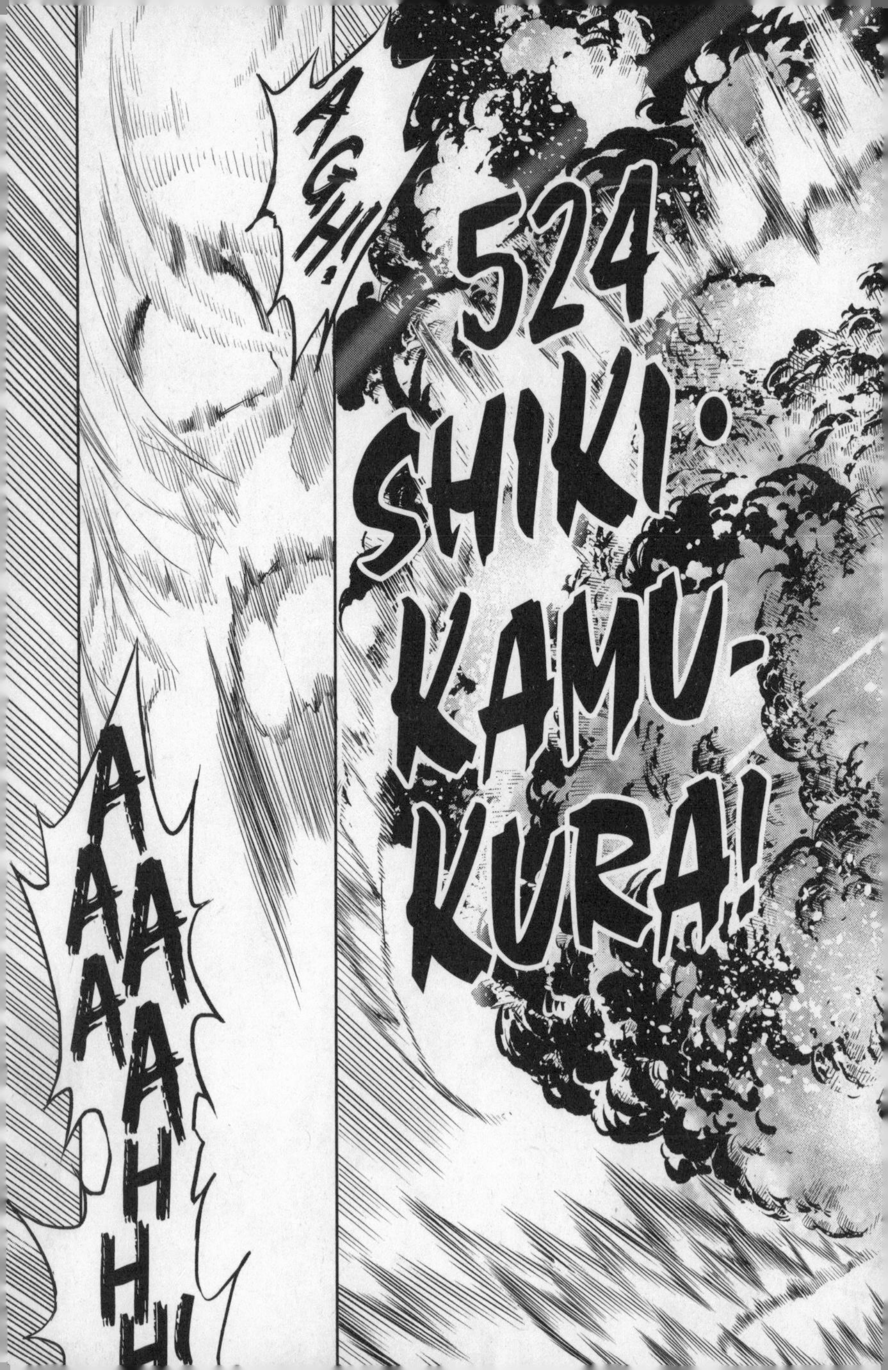
524 SHIKI: KAMU-KURA!
AGH!
AAAAAAHHH

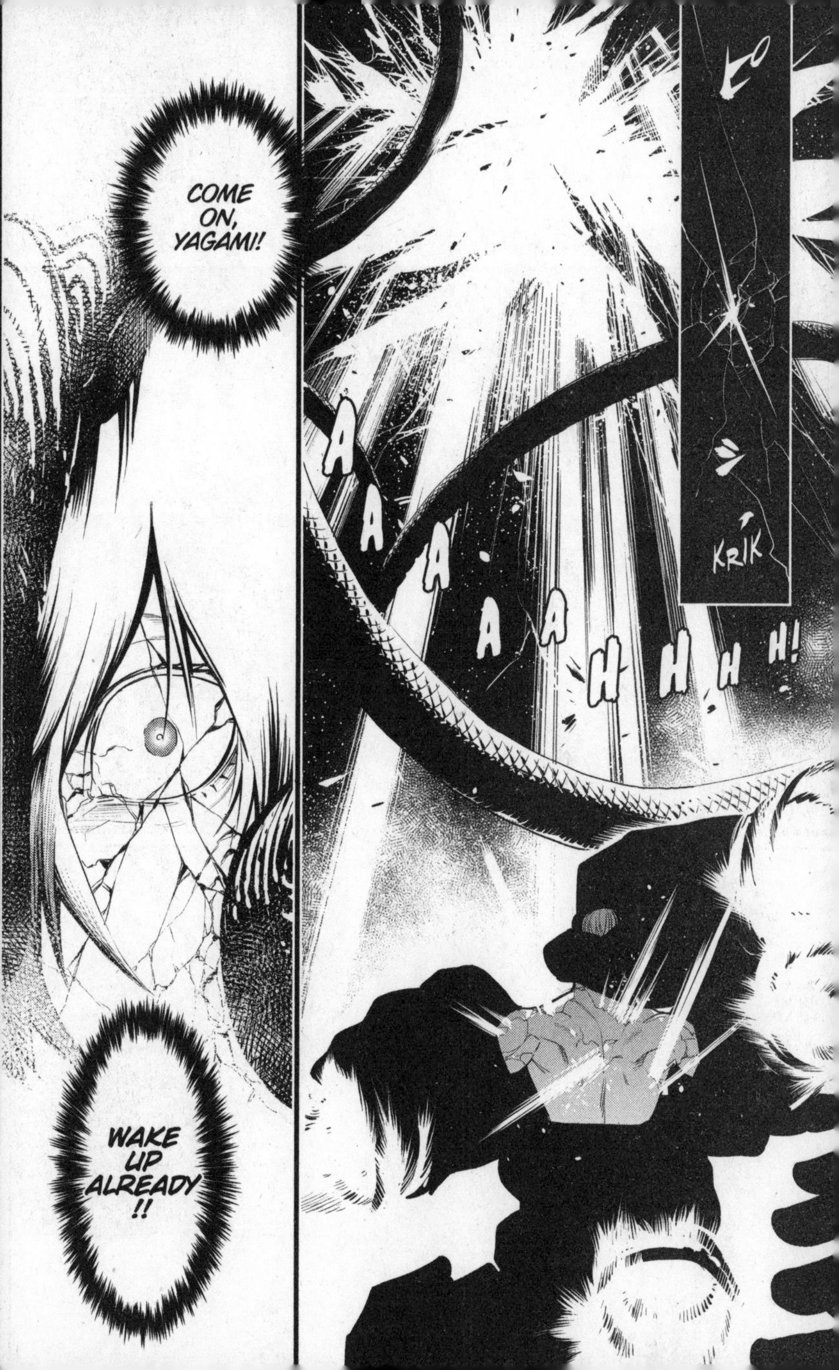
KRIK
AAAAAHHHH!
COME ON, YAGAMI!
WAKE UP ALREADY!!

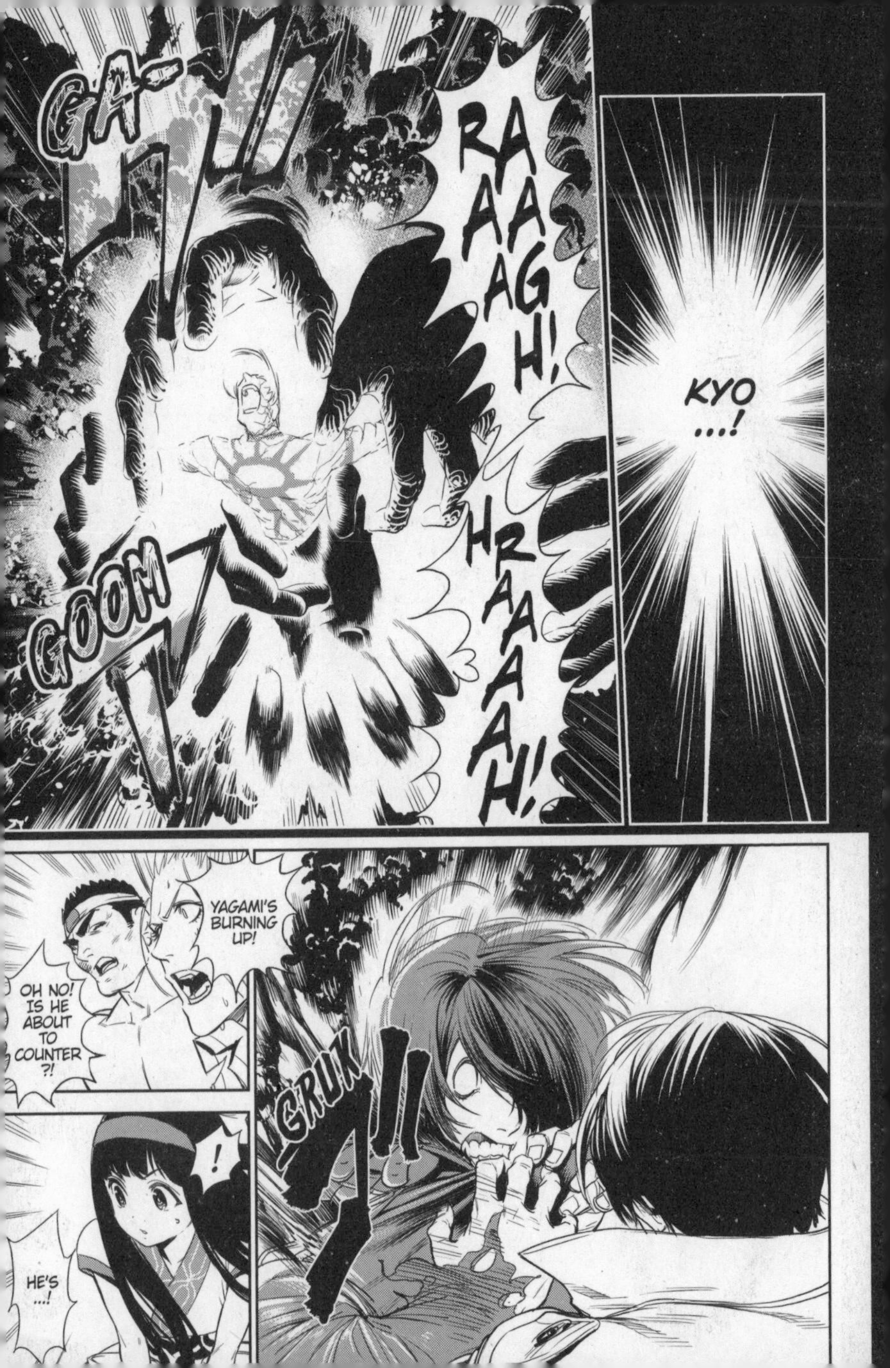
KYO ...!
RAAAAGH!
GA-
HRAAAAH!
GOOM
GRUK
YAGAMI'S BURNING UP!
OH NO! IS HE ABOUT TO COUNTER?!
!
HE'S ...!

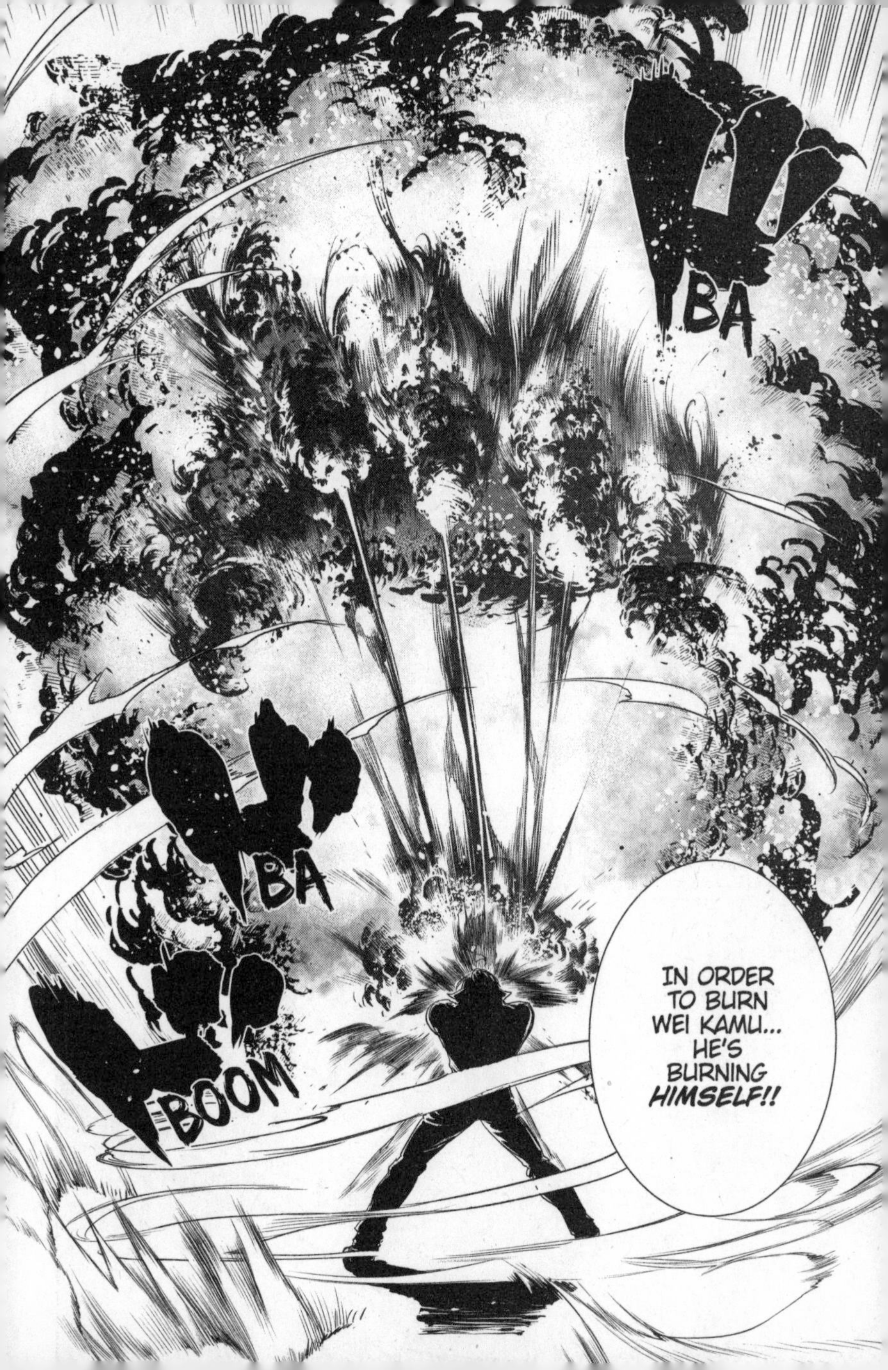
BA
IN ORDER TO BURN WEI KAMU... HE'S BURNING ***HIMSELF!!***
BA
BOOM

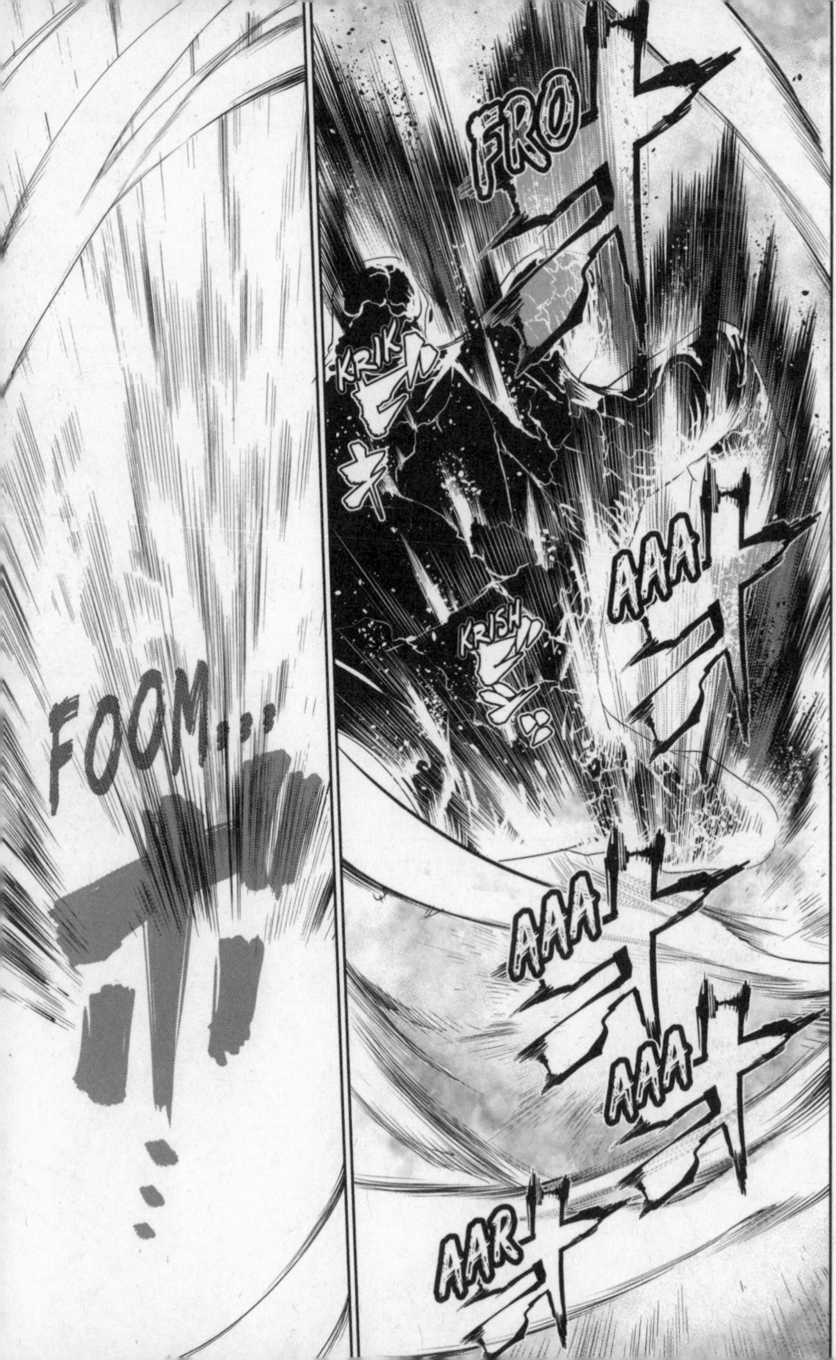
FRO
KRIK
AAA
KRISH
AAA
AAA
AAR
FOOM...!!

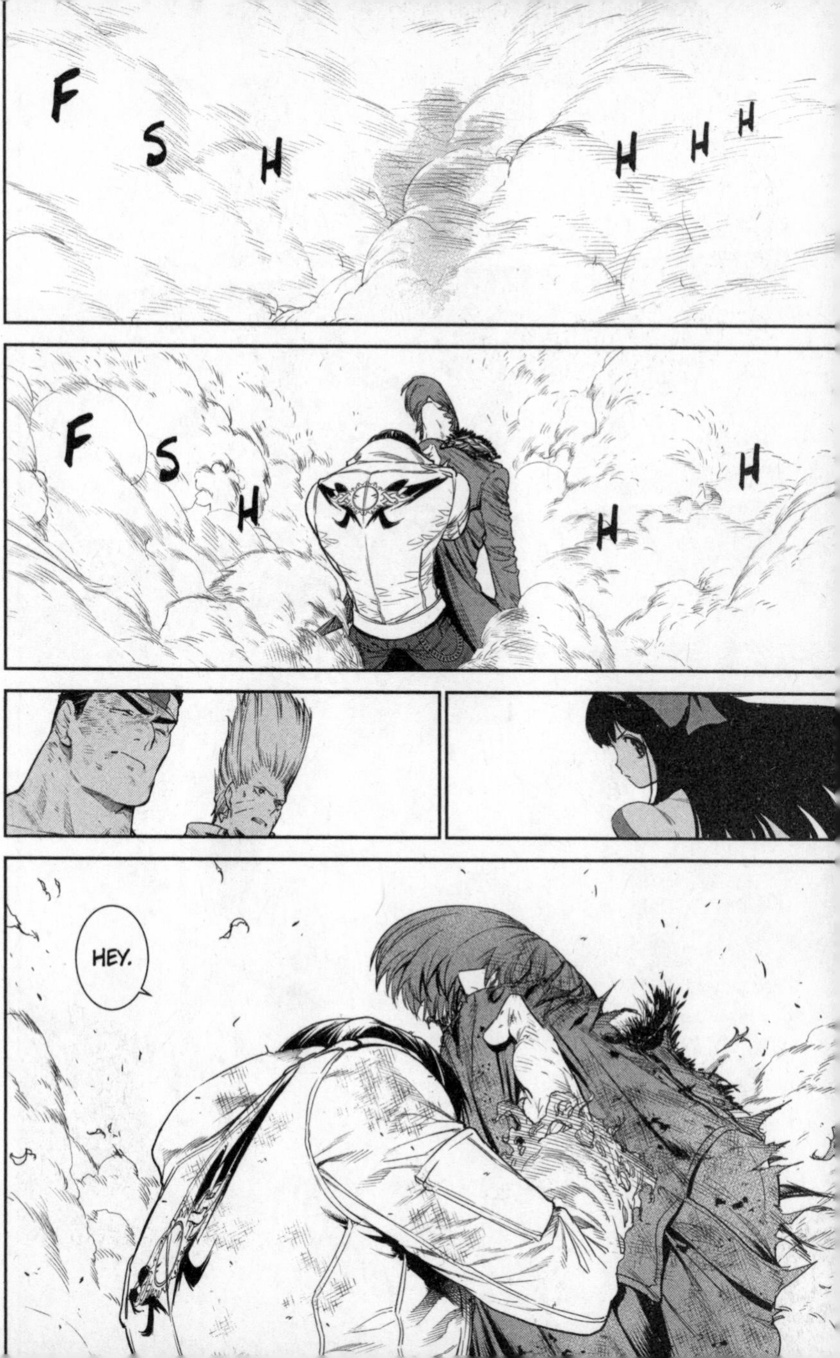
FSHHHH
FSHHH
HEY.

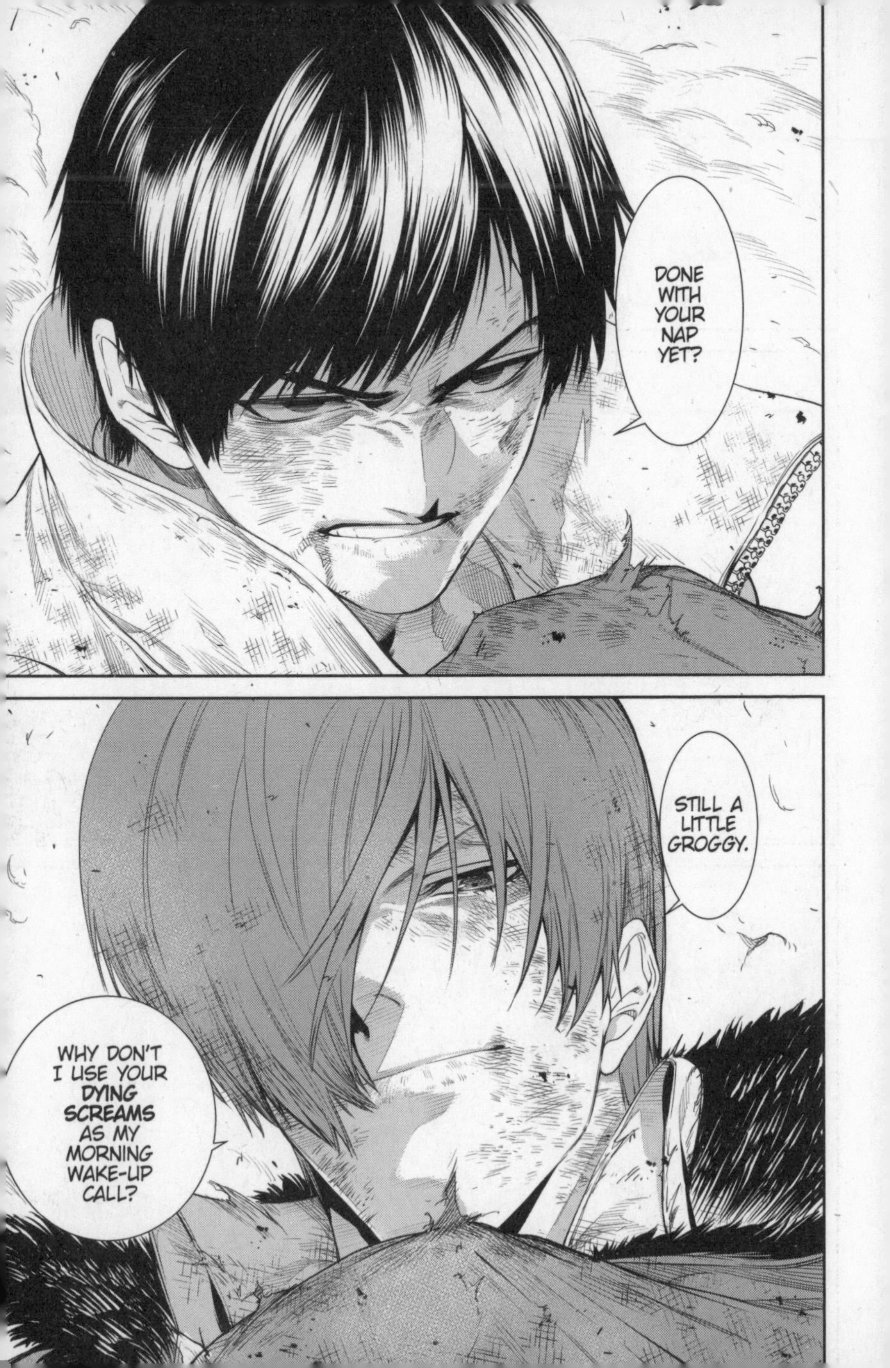
DONE WITH YOUR NAP YET?
STILL A LITTLE GROGGY.
WHY DON'T I USE YOUR DYING SCREAMS AS MY MORNING WAKE-UP CALL?

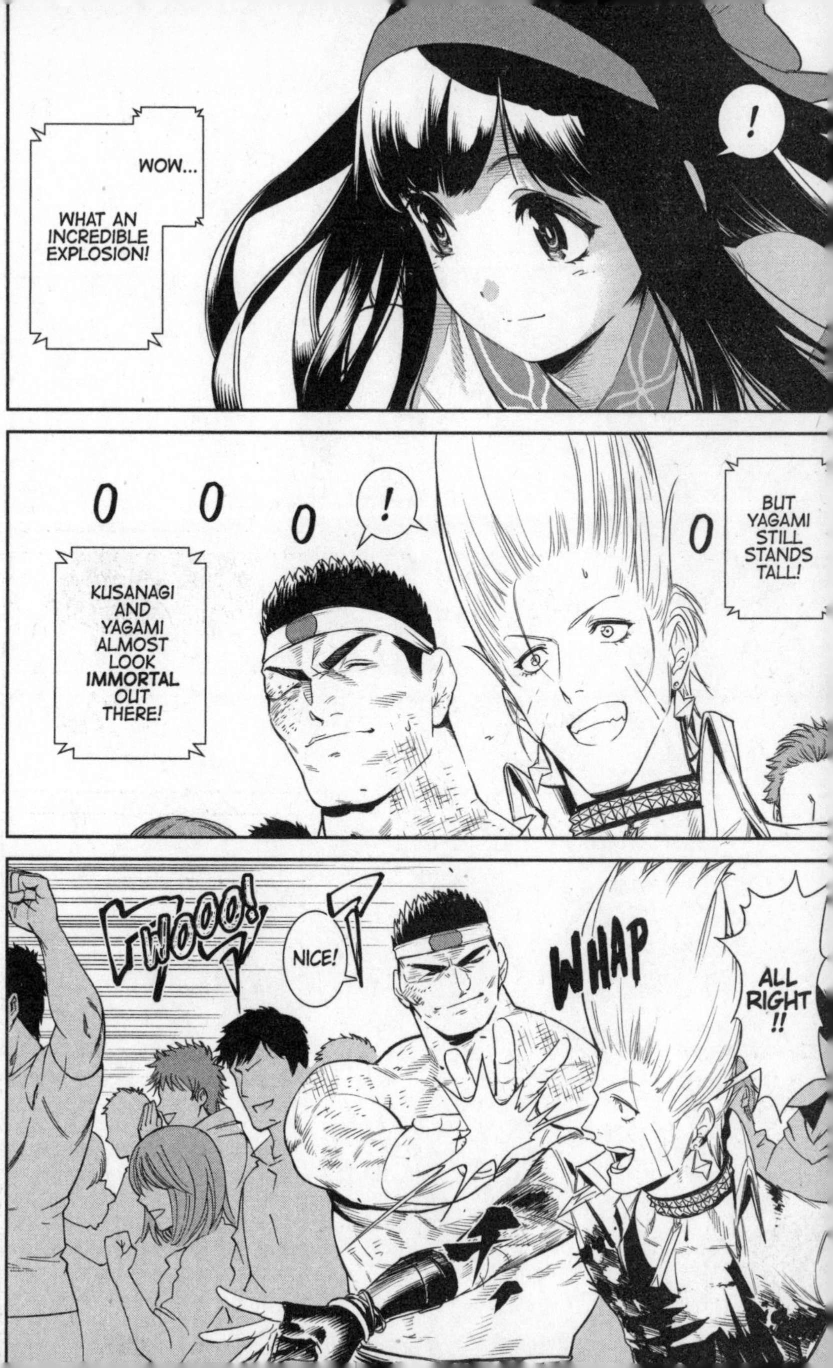
!
WOW...
WHAT AN INCREDIBLE EXPLOSION!
BUT YAGAMI STILL STANDS TALL!
O O O O
!
KUSANAGI AND YAGAMI ALMOST LOOK IMMORTAL OUT THERE!
ALL RIGHT!!
WHAP
NICE!
WOOO!

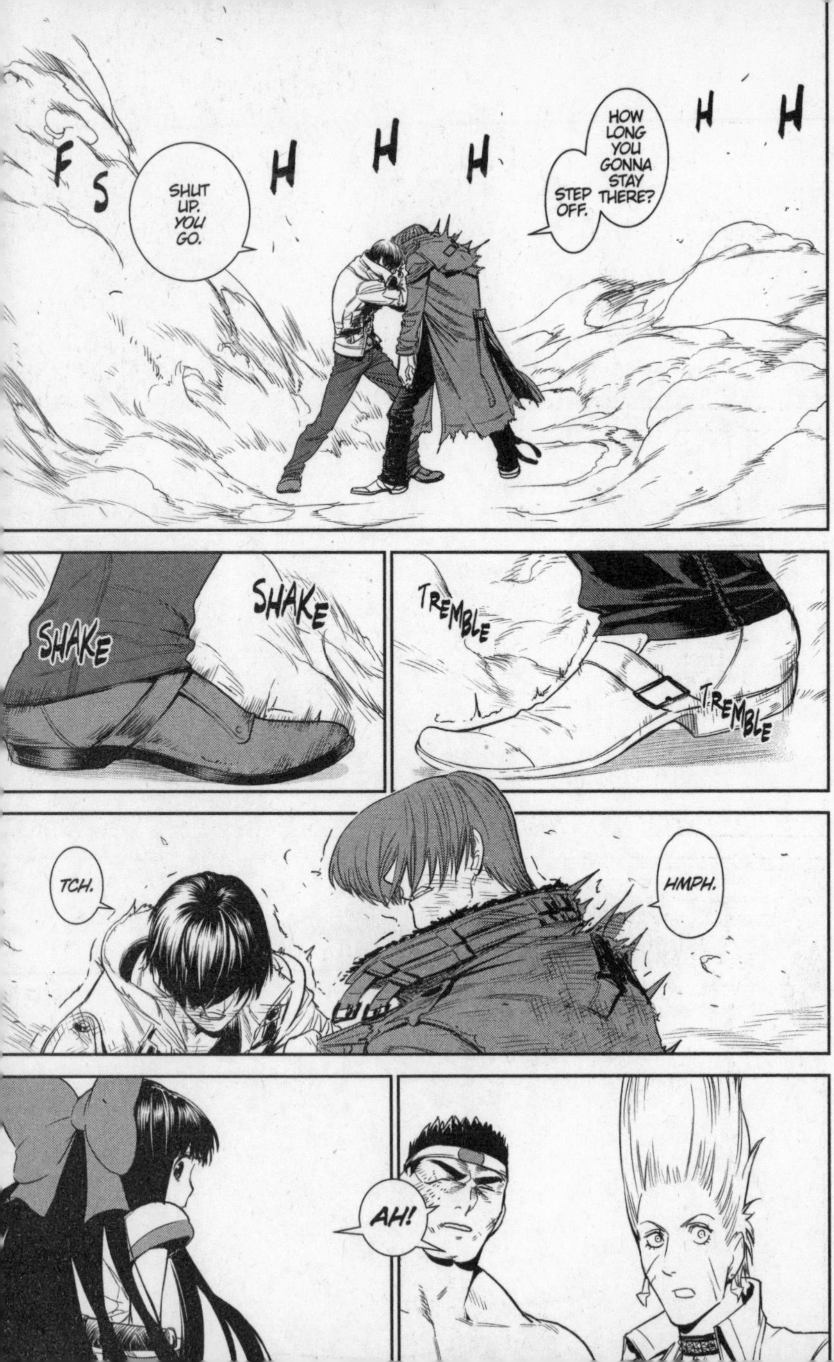
FSHHHHHH
HOW LONG YOU GONNA STAY THERE? STEP OFF.
SHUT UP. YOU GO.
TREMBLE
TREMBLE
SHAKE
SHAKE
HMPH.
TCH.
AH!

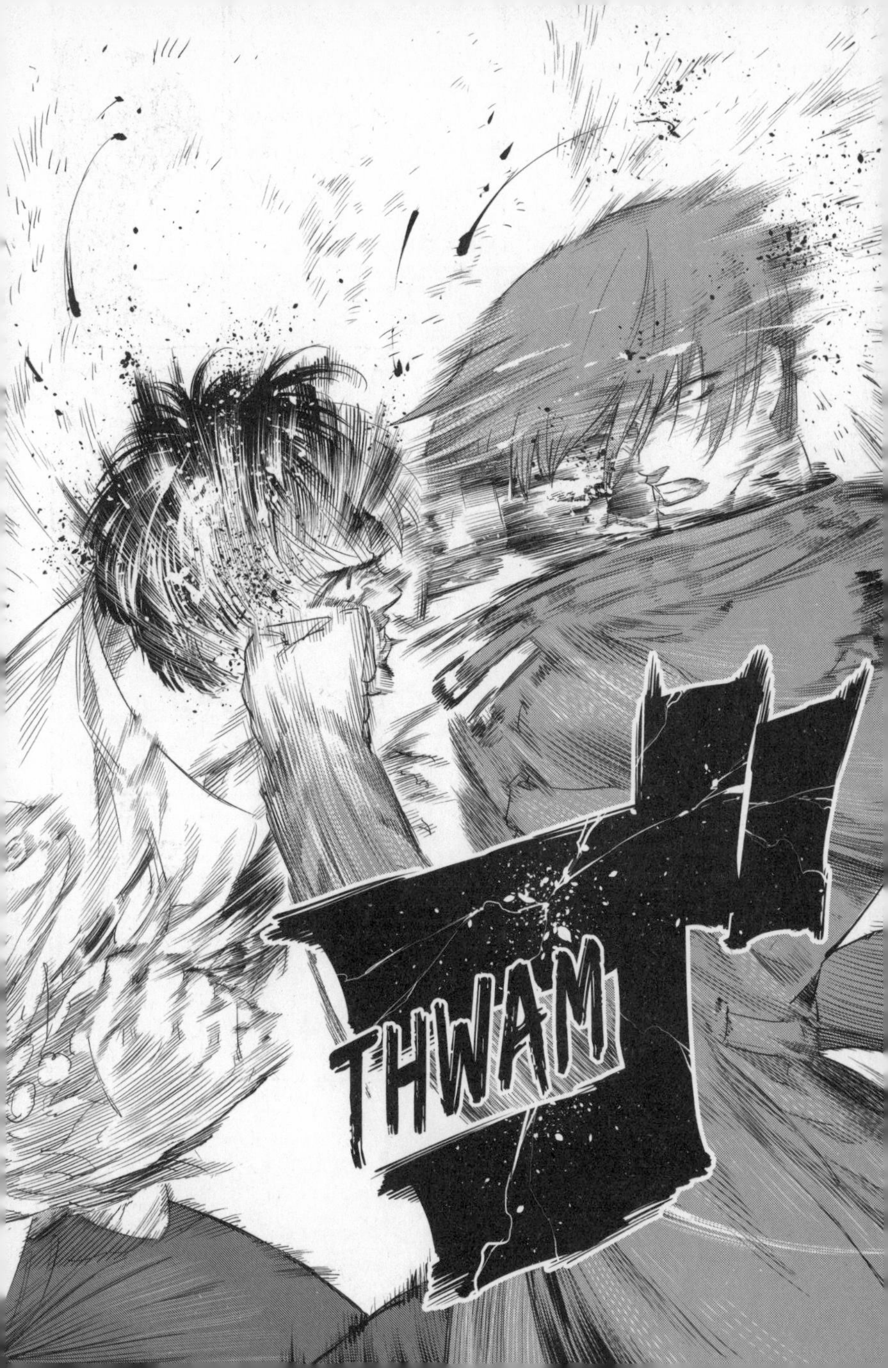
THWAM

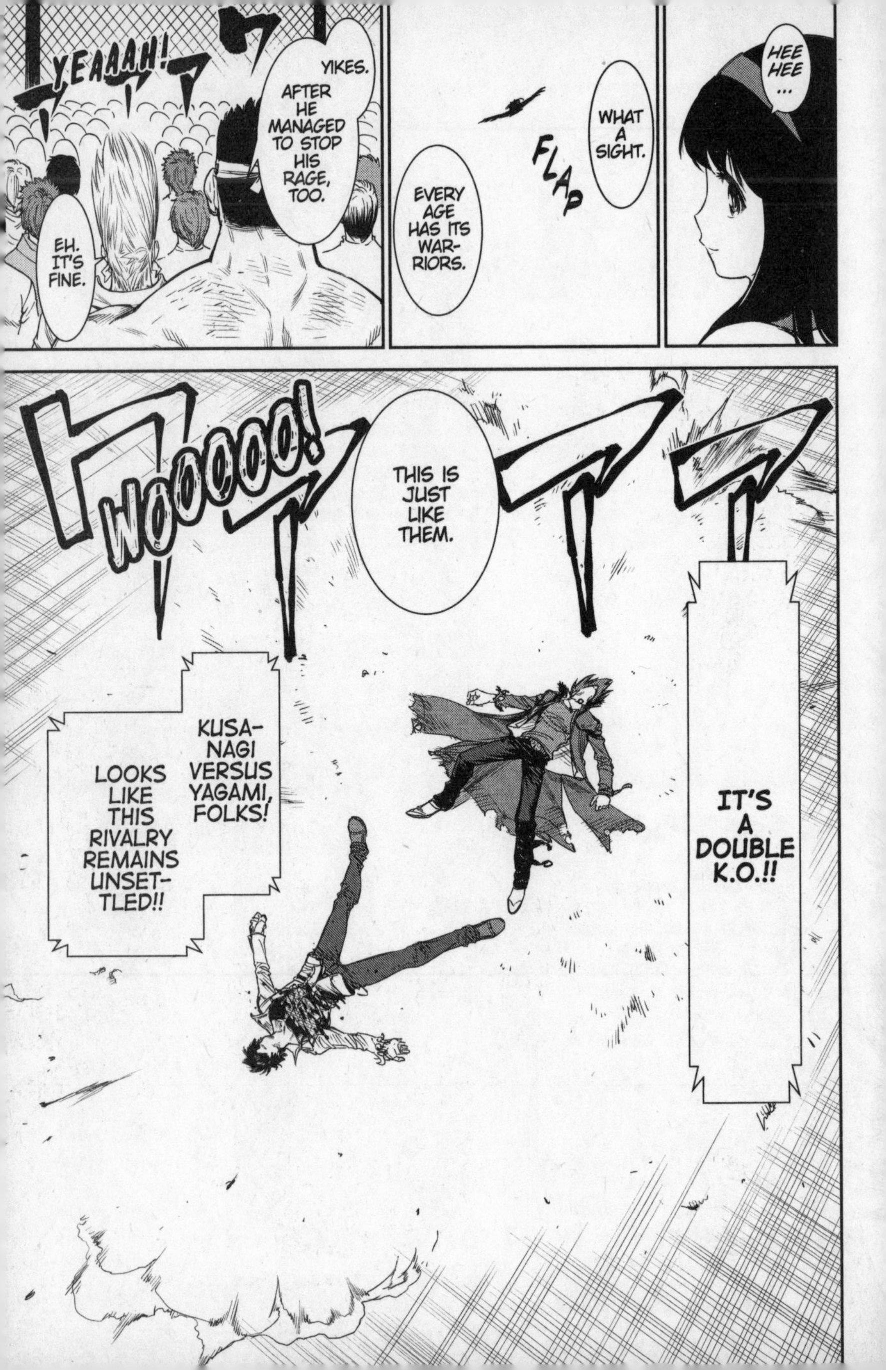
HEE HEE ...
WHAT A SIGHT.
FLAP
EVERY AGE HAS ITS WAR-RIORS.
YIKES.
AFTER HE MANAGED TO STOP HIS RAGE, TOO.
YEAAAH!
EH. IT'S FINE.
IT'S A DOUBLE K.O.!!
THIS IS JUST LIKE THEM.
WOOOOO!
KUSA-NAGI VERSUS YAGAMI, FOLKS!
LOOKS LIKE THIS RIVALRY REMAINS UNSET-TLED!!

MOVE LIST

AIHA
N-OU
EN!!

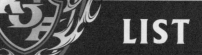

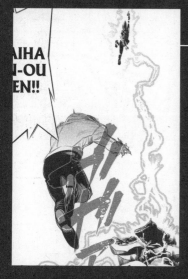

Raiha Jin-Ou Ken

Benimaru uses his highly conductive body as a lightning rod and twists the thunder onto his opponent.

User: Benimaru Nikaido

Command:
↓↙←↙↓↘→+ LP + HP

524 Shiki • Kamukura

A close-range secret art in which Kyo grabs his opponent by the collar, blasts them with a huge explosion, and hits them with fire repeatedly.

User: Kyo Kusanagi

Command:
→↘↓↙←→↘↓↙←+
LP + HP ※(close range)

(Seen in games such as *KOF 2001*, *KOF 2002*, *KOF Neowave*, *KOF 2002 UM*, *KOF XI*, *KOF Maximum Impact*, and *KOF Maximum Impact Regulation "A"*)

EXPLOOOOOOODE!!
524
HIKI·
AMU-
URA

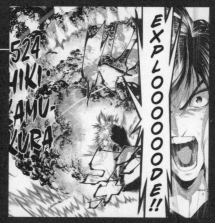

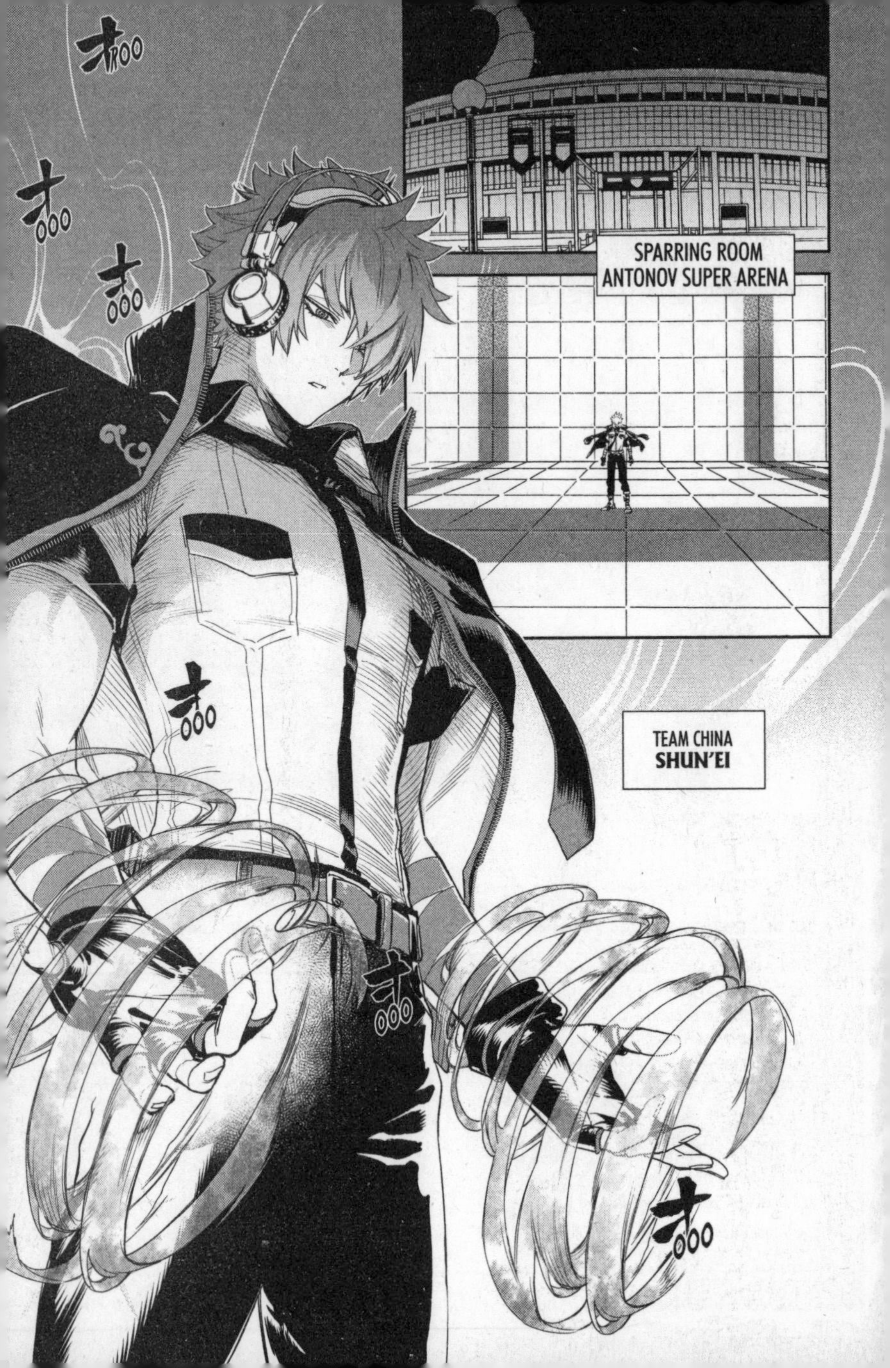
SPARRING ROOM
ANTONOV SUPER ARENA
TEAM CHINA
SHUN'EI
オROO
オOOO
オOOO
オOOO
オOOO
オOOO

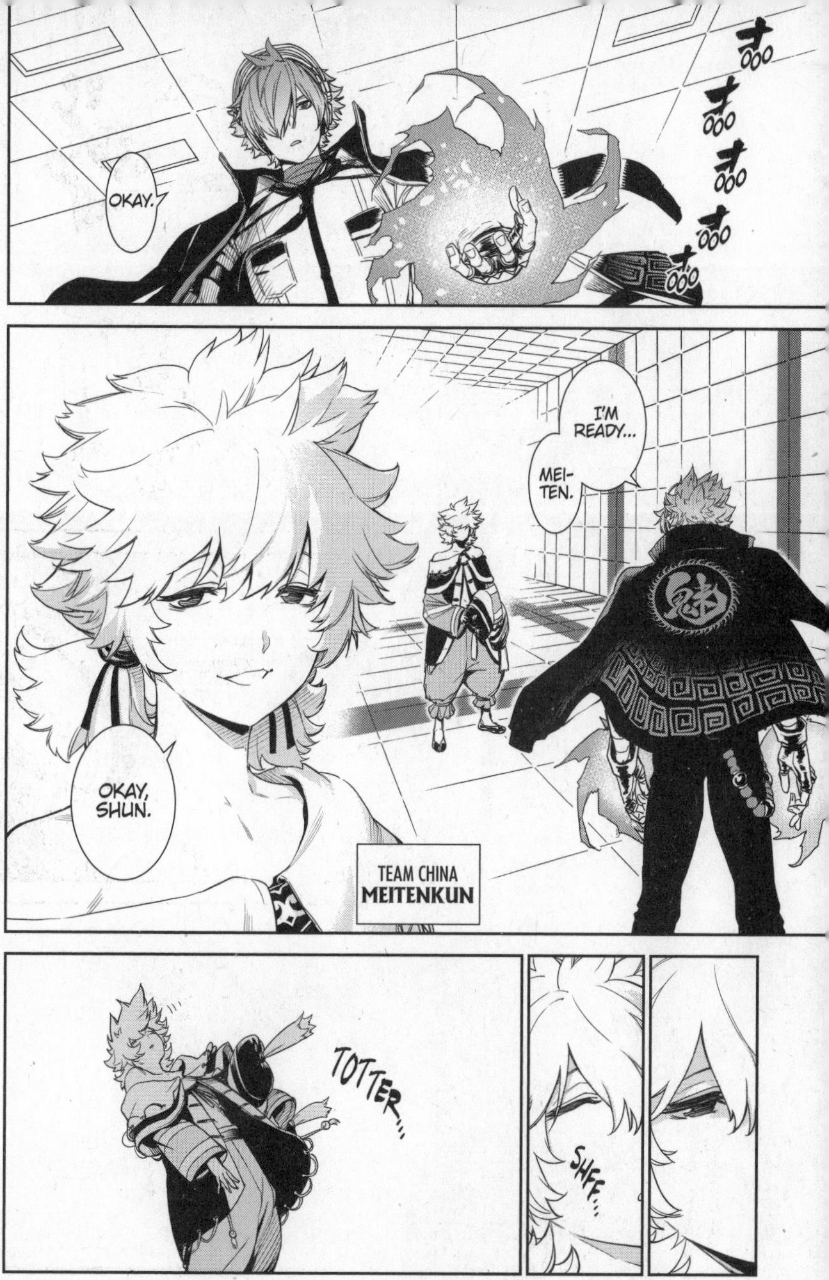
OKAY.
I'M READY...
MEI-TEN.
OKAY, SHUN.
TEAM CHINA
MEITENKUN
SHFF...
TOTTER...

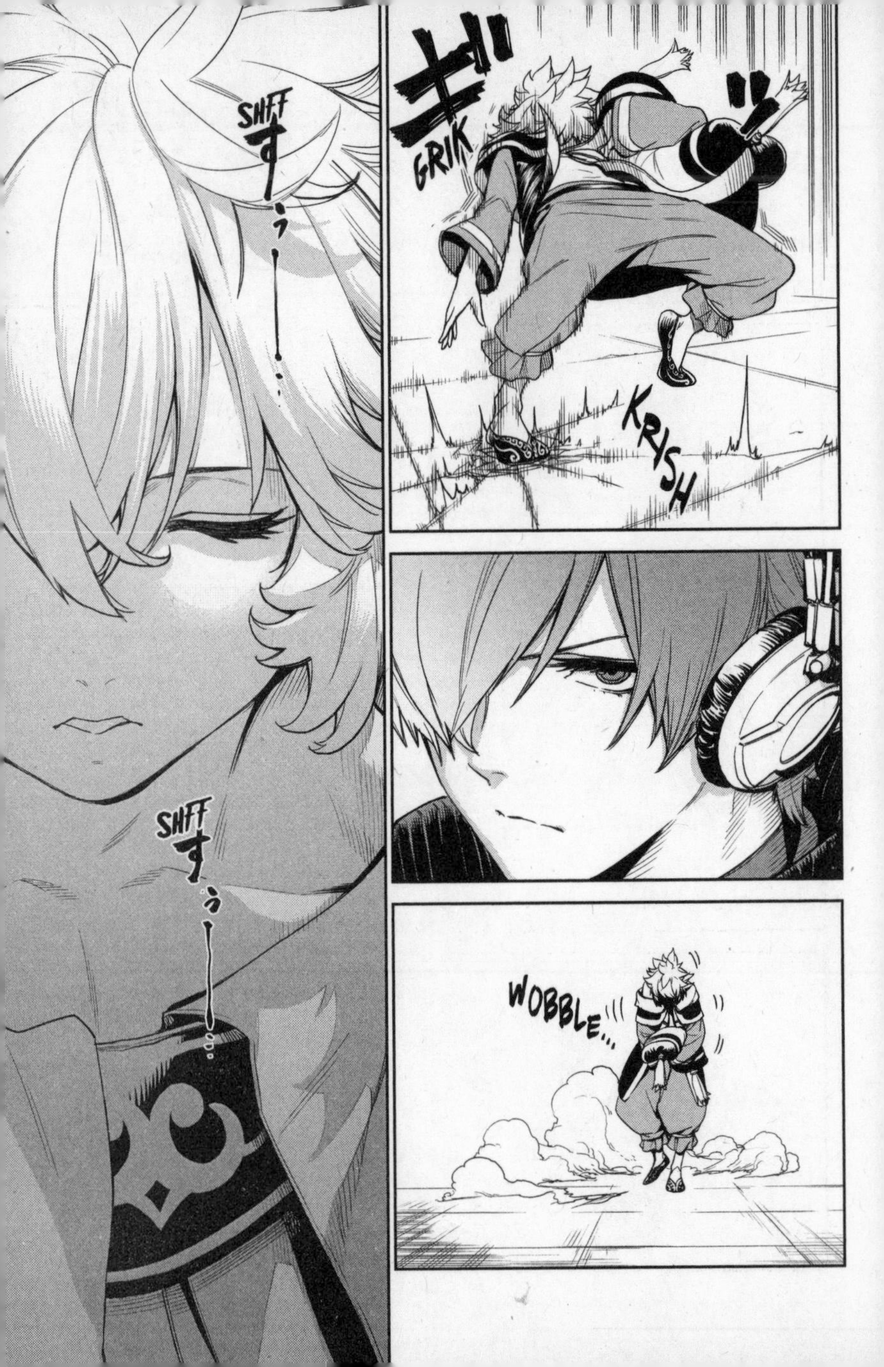
ギッ
GRIK
KRISH
WOBBLE...
SHFF すぅー…
SHFF すぅー…

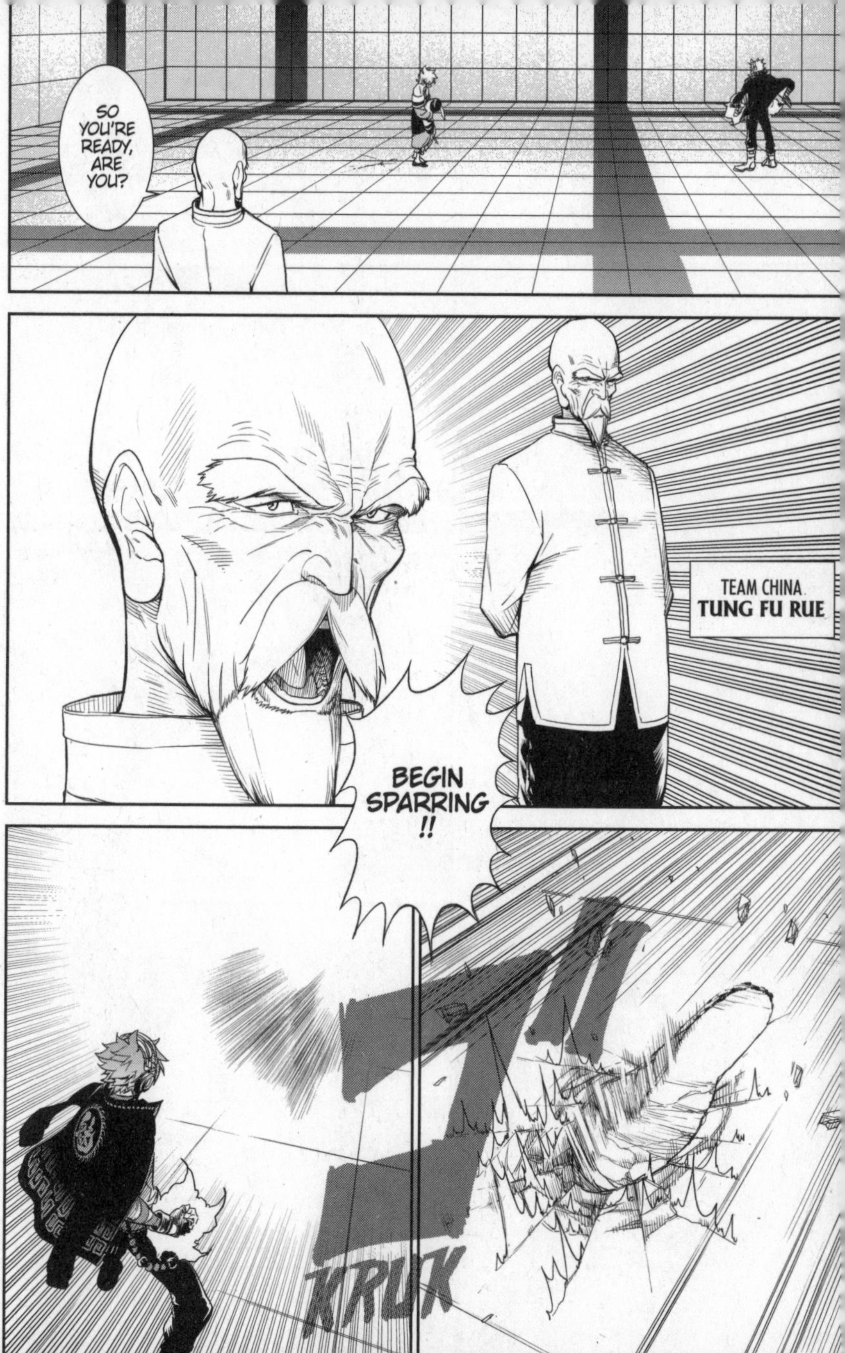
SO YOU'RE READY, ARE YOU?
TEAM CHINA
TUNG FU RUE
BEGIN SPARRING!!
KRUK

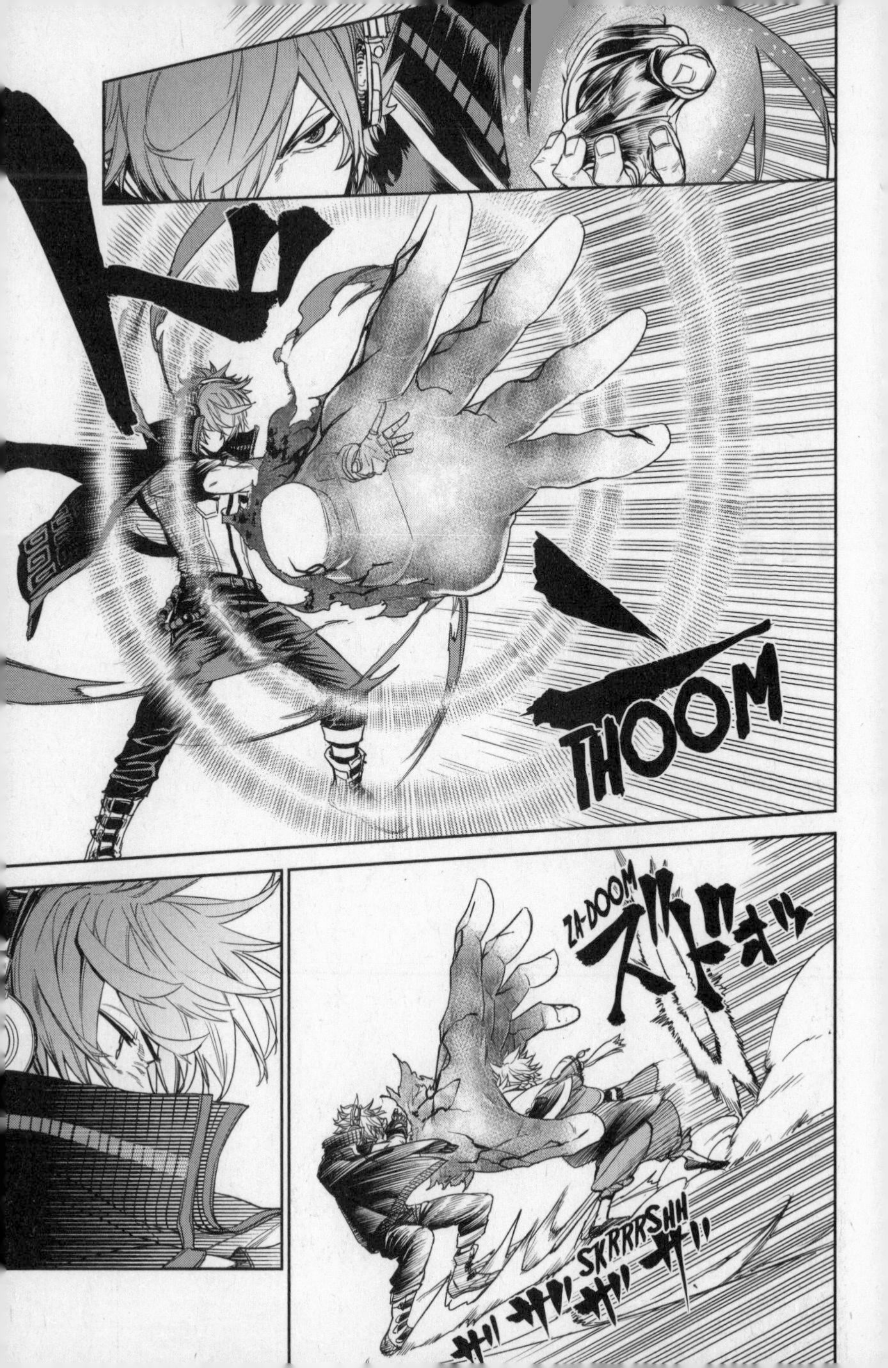
THOOM
ZA-DOOM
SKRRRSHH

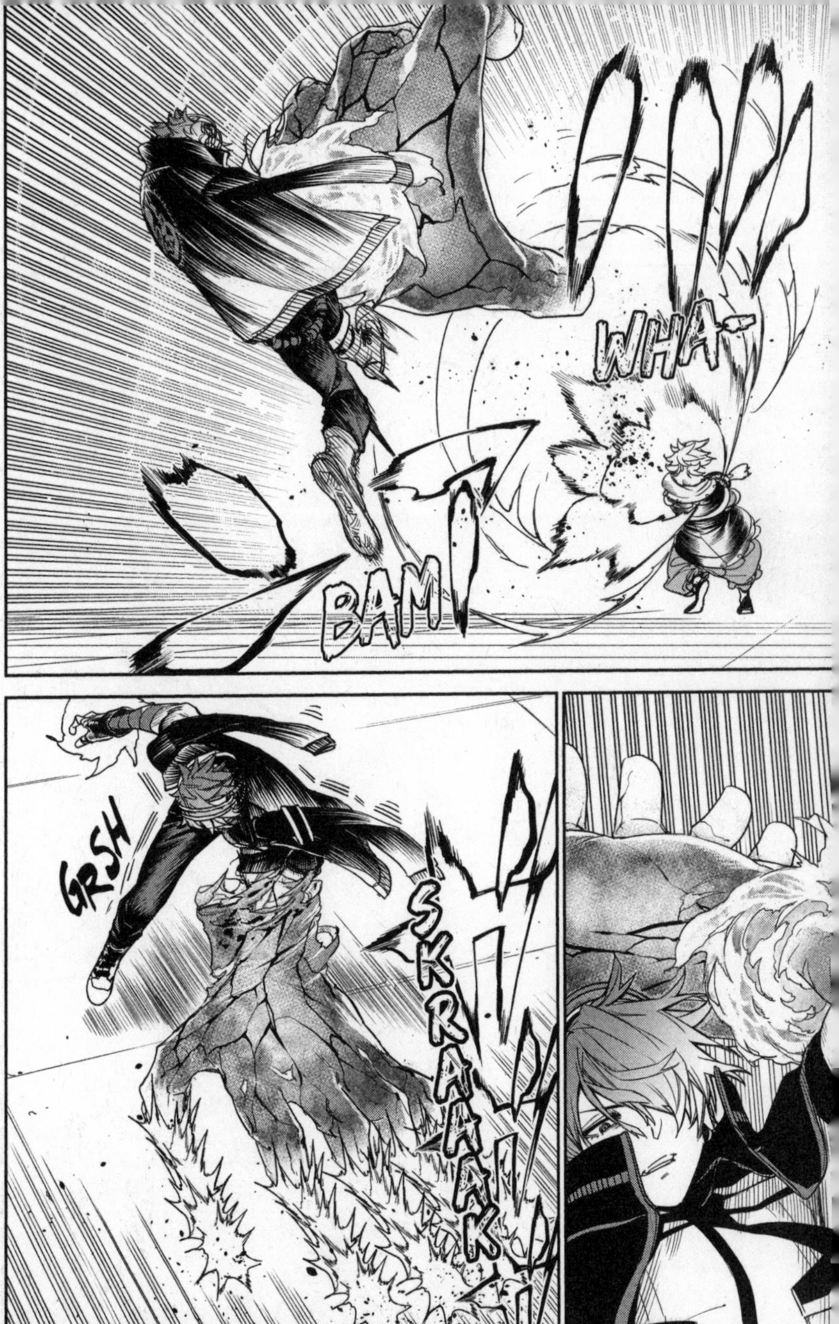
WHA-
BAM
SKRAAAAK
GRSH

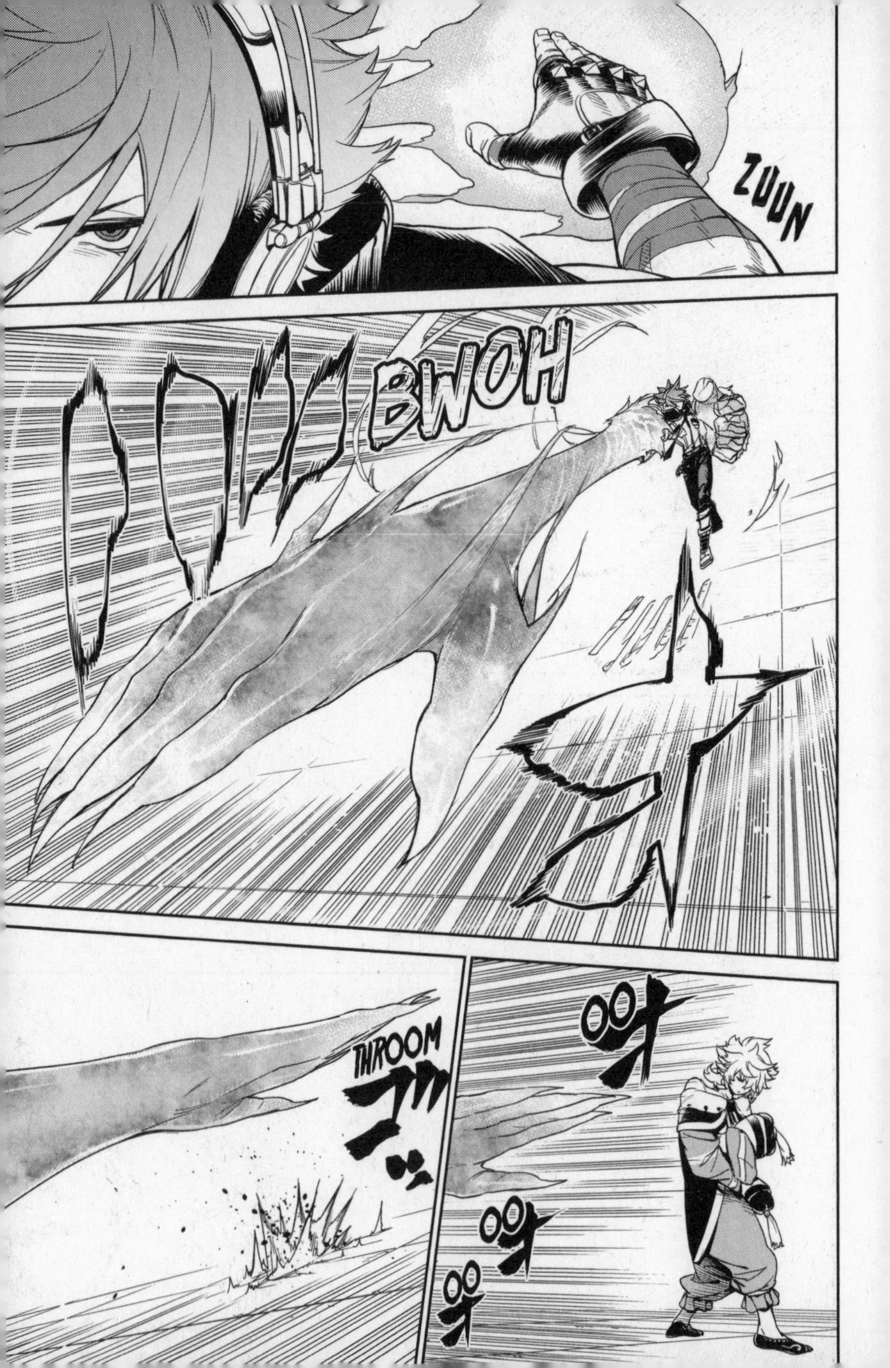
ZUUN
BWOH
THROOM

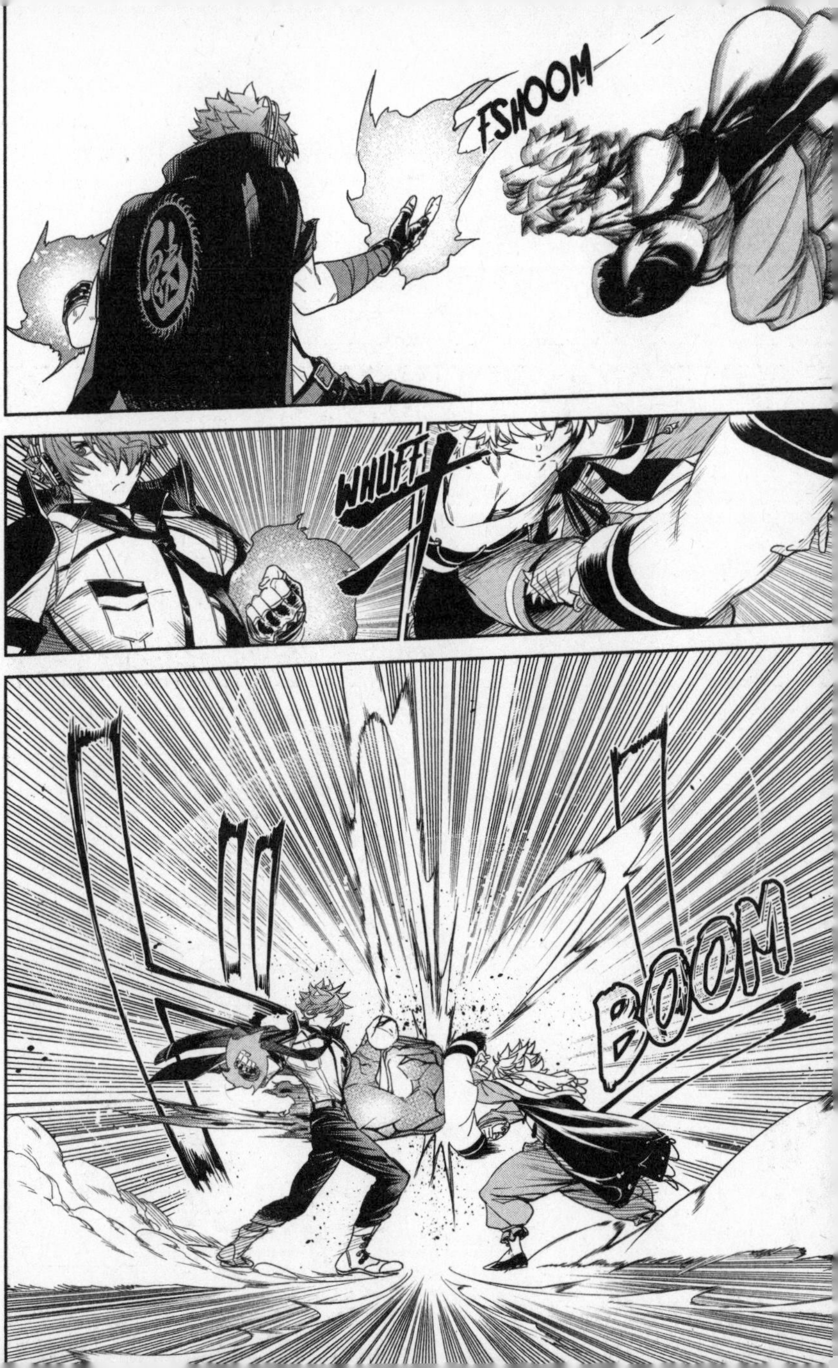
FSHOOM
WHUFF
BOOM

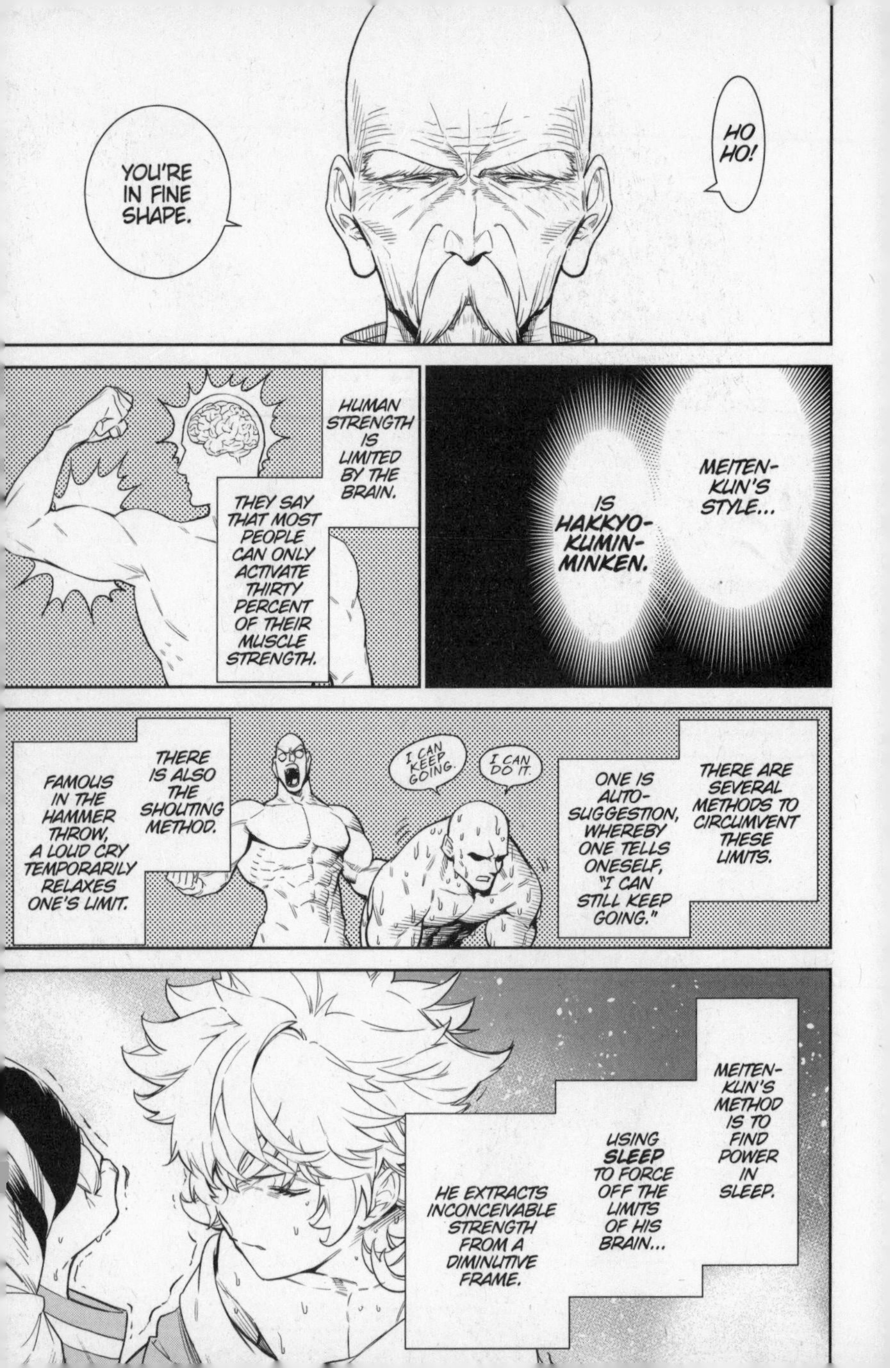
HO HO!
YOU'RE IN FINE SHAPE.
MEITEN-KUN'S STYLE...
IS HAKKYO-KUMIN-MINKEN.
HUMAN STRENGTH IS LIMITED BY THE BRAIN.
THEY SAY THAT MOST PEOPLE CAN ONLY ACTIVATE THIRTY PERCENT OF THEIR MUSCLE STRENGTH.
THERE ARE SEVERAL METHODS TO CIRCUMVENT THESE LIMITS.
ONE IS AUTO-SUGGESTION, WHEREBY ONE TELLS ONESELF, "I CAN STILL KEEP GOING."
I CAN DO IT.
I CAN KEEP GOING.
THERE IS ALSO THE SHOUTING METHOD.
FAMOUS IN THE HAMMER THROW, A LOUD CRY TEMPORARILY RELAXES ONE'S LIMIT.
MEITEN-KUN'S METHOD IS TO FIND POWER IN SLEEP.
USING SLEEP TO FORCE OFF THE LIMITS OF HIS BRAIN...
HE EXTRACTS INCONCEIVABLE STRENGTH FROM A DIMINUTIVE FRAME.

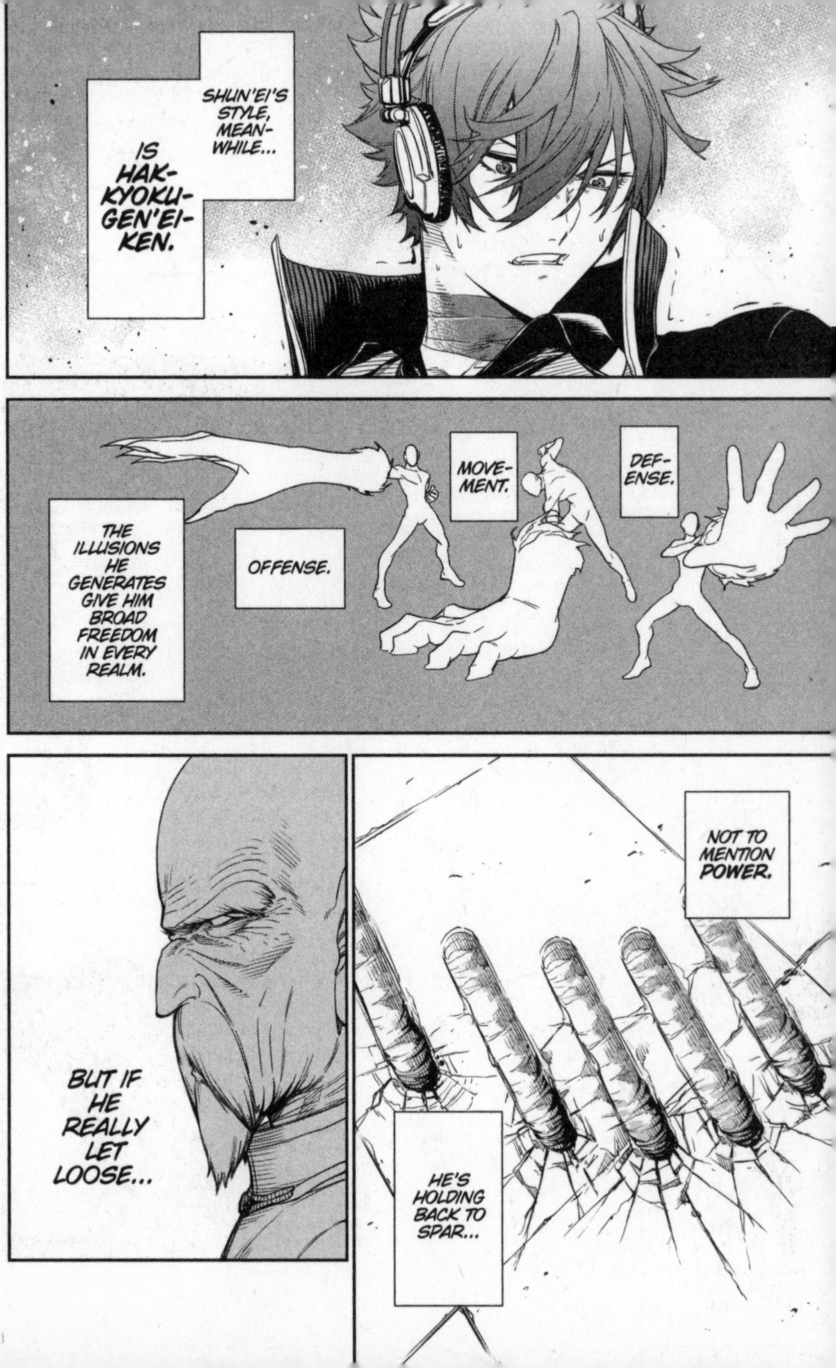
SHUN'EI'S STYLE, MEANWHILE...
IS HAKKYOKUGEN'EIKEN.
DEFENSE.
MOVEMENT.
OFFENSE.
THE ILLUSIONS HE GENERATES GIVE HIM BROAD FREEDOM IN EVERY REALM.
NOT TO MENTION POWER.
HE'S HOLDING BACK TO SPAR...
BUT IF HE REALLY LET LOOSE...

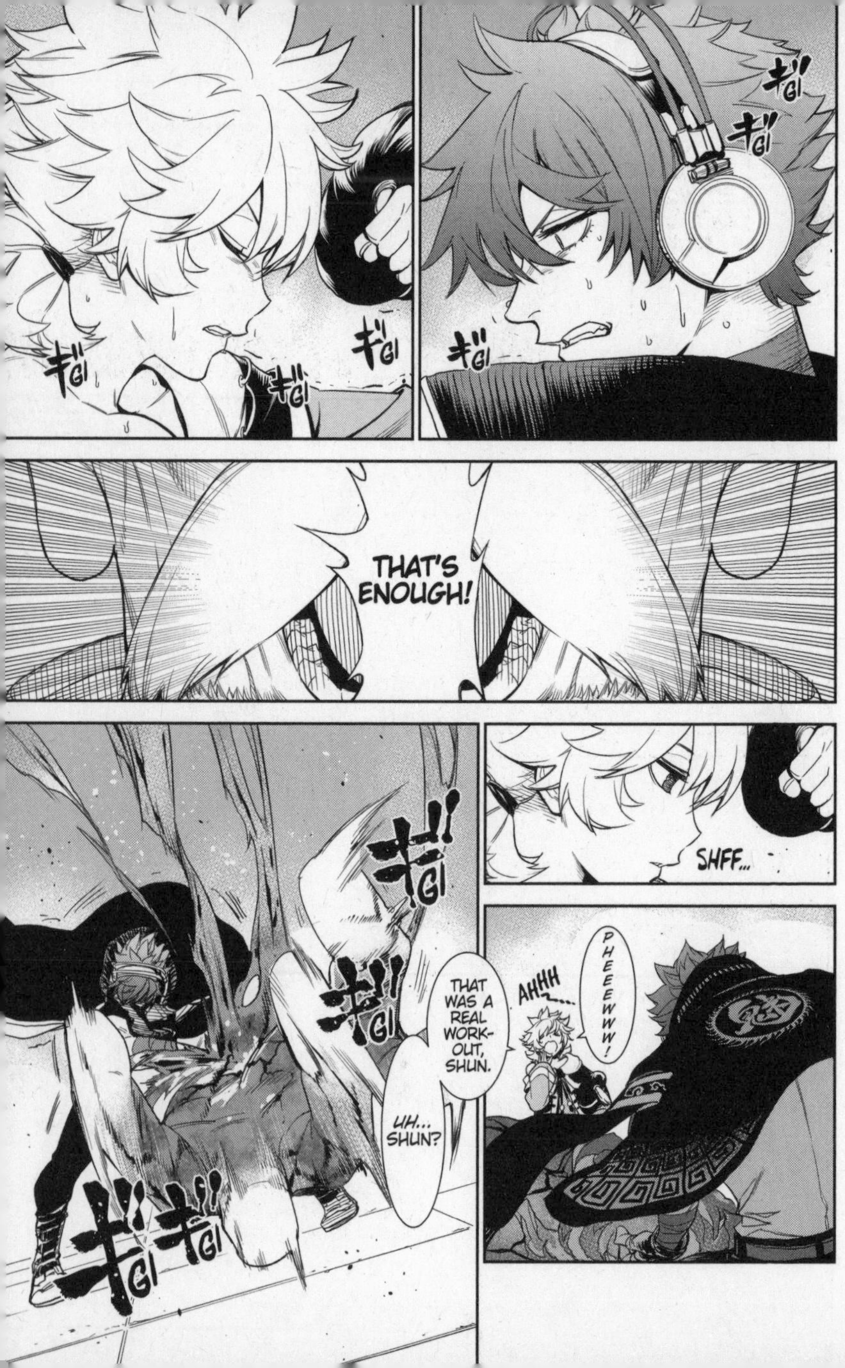
ギ GI
ギ GI
ギ GI
ギ GI
ギ GI
ギ GI
THAT'S ENOUGH!
SHFF...
PHEEEEWWW!
AHHH~...
THAT WAS A REAL WORK-OUT, SHUN.
UH... SHUN?
ギ GI
ギ GI
ギ GI
ギ GI

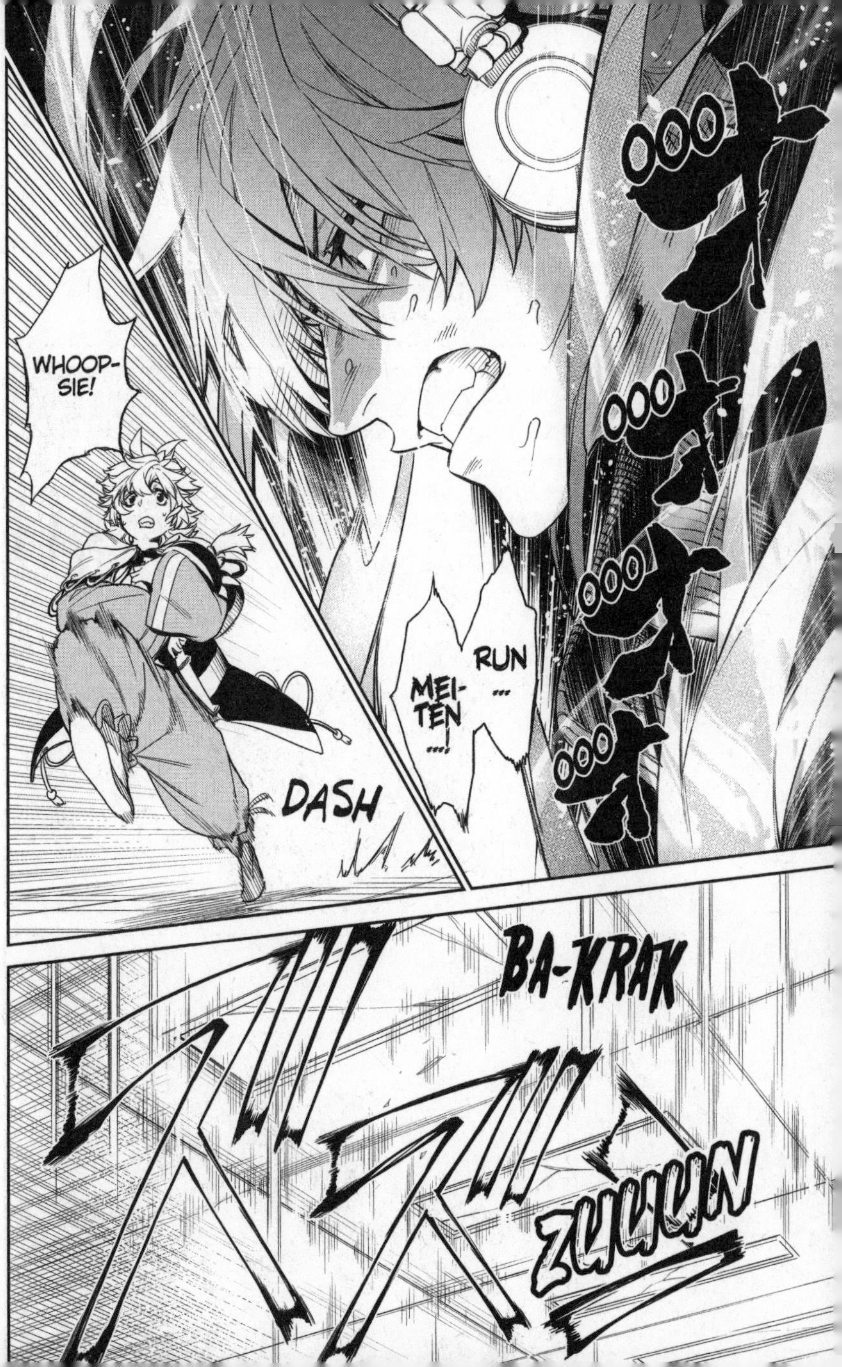
RUN... MEITEN...!
WHOOP-SIE!
DASH
BA-KRAK
ZUUUN

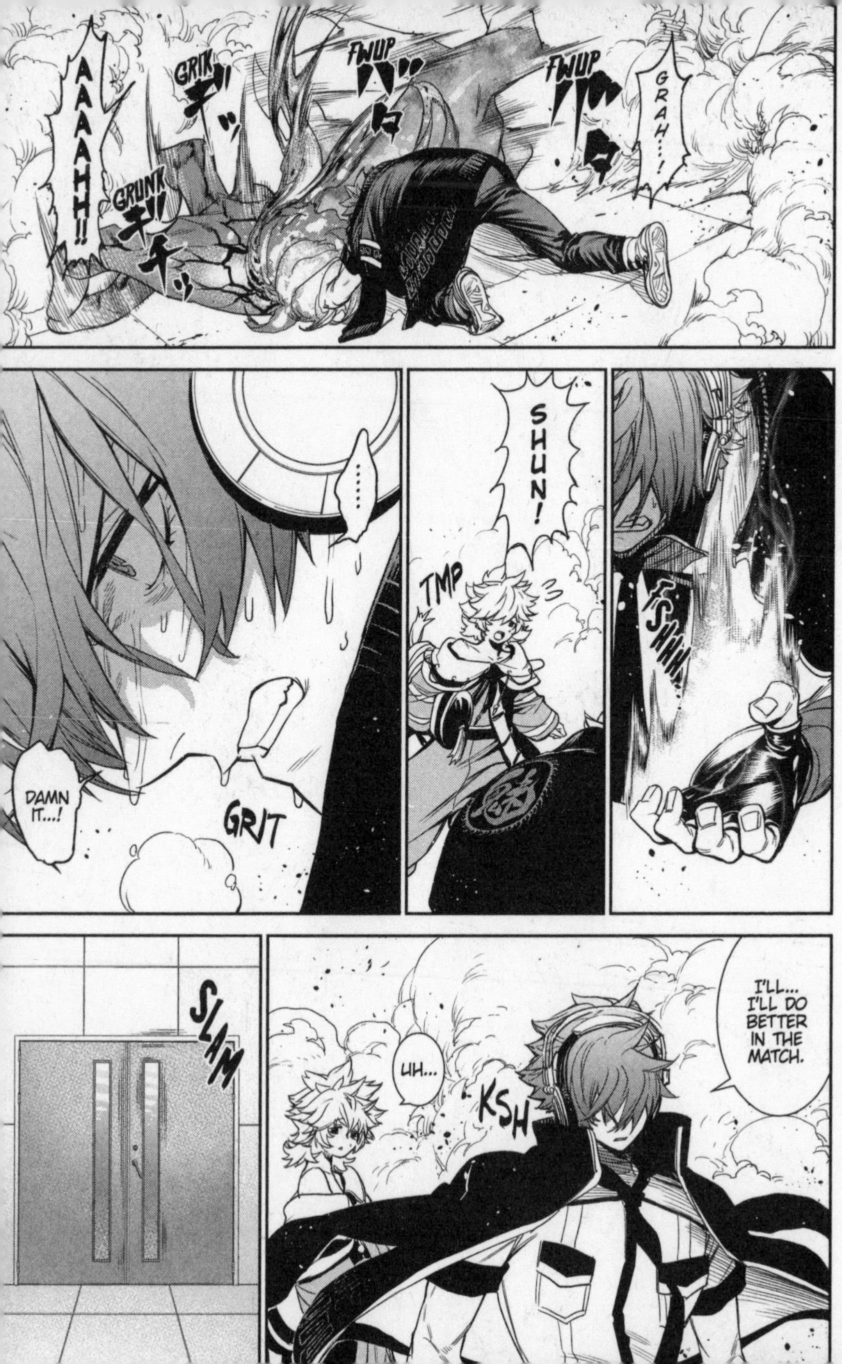
GRAH...!
FWUP
FWUP
GRIK
AAAAHH!!
GRUNK
FSHHH
SHUN!
TMP
......
DAMN IT...!
GRIT
I'LL... I'LL DO BETTER IN THE MATCH.
UH...
KSH
SLAM

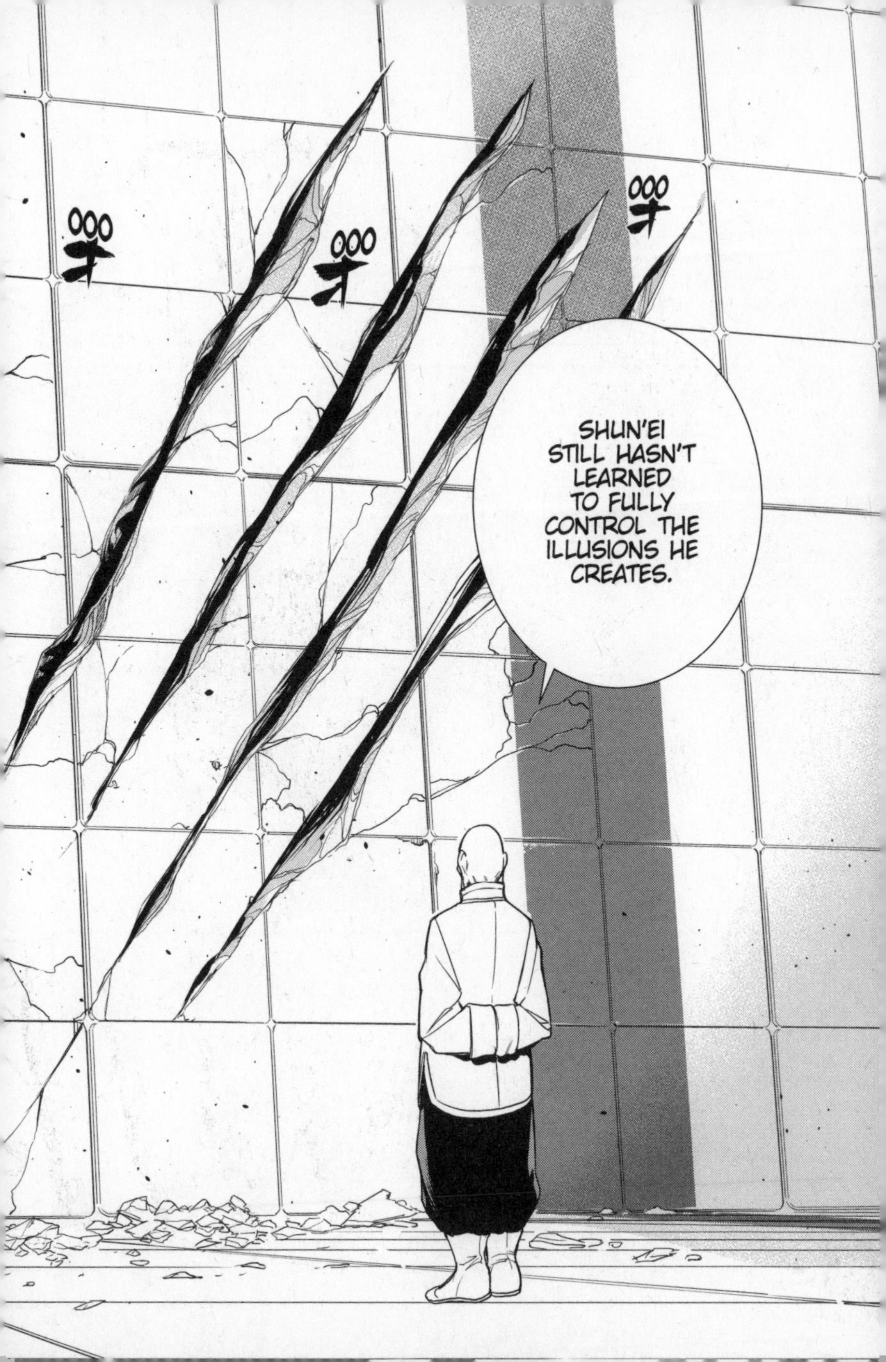
OOO
OOO
OOO
SHUN'EI STILL HASN'T LEARNED TO FULLY CONTROL THE ILLUSIONS HE CREATES.

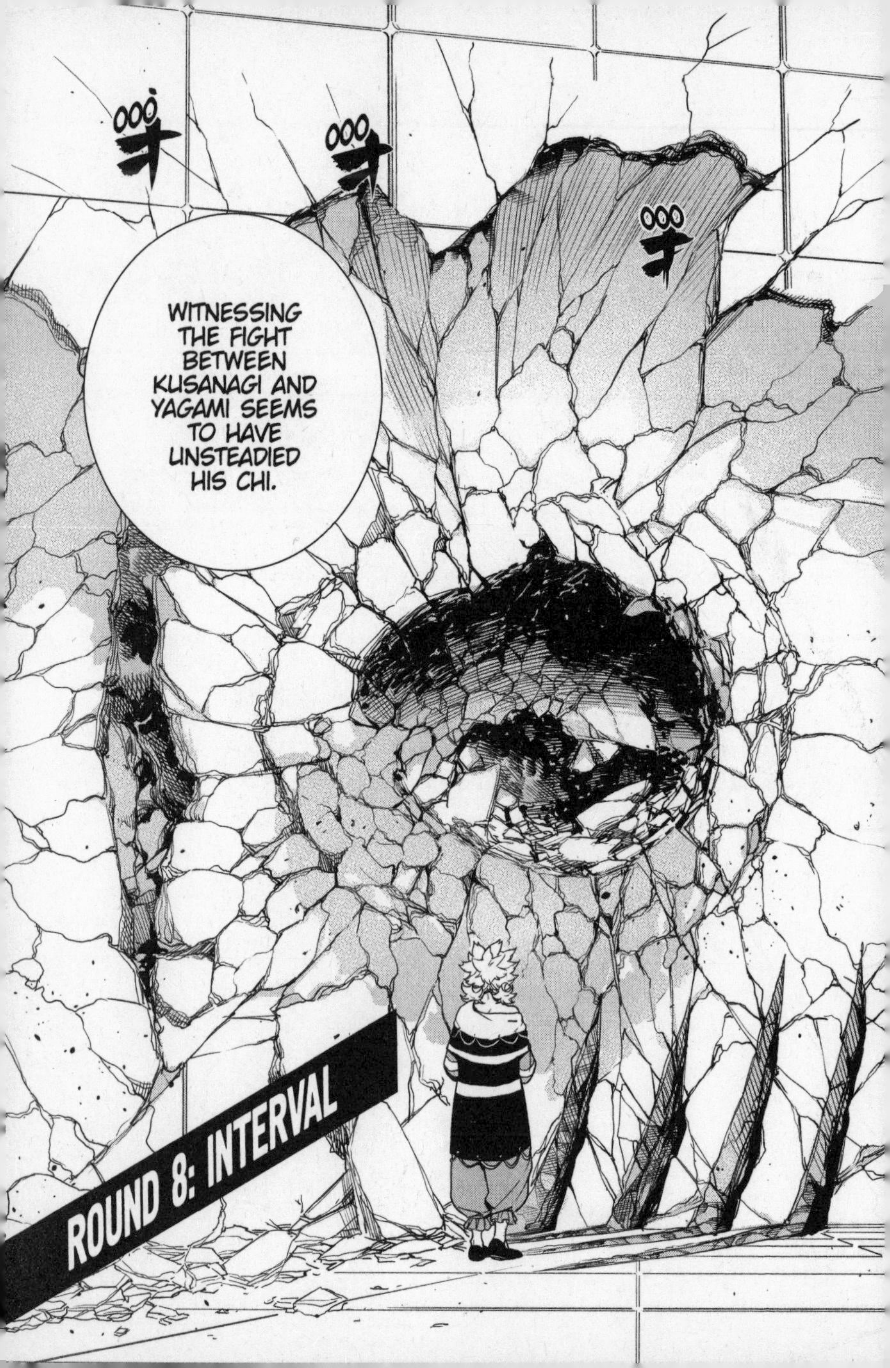
WITNESSING THE FIGHT BETWEEN KUSANAGI AND YAGAMI SEEMS TO HAVE UNSTEADIED HIS CHI.
ROUND 8: INTERVAL

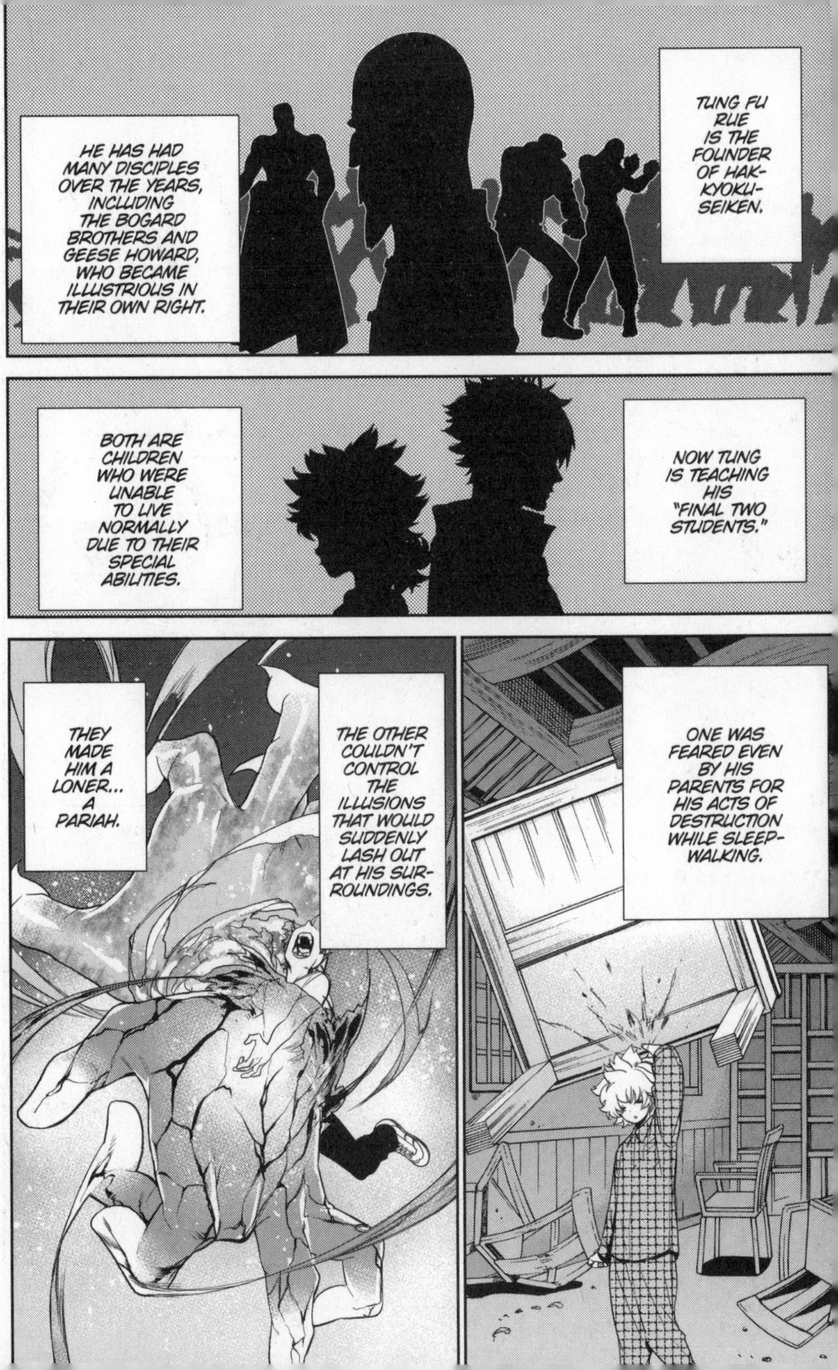
TUNG FU RUE IS THE FOUNDER OF HAK-KYOKU-SEIKEN.
HE HAS HAD MANY DISCIPLES OVER THE YEARS, INCLUDING THE BOGARD BROTHERS AND GEESE HOWARD, WHO BECAME ILLUSTRIOUS IN THEIR OWN RIGHT.
NOW TUNG IS TEACHING HIS "FINAL TWO STUDENTS."
BOTH ARE CHILDREN WHO WERE UNABLE TO LIVE NORMALLY DUE TO THEIR SPECIAL ABILITIES.
ONE WAS FEARED EVEN BY HIS PARENTS FOR HIS ACTS OF DESTRUCTION WHILE SLEEP-WALKING.
THE OTHER COULDN'T CONTROL THE ILLUSIONS THAT WOULD SUDDENLY LASH OUT AT HIS SUR-ROUNDINGS.
THEY MADE HIM A LONER... A PARIAH.

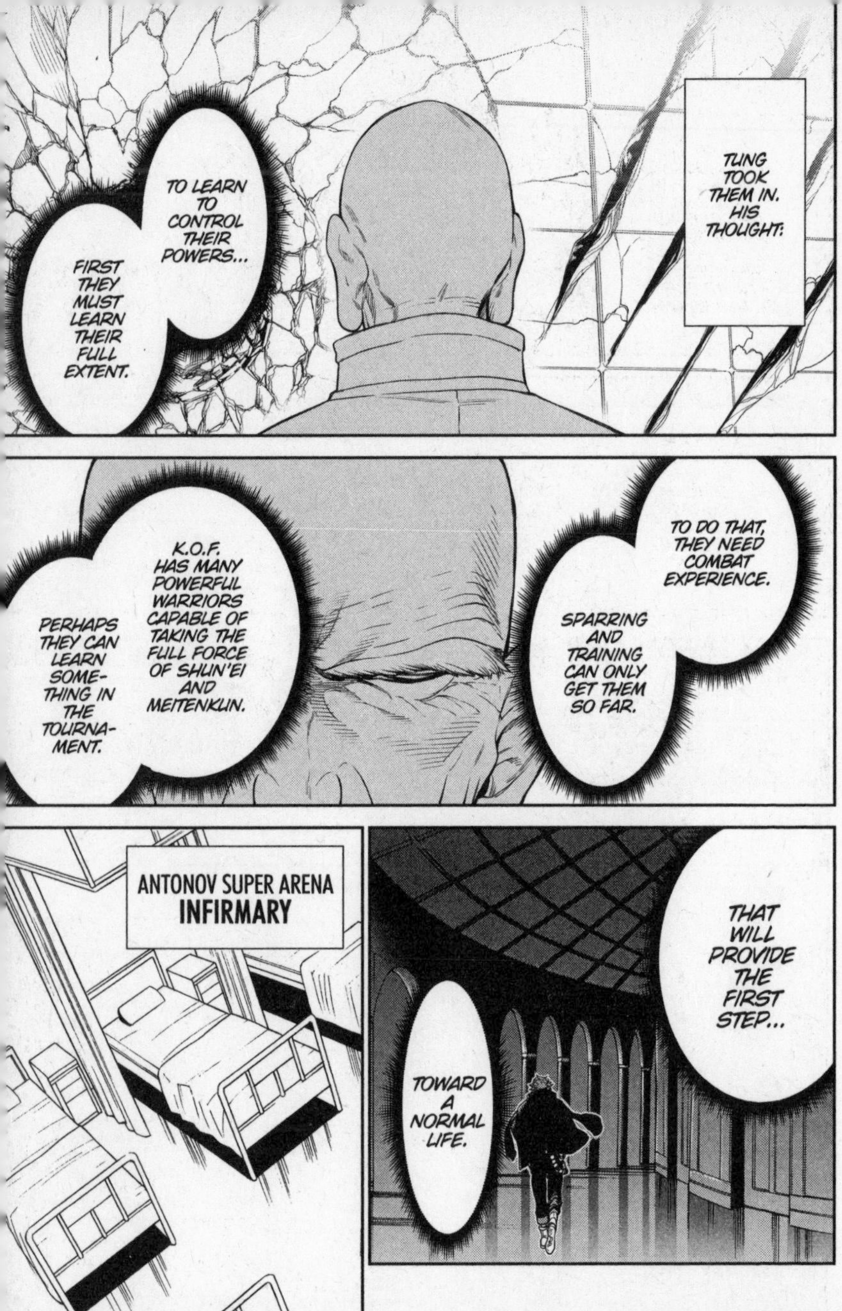
TUNG TOOK THEM IN. HIS THOUGHT:
TO LEARN TO CONTROL THEIR POWERS...
FIRST THEY MUST LEARN THEIR FULL EXTENT.
TO DO THAT, THEY NEED COMBAT EXPERIENCE.
SPARRING AND TRAINING CAN ONLY GET THEM SO FAR.
K.O.F. HAS MANY POWERFUL WARRIORS CAPABLE OF TAKING THE FULL FORCE OF SHUN'EI AND MEITENKUN.
PERHAPS THEY CAN LEARN SOME-THING IN THE TOURNA-MENT.
THAT WILL PROVIDE THE FIRST STEP...
TOWARD A NORMAL LIFE.
ANTONOV SUPER ARENA
INFIRMARY

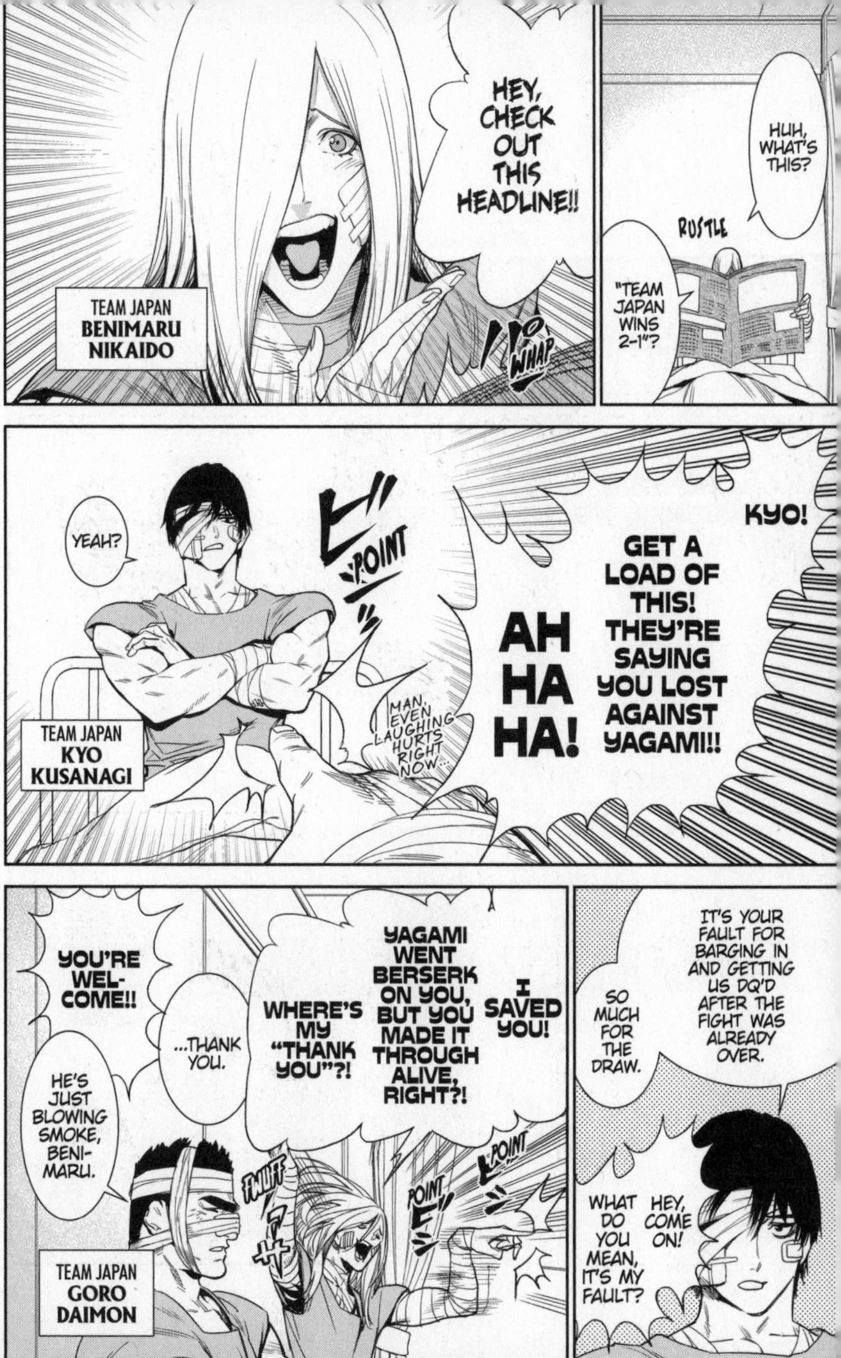
HUH, WHAT'S THIS?
RUSTLE
"TEAM JAPAN WINS 2-1"?
HEY, CHECK OUT THIS HEADLINE!!
TEAM JAPAN BENIMARU NIKAIDO
WHAP
KYO!
GET A LOAD OF THIS! THEY'RE SAYING YOU LOST AGAINST YAGAMI!!
AH HA HA!
MAN, EVEN LAUGHING HURTS RIGHT NOW...
POINT
YEAH?
TEAM JAPAN KYO KUSANAGI
IT'S YOUR FAULT FOR BARGING IN AND GETTING US DQ'D AFTER THE FIGHT WAS ALREADY OVER.
SO MUCH FOR THE DRAW.
HEY, COME ON!
WHAT DO YOU MEAN, IT'S MY FAULT?
I SAVED YOU!
YAGAMI WENT BERSERK ON YOU, BUT YOU MADE IT THROUGH ALIVE, RIGHT?!
WHERE'S MY "THANK YOU"?!
...THANK YOU.
YOU'RE WEL-COME!!
HE'S JUST BLOWING SMOKE, BENI-MARU.
POINT
POINT
FWUFF
TEAM JAPAN GORO DAIMON

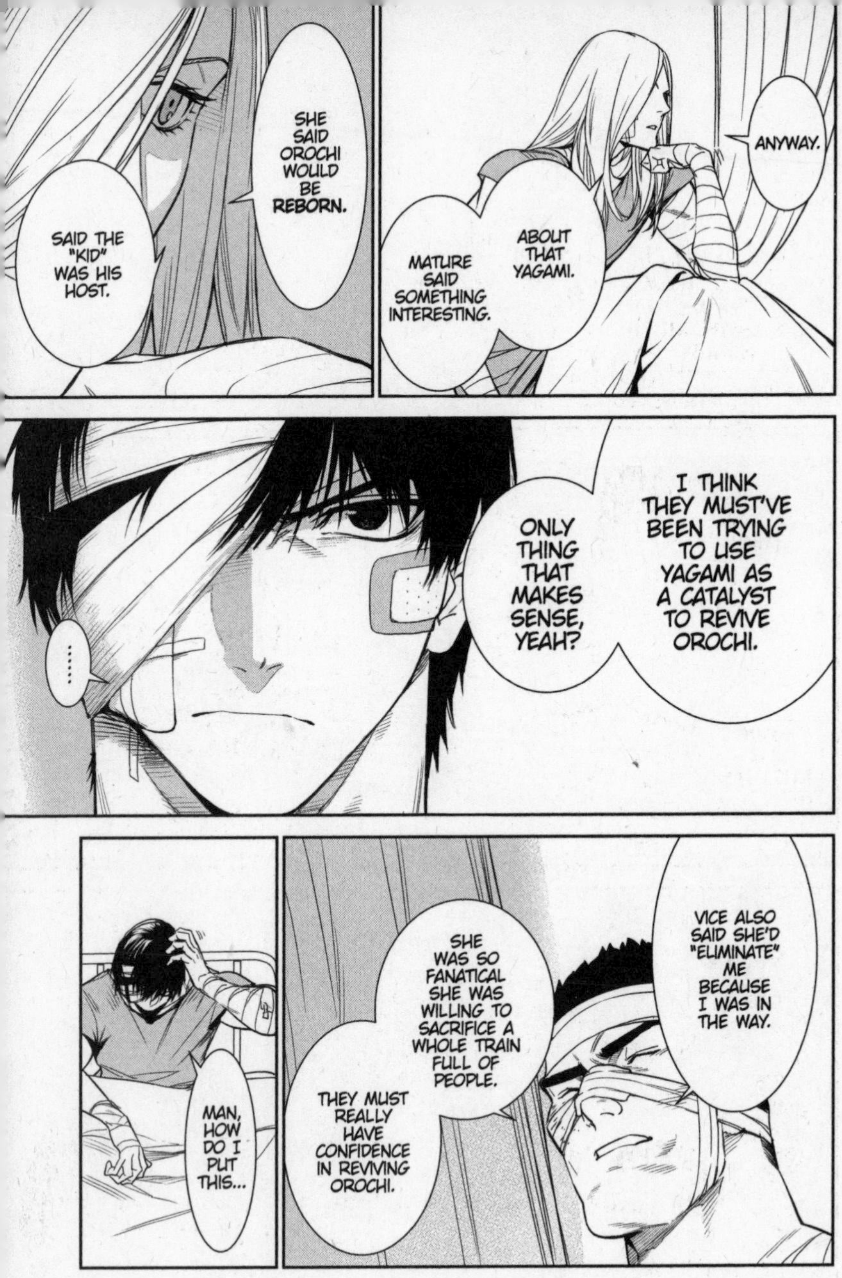
ANYWAY.
ABOUT THAT YAGAMI.
MATURE SAID SOMETHING INTERESTING.
SHE SAID OROCHI WOULD BE REBORN.
SAID THE "KID" WAS HIS HOST.
I THINK THEY MUST'VE BEEN TRYING TO USE YAGAMI AS A CATALYST TO REVIVE OROCHI.
ONLY THING THAT MAKES SENSE, YEAH?
......
VICE ALSO SAID SHE'D "ELIMINATE" ME BECAUSE I WAS IN THE WAY.
SHE WAS SO FANATICAL SHE WAS WILLING TO SACRIFICE A WHOLE TRAIN FULL OF PEOPLE.
THEY MUST REALLY HAVE CONFIDENCE IN REVIVING OROCHI.
MAN, HOW DO I PUT THIS...

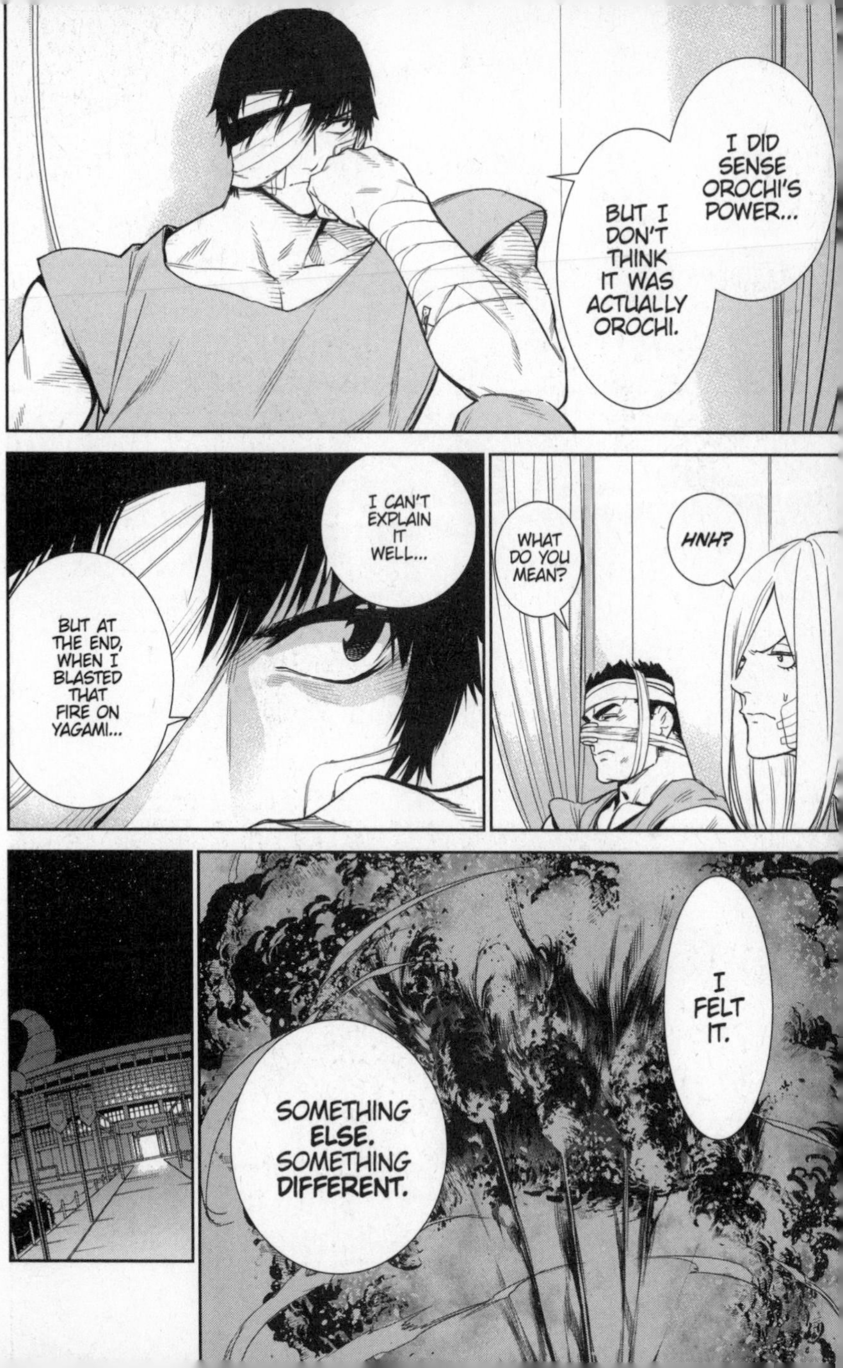
I DID SENSE OROCHI'S POWER...
BUT I DON'T THINK IT WAS ACTUALLY OROCHI.
HNH?
WHAT DO YOU MEAN?
I CAN'T EXPLAIN IT WELL...
BUT AT THE END, WHEN I BLASTED THAT FIRE ON YAGAMI...
I FELT IT.
SOMETHING ELSE. SOMETHING DIFFERENT.

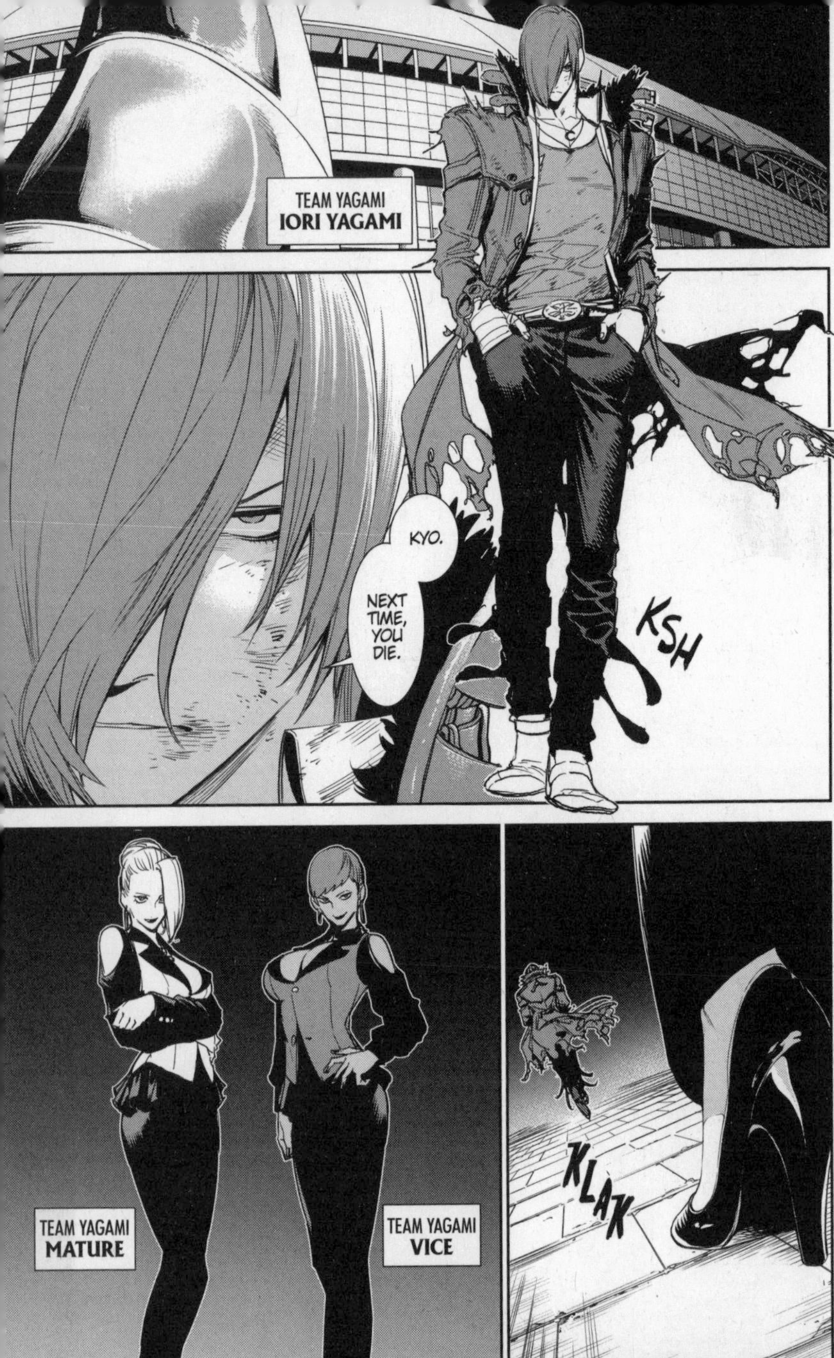
TEAM YAGAMI
IORI YAGAMI
KSH
KYO.
NEXT TIME, YOU DIE.
KLAK
TEAM YAGAMI
VICE
TEAM YAGAMI
MATURE

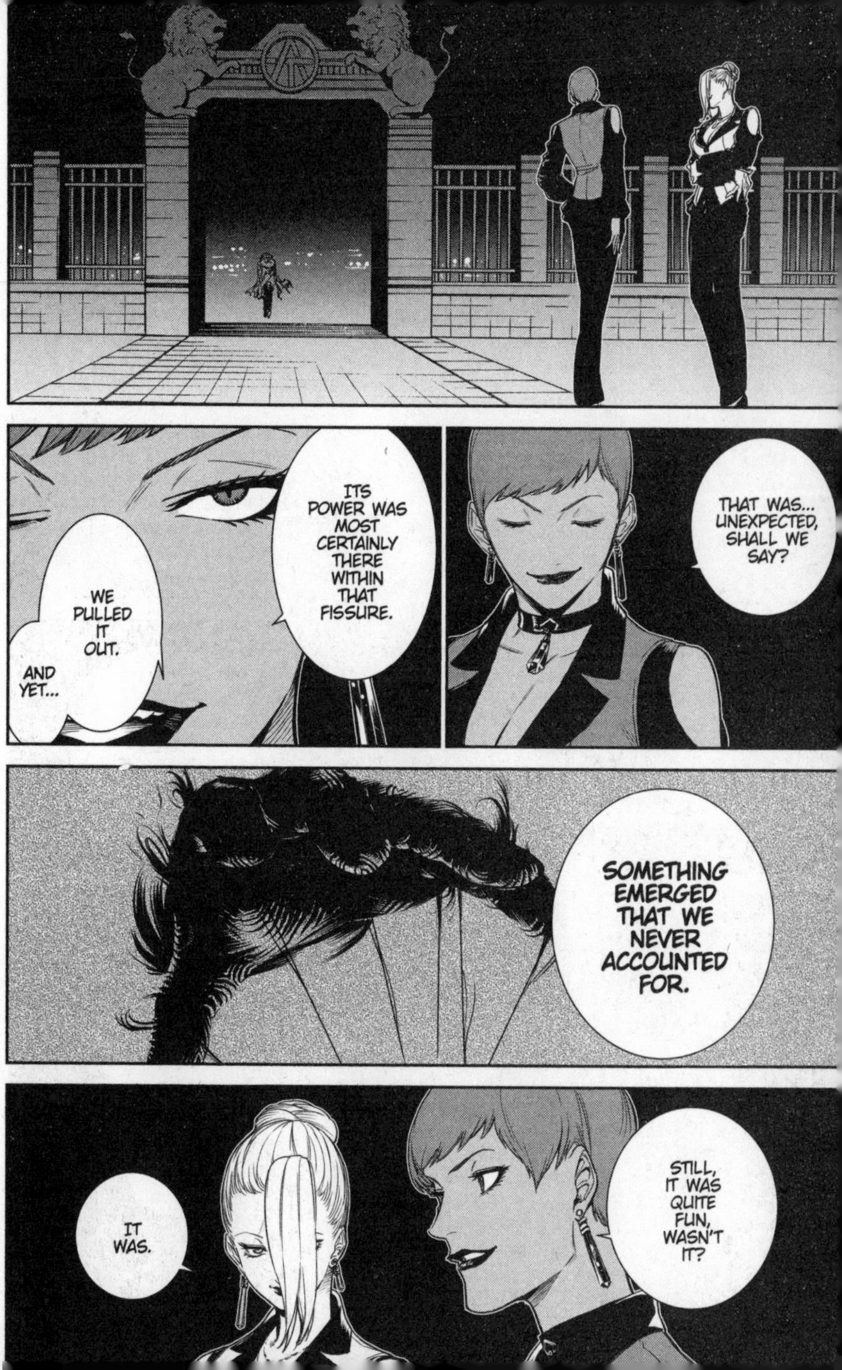
THAT WAS... UNEXPECTED, SHALL WE SAY?
ITS POWER WAS MOST CERTAINLY THERE WITHIN THAT FISSURE.
WE PULLED IT OUT.
AND YET...
SOMETHING EMERGED THAT WE NEVER ACCOUNTED FOR.
STILL, IT WAS QUITE FUN, WASN'T IT?
IT WAS.

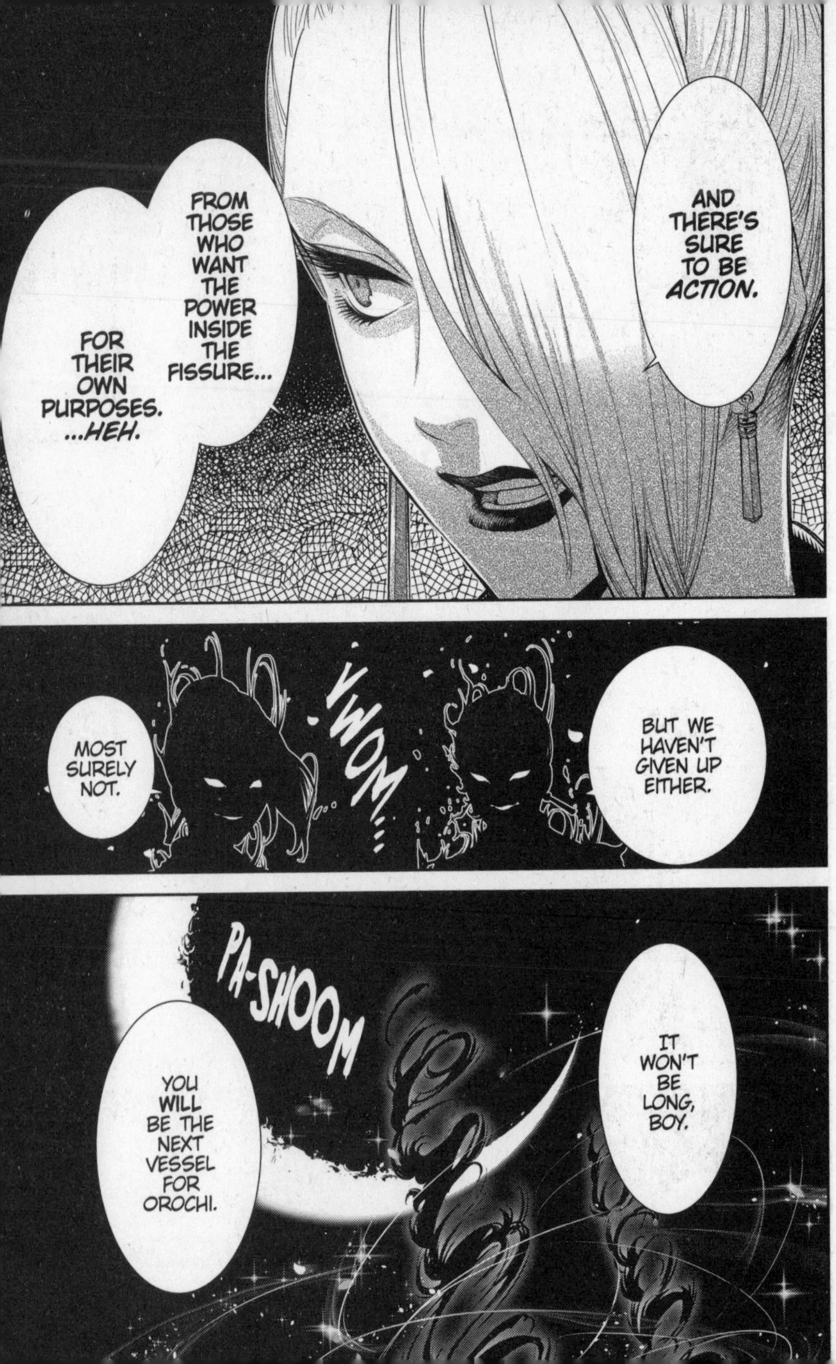
AND THERE'S SURE TO BE *ACTION.*
FROM THOSE WHO WANT THE POWER INSIDE THE FISSURE...
FOR THEIR OWN PURPOSES. ...*HEH.*
BUT WE HAVEN'T GIVEN UP EITHER.
VWOM...
MOST SURELY NOT.
IT WON'T BE LONG, BOY.
PA-SHOOM
YOU WILL BE THE NEXT VESSEL FOR OROCHI.

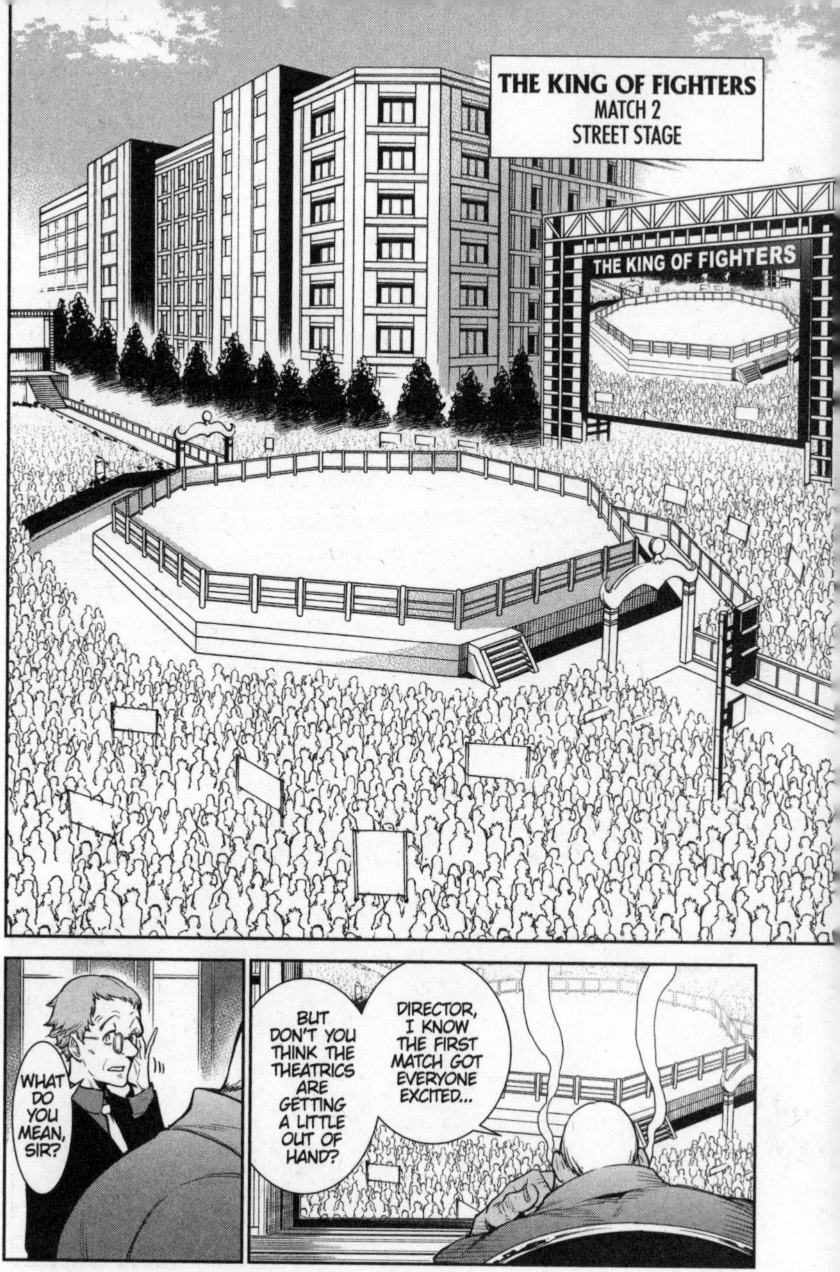
THE KING OF FIGHTERS MATCH 2 STREET STAGE
THE KING OF FIGHTERS
DIRECTOR, I KNOW THE FIRST MATCH GOT EVERYONE EXCITED...
BUT DON'T YOU THINK THE THEATRICS ARE GETTING A LITTLE OUT OF HAND?
WHAT DO YOU MEAN, SIR?

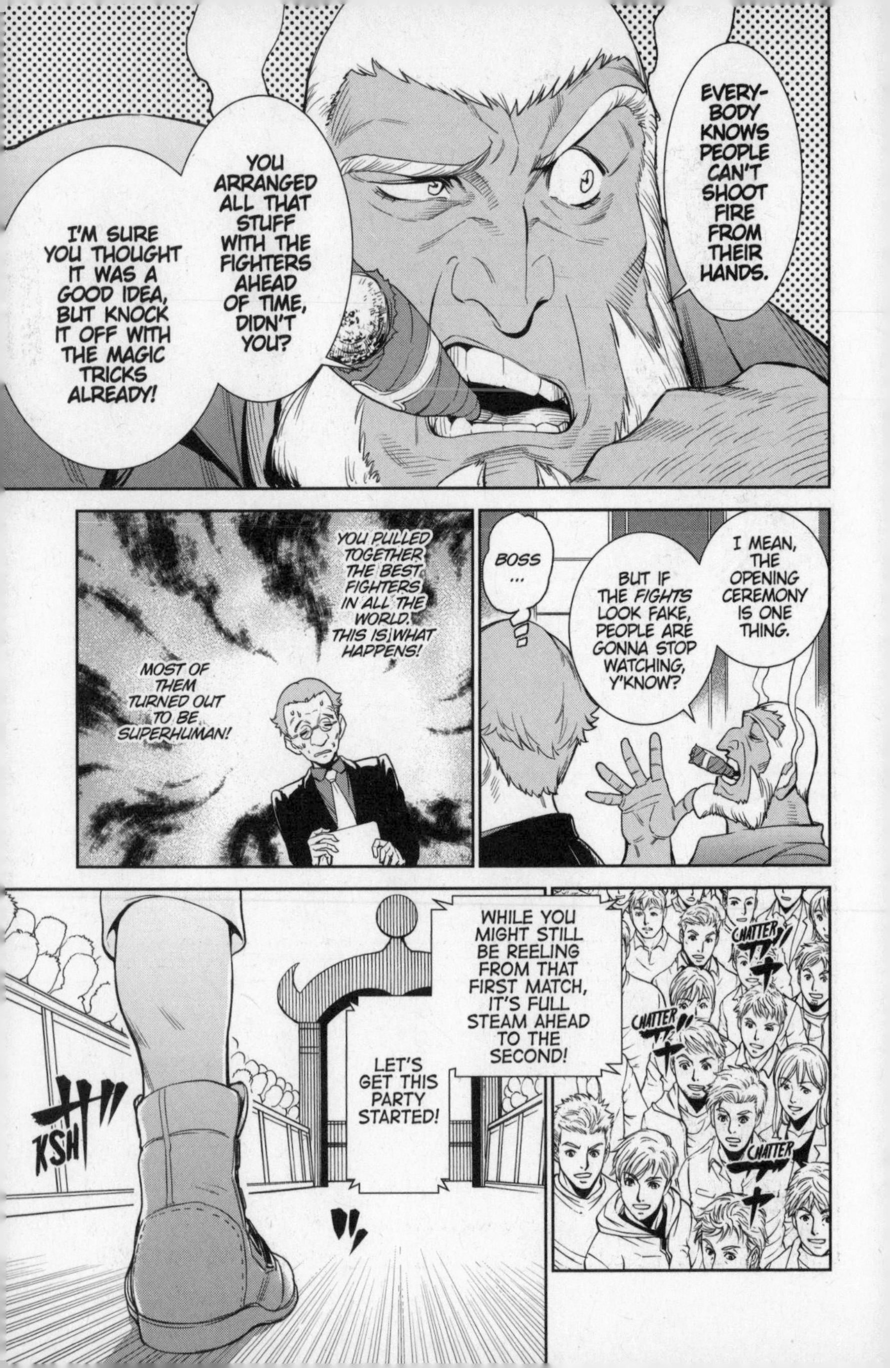
EVERY-BODY KNOWS PEOPLE CAN'T SHOOT FIRE FROM THEIR HANDS.
YOU ARRANGED ALL THAT STUFF WITH THE FIGHTERS AHEAD OF TIME, DIDN'T YOU?
I'M SURE YOU THOUGHT IT WAS A GOOD IDEA, BUT KNOCK IT OFF WITH THE MAGIC TRICKS ALREADY!
I MEAN, THE OPENING CEREMONY IS ONE THING.
BUT IF THE *FIGHTS* LOOK FAKE, PEOPLE ARE GONNA STOP WATCHING, Y'KNOW?
BOSS...
YOU PULLED TOGETHER THE BEST FIGHTERS IN ALL THE WORLD. THIS IS WHAT HAPPENS!
MOST OF THEM TURNED OUT TO BE SUPERHUMAN!
CHATTER
CHATTER
CHATTER
WHILE YOU MIGHT STILL BE REELING FROM THAT FIRST MATCH, IT'S FULL STEAM AHEAD TO THE SECOND!
LET'S GET THIS PARTY STARTED!
KSH

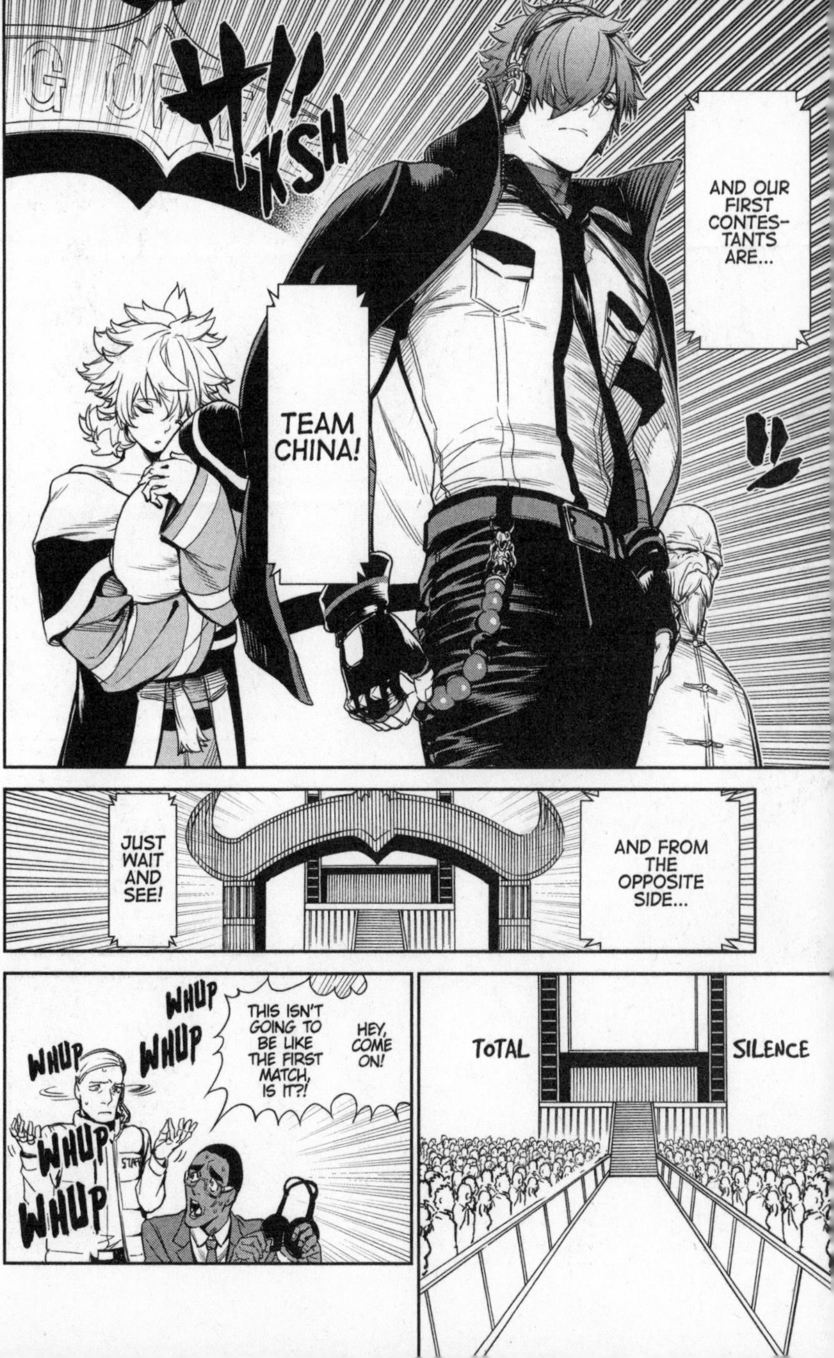
KSH
AND OUR FIRST CONTES-TANTS ARE...
TEAM CHINA!
AND FROM THE OPPOSITE SIDE...
JUST WAIT AND SEE!
TOTAL SILENCE
HEY, COME ON!
THIS ISN'T GOING TO BE LIKE THE FIRST MATCH, IS IT?!
WHUP
WHUP
WHUP
WHUP
WHUP
STAFF

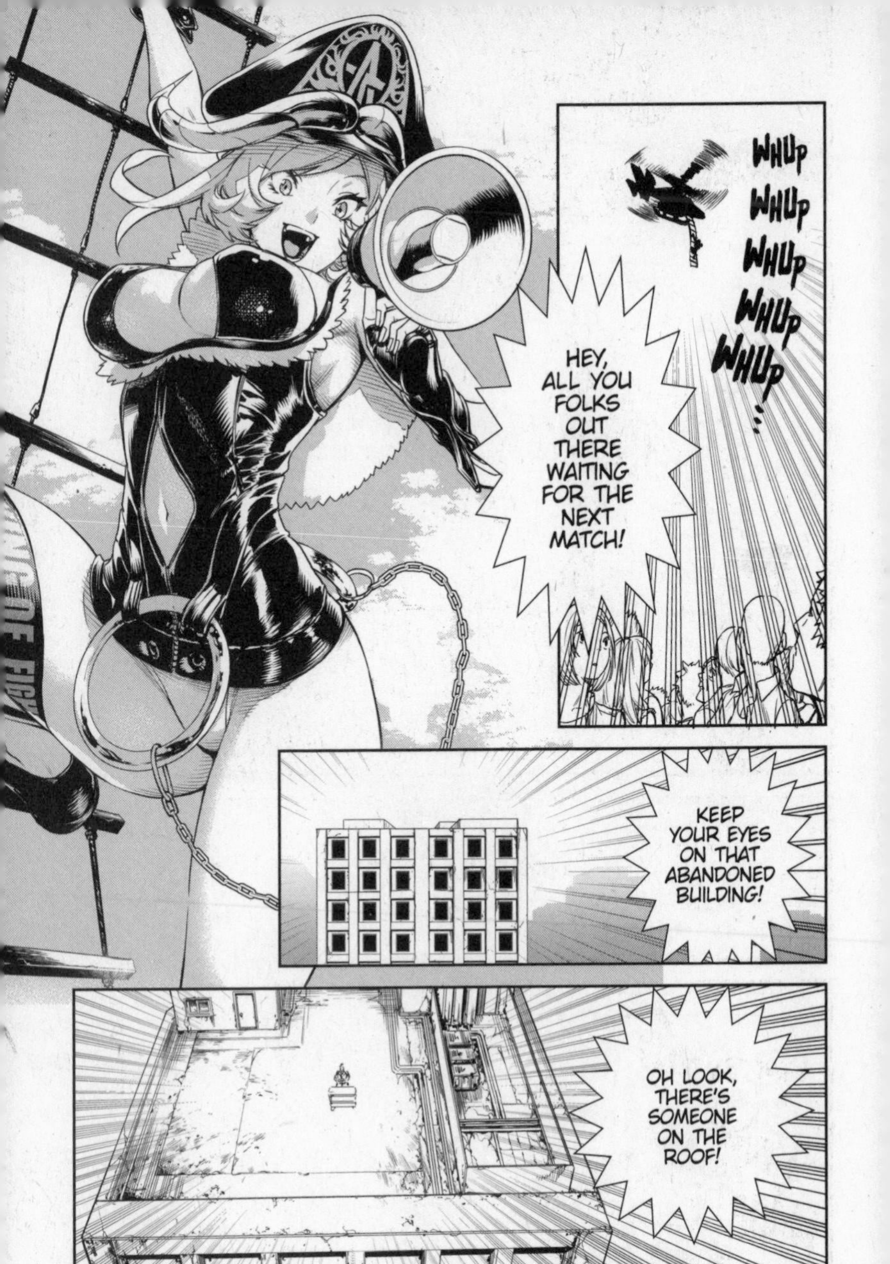
WHUP WHUP WHUP WHUP WHUP
HEY, ALL YOU FOLKS OUT THERE WAITING FOR THE NEXT MATCH!
KEEP YOUR EYES ON THAT ABANDONED BUILDING!
OH LOOK, THERE'S SOMEONE ON THE ROOF!

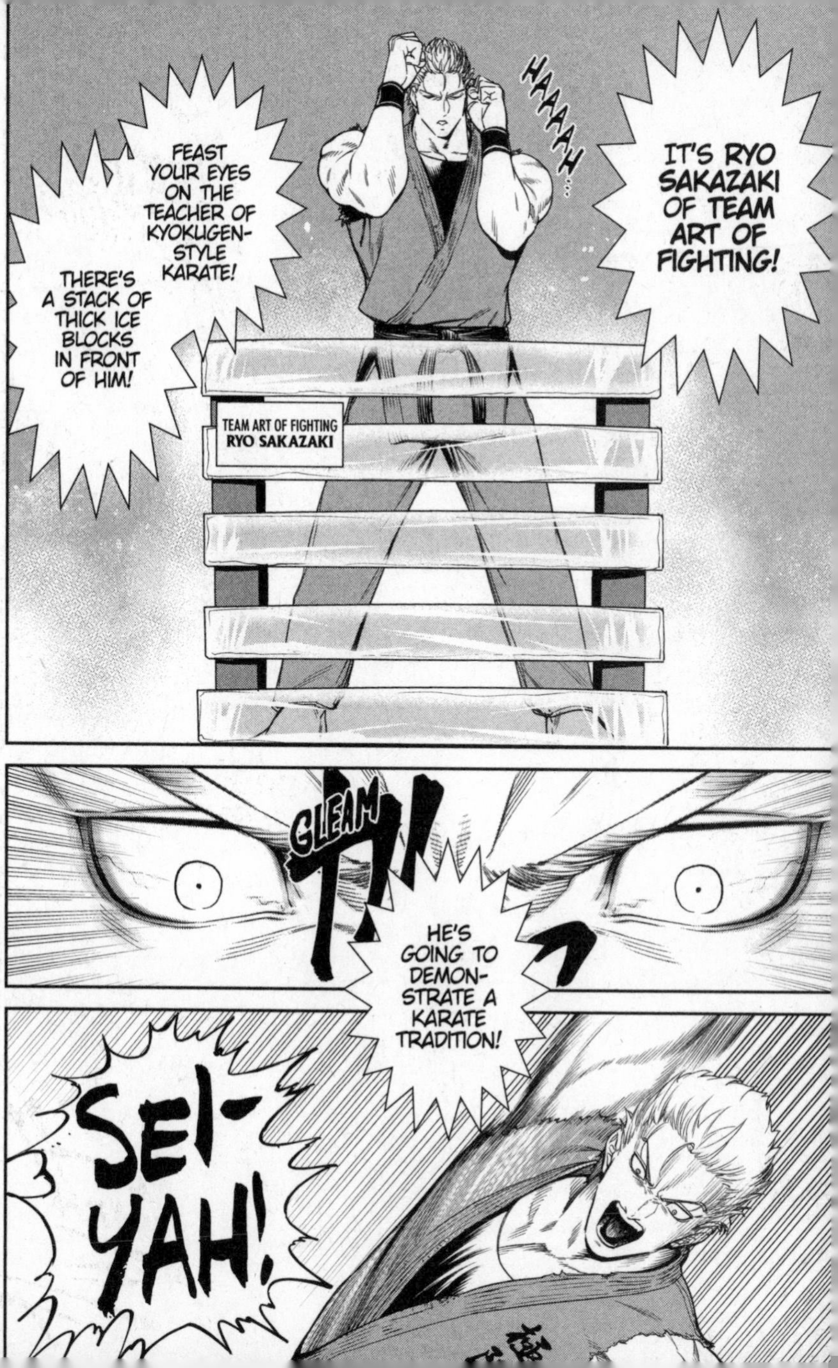
HAAAAAH...
IT'S RYO SAKAZAKI OF TEAM ART OF FIGHTING!
FEAST YOUR EYES ON THE TEACHER OF KYOKUGEN-STYLE KARATE!
THERE'S A STACK OF THICK ICE BLOCKS IN FRONT OF HIM!
TEAM ART OF FIGHTING
RYO SAKAZAKI
GLEAM
HE'S GOING TO DEMONSTRATE A KARATE TRADITION!
SEI-YAH!

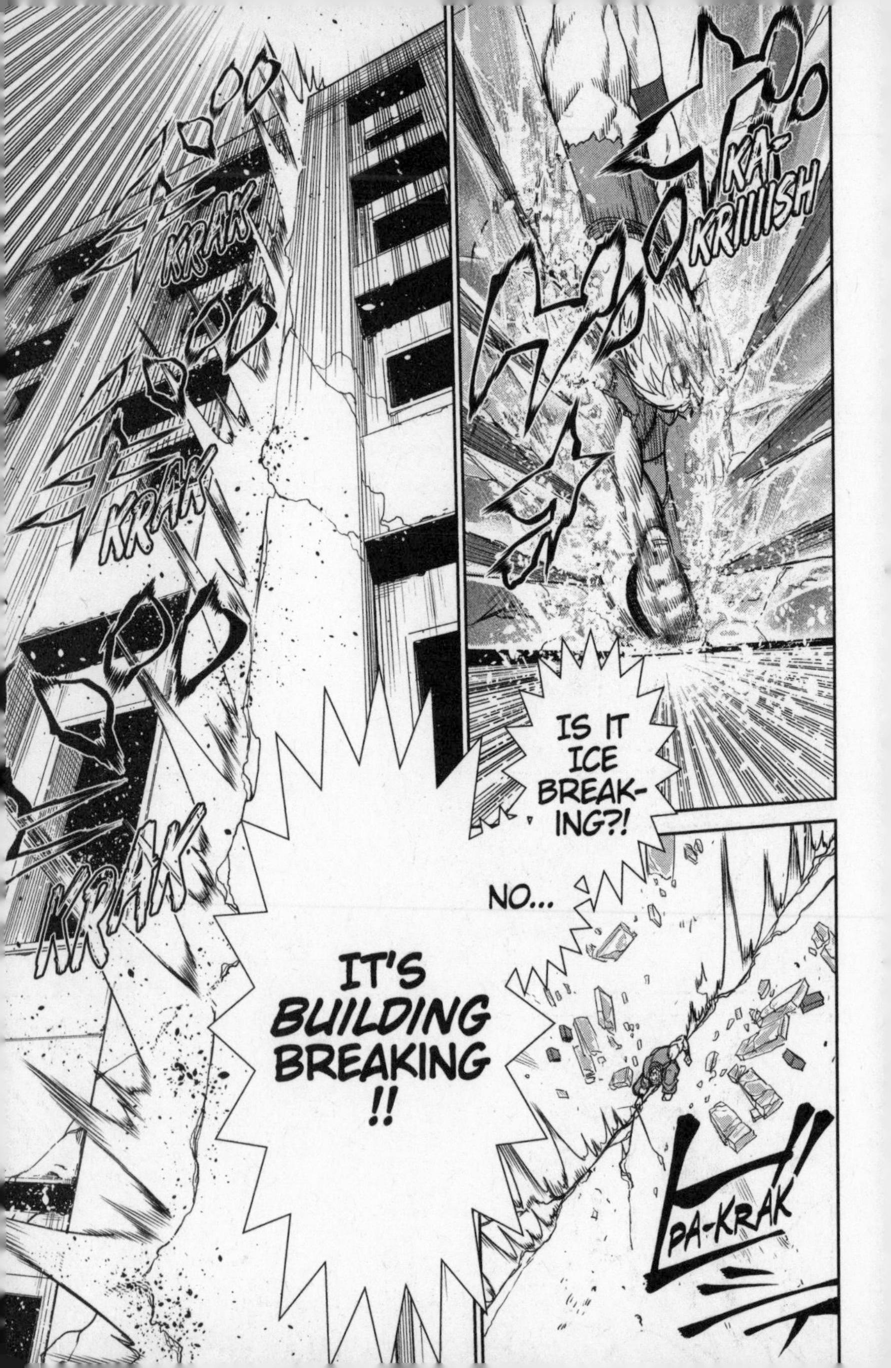
KA-KRIIIISH
IS IT ICE BREAKING?!
NO...
PA-KRAK
KRAK
KRAK
KRAK
IT'S BUILDING BREAKING!!

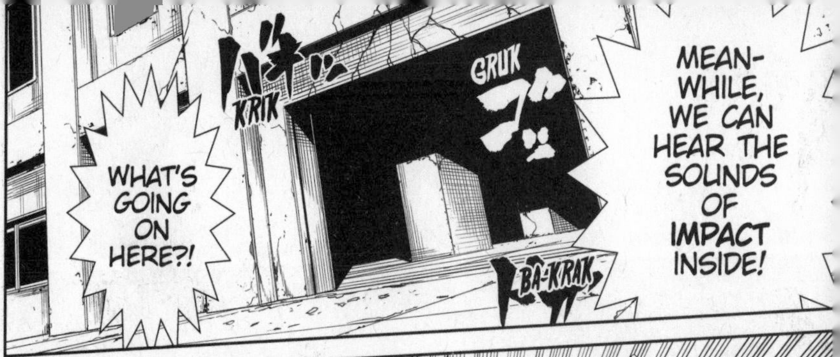
MEAN-WHILE, WE CAN HEAR THE SOUNDS OF IMPACT INSIDE!
GRUK
KRIK
BA-KRAK
WHAT'S GOING ON HERE?!
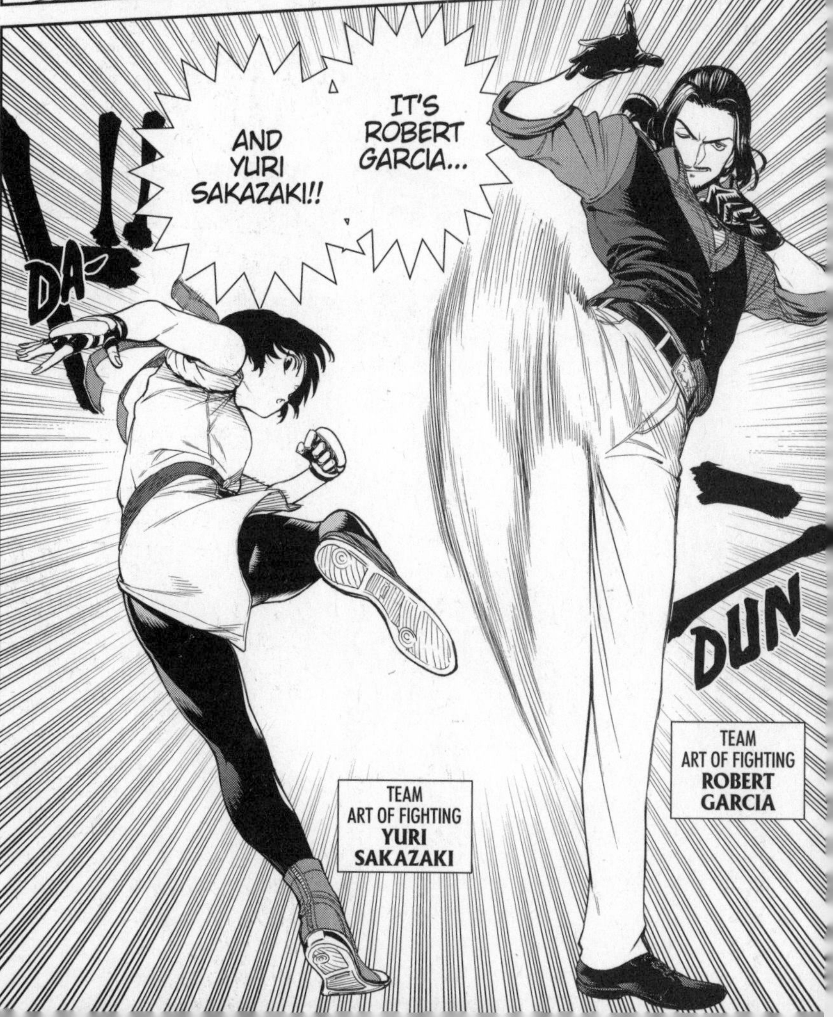
IT'S ROBERT GARCIA...
AND YURI SAKAZAKI!!
DUN
DA
TEAM ART OF FIGHTING ROBERT GARCIA
TEAM ART OF FIGHTING YURI SAKAZAKI

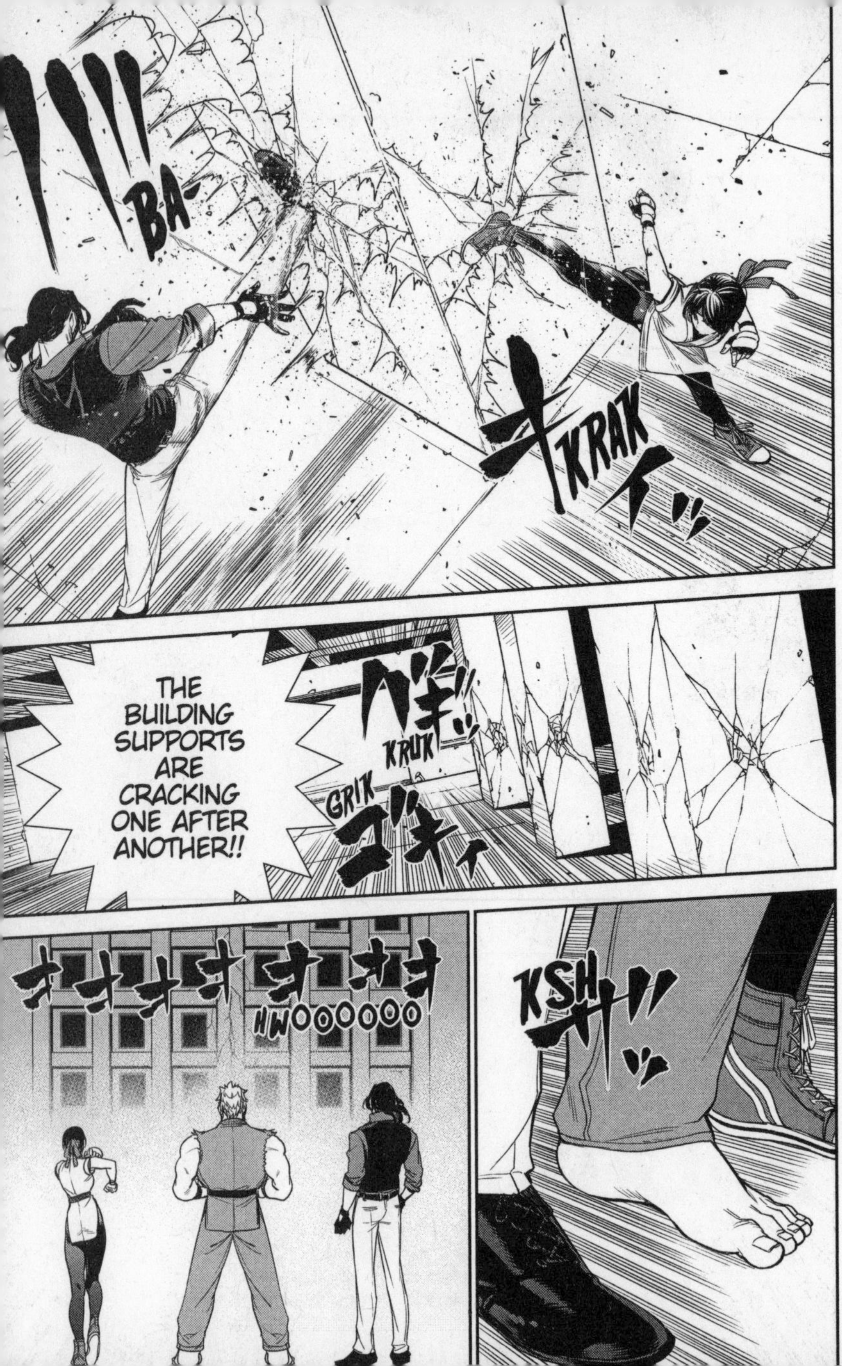
BA-
KRAK
THE BUILDING SUPPORTS ARE CRACKING ONE AFTER ANOTHER!!
ベギッ
KRUK
GRIK
ゴキィ
KSH
オオオオオオオオ
HWOOOOOO

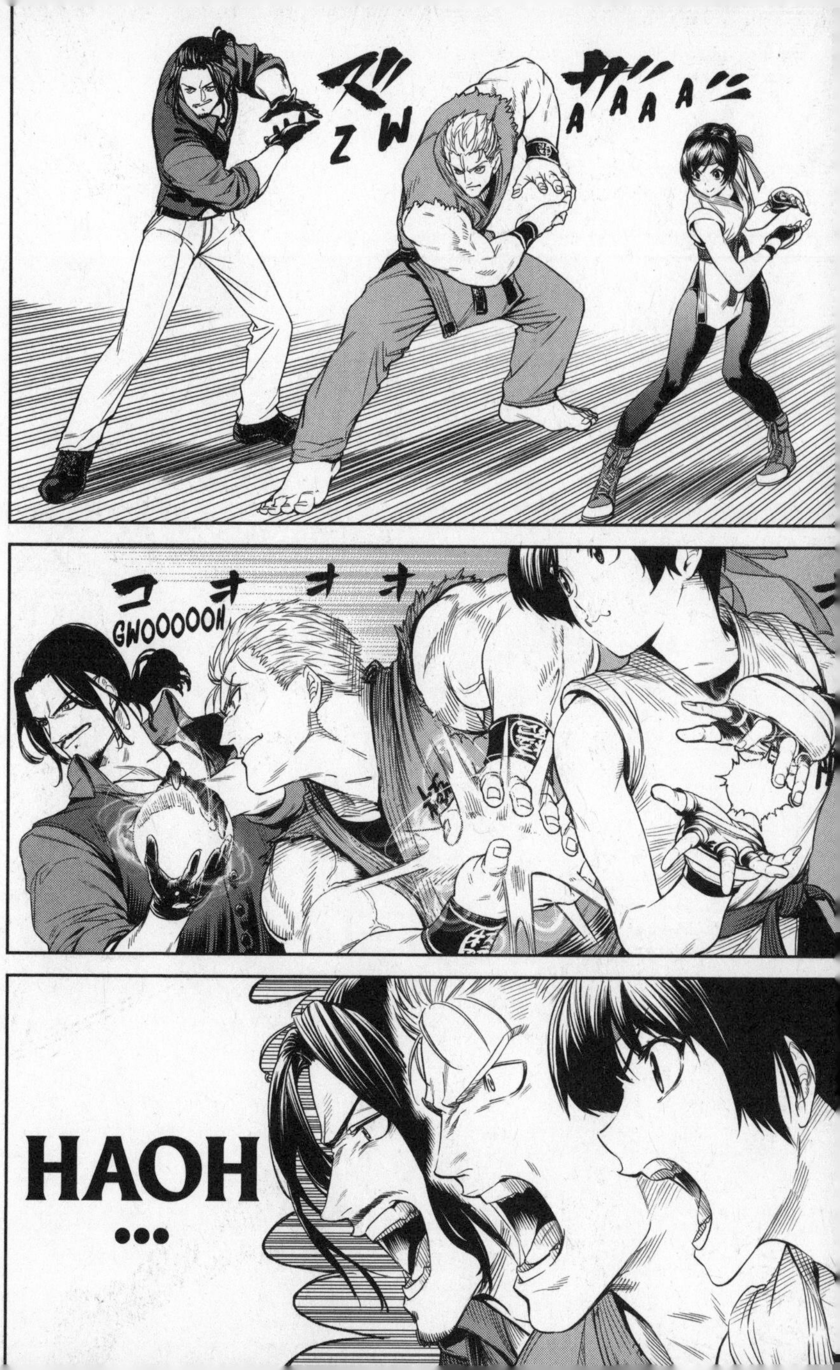
AAAA
ZW
コォォォ
GWOOOOOH
HAOH
...

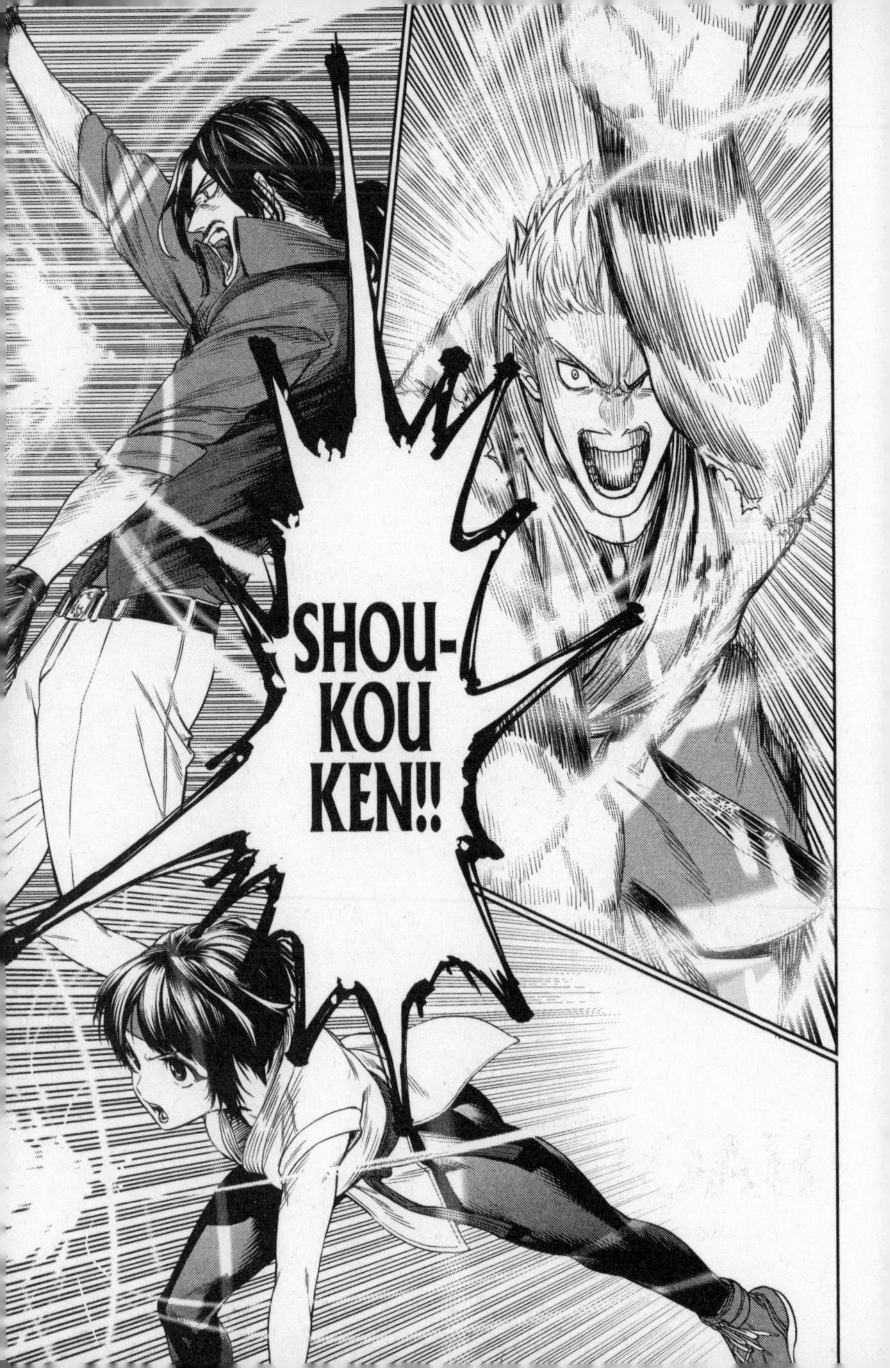
SHOU-KOU KEN!!

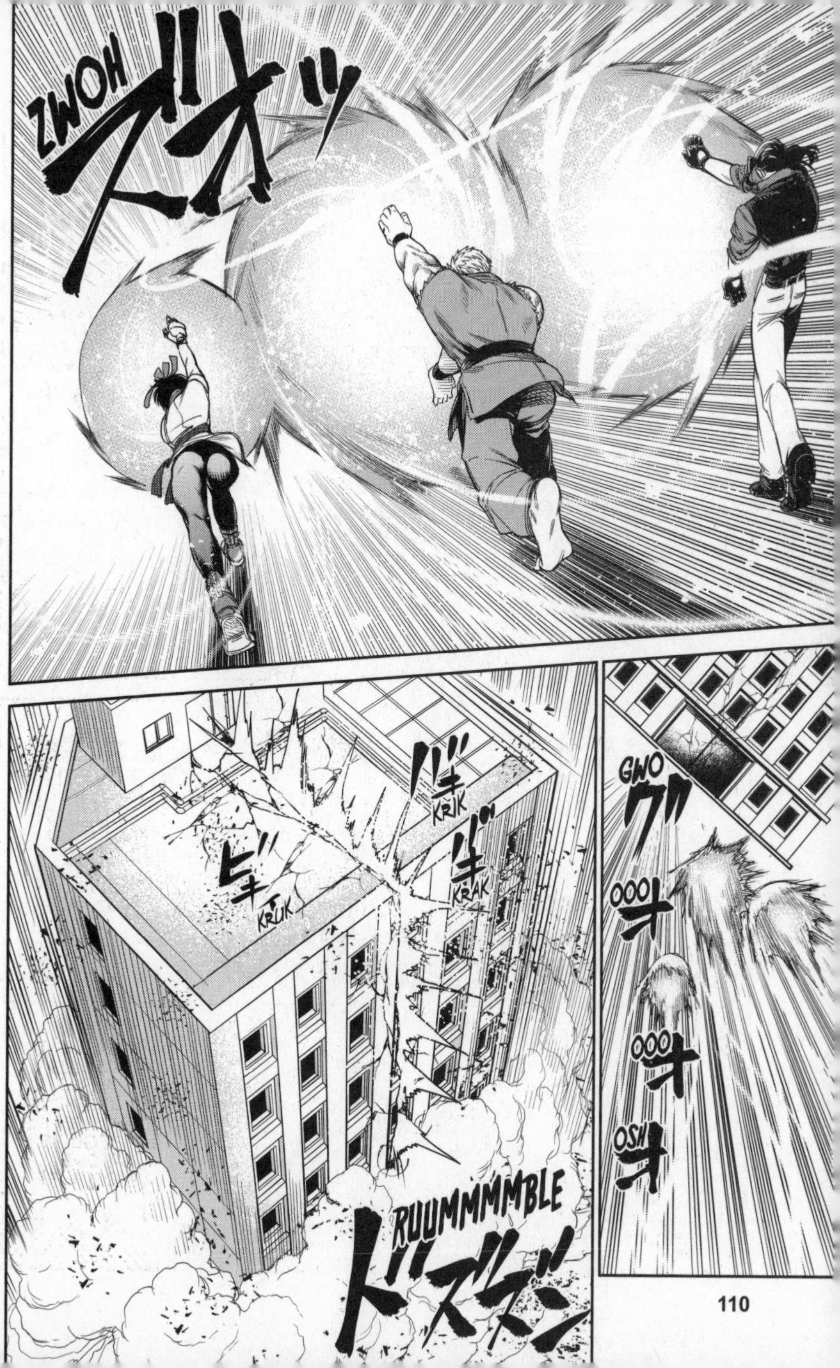
ZWOH
GWO
OOO
OOO
OSH
KRIK
KRAK
KRUK
RUUMMMMBLE

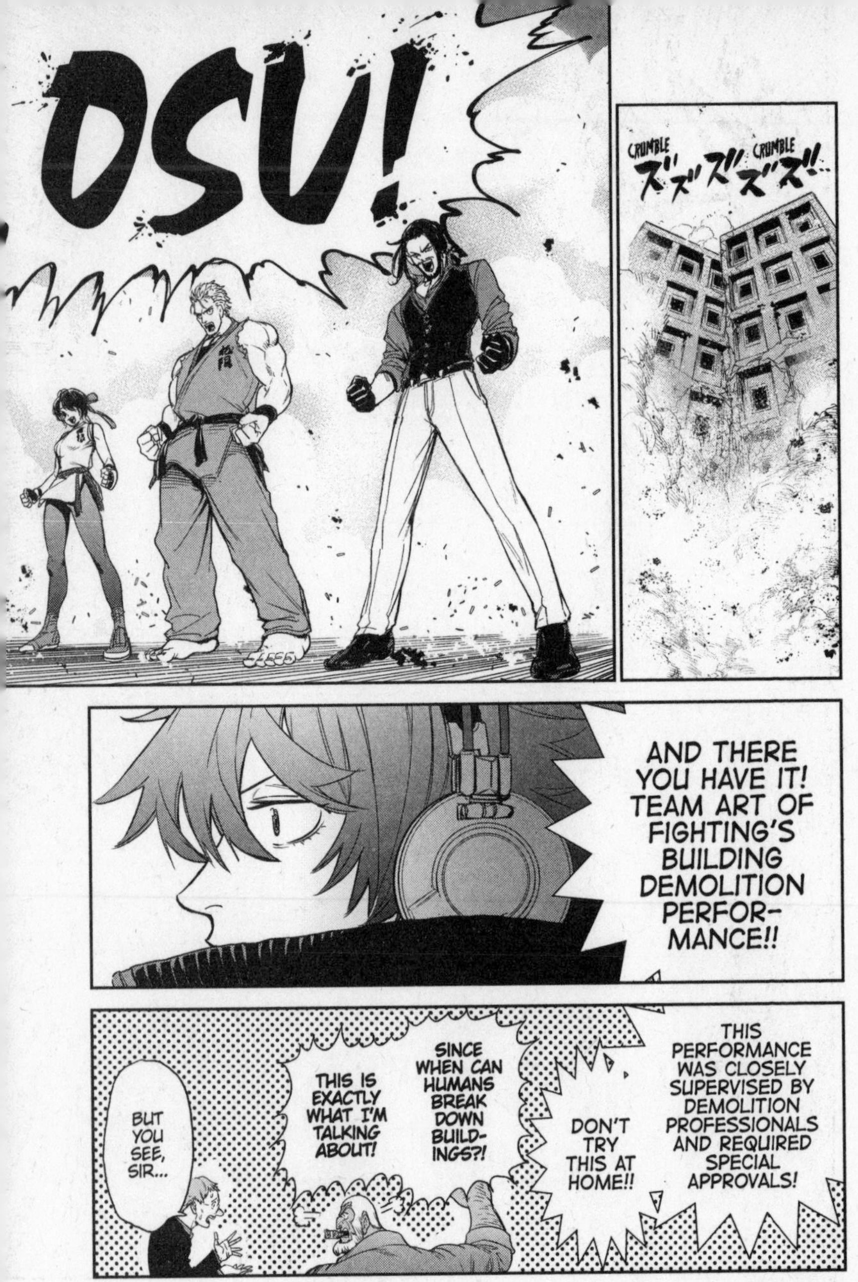
CRUMBLE
ズズズズズ!!
CRUMBLE
OSU!
AND THERE YOU HAVE IT! TEAM ART OF FIGHTING'S BUILDING DEMOLITION PERFOR-MANCE!!
THIS PERFORMANCE WAS CLOSELY SUPERVISED BY DEMOLITION PROFESSIONALS AND REQUIRED SPECIAL APPROVALS!
DON'T TRY THIS AT HOME!!
SINCE WHEN CAN HUMANS BREAK DOWN BUILD-INGS?!
THIS IS EXACTLY WHAT I'M TALKING ABOUT!
BUT YOU SEE, SIR...

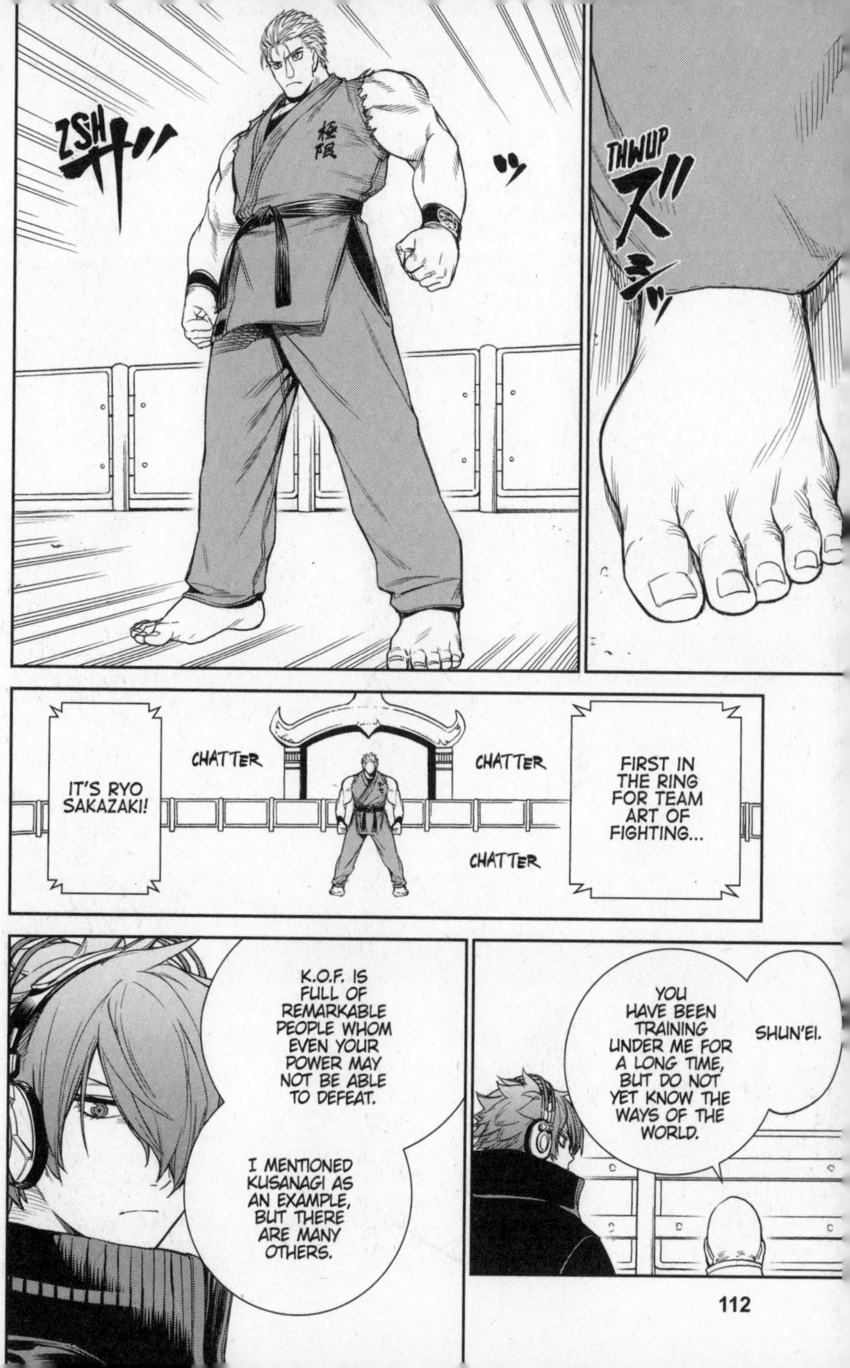
THWUP
ZSH
CHATTER
FIRST IN THE RING FOR TEAM ART OF FIGHTING...
CHATTER
CHATTER
IT'S RYO SAKAZAKI!
SHUN'EI.
YOU HAVE BEEN TRAINING UNDER ME FOR A LONG TIME, BUT DO NOT YET KNOW THE WAYS OF THE WORLD.
K.O.F. IS FULL OF REMARKABLE PEOPLE WHOM EVEN YOUR POWER MAY NOT BE ABLE TO DEFEAT.
I MENTIONED KUSANAGI AS AN EXAMPLE, BUT THERE ARE MANY OTHERS.

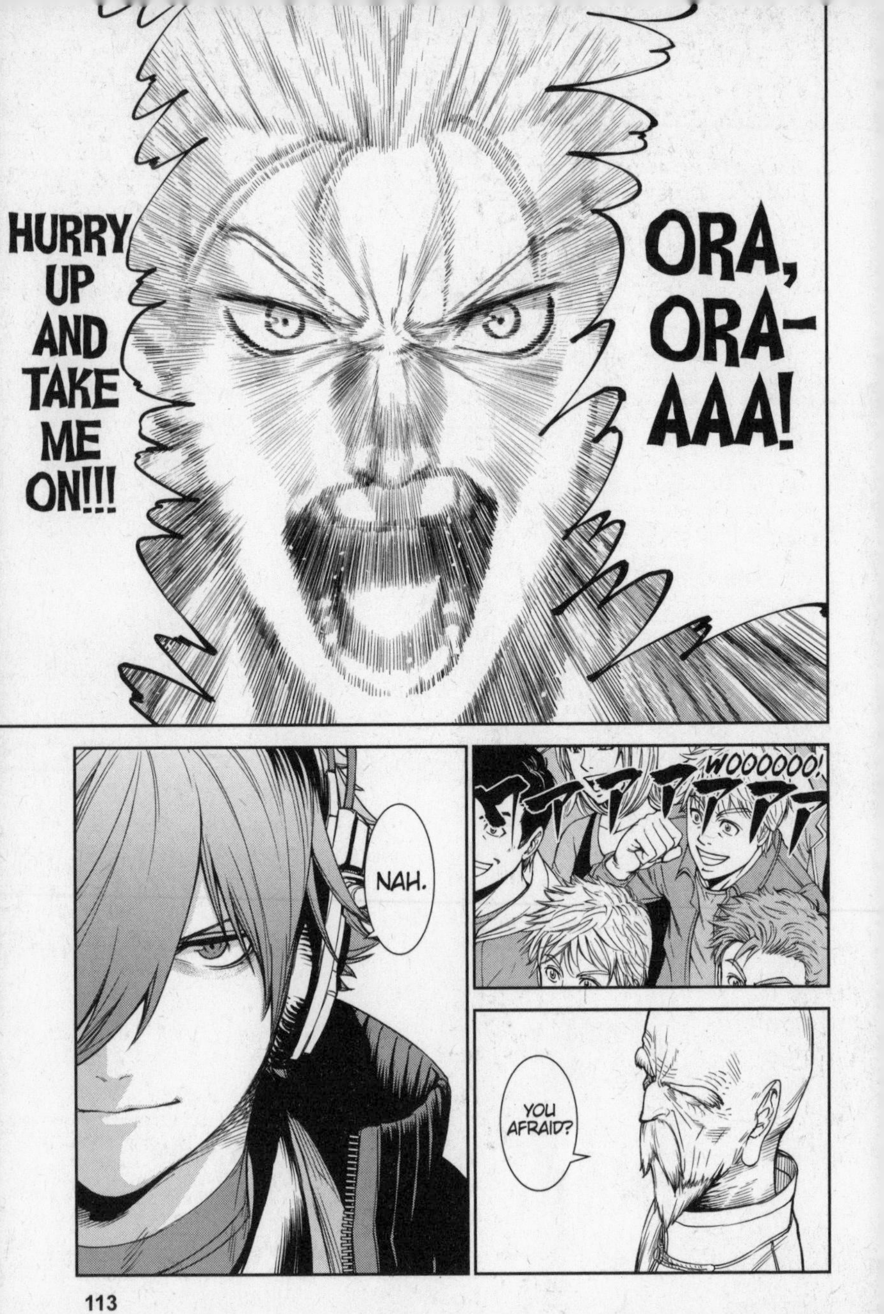
ORA, ORA-AAA!
HURRY UP AND TAKE ME ON!!!
WOOOOOO!
YOU AFRAID?
NAH.

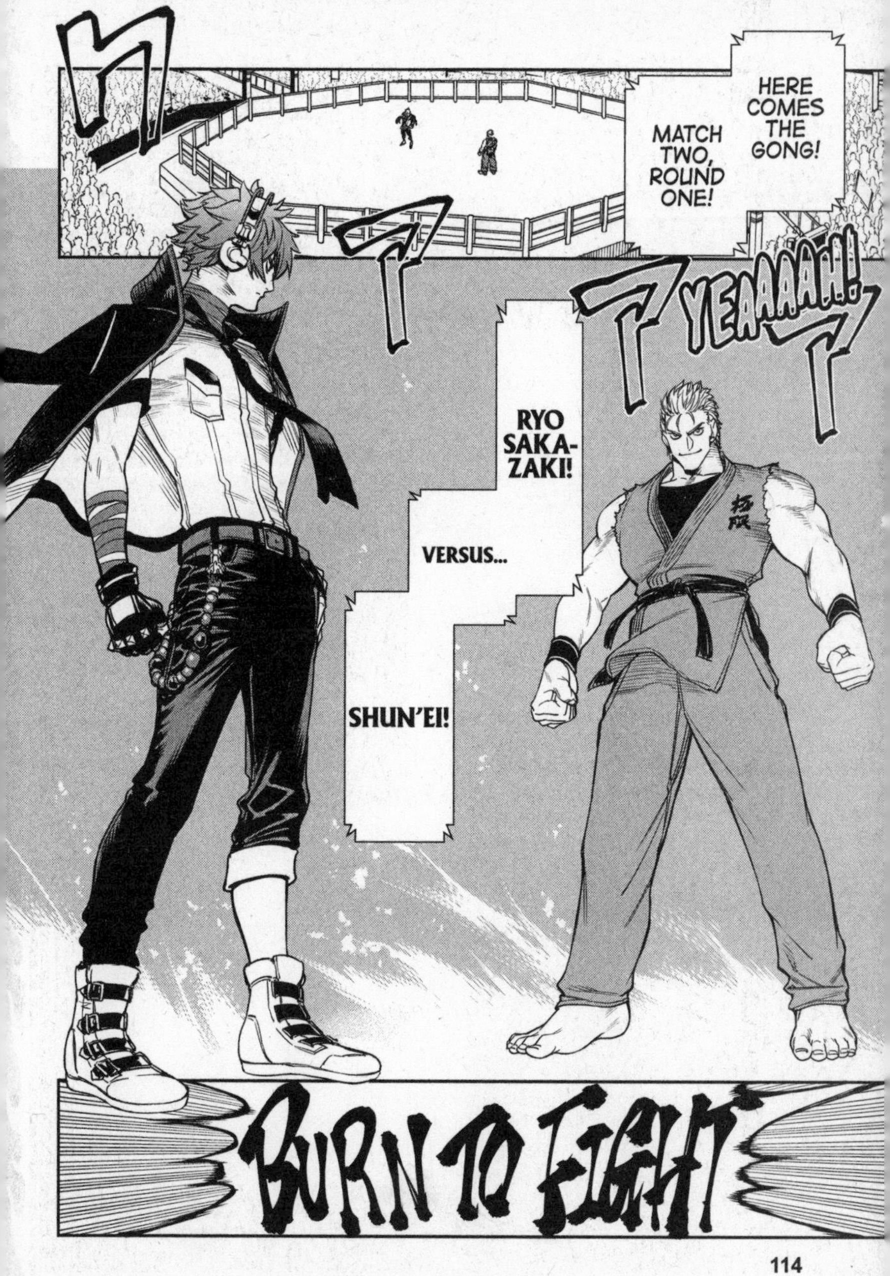
HERE COMES THE GONG!
MATCH TWO, ROUND ONE!
YEAAAAH!
RYO SAKA-ZAKI!
VERSUS...
SHUN'EI!
BURN TO FIGHT

MOVE 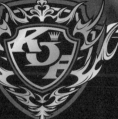 LIST

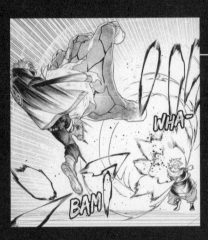

Sen-Siss Hou

A Hakkyokuseiken lunge attack imparted directly from Tung Fu Rue. Here, the movement is modified slightly for sparring purposes.

User: Meitenkun

Command:
← (HOLD) → + **LP** or **HP**

Aqua Spear

A mid-range attack piercing the opponent with illusory claws that extend straight forward.

User: Shun'ei

Command:
↓ ↘ → + **LP** or **HP**

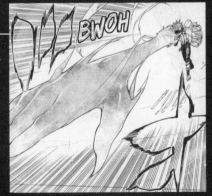

MOVE LIST

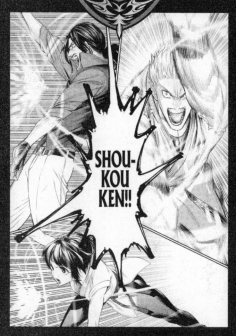

SHOU-KOU KEN!!

Haoh Shoukou Ken

A supreme, iconic secret art of Kyokugen-style karate. Chi is collected from throughout the body and blasted forward in a huge mass from the extended palms.

Users: Ryo Sakazaki, Robert Garcia, Yuri Sakazaki

Command:
→ ← ↙ ↓ ↘ → + LP or HP

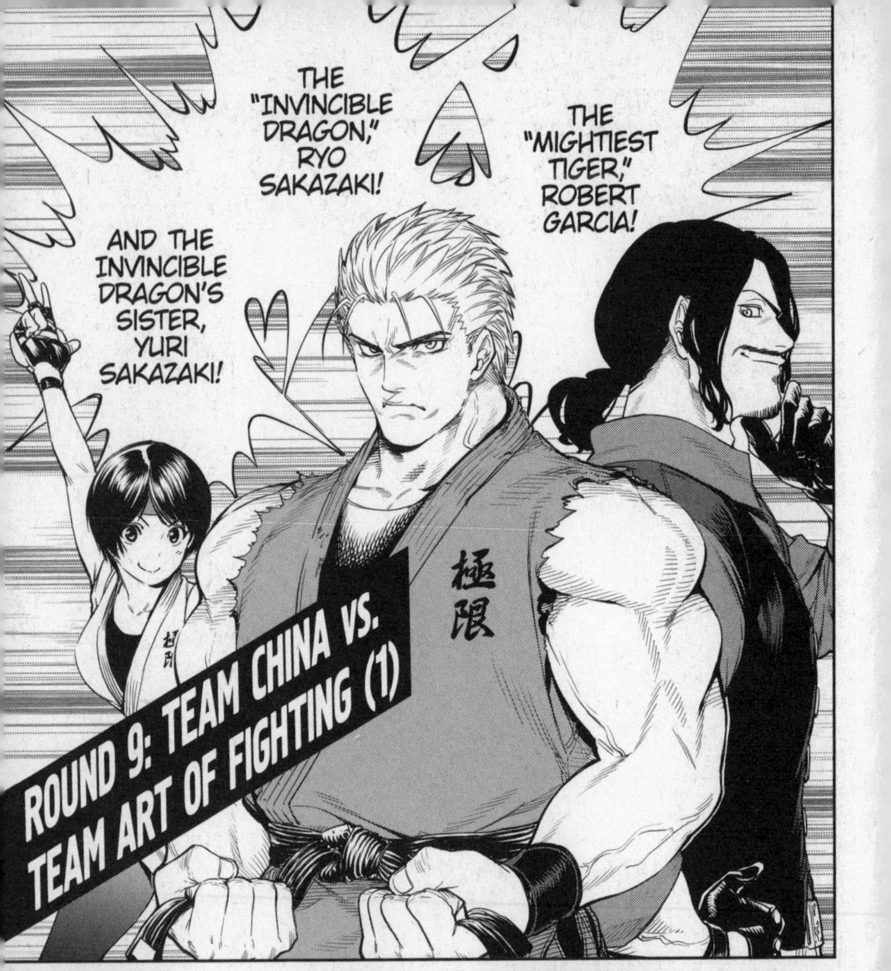
THE "MIGHTIEST TIGER," ROBERT GARCIA!
THE "INVINCIBLE DRAGON," RYO SAKAZAKI!
AND THE INVINCIBLE DRAGON'S SISTER, YURI SAKAZAKI!
極限
ROUND 9: TEAM CHINA VS. TEAM ART OF FIGHTING (1)

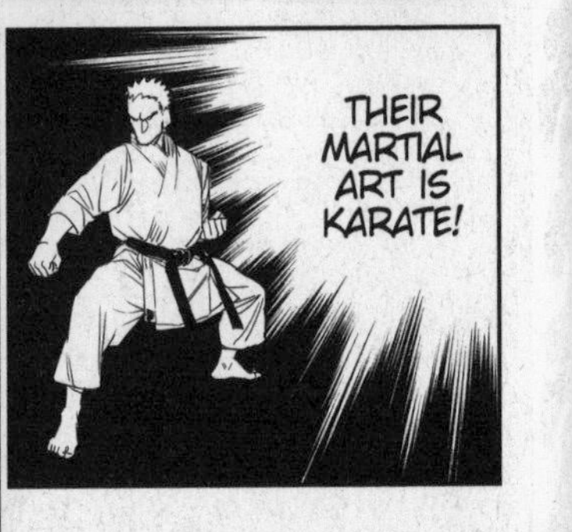
THEIR MARTIAL ART IS KARATE!

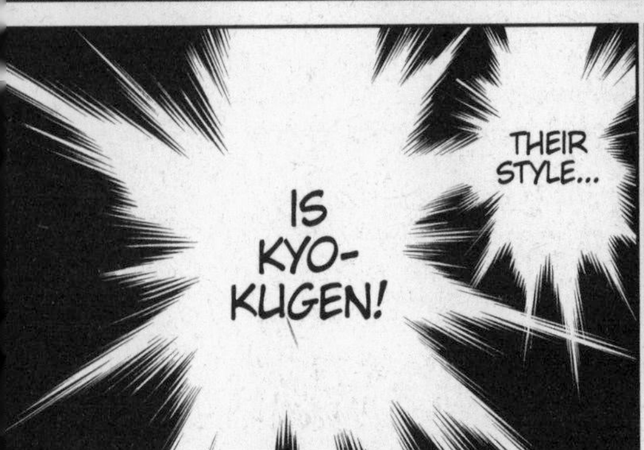
THEIR STYLE...
IS KYO-KUGEN!

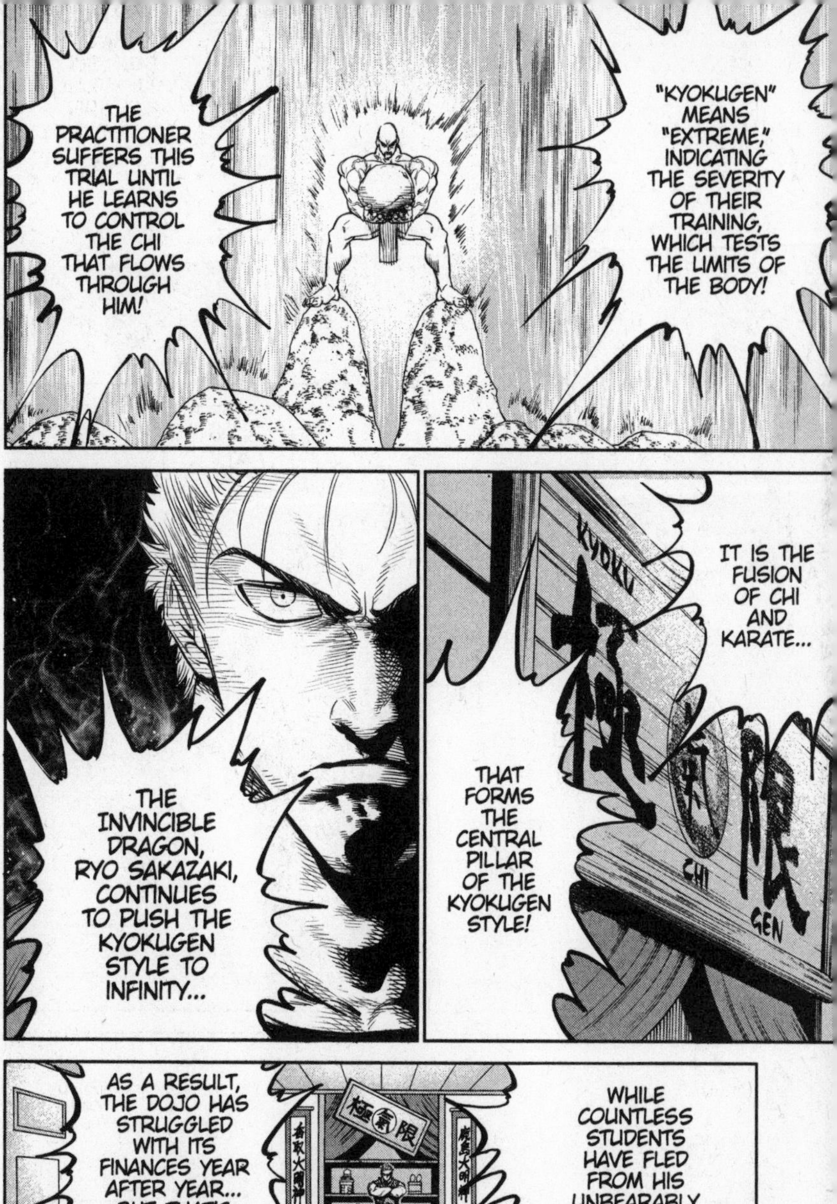
"KYOKUGEN" MEANS "EXTREME," INDICATING THE SEVERITY OF THEIR TRAINING, WHICH TESTS THE LIMITS OF THE BODY!
THE PRACTITIONER SUFFERS THIS TRIAL UNTIL HE LEARNS TO CONTROL THE CHI THAT FLOWS THROUGH HIM!
KYOKU
CHI
GEN
IT IS THE FUSION OF CHI AND KARATE...
THAT FORMS THE CENTRAL PILLAR OF THE KYOKUGEN STYLE!
THE INVINCIBLE DRAGON, RYO SAKAZAKI, CONTINUES TO PUSH THE KYOKUGEN STYLE TO INFINITY...
WHILE COUNTLESS STUDENTS HAVE FLED FROM HIS UNBEARABLY STRICT INSTRUCTION!
AS A RESULT, THE DOJO HAS STRUGGLED WITH ITS FINANCES YEAR AFTER YEAR... BUT THAT'S NEITHER HERE NOR THERE!

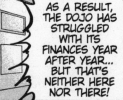

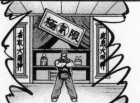

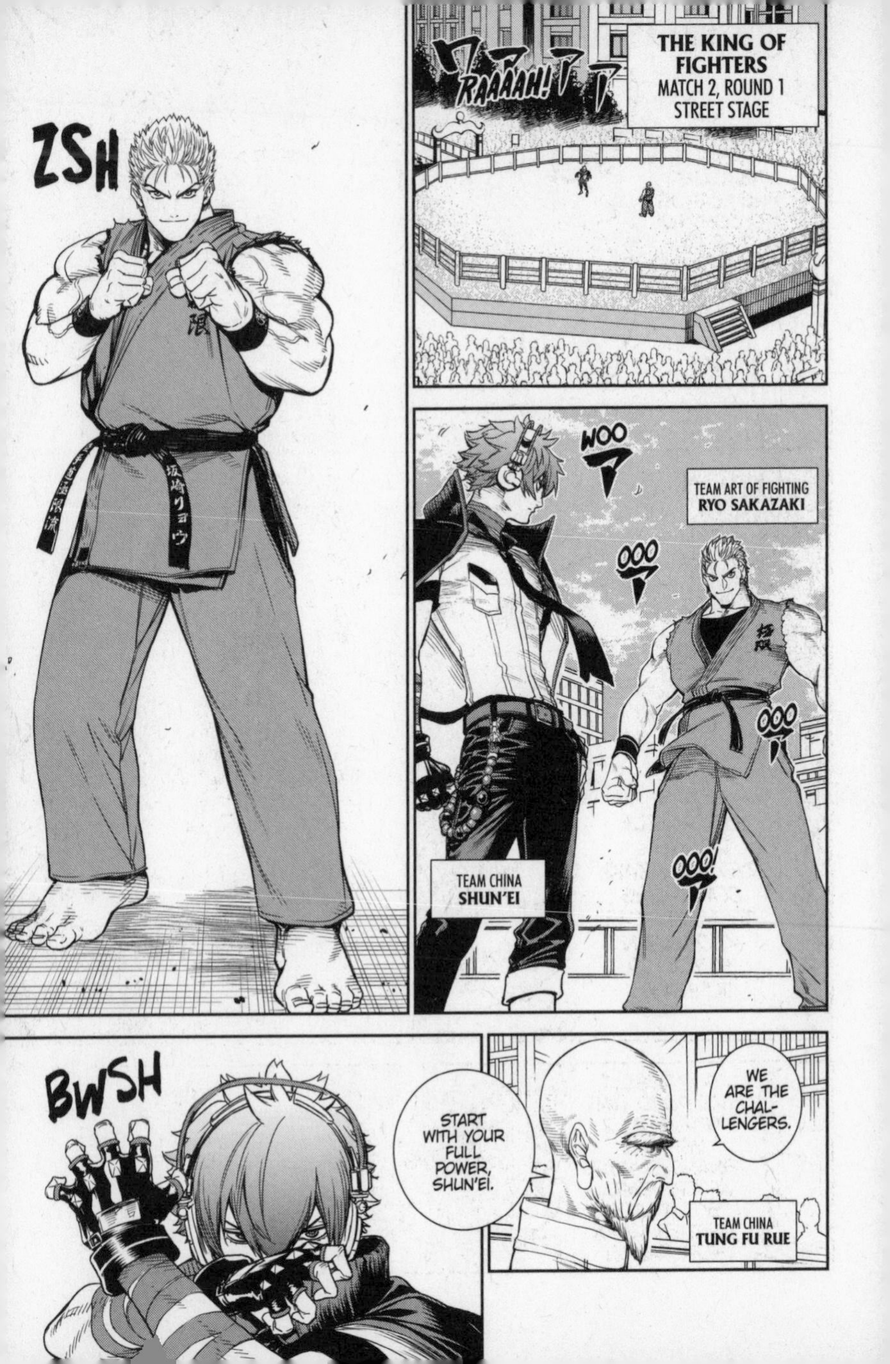
RAAAAH!
THE KING OF FIGHTERS
MATCH 2, ROUND 1
STREET STAGE
WOO
TEAM ART OF FIGHTING
RYO SAKAZAKI
OOO
OOO
OOO!
TEAM CHINA
SHUN'EI
ZSH
WE ARE THE CHAL-LENGERS.
START WITH YOUR FULL POWER, SHUN'EI.
TEAM CHINA
TUNG FU RUE
BWSH

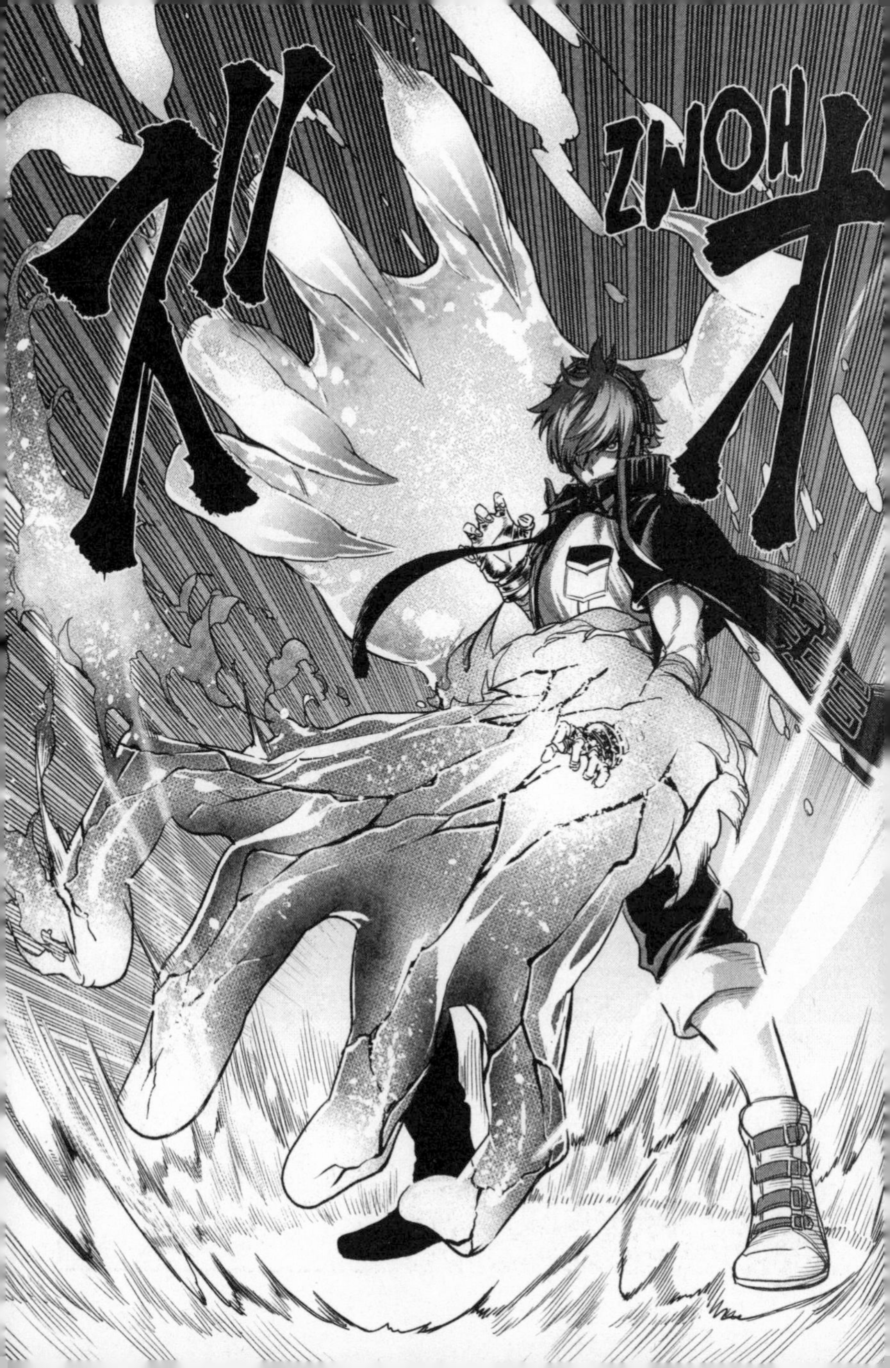
ZWOH

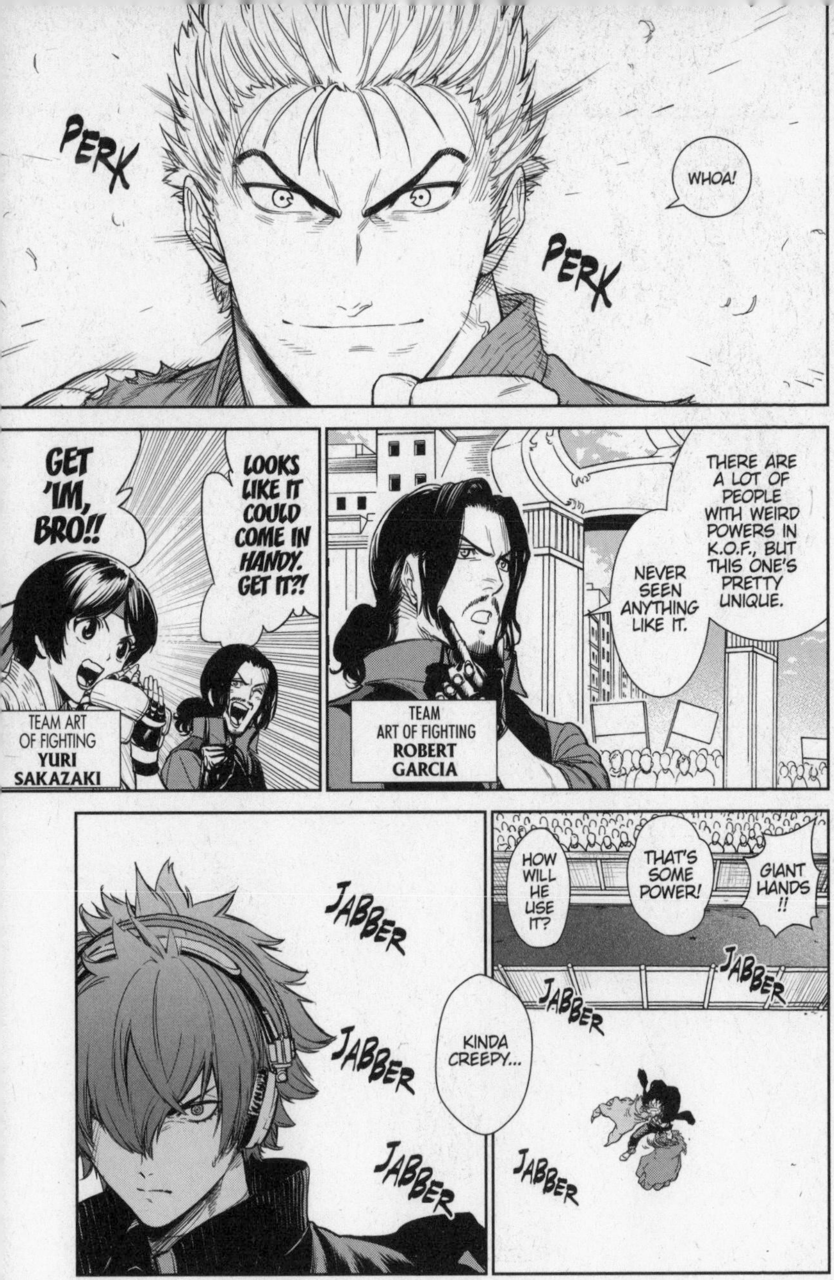
WHOA!
PERK
PERK
THERE ARE A LOT OF PEOPLE WITH WEIRD POWERS IN K.O.F., BUT THIS ONE'S PRETTY UNIQUE.
NEVER SEEN ANYTHING LIKE IT.
TEAM ART OF FIGHTING ROBERT GARCIA
LOOKS LIKE IT COULD COME IN HANDY. GET IT?!
GET 'IM, BRO!!
TEAM ART OF FIGHTING YURI SAKAZAKI
GIANT HANDS!!
THAT'S SOME POWER!
HOW WILL HE USE IT?
JABBER
JABBER
KINDA CREEPY...
JABBER
JABBER
JABBER
JABBER

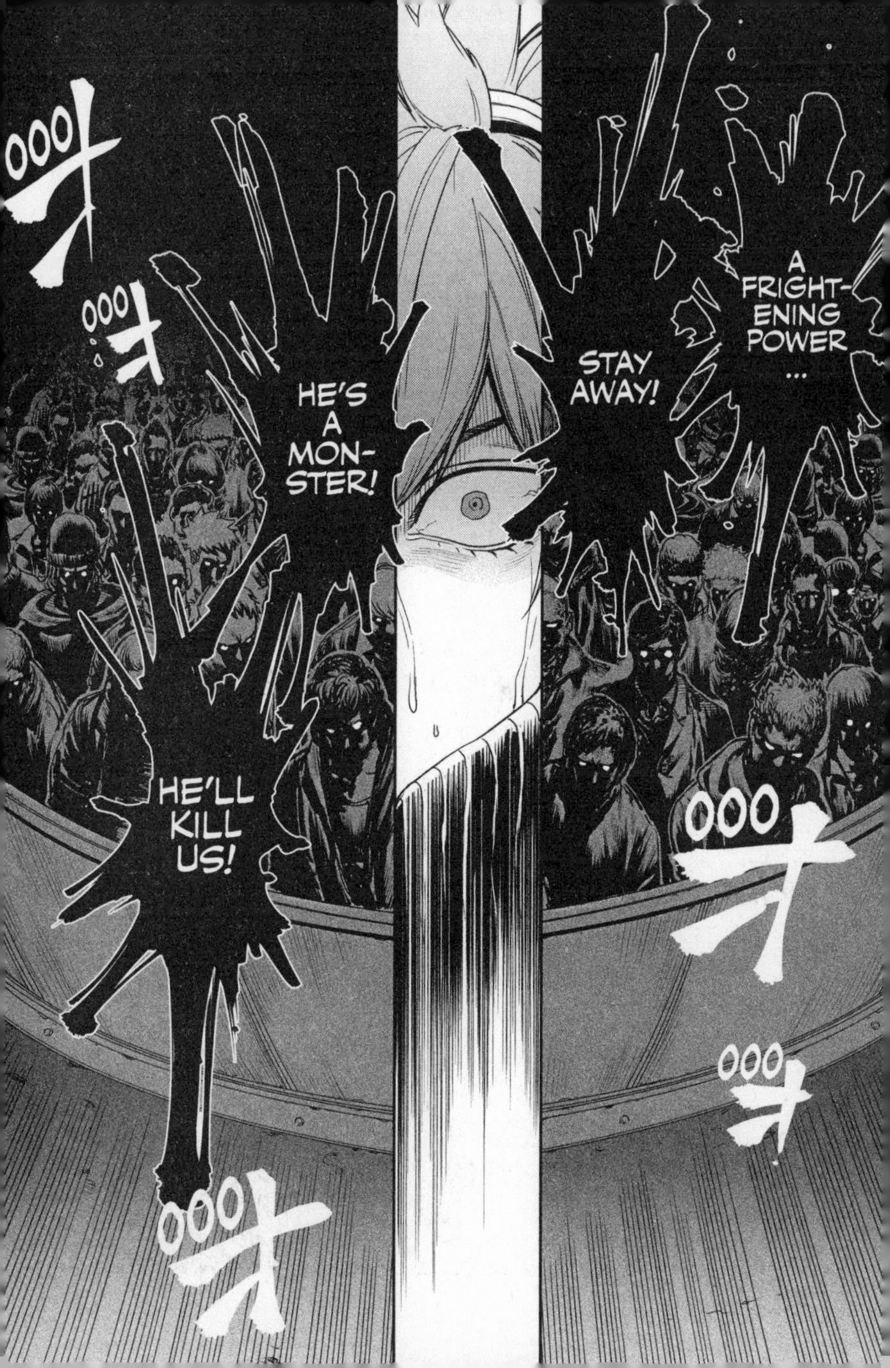
A FRIGHTENING POWER ...
STAY AWAY!
OOOオ
OOOオ
HE'S A MONSTER!
OOOオ
OOOオ
HE'LL KILL US!
OOOオ

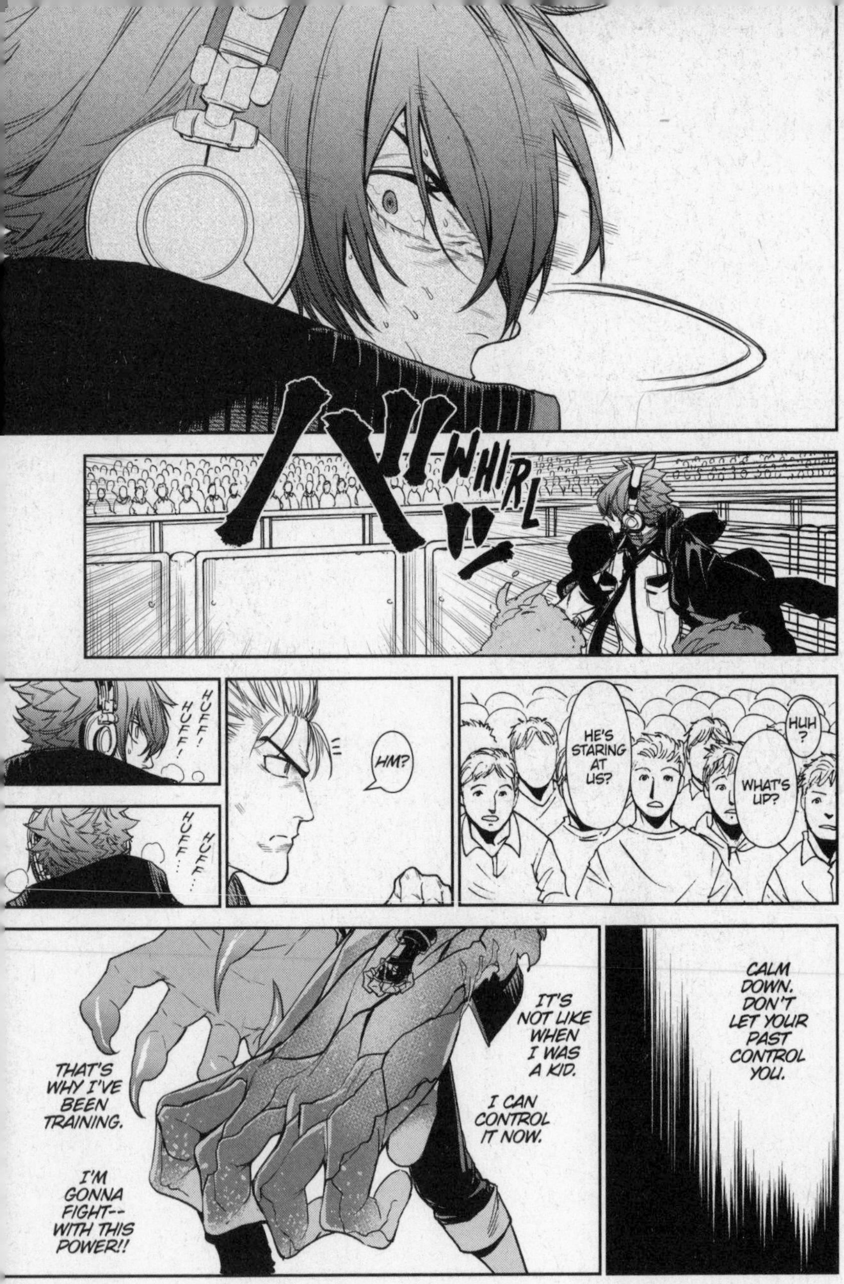
WHIRL
HUH?
WHAT'S UP?
HE'S STARING AT US?
HM?
HUFF! HUFF!
HUFF... HUFF...
CALM DOWN. DON'T LET YOUR PAST CONTROL YOU.
IT'S NOT LIKE WHEN I WAS A KID.
I CAN CONTROL IT NOW.
THAT'S WHY I'VE BEEN TRAINING.
I'M GONNA FIGHT-- WITH THIS POWER!!

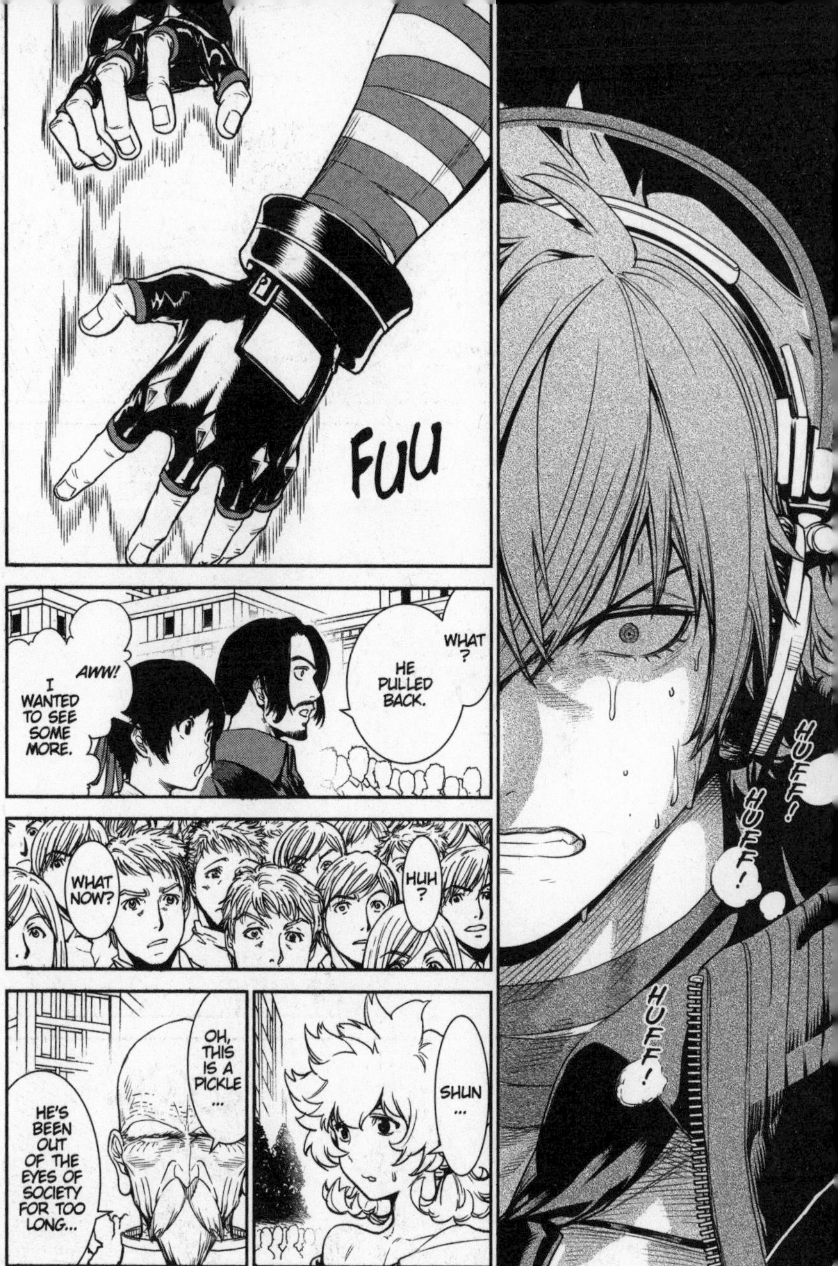
HUFF!
HUFF!
HUFF!
FUU
WHAT? HE PULLED BACK.
AWW! I WANTED TO SEE SOME MORE.
HUH?
WHAT NOW?
SHUN...
OH, THIS IS A PICKLE...
HE'S BEEN OUT OF THE EYES OF SOCIETY FOR TOO LONG...

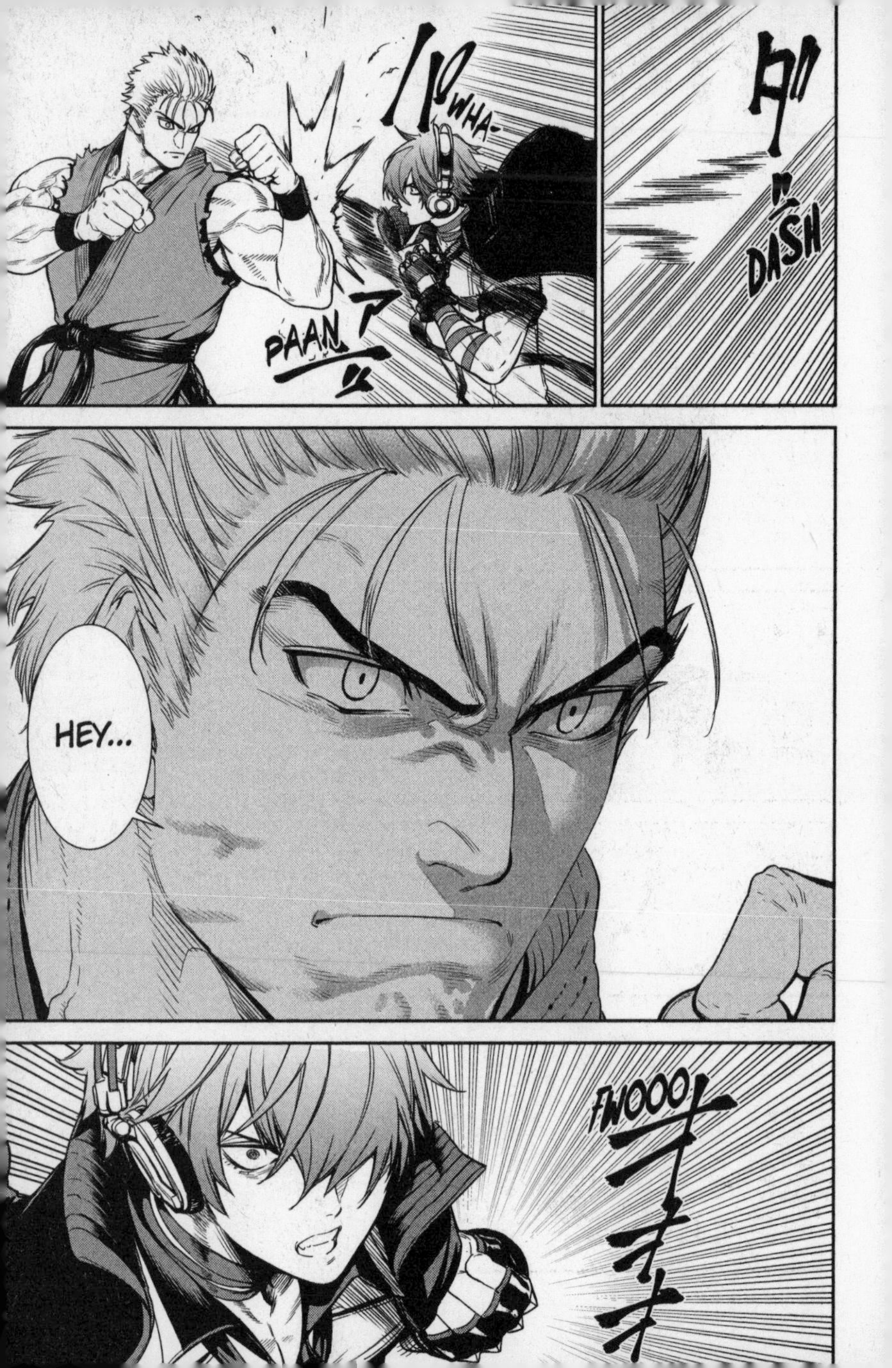
DASH
WHA-
PAAN
HEY...
FWOOO

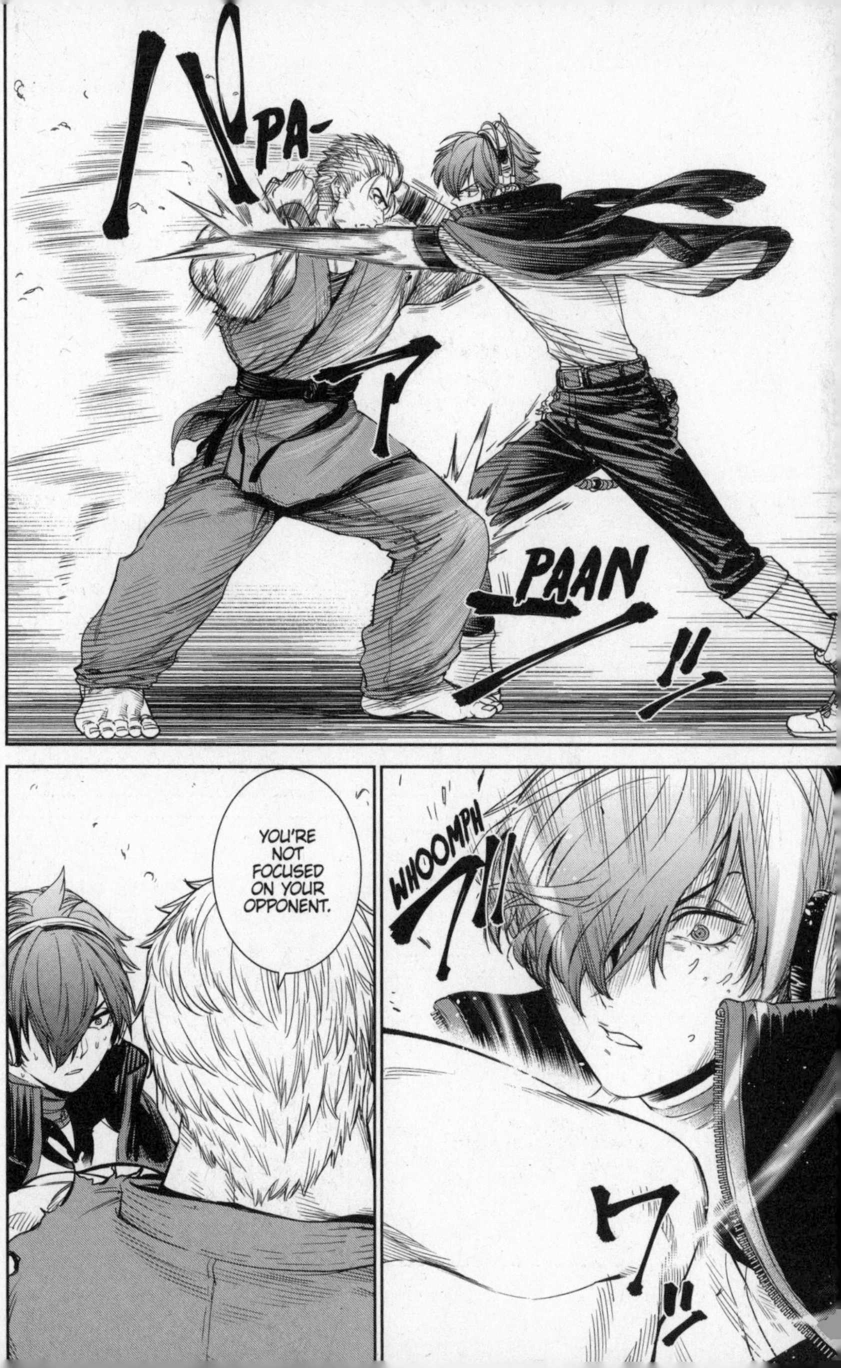
PA-
PAAN
WHOOMPH
YOU'RE NOT FOCUSED ON YOUR OPPONENT.

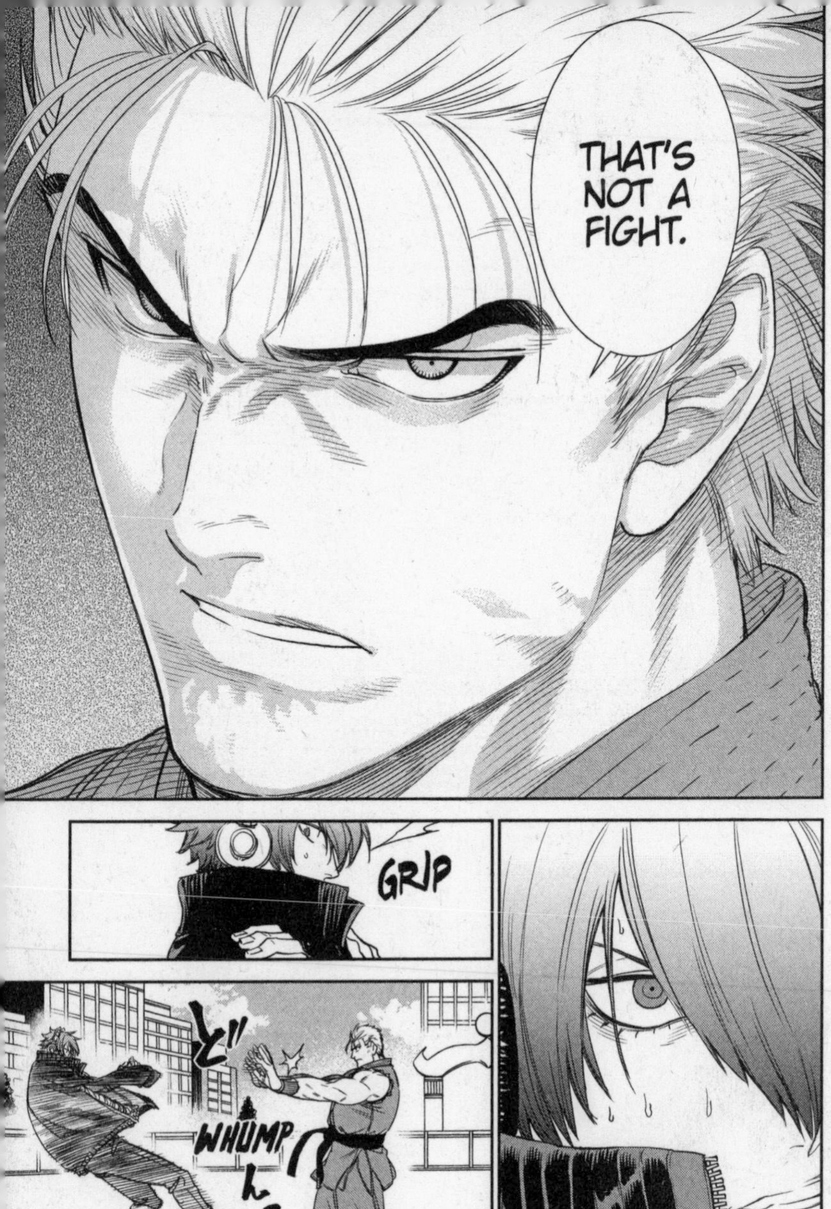
THAT'S NOT A FIGHT.
GRIP
ど
WHUMP
んっ

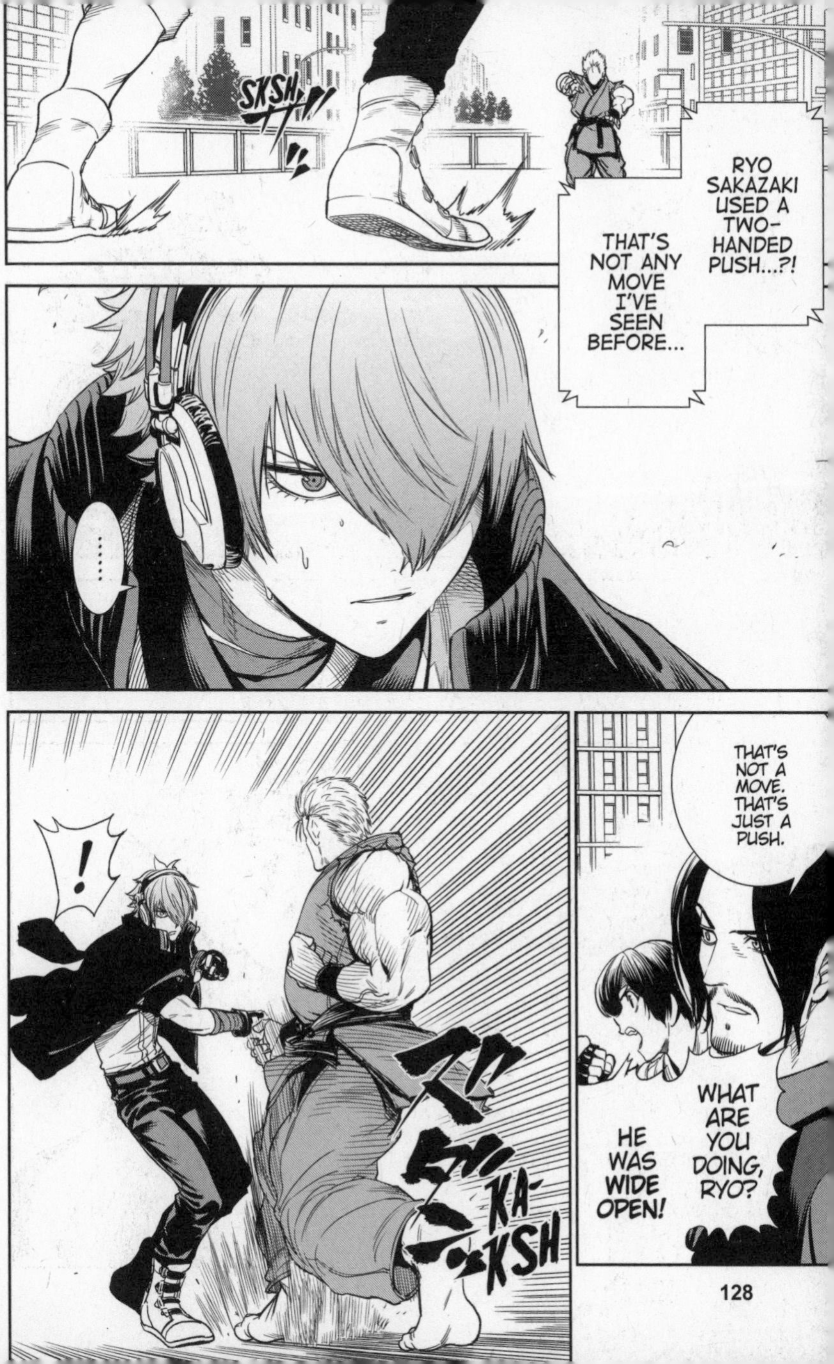
SKSH
RYO SAKAZAKI USED A TWO-HANDED PUSH...?!
THAT'S NOT ANY MOVE I'VE SEEN BEFORE...
......
THAT'S NOT A MOVE. THAT'S JUST A PUSH.
WHAT ARE YOU DOING, RYO?
HE WAS WIDE OPEN!
!
KA-KSH

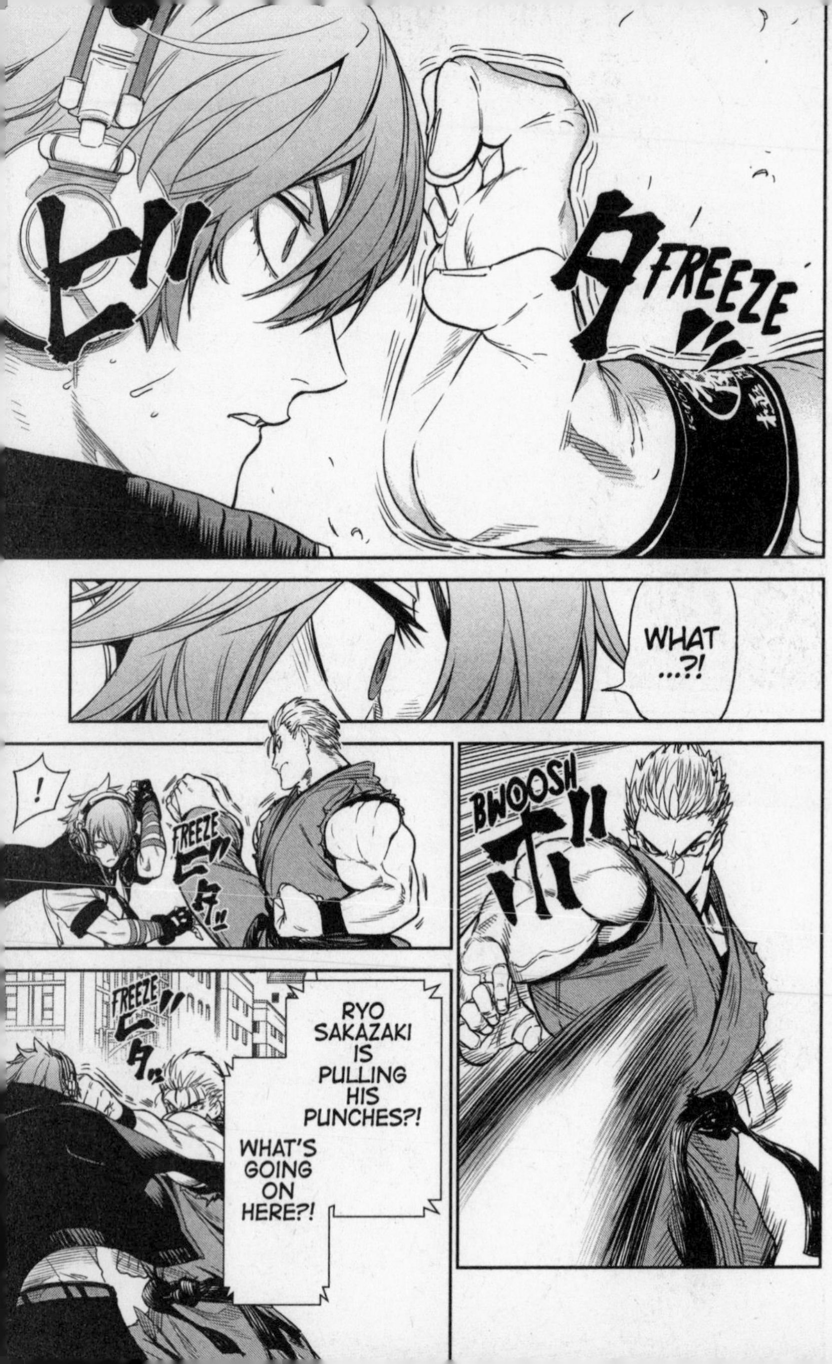
FREEZE
WHAT ...?!
BWOOSH
!
FREEZE
FREEZE
RYO SAKAZAKI IS PULLING HIS PUNCHES?!
WHAT'S GOING ON HERE?!

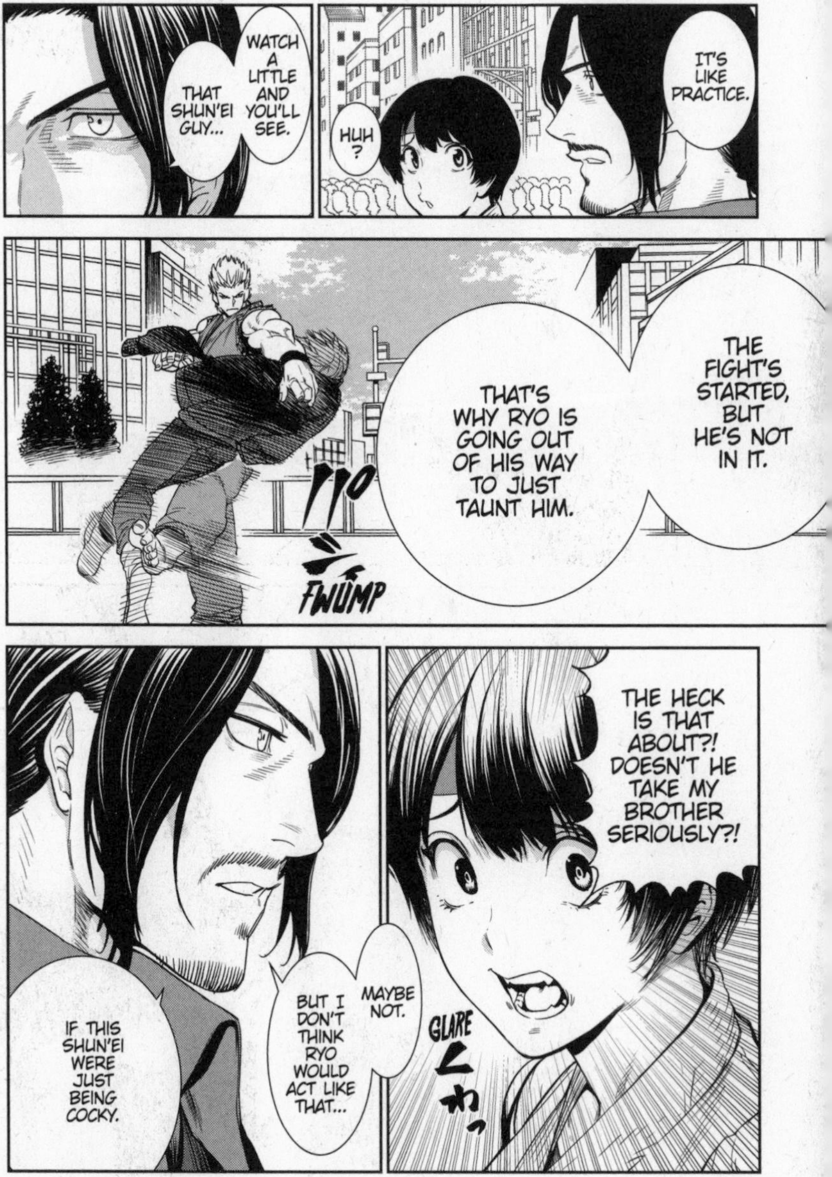

IT'S LIKE PRACTICE.
HUH?
WATCH A LITTLE AND YOU'LL SEE.
THAT SHUN'EI GUY...
THE FIGHT'S STARTED, BUT HE'S NOT IN IT.
THAT'S WHY RYO IS GOING OUT OF HIS WAY TO JUST TAUNT HIM.
FWUMP
THE HECK IS THAT ABOUT?! DOESN'T HE TAKE MY BROTHER SERIOUSLY?!
GLARE
くわっ
MAYBE NOT.
BUT I DON'T THINK RYO WOULD ACT LIKE THAT...
IF THIS SHUN'EI WERE JUST BEING COCKY.

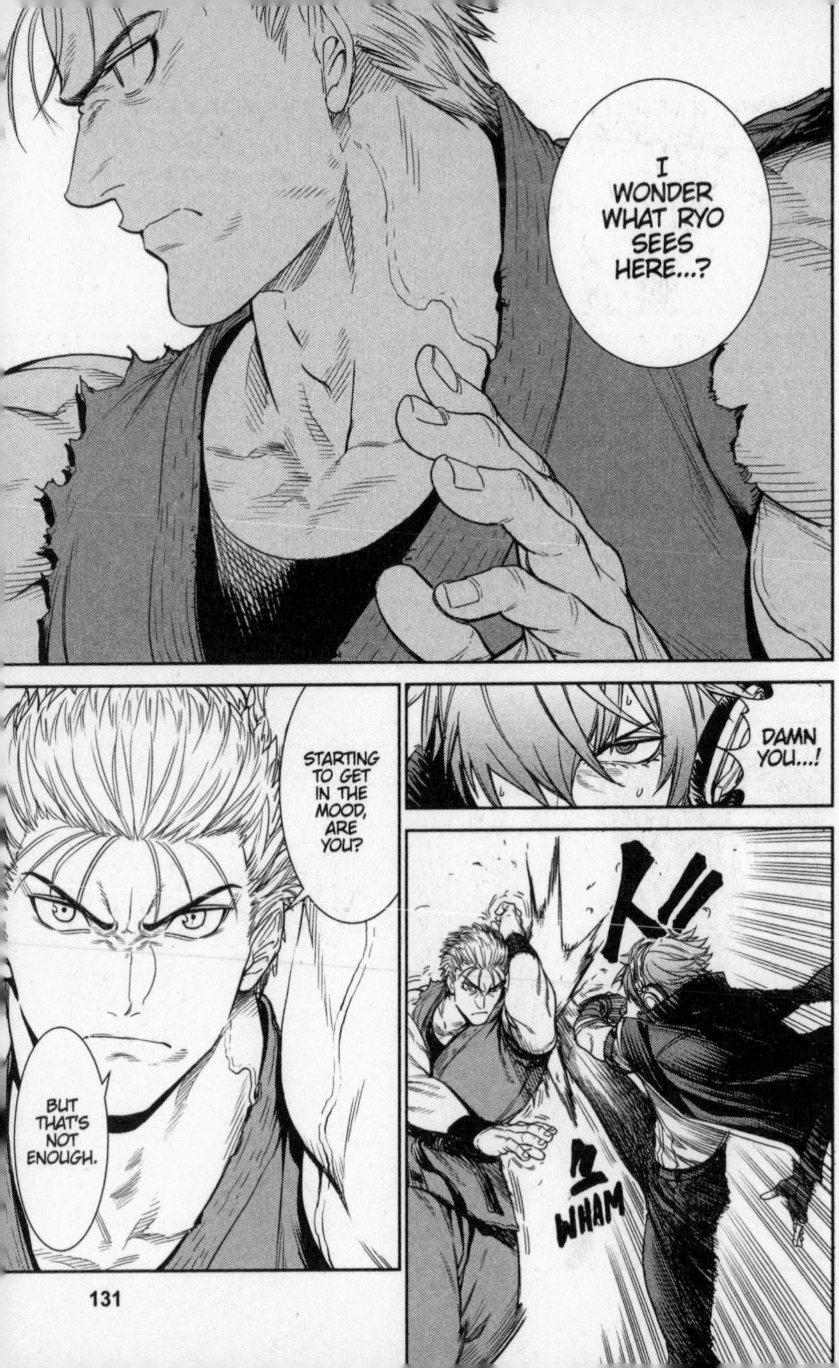
I WONDER WHAT RYO SEES HERE...?
DAMN YOU...!
WHAM
STARTING TO GET IN THE MOOD, ARE YOU?
BUT THAT'S NOT ENOUGH.

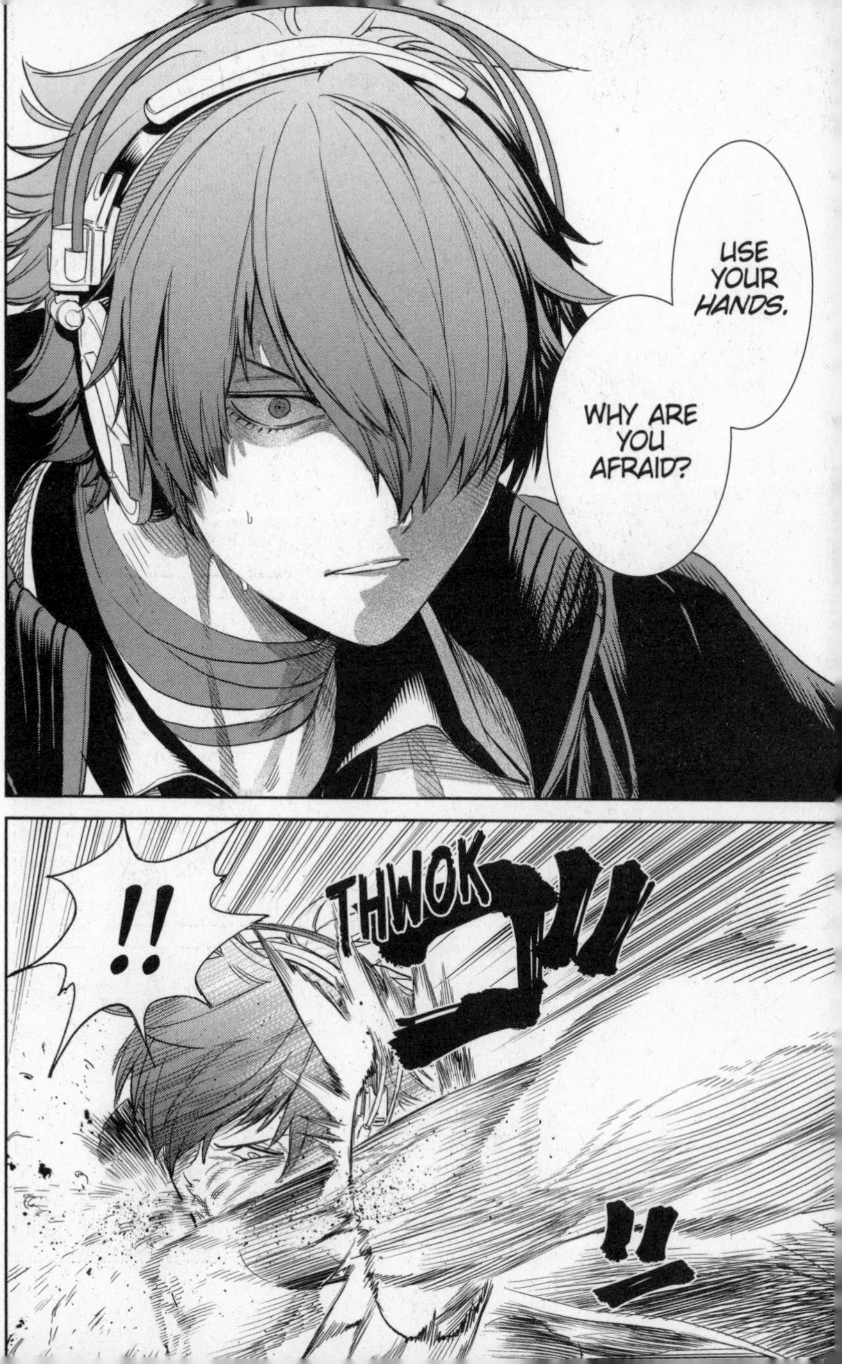
USE YOUR HANDS.
WHY ARE YOU AFRAID?
!!
THWOK

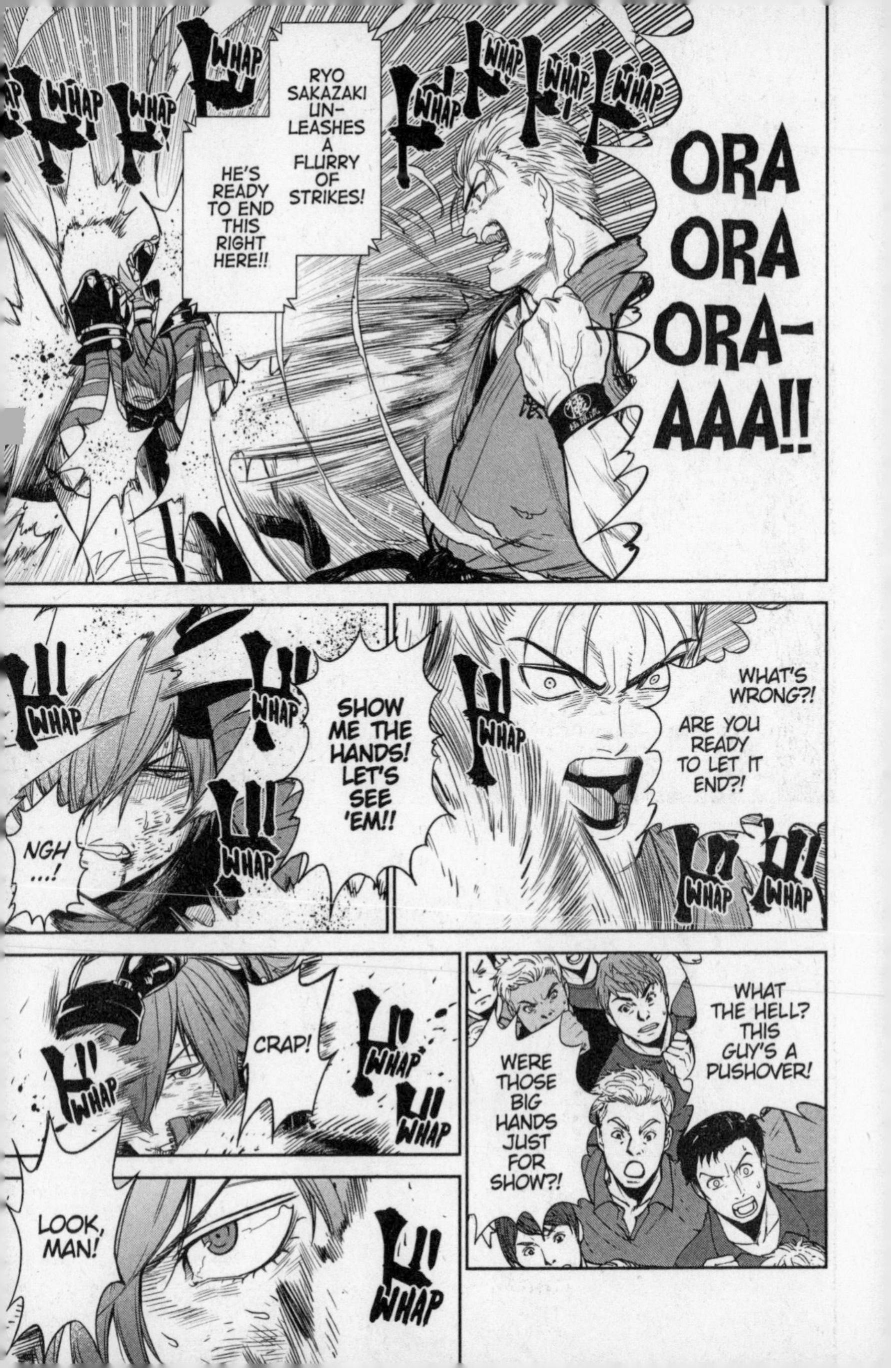
ORA ORA ORA-AAA!!
WHAP WHAP WHAP
WHAP
RYO SAKAZAKI UN-LEASHES A FLURRY OF STRIKES!
HE'S READY TO END THIS RIGHT HERE!!
WHAP
WHAP WHAP
WHAP'S WRONG?!
ARE YOU READY TO LET IT END?!
WHAP WHAP
WHAP
SHOW ME THE HANDS! LET'S SEE 'EM!!
WHAP
WHAP
WHAP
NGH ...!
WHAT THE HELL? THIS GUY'S A PUSHOVER!
WERE THOSE BIG HANDS JUST FOR SHOW?!
WHAP
WHAP
CRAP!
WHAP
LOOK, MAN!
WHAP

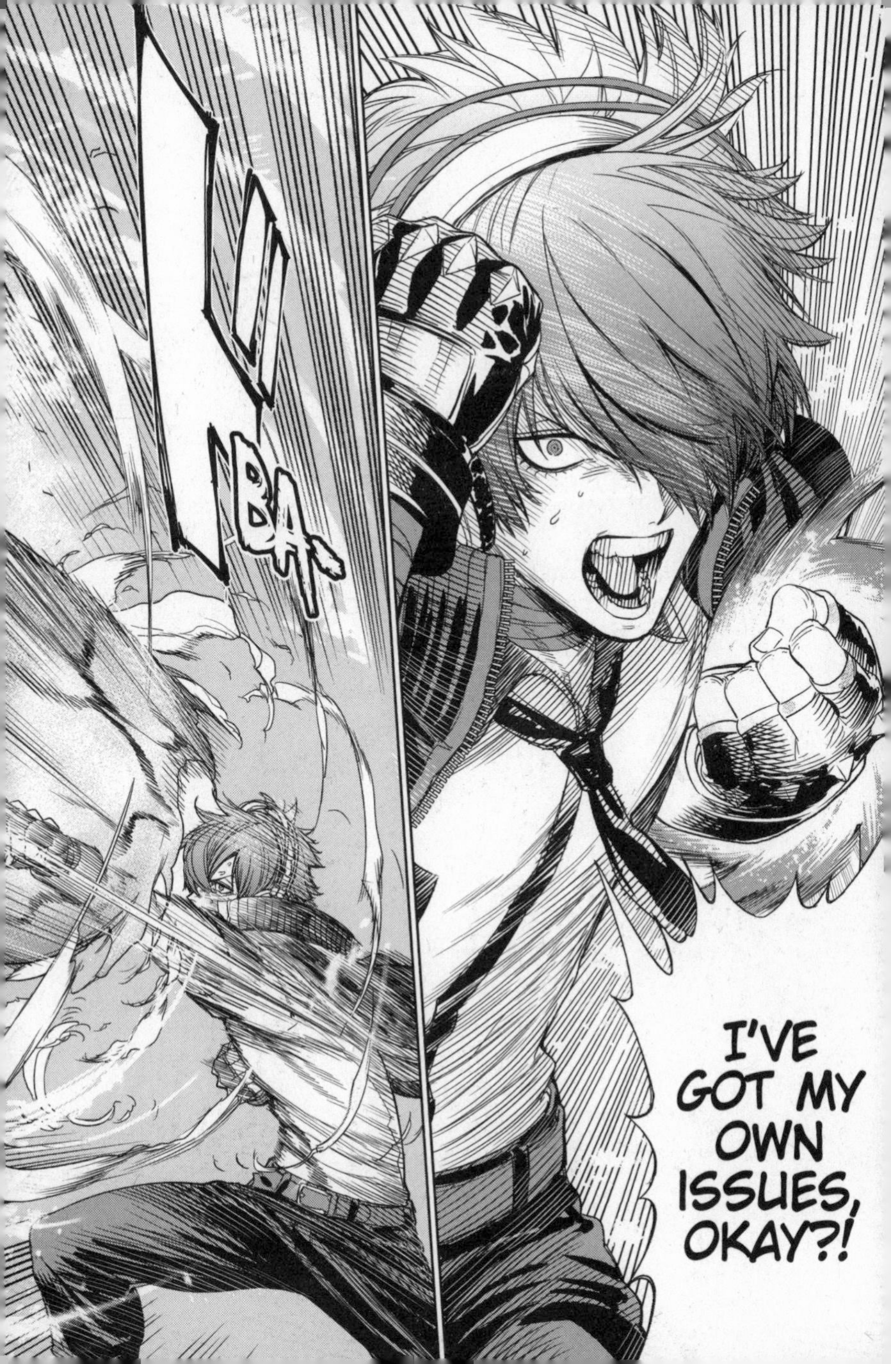
I'VE GOT MY OWN ISSUES, OKAY?!
BA

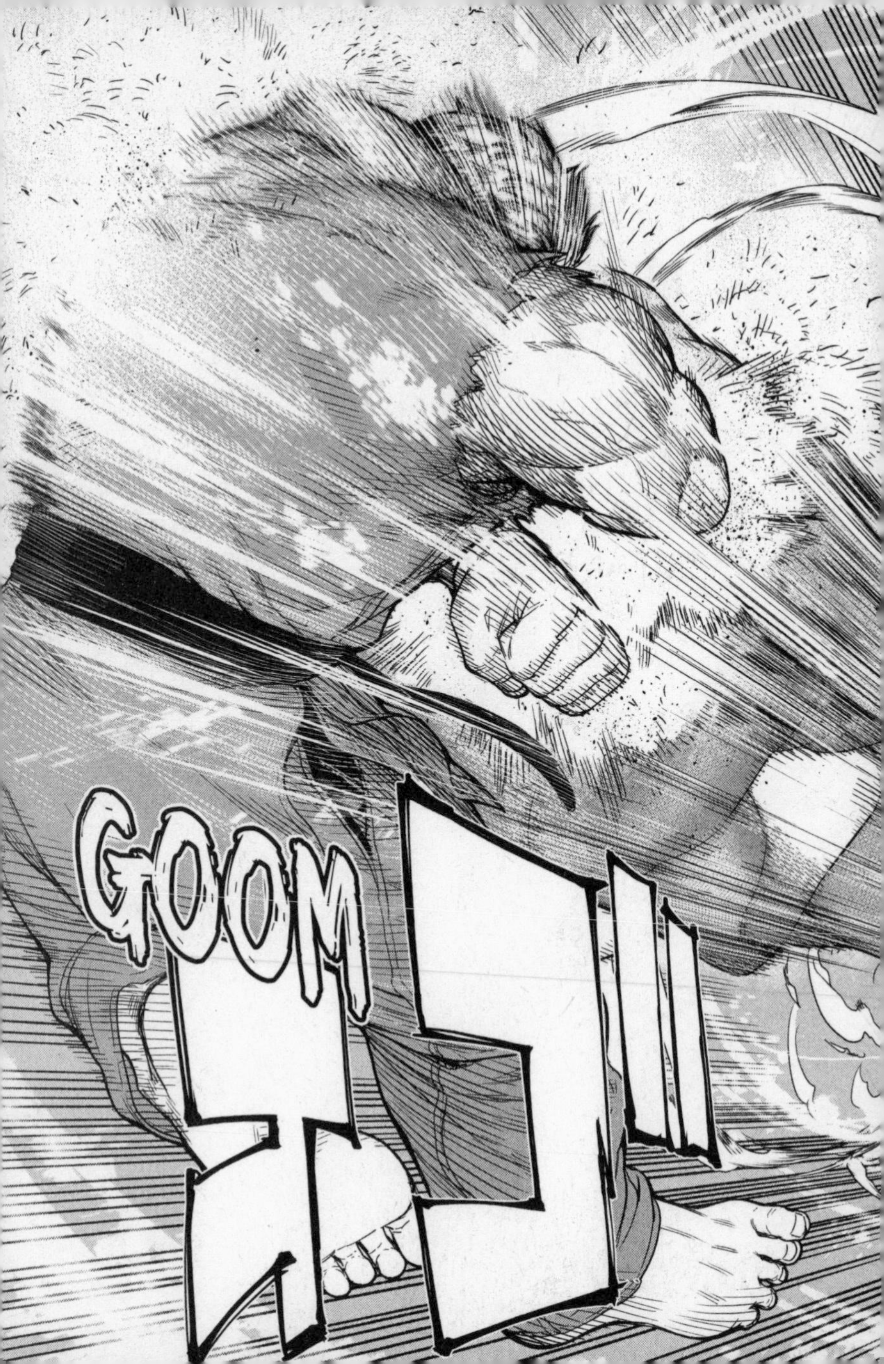
GOOM

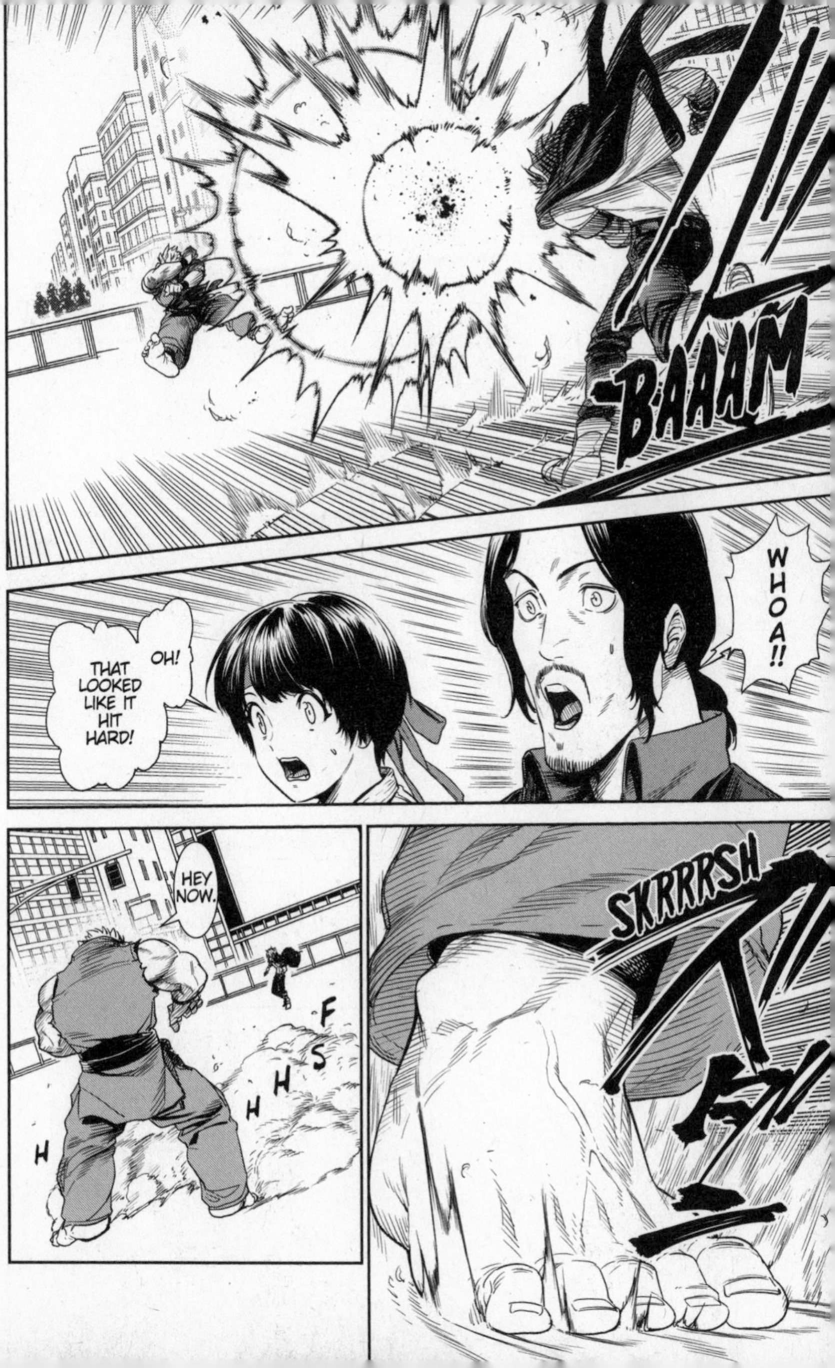
BAAAM
WHOA!!
OH!
THAT LOOKED LIKE IT HIT HARD!
SKRRRSH
HEY NOW.
FSHHH

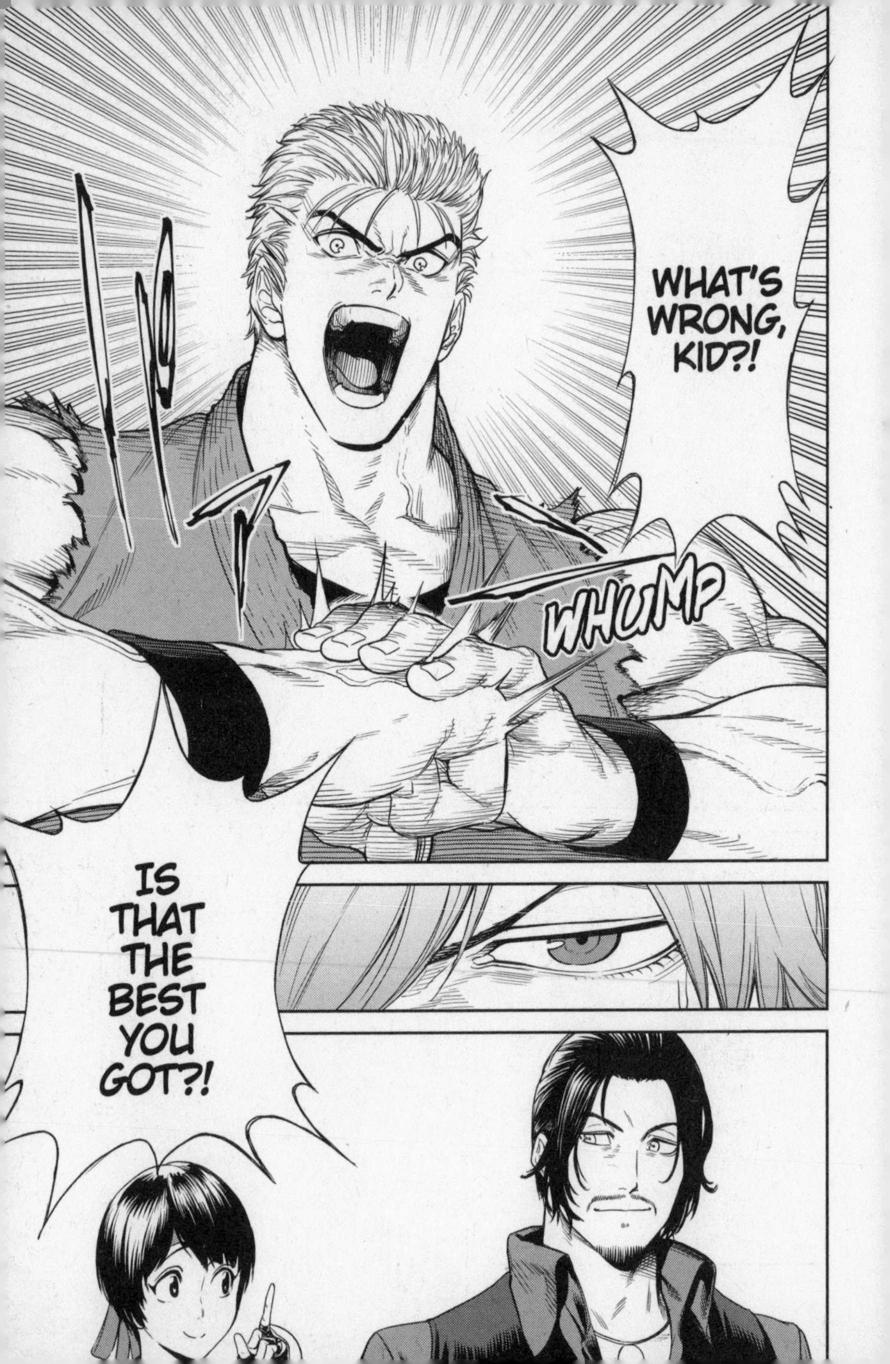
WHAT'S WRONG, KID?!
WHUMP
IS THAT THE BEST YOU GOT?!

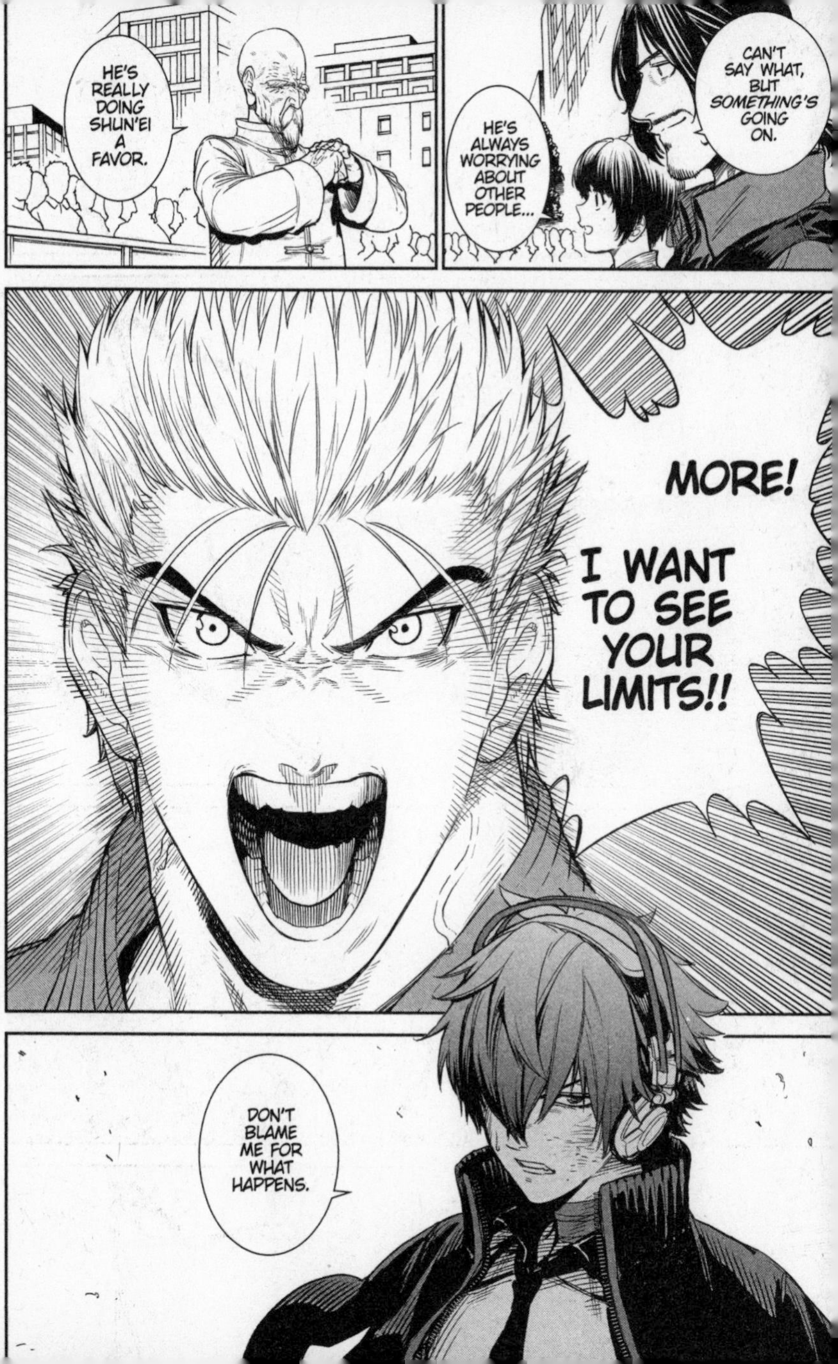
CAN'T SAY WHAT, BUT SOMETHING'S GOING ON.
HE'S ALWAYS WORRYING ABOUT OTHER PEOPLE...
HE'S REALLY DOING SHUN'EI A FAVOR.
MORE!
I WANT TO SEE YOUR LIMITS!!
DON'T BLAME ME FOR WHAT HAPPENS.

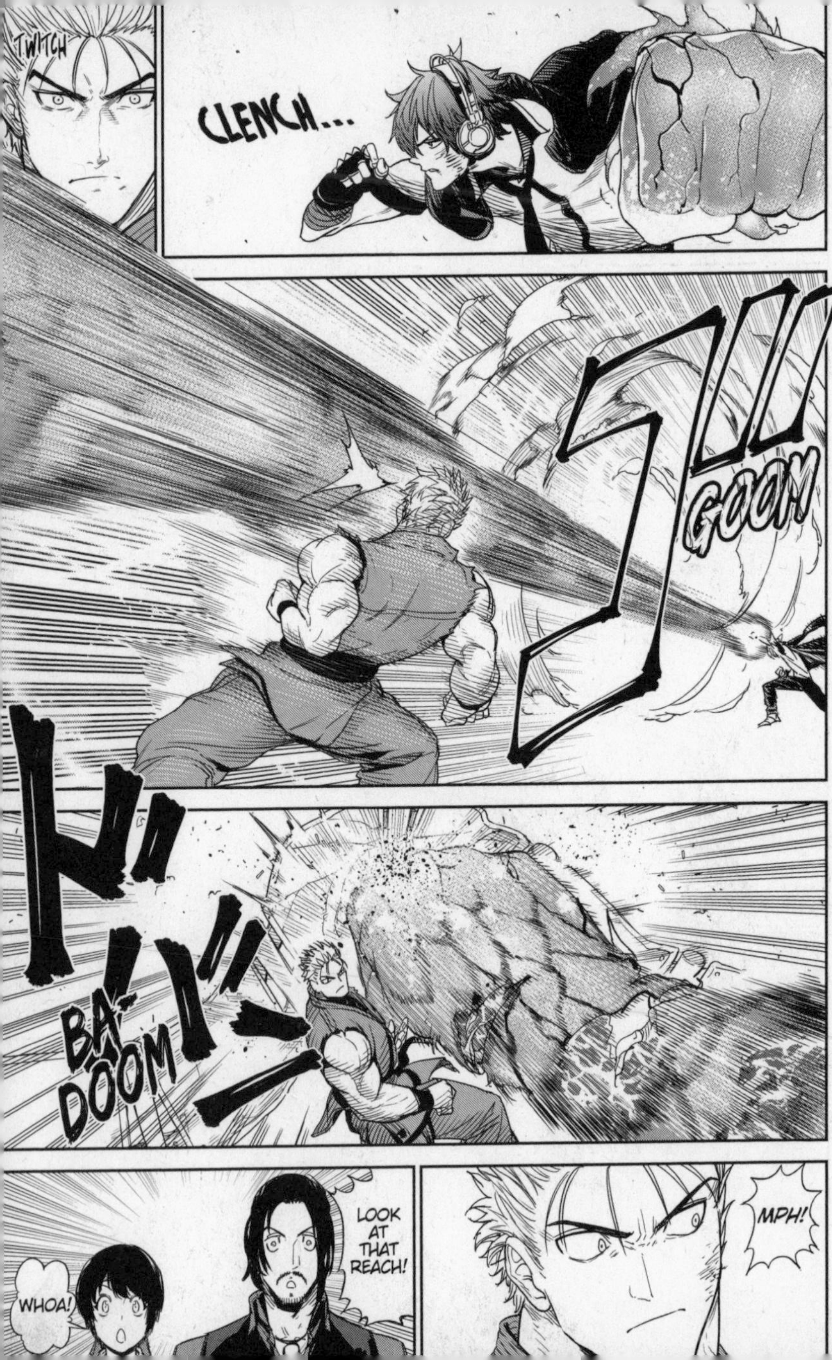
CLENCH...
TWITCH
GOOM
BA-DOOM
MPH!
LOOK AT THAT REACH!
WHOA!

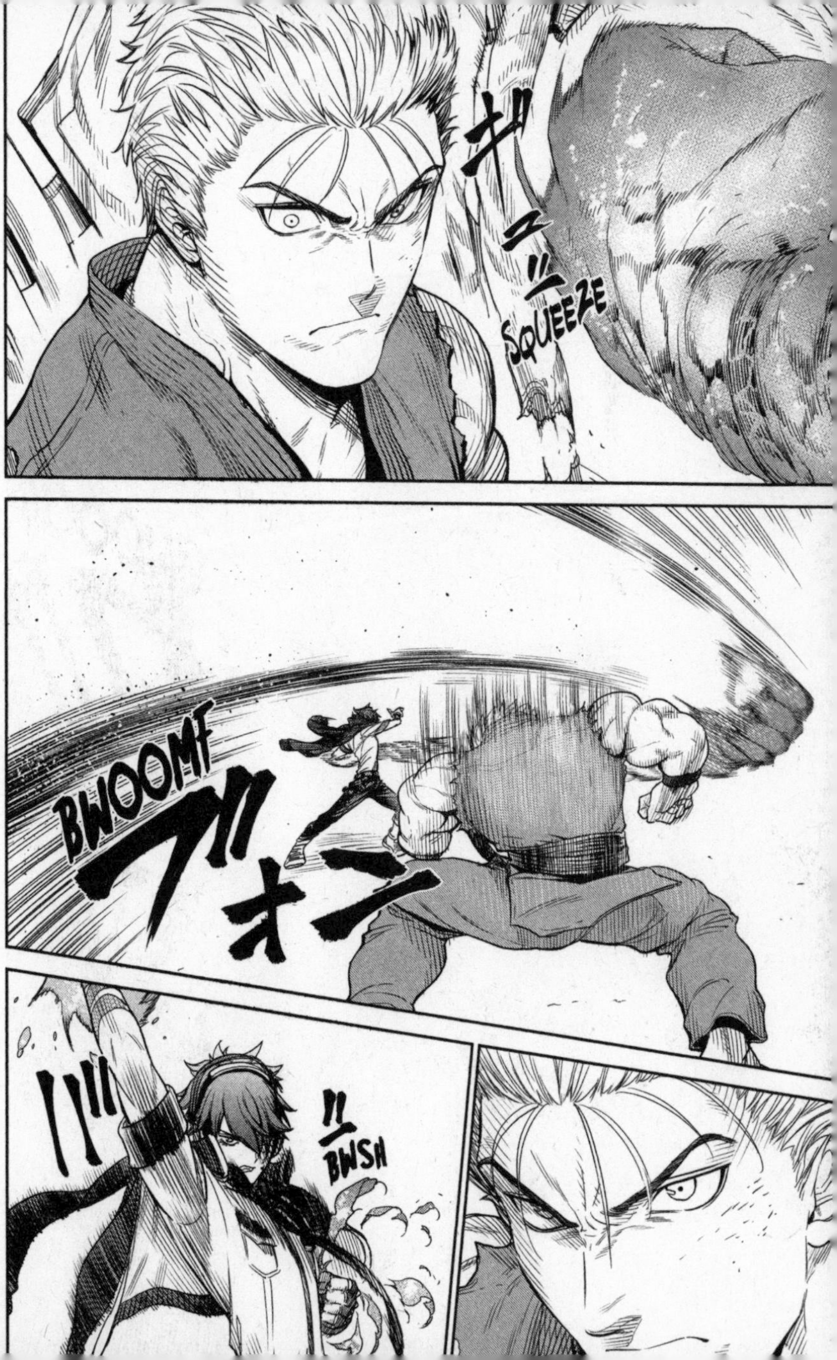
SQUEEZE
BWOOMF
BWSH

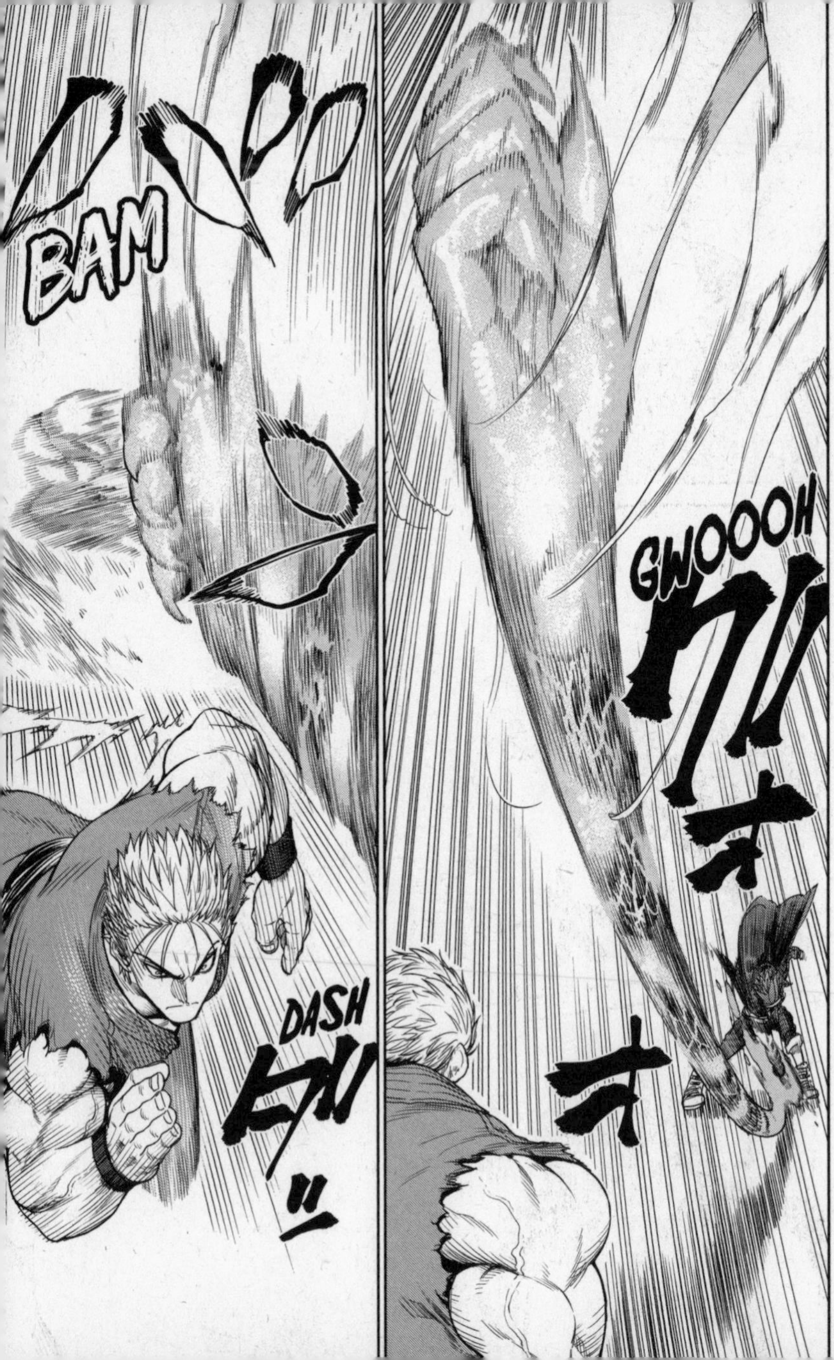
GWOOOH
BAM
DASH

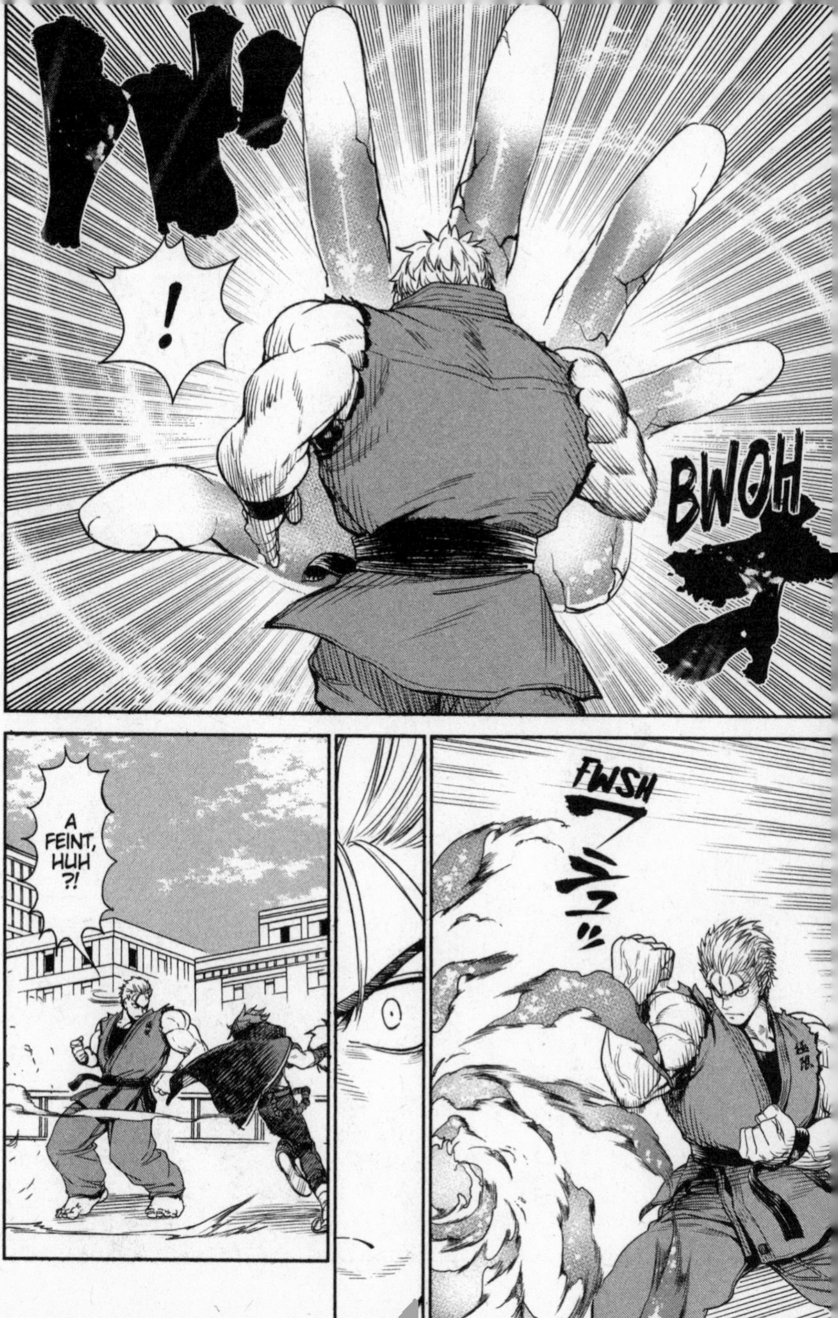
!
BWOH
FWSH
A FEINT, HUH?!

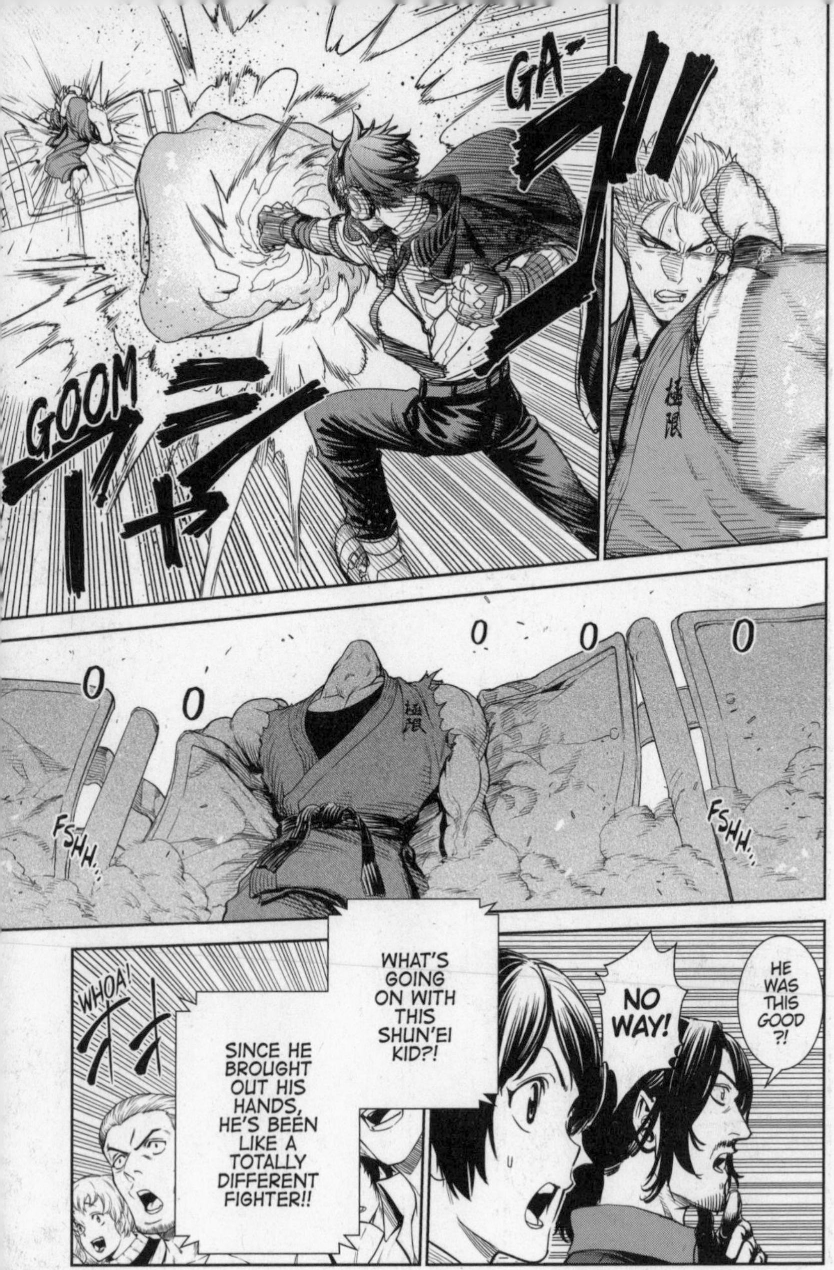
GA-
GOOM
O O O
O O
FSHH..
FSHH...
HE WAS THIS GOOD?!
NO WAY!
WHAT'S GOING ON WITH THIS SHUN'EI KID?!
SINCE HE BROUGHT OUT HIS HANDS, HE'S BEEN LIKE A TOTALLY DIFFERENT FIGHTER!!
WHOA!

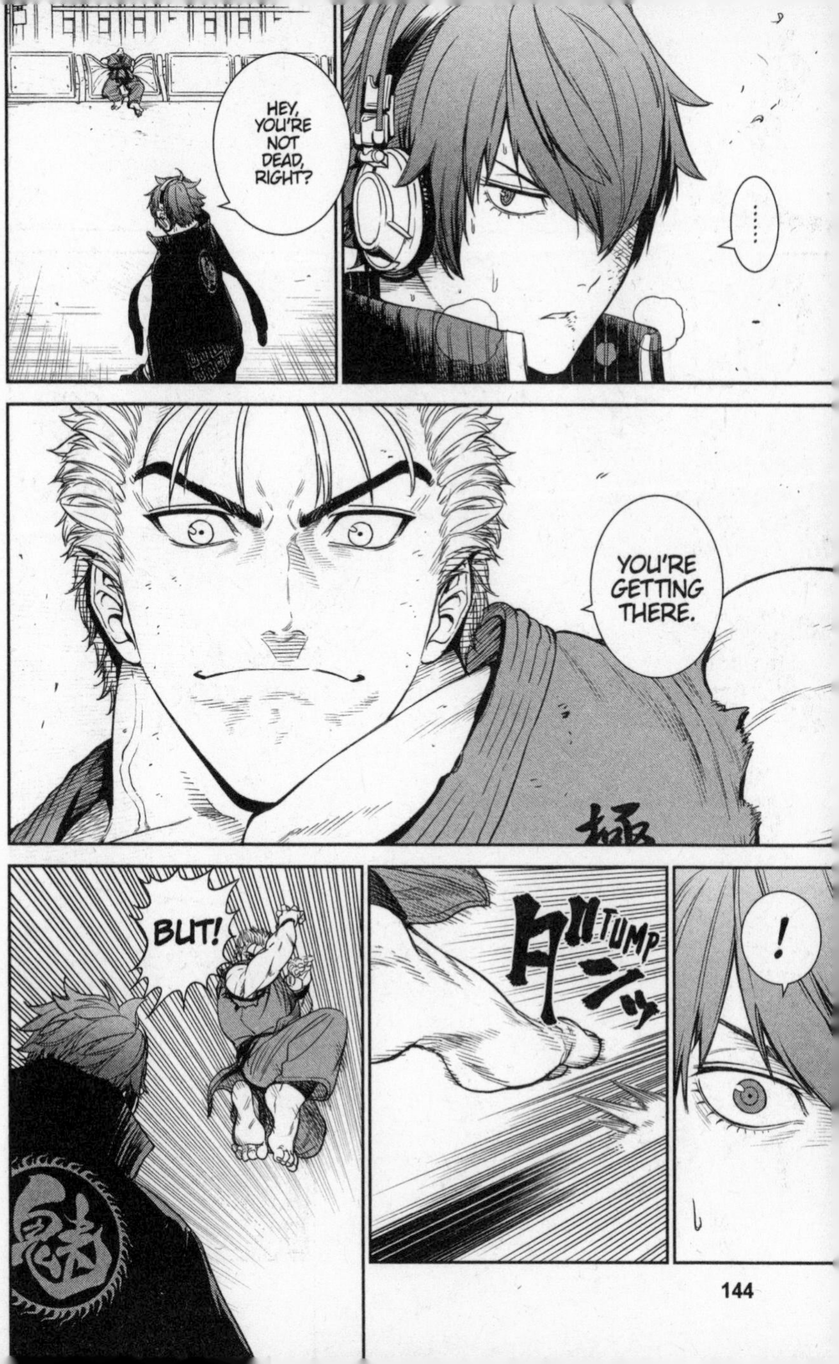
……
HEY, YOU'RE NOT DEAD, RIGHT?
YOU'RE GETTING THERE.
!
タンッ TUMP
BUT!

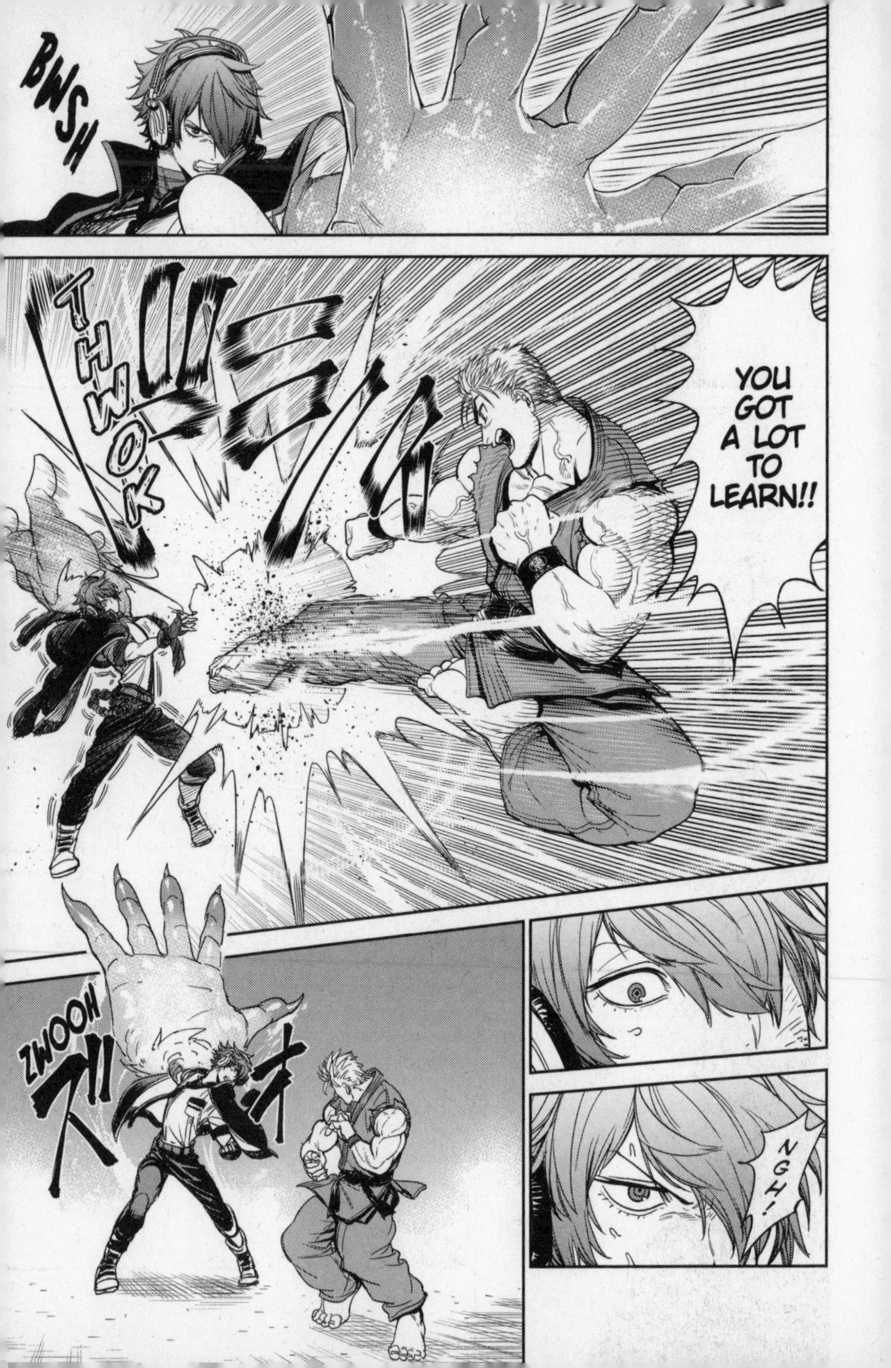
BWSH
YOU GOT A LOT TO LEARN!!
THWOK
NGH!
ZWOOH

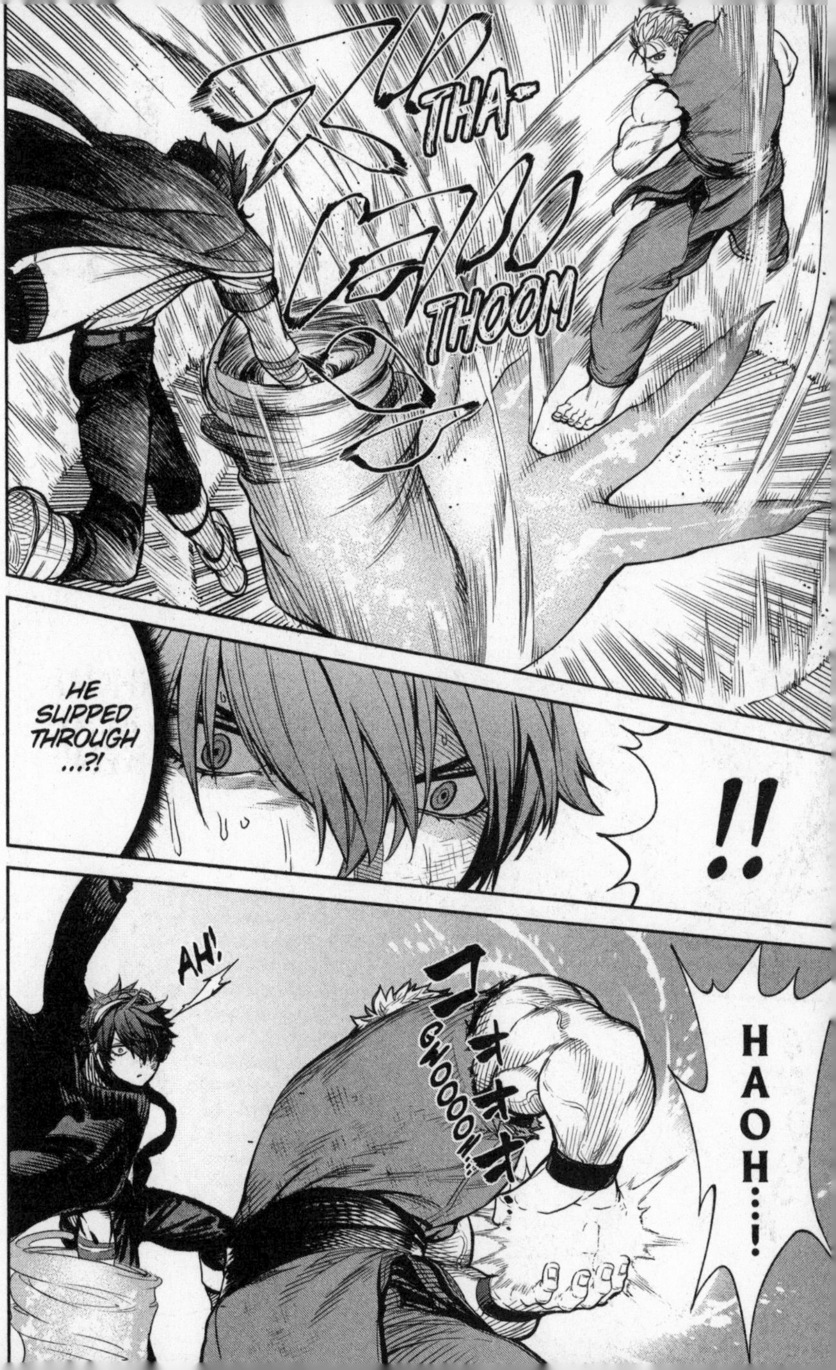
THA-THOOM
!!
HE SLIPPED THROUGH ...?!
HAOH...!
コオオオ
GWOOOOH...
AH!

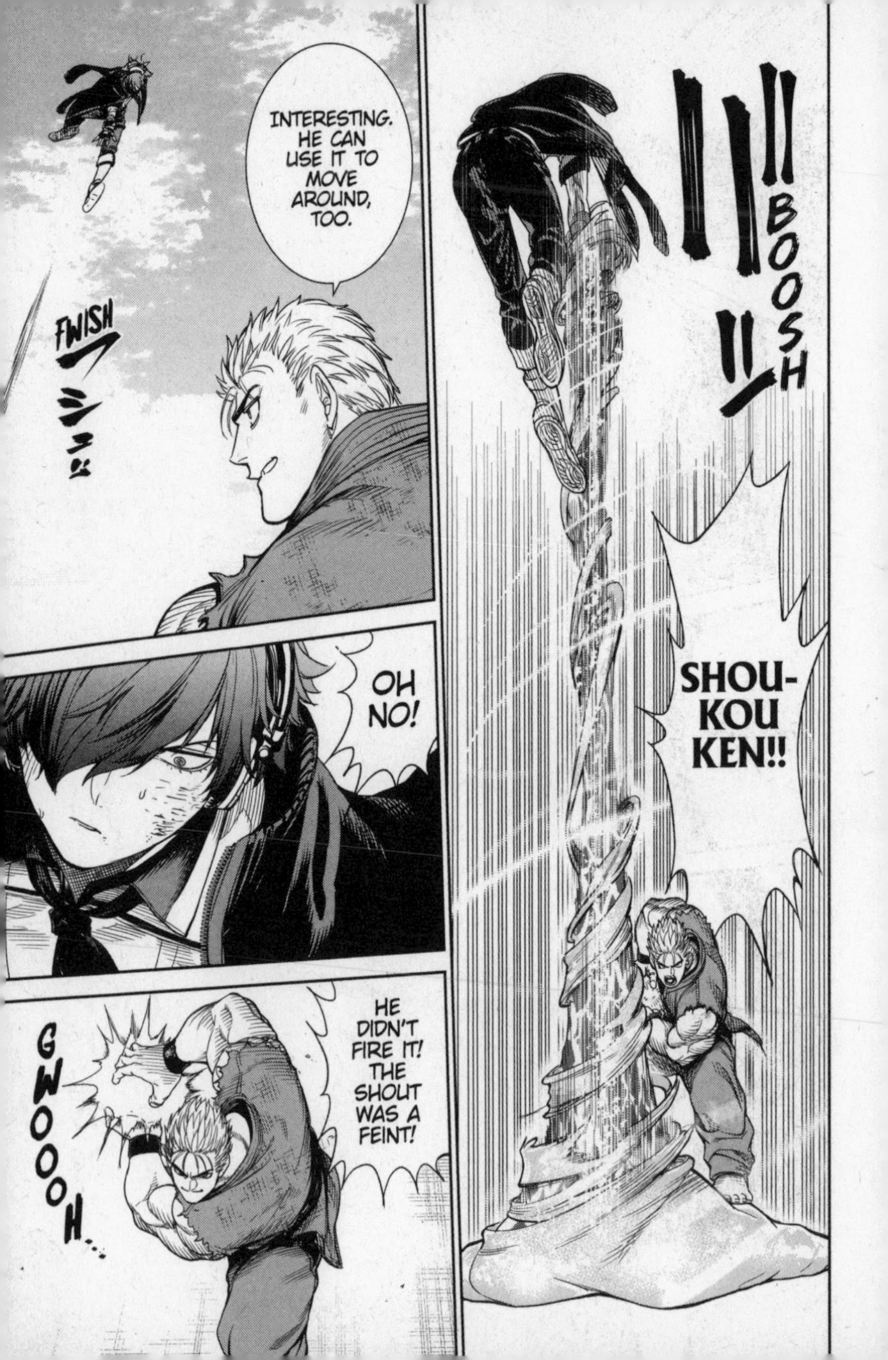
INTERESTING. HE CAN USE IT TO MOVE AROUND, TOO.
FWISH
OH NO!
HE DIDN'T FIRE IT! THE SHOUT WAS A FEINT!
GWOOOOH...
SHOU-KOU KEN!!
BOOSH

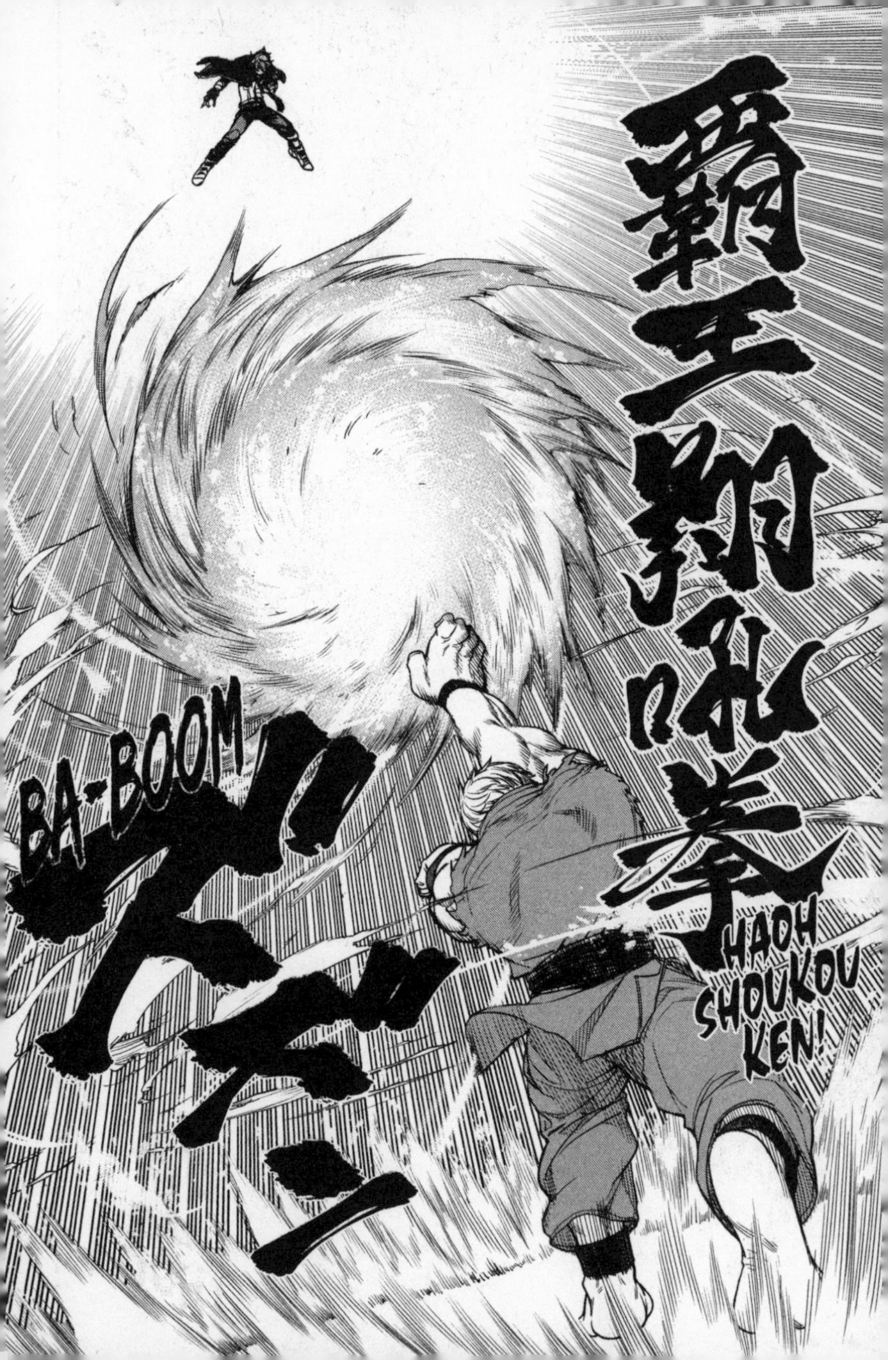
覇王翔吼拳
HAOH SHOUKOU KEN!
BA-BOOM

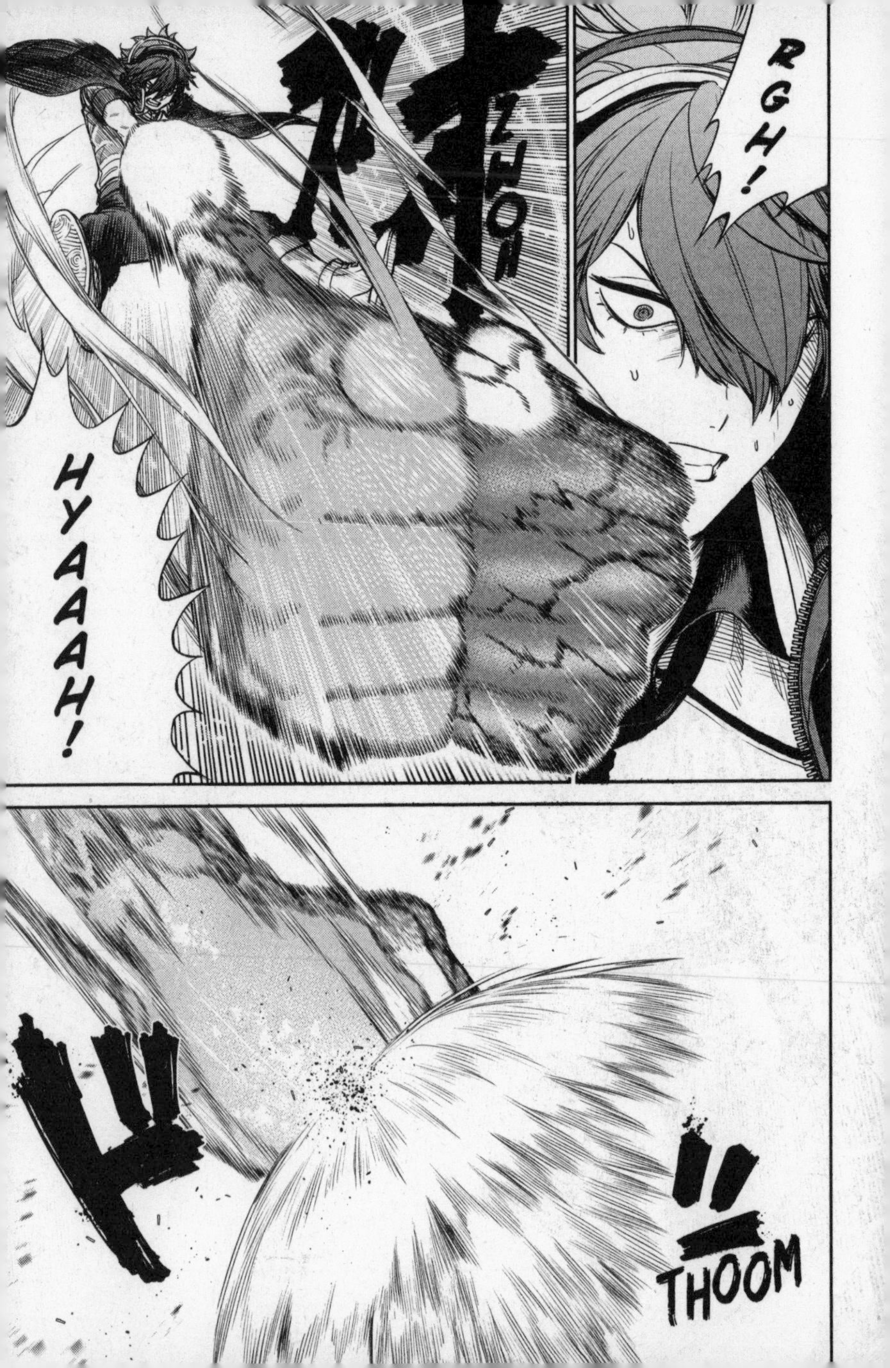

RGH!
ZHOM
HYAAAAH!
THOOM

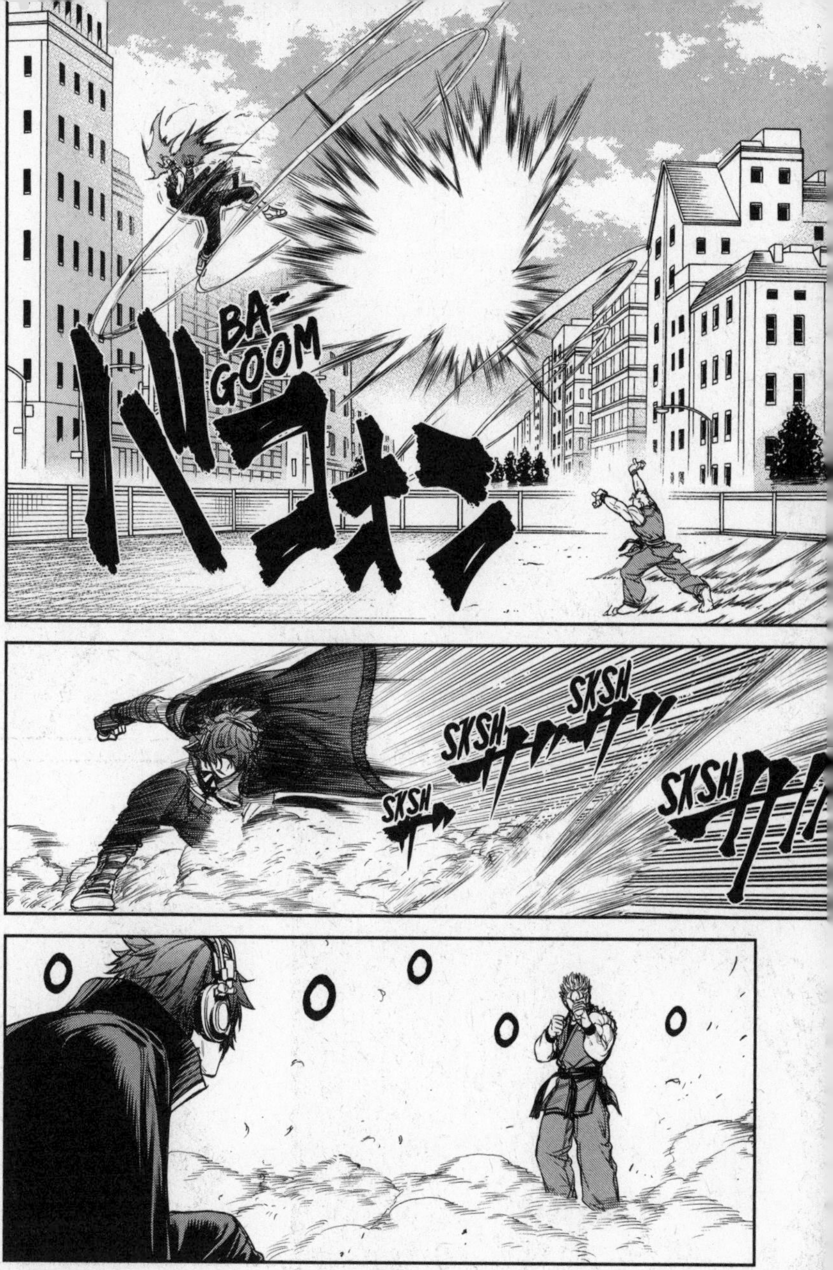
BA-GOOM
SKSH
SKSH
SKSH
SKSH

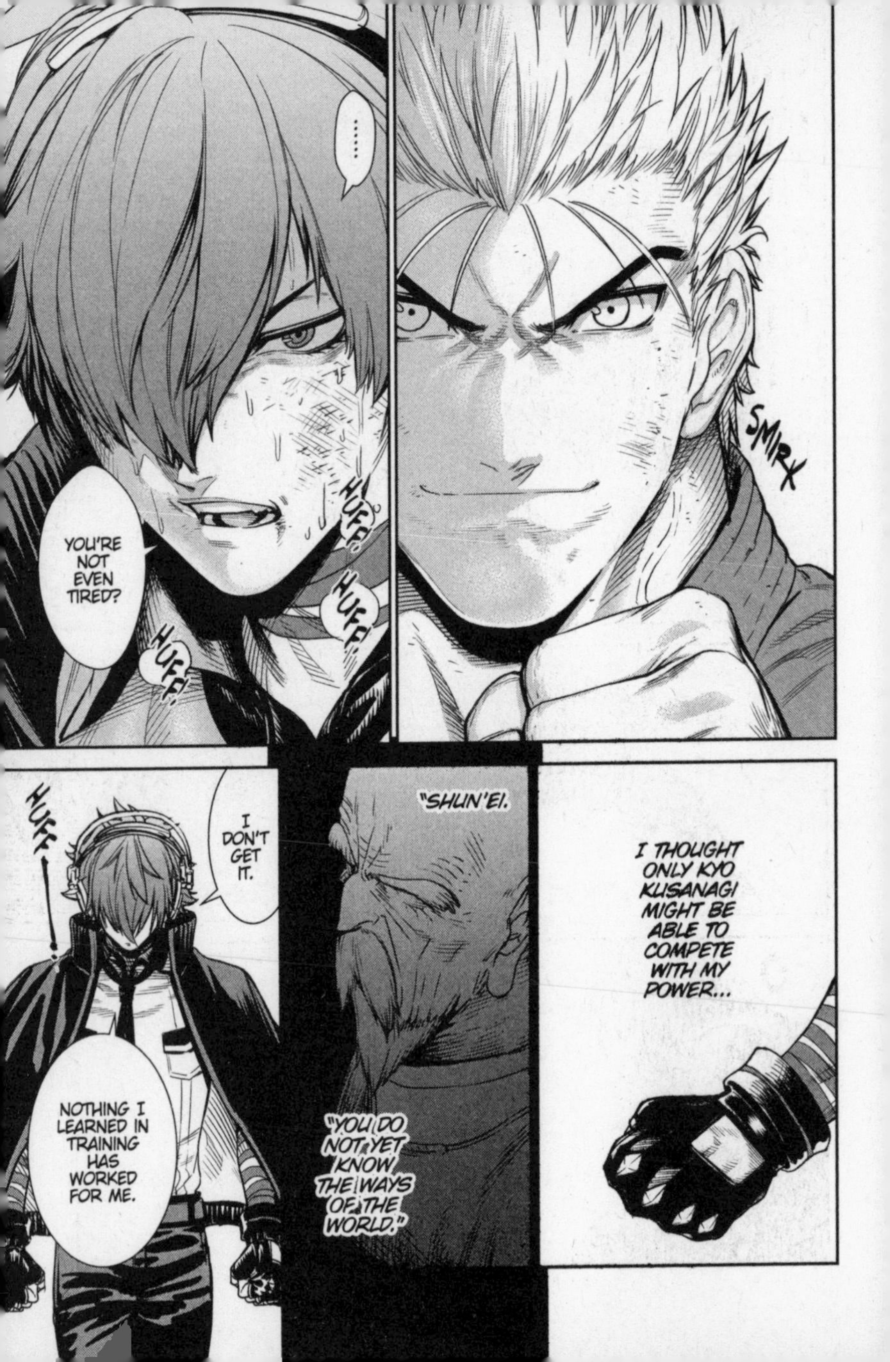
SMIRK
......
YOU'RE NOT EVEN TIRED?
HUFF!
HUFF!
HUFF!
I THOUGHT ONLY KYO KUSANAGI MIGHT BE ABLE TO COMPETE WITH MY POWER...
"SHUN'EI.
"YOU DO NOT YET KNOW THE WAYS OF THE WORLD."
HUFF...!
I DON'T GET IT.
NOTHING I LEARNED IN TRAINING HAS WORKED FOR ME.

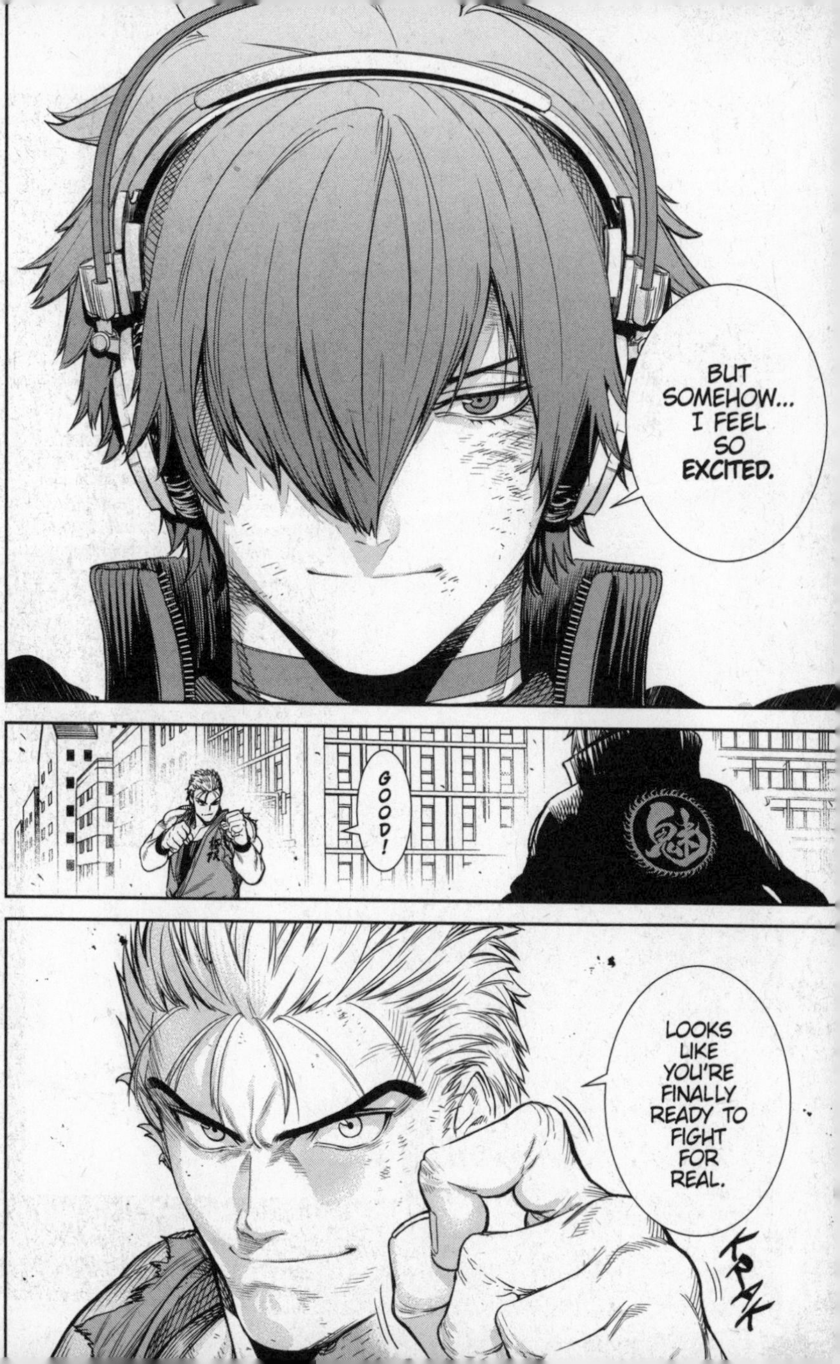
BUT SOMEHOW... I FEEL SO EXCITED.
GOOD!
LOOKS LIKE YOU'RE FINALLY READY TO FIGHT FOR REAL.
KRAK

MOVE LIST

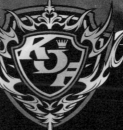

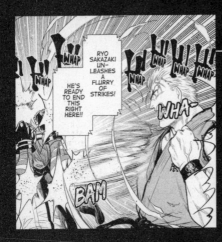

RYO SAKAZAKI UN-LEASHES A FLURRY OF STRIKES!
HE'S READY TO END THIS RIGHT HERE!!
WHAP
WHAP
WHAP
WHAP
WHAP
WHAP
WHA-
BAM

Zanretsuken

A torrent of countless strikes launched against an opponent. If even one gets through, it's hard to evade the blows that follow.

User: Ryo Sakazaki

Command:
→←→+ LP or HP

Hien Shippuu Kyaku

A Kyokugen technique of launching oneself toward the opponent with a jump kick. A spin kick can be added.

Users: Ryo Sakazaki, Robert Garcia

Command:
→↘↓↙←+ LK or HK

THWOK

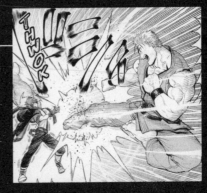

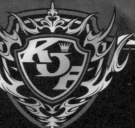

MOVE LIST

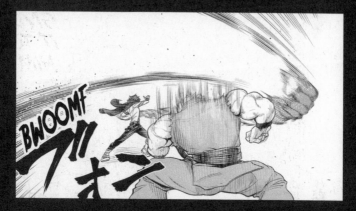

Blau Wing

A sweep of the forward space with an illusory arm.
Normally performed from the air.

User: Shun'ei

Command:
In the air: ↓ ↘ → + LP or HP

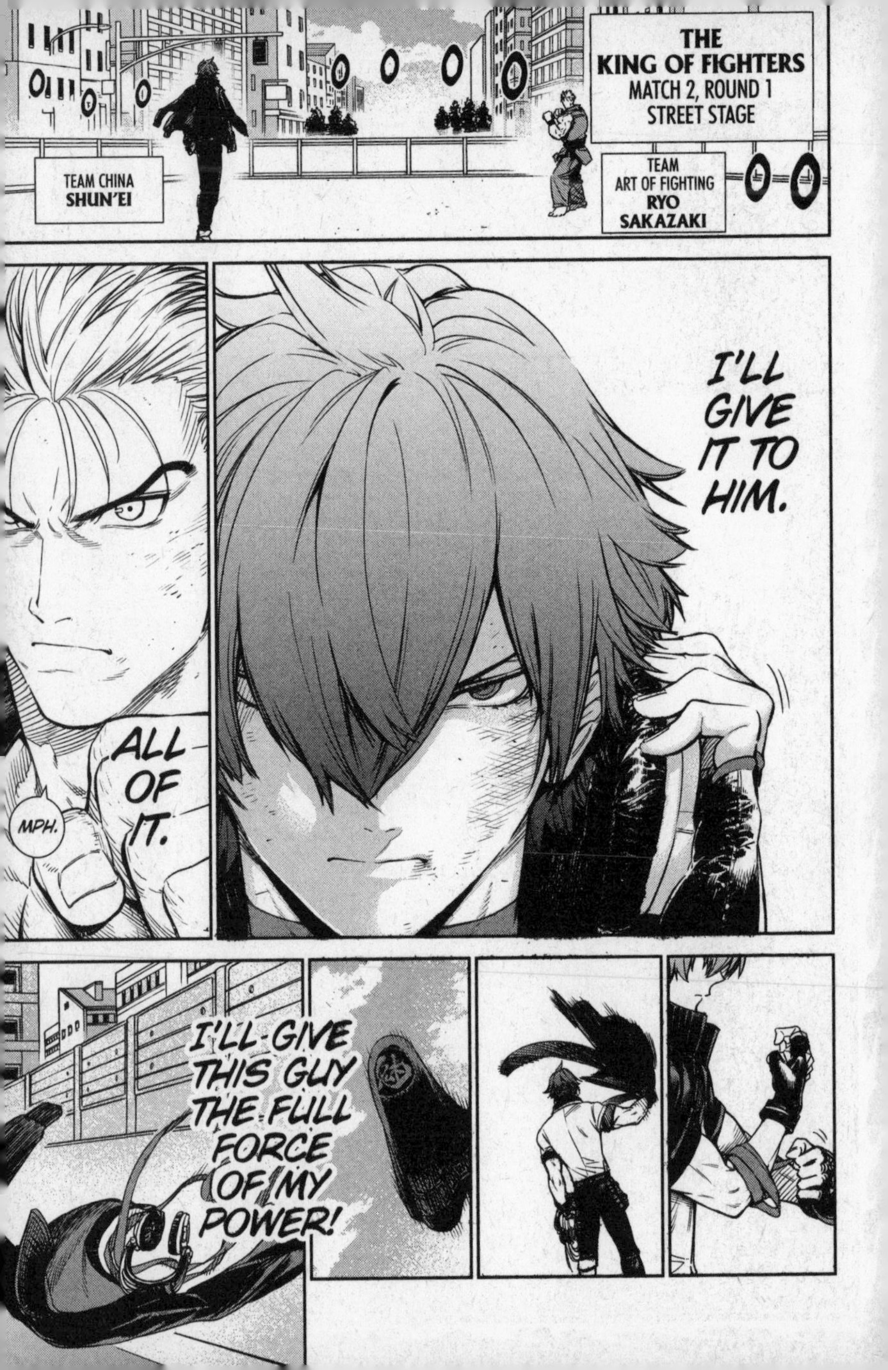
THE KING OF FIGHTERS
MATCH 2, ROUND 1
STREET STAGE
TEAM ART OF FIGHTING
RYO SAKAZAKI
TEAM CHINA
SHUN'EI
I'LL GIVE IT TO HIM.
ALL OF IT.
MPH.
I'LL GIVE THIS GUY THE FULL FORCE OF MY POWER!

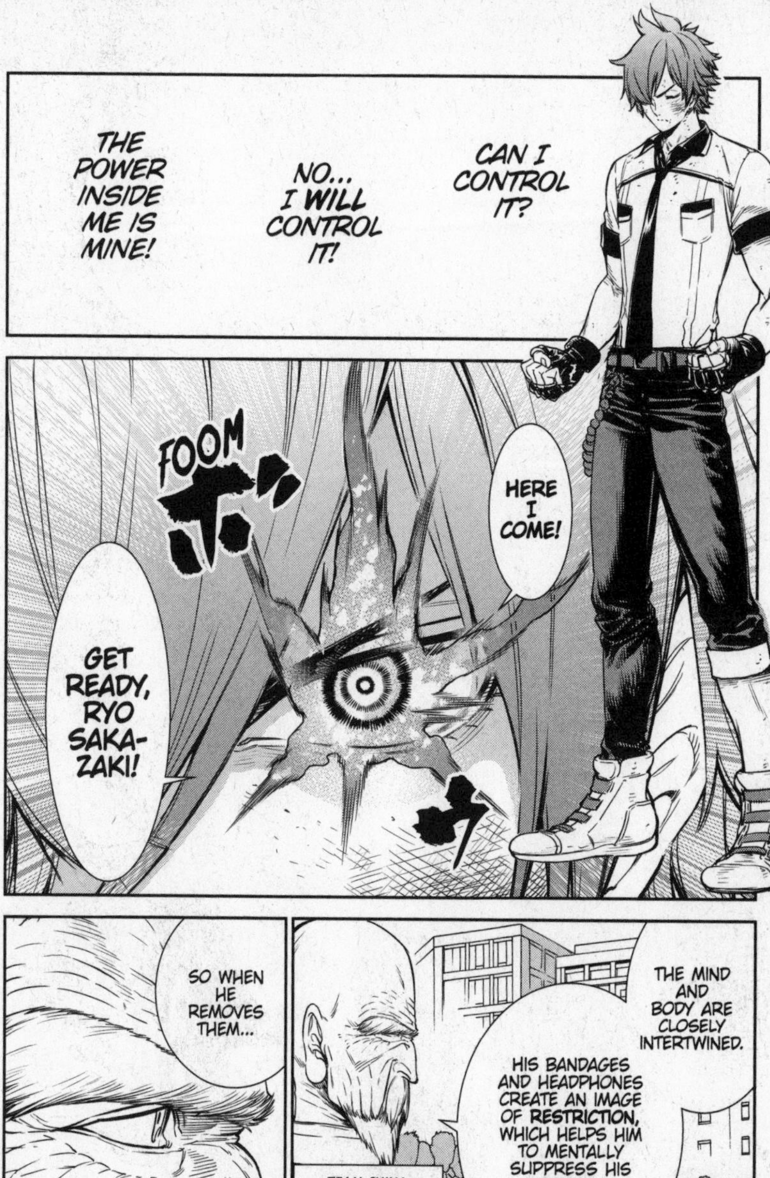
CAN I CONTROL IT?
NO... I WILL CONTROL IT!
THE POWER INSIDE ME IS MINE!
HERE I COME!
FOOM
GET READY, RYO SAKAZAKI!
THE MIND AND BODY ARE CLOSELY INTERTWINED.
HIS BANDAGES AND HEADPHONES CREATE AN IMAGE OF RESTRICTION, WHICH HELPS HIM TO MENTALLY SUPPRESS HIS POWER.
TEAM CHINA TUNG FU RUE
SO WHEN HE REMOVES THEM...

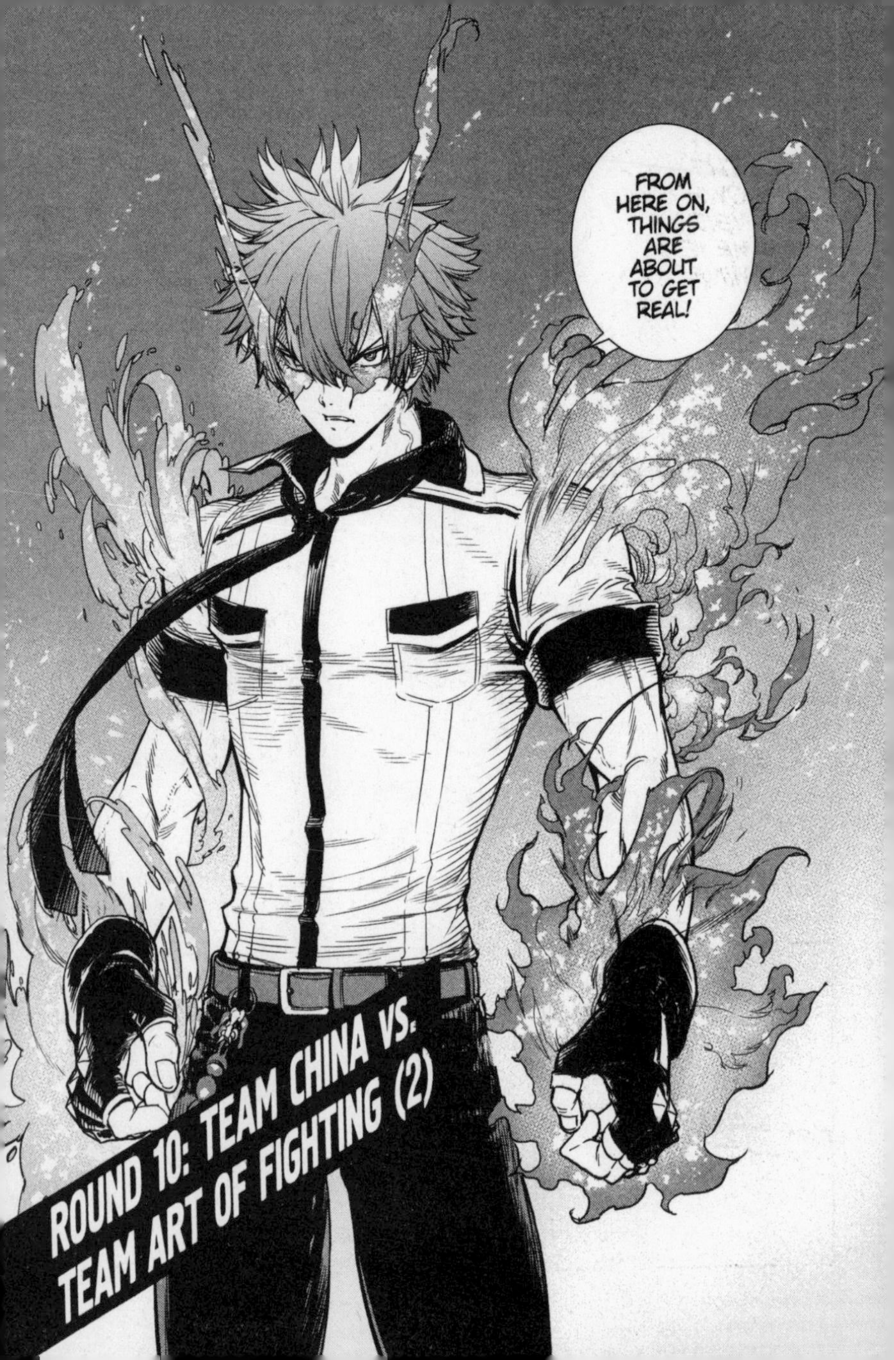
FROM HERE ON, THINGS ARE ABOUT TO GET REAL!
ROUND 10: TEAM CHINA VS. TEAM ART OF FIGHTING (2)

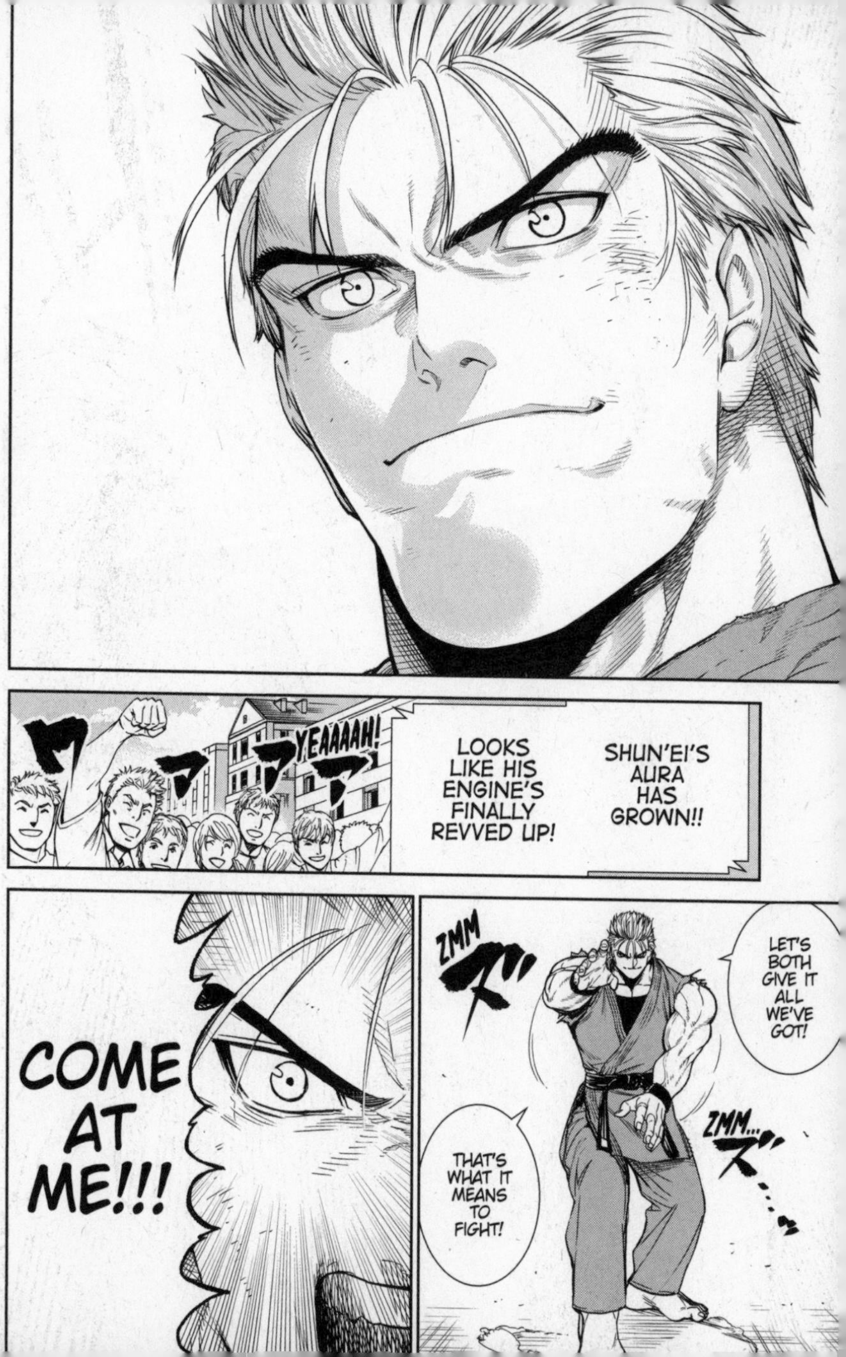
SHUN'EI'S AURA HAS GROWN!!
LOOKS LIKE HIS ENGINE'S FINALLY REVVED UP!
YEAAAAH!
ZMM
LET'S BOTH GIVE IT ALL WE'VE GOT!
THAT'S WHAT IT MEANS TO FIGHT!
ZMM...
COME AT ME!!!

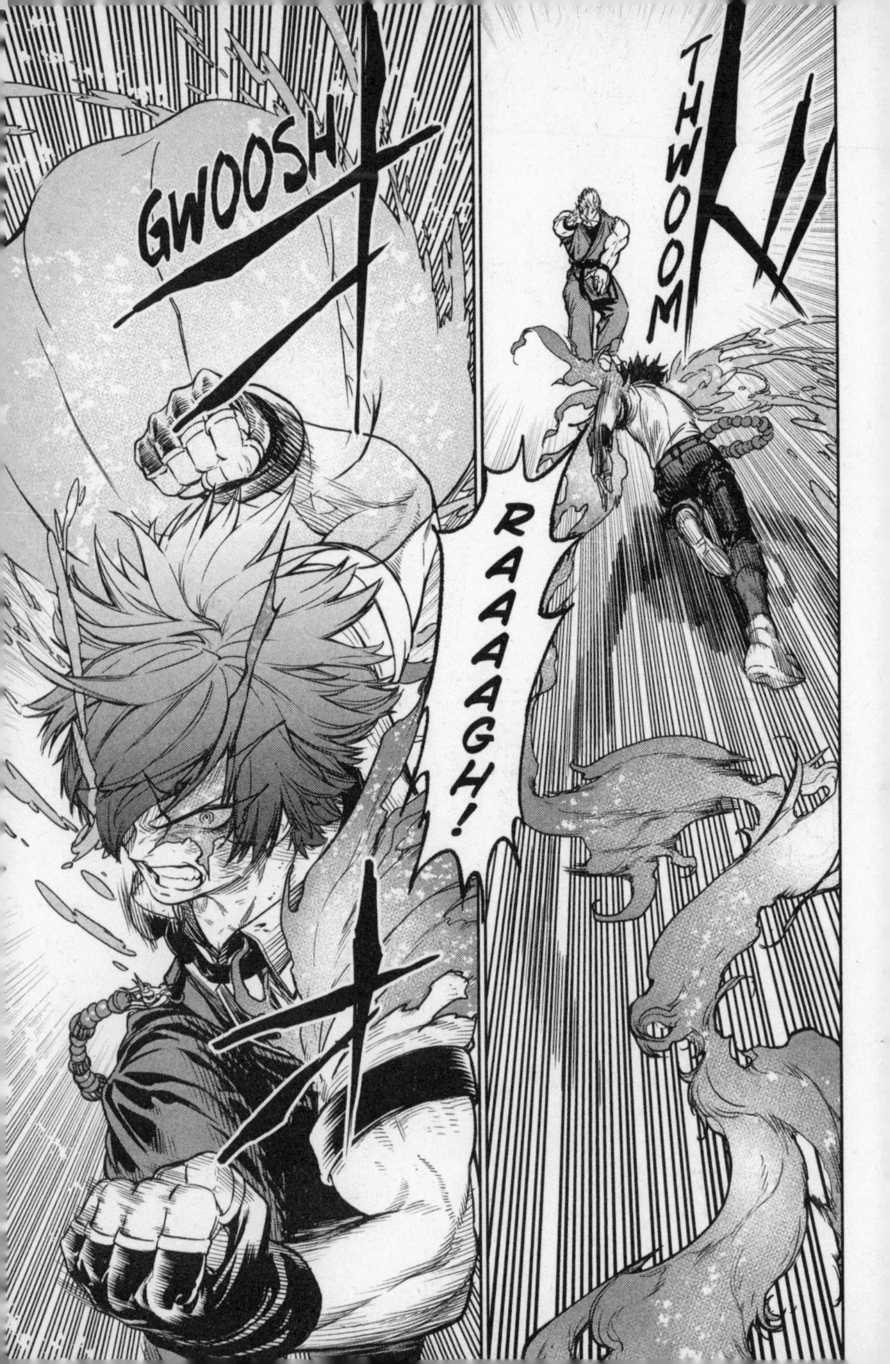
THWOOM
RAAAAGH!
GWOOSH

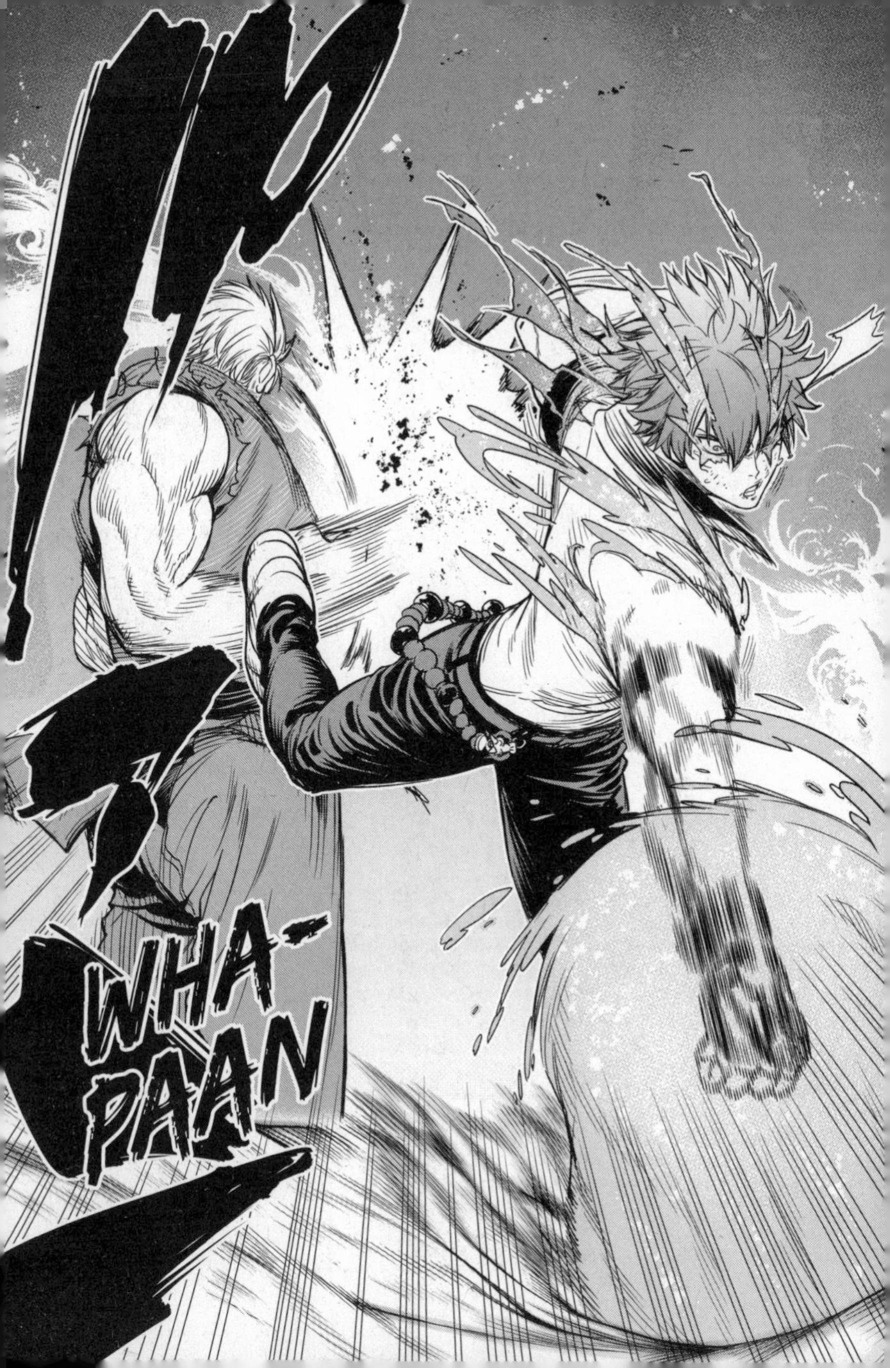
WHA-
PAAN

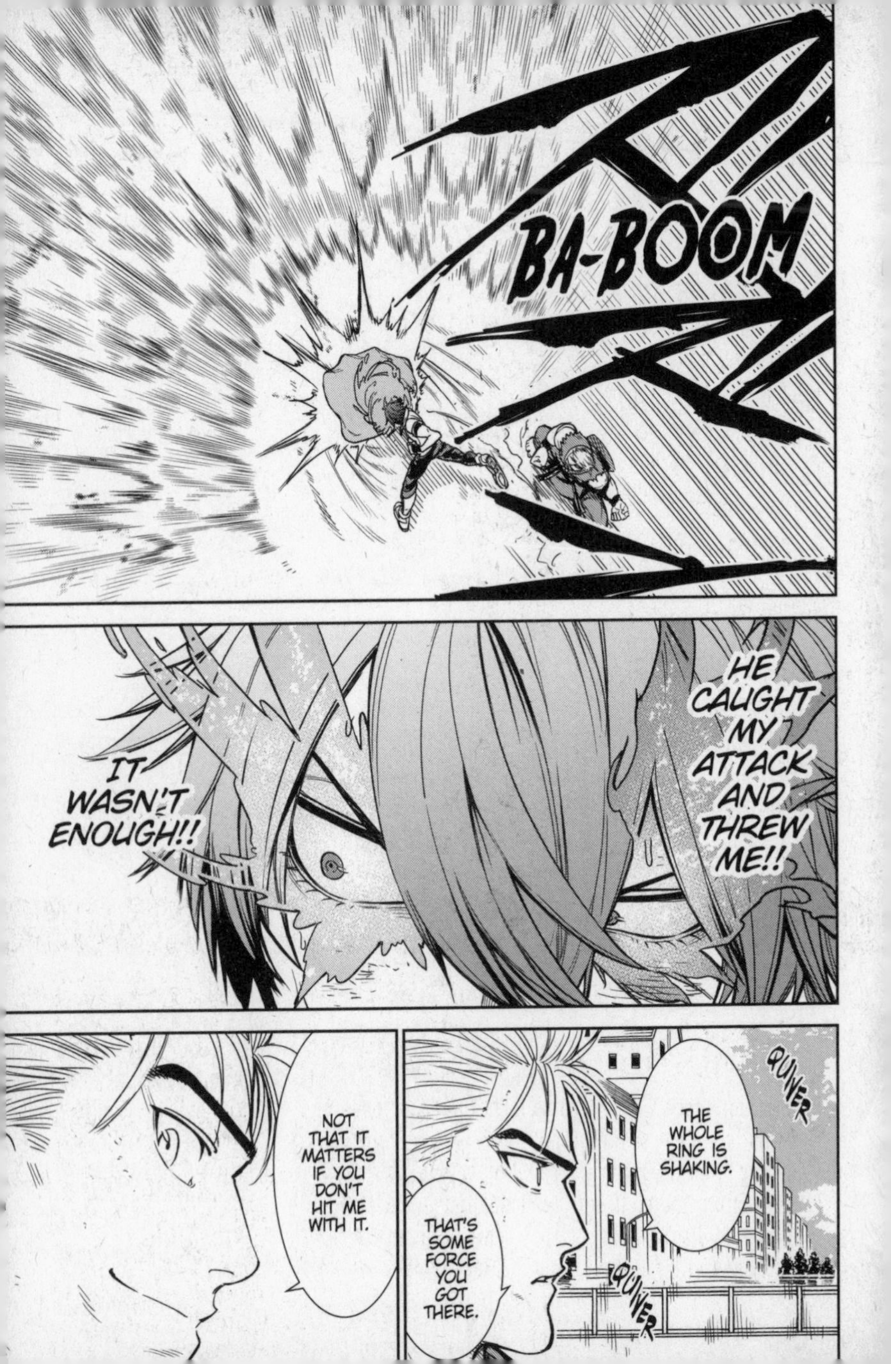
BA-BOOM
HE CAUGHT MY ATTACK AND THREW ME!!
IT WASN'T ENOUGH!!
QUIVER
THE WHOLE RING IS SHAKING.
THAT'S SOME FORCE YOU GOT THERE.
QUIVER
NOT THAT IT MATTERS IF YOU DON'T HIT ME WITH IT.

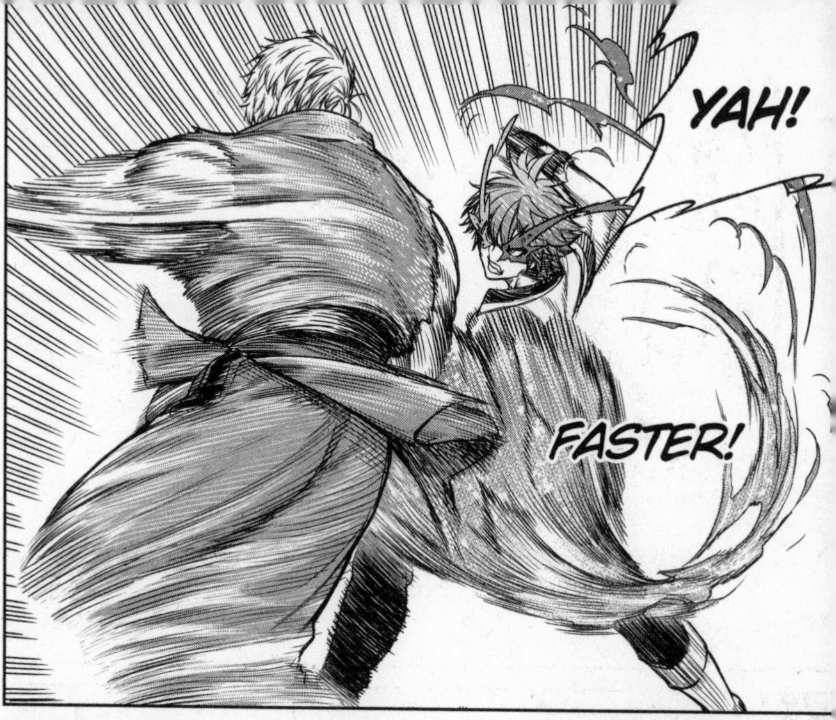
YAH!
FASTER!
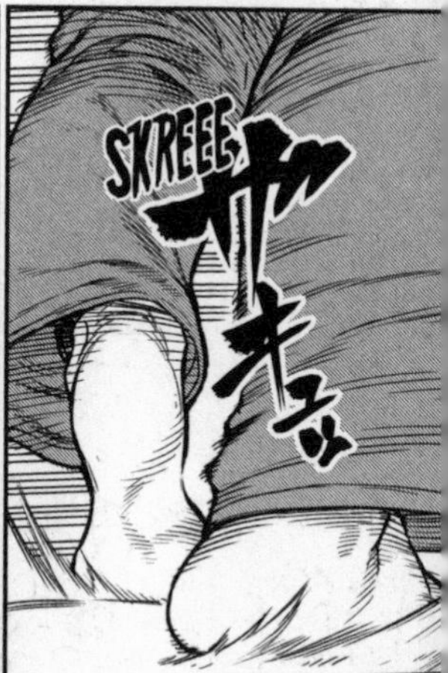
SKREEE
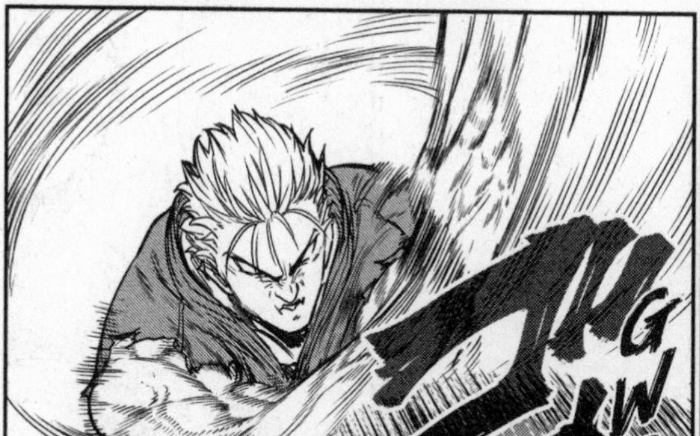
GWOOOM

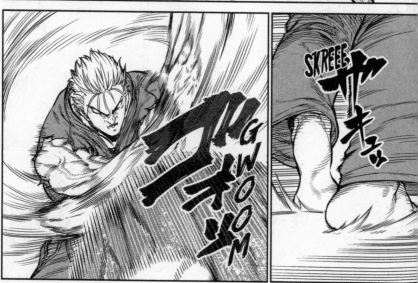

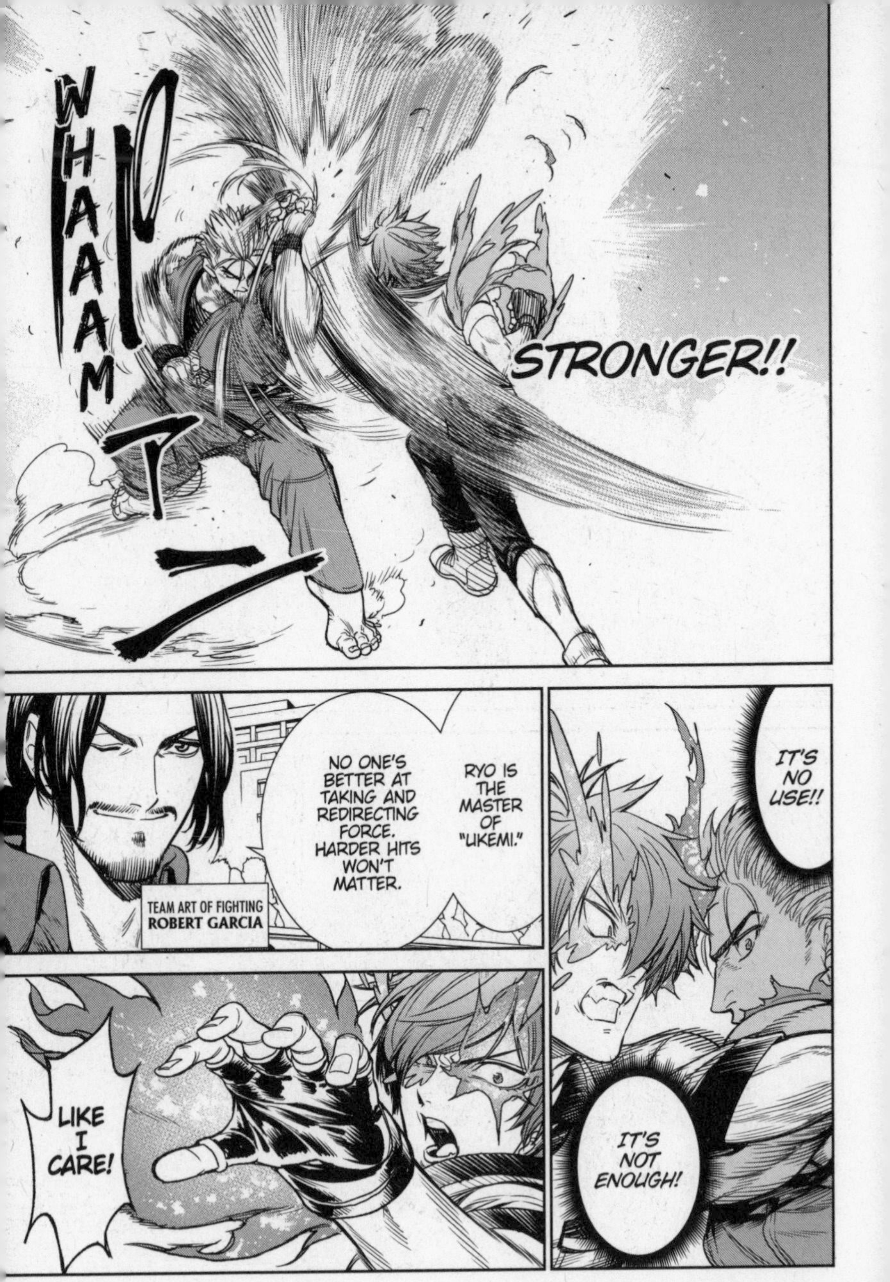
STRONGER!!
WHAAAM
IT'S NO USE!!
IT'S NOT ENOUGH!
RYO IS THE MASTER OF "UKEMI."
NO ONE'S BETTER AT TAKING AND REDIRECTING FORCE. HARDER HITS WON'T MATTER.
TEAM ART OF FIGHTING
ROBERT GARCIA
LIKE I CARE!

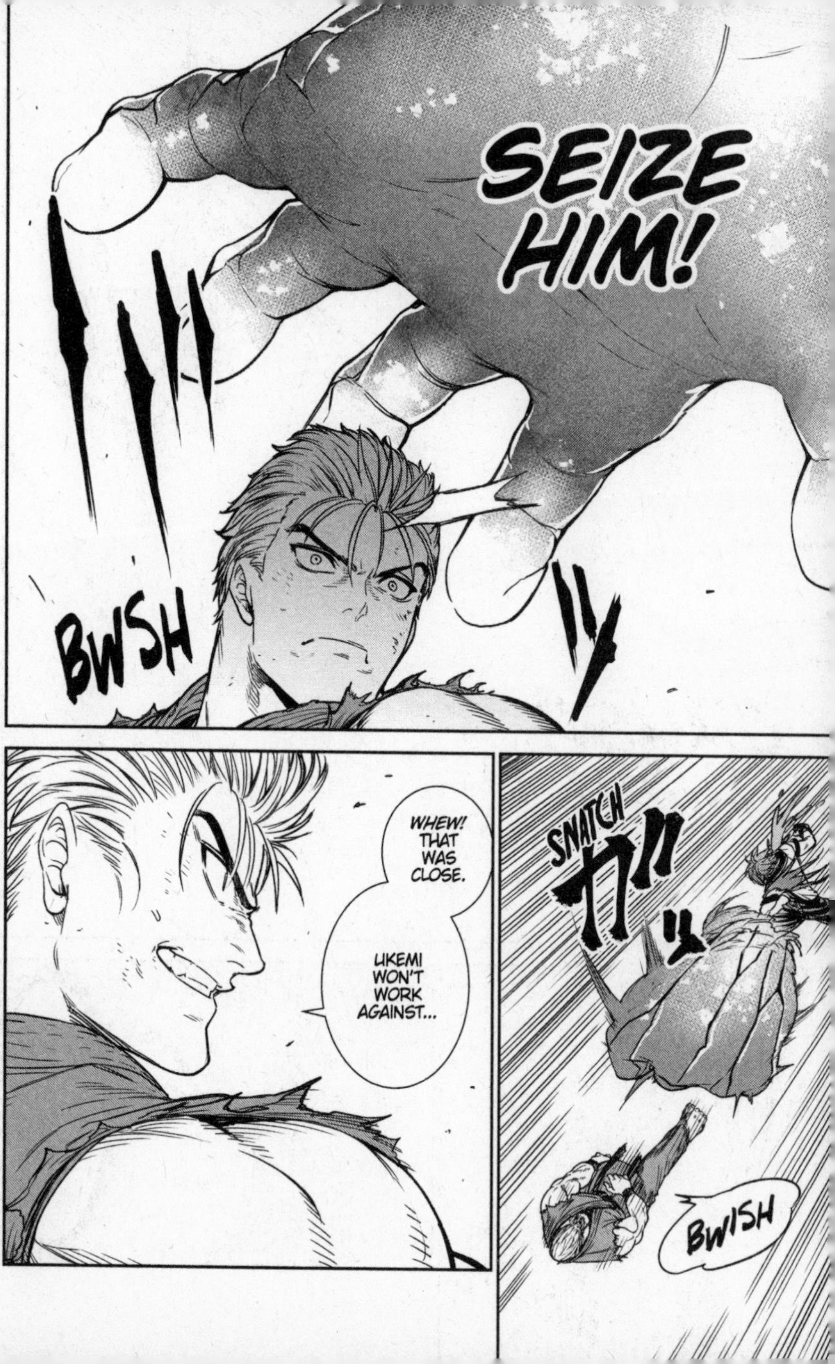
SEIZE HIM!
BWSH
SNATCH
BWISH
WHEW! THAT WAS CLOSE.
UKEMI WON'T WORK AGAINST...

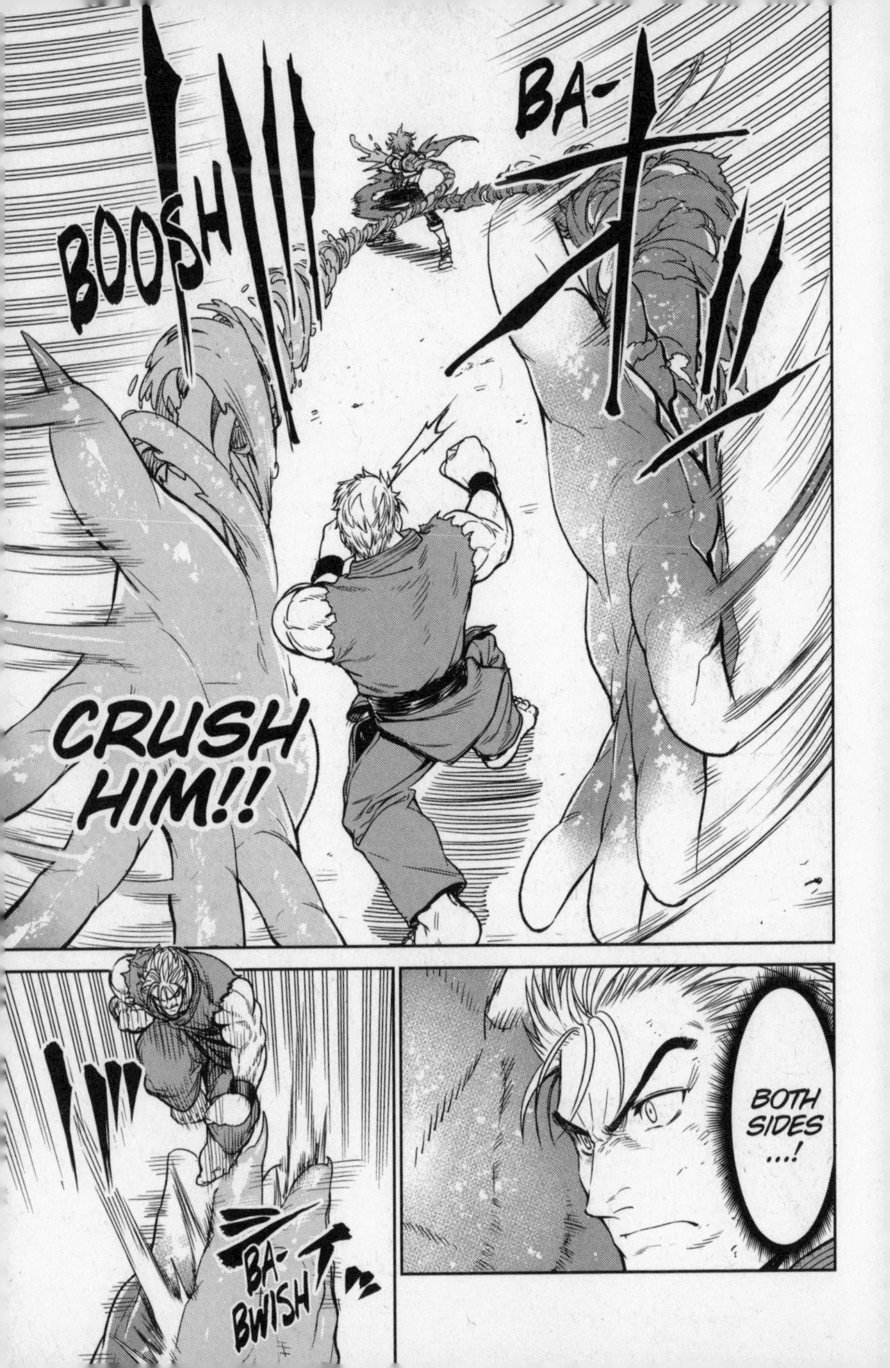
BA-
BOOSH
CRUSH HIM!!
BOTH SIDES ...!
BA-BWISH

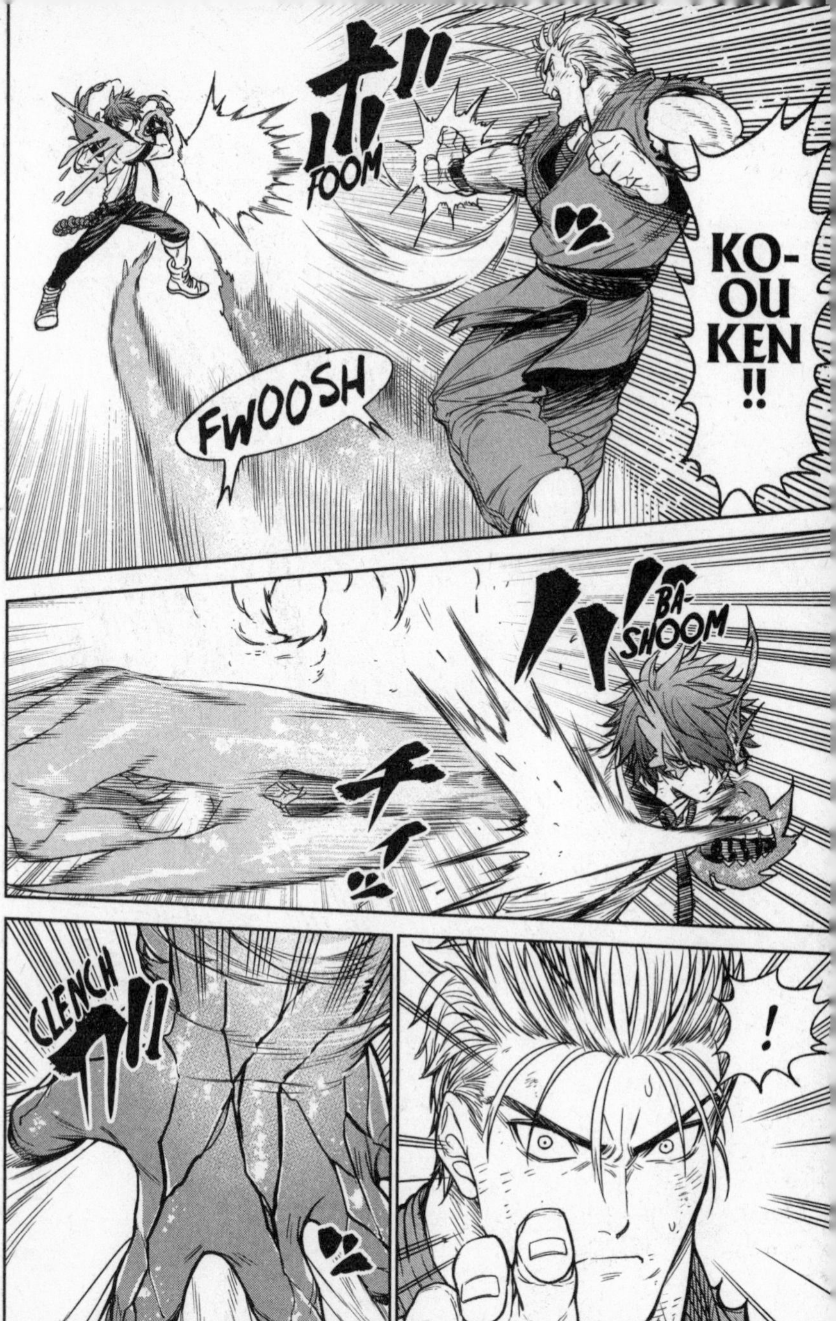
KO-OU KEN!!
FOOM
FWOOSH
BA-SHOOM
!
CLENCH

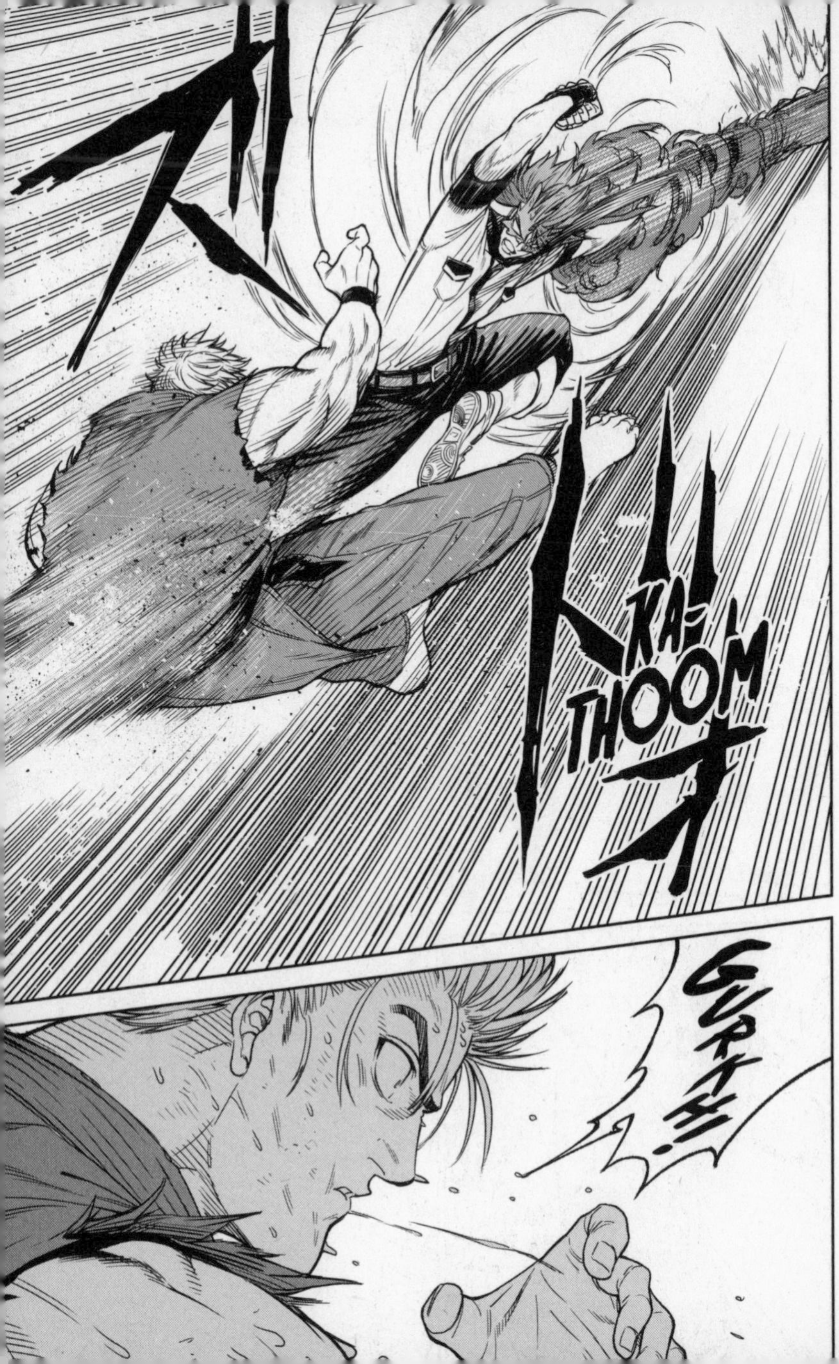
KA-THOOM
GURKH!!

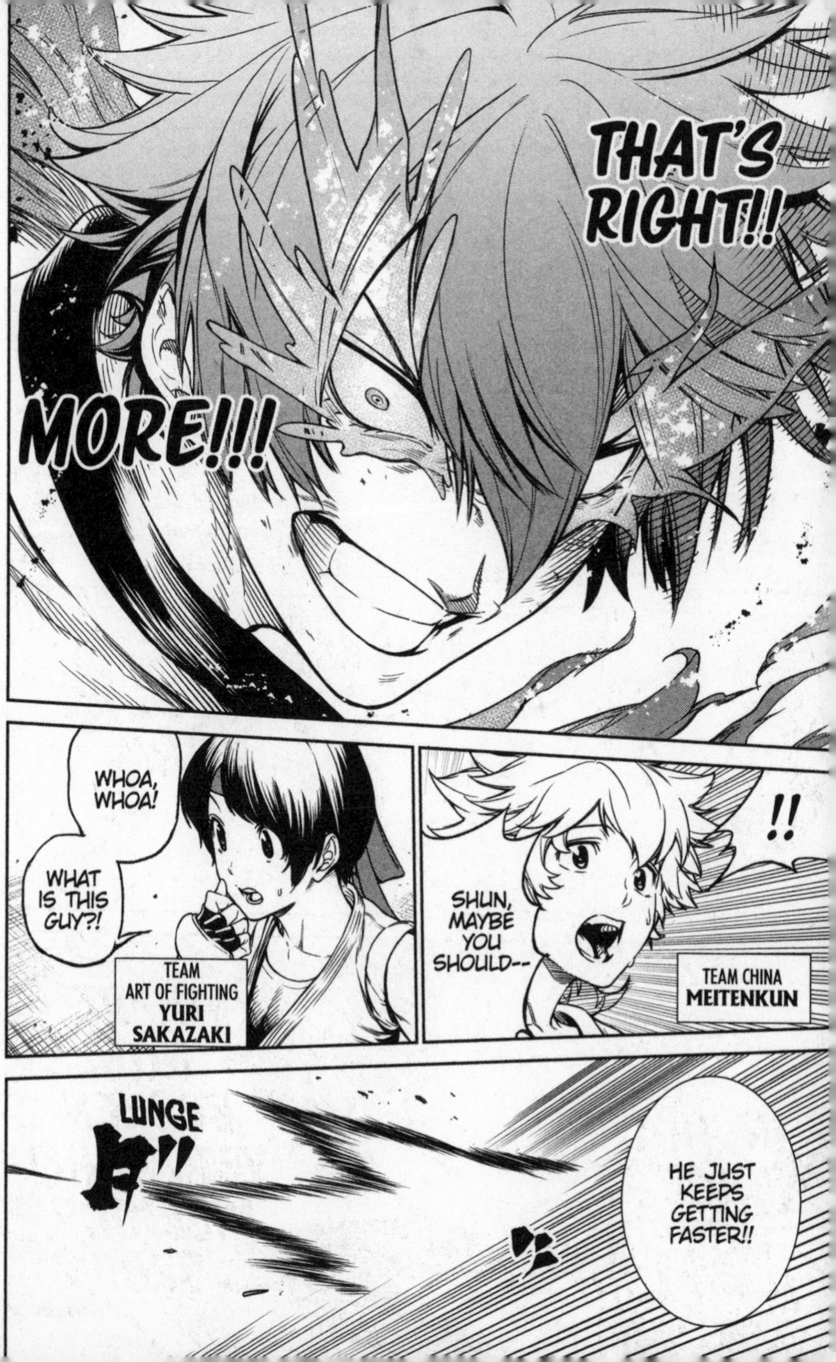
THAT'S RIGHT!!
MORE!!!
!!
SHUN, MAYBE YOU SHOULD--
TEAM CHINA MEITENKUN
WHOA, WHOA!
WHAT IS THIS GUY?!
TEAM ART OF FIGHTING YURI SAKAZAKI
HE JUST KEEPS GETTING FASTER!!
LUNGE

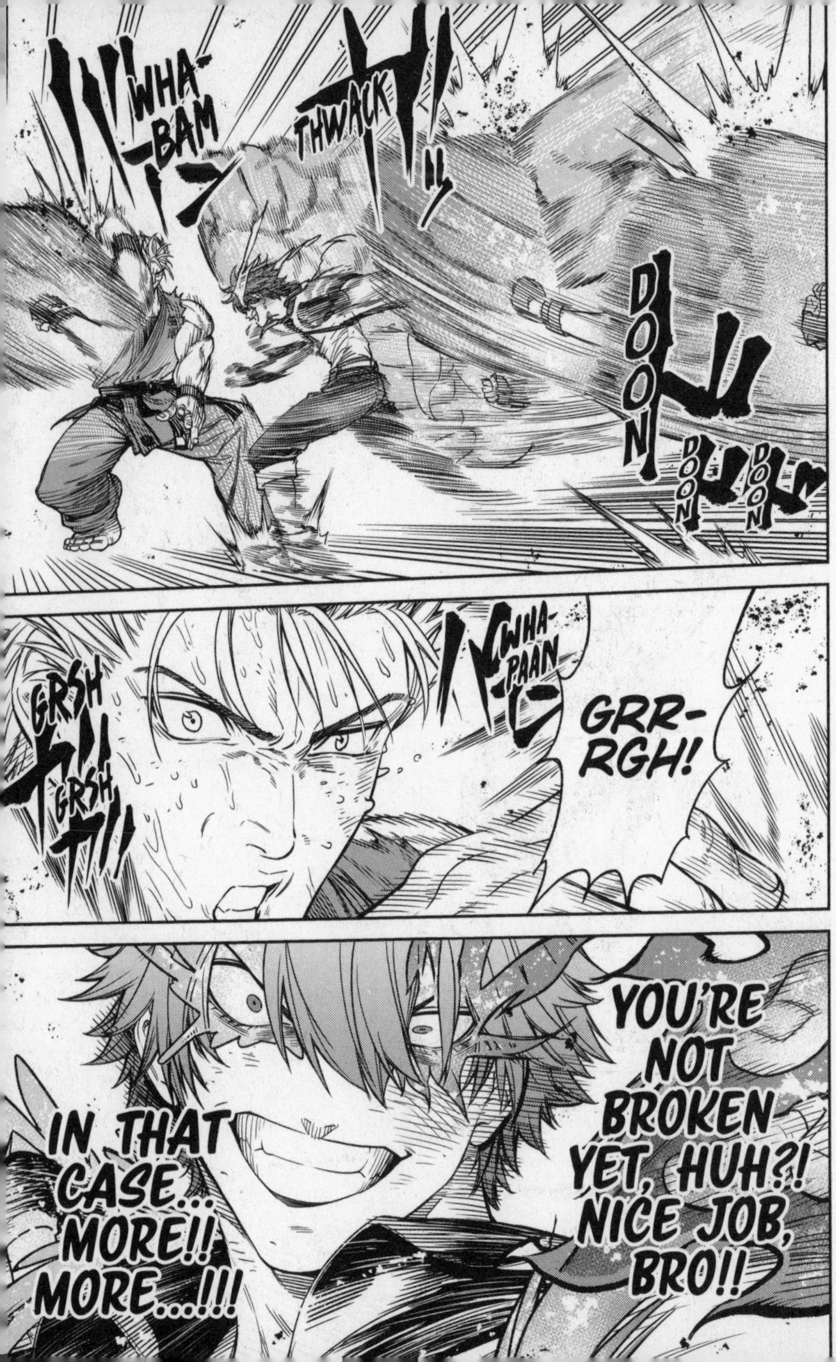
THWACK
WHA-BAM
DOOON
DOOON
DOOON
GRR-RGH!
WHA-PAAN
GRSH
GRSH
YOU'RE NOT BROKEN YET, HUH?! NICE JOB, BRO!!
IN THAT CASE... MORE!! MORE...!!!

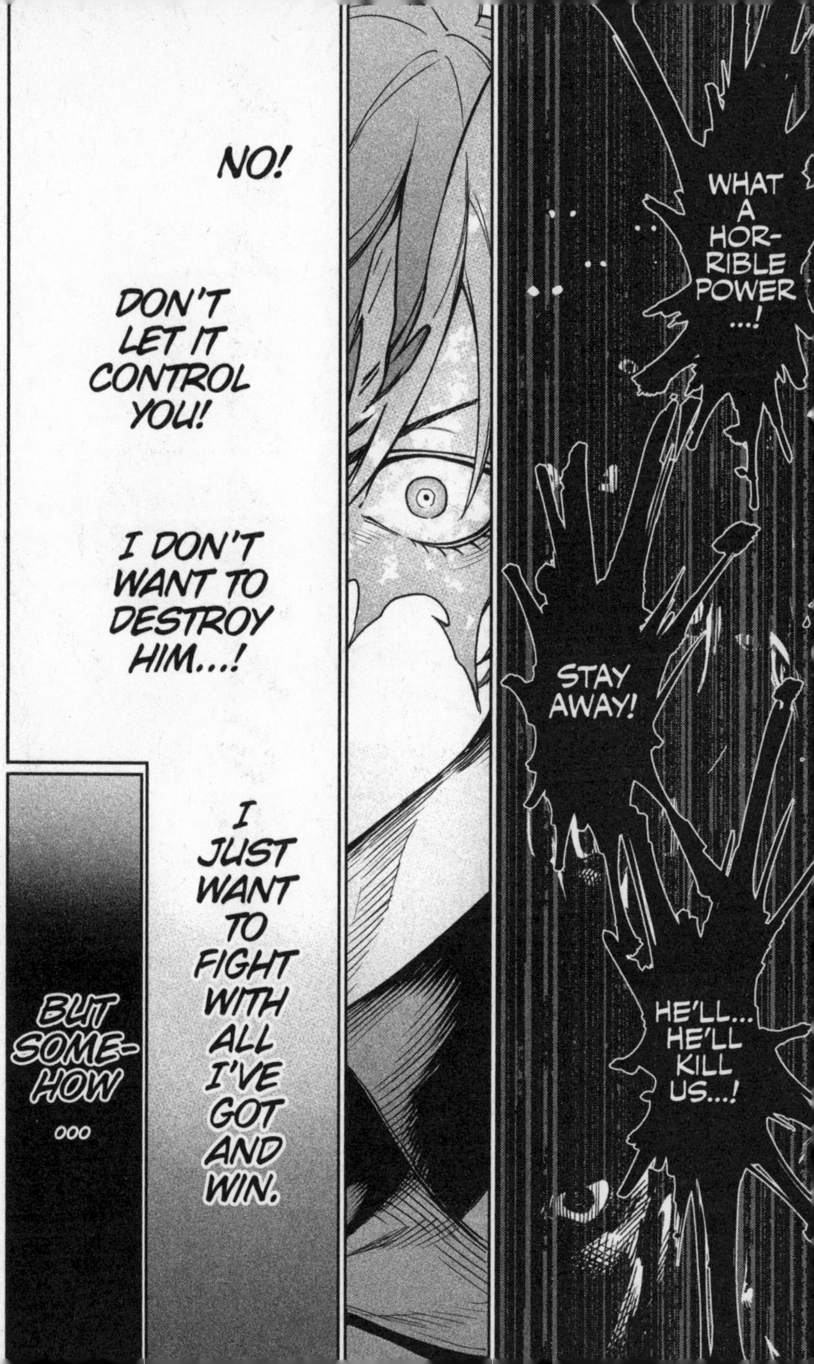
WHAT A HOR-RIBLE POWER...!
STAY AWAY!
HE'LL... HE'LL KILL US...!
NO!
DON'T LET IT CONTROL YOU!
I DON'T WANT TO DESTROY HIM...!
I JUST WANT TO FIGHT WITH ALL I'VE GOT AND WIN.
BUT SOME-HOW...

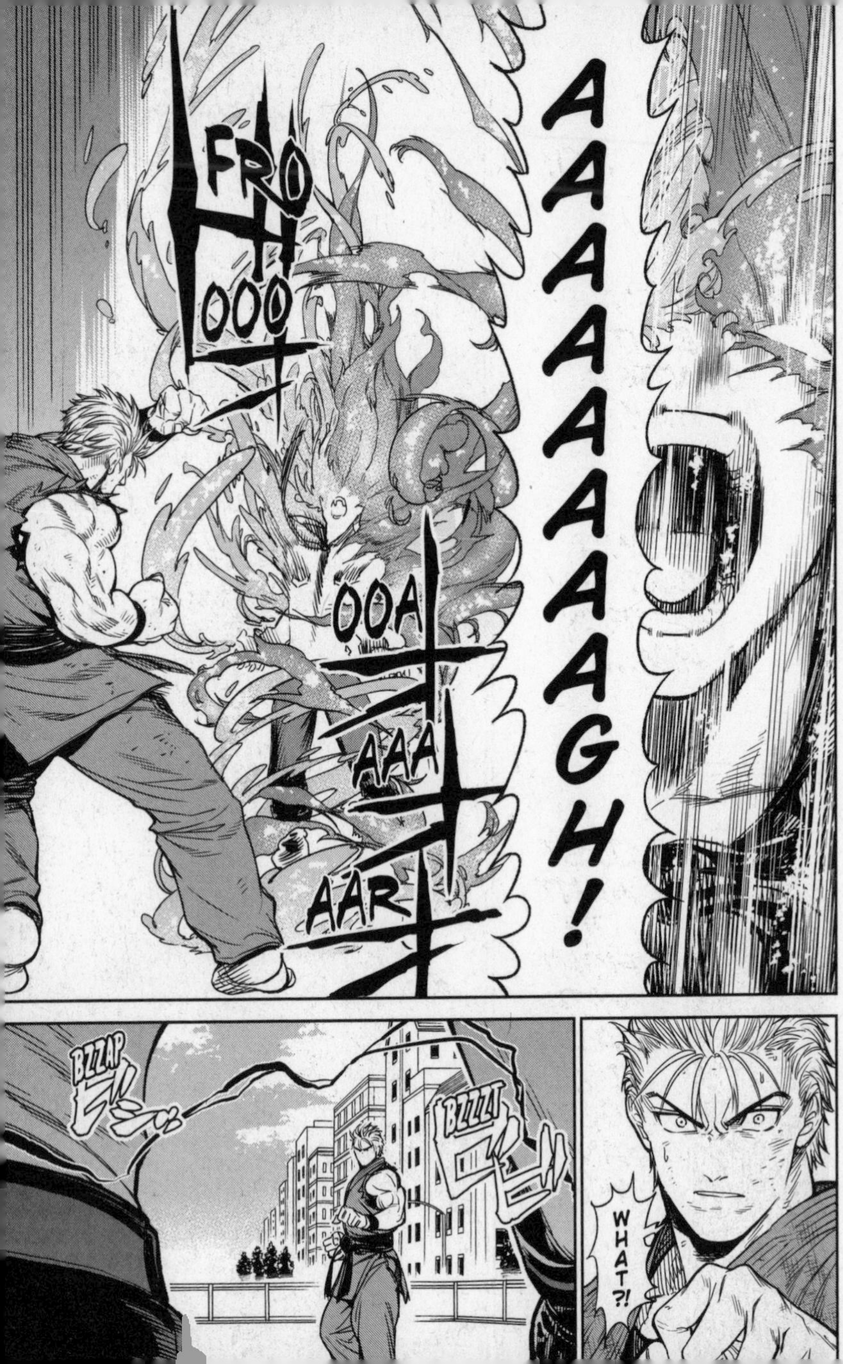
AAAAAAAAGH!
FRO
OOO
OOA
AAA
AAR
WHAT?!
BZZAP
BZZZT

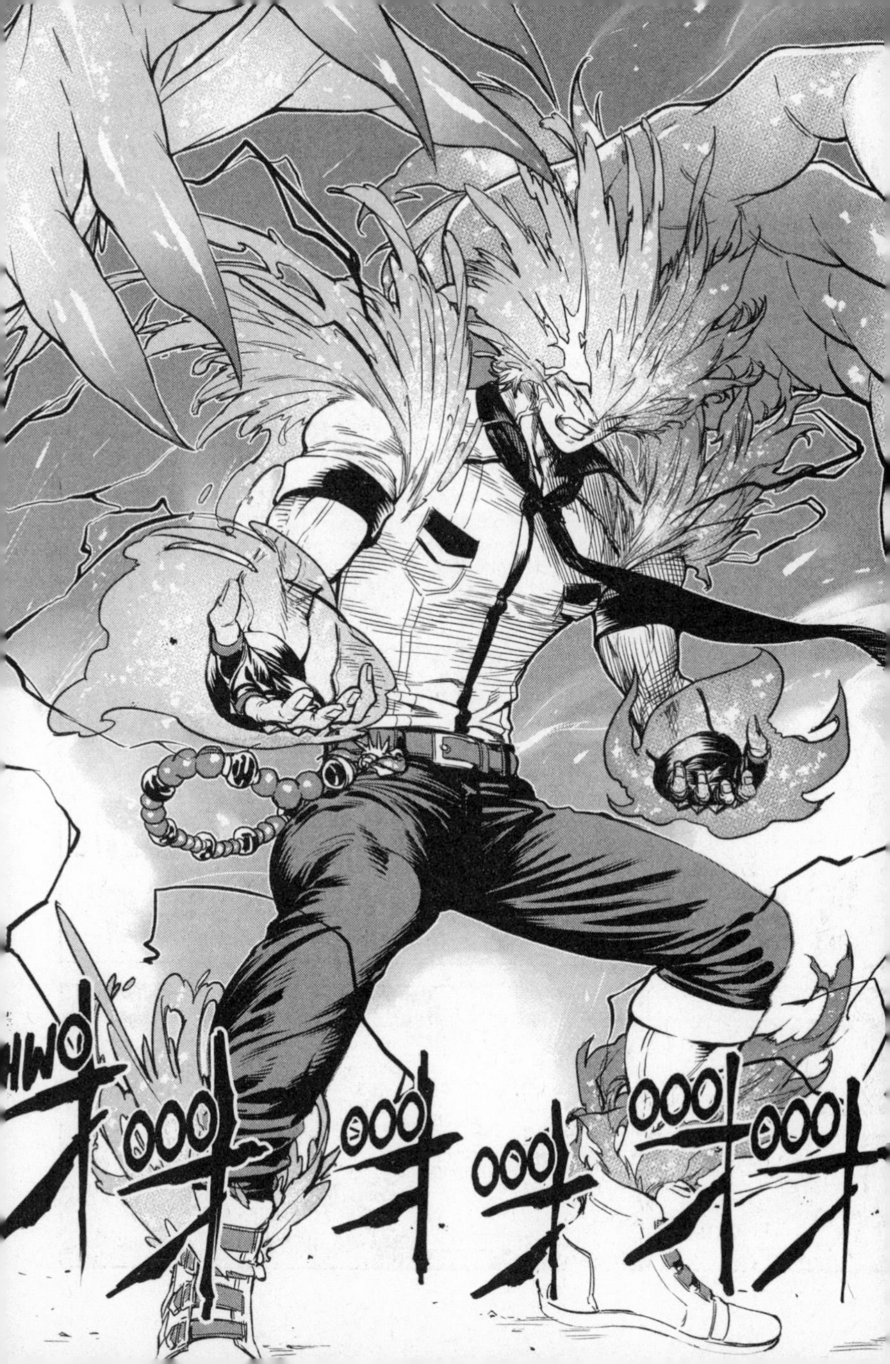
HWOOOOOOOOOOOOOOOOO

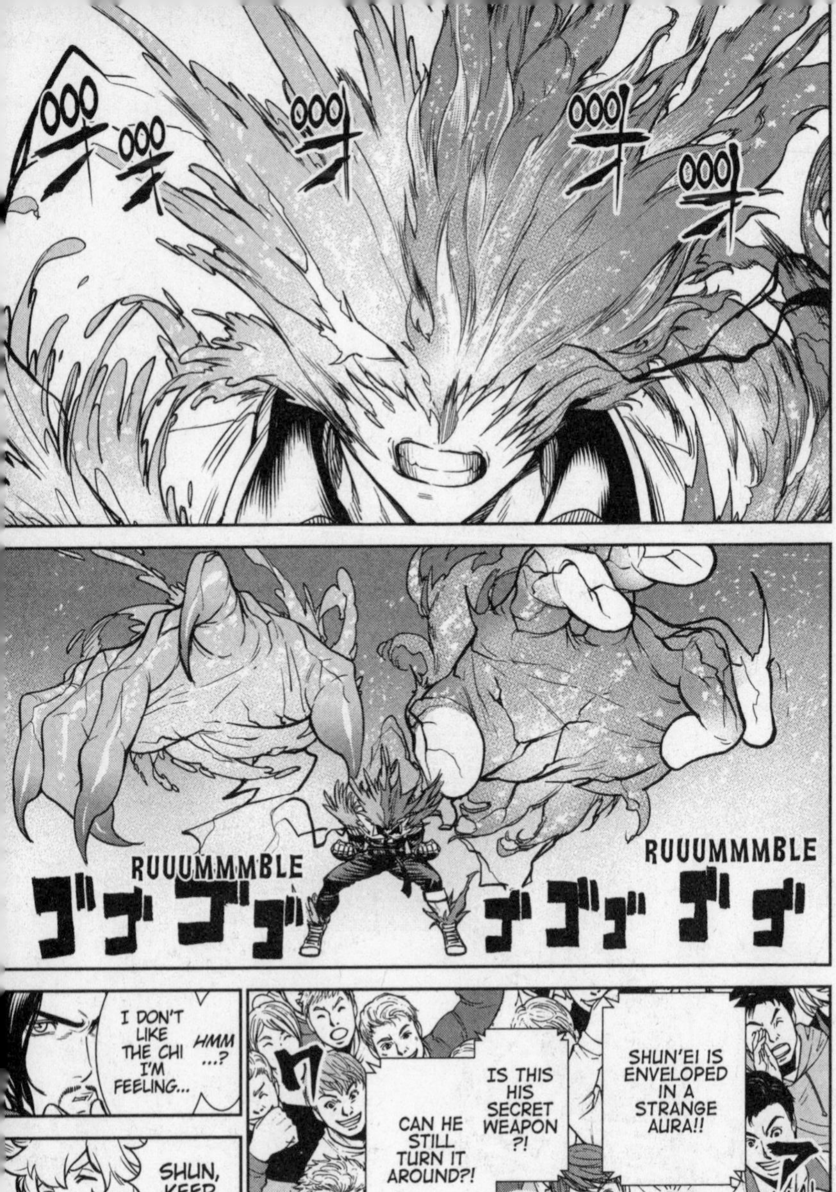

RUUUMMMBLE
RUUUMMMBLE
SHUN'EI IS ENVELOPED IN A STRANGE AURA!!
IS THIS HIS SECRET WEAPON?!
CAN HE STILL TURN IT AROUND?!
WHOOAAA!
HMM ...?
I DON'T LIKE THE CHI I'M FEELING...
SHUN, KEEP IT TO-GETHER!

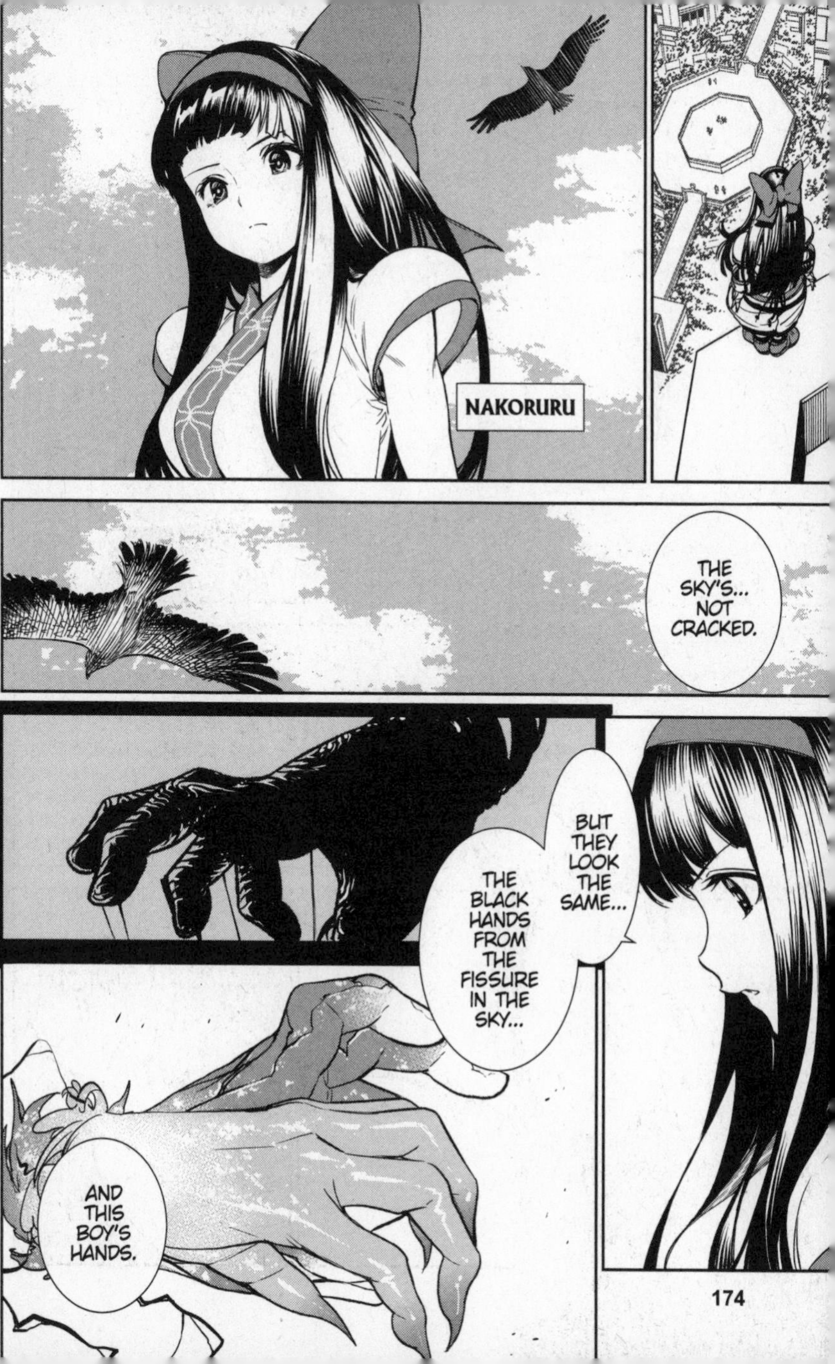
NAKORURU
THE SKY'S... NOT CRACKED.
BUT THEY LOOK THE SAME...
THE BLACK HANDS FROM THE FISSURE IN THE SKY...
AND THIS BOY'S HANDS.

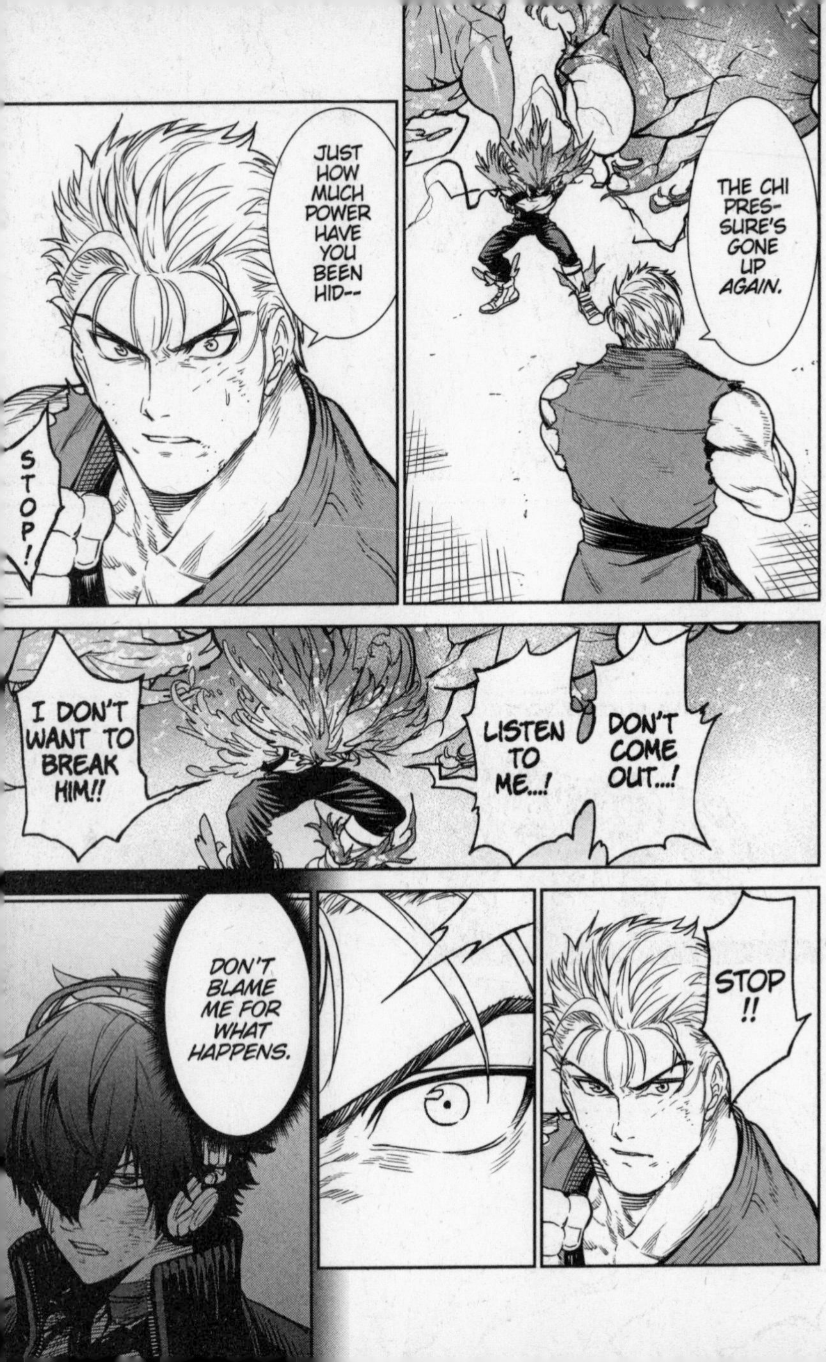

THE CHI PRES-SURE'S GONE UP AGAIN.
JUST HOW MUCH POWER HAVE YOU BEEN HID--
STOP!
DON'T COME OUT...!
LISTEN TO ME...!
I DON'T WANT TO BREAK HIM!!
STOP !!
DON'T BLAME ME FOR WHAT HAPPENS.

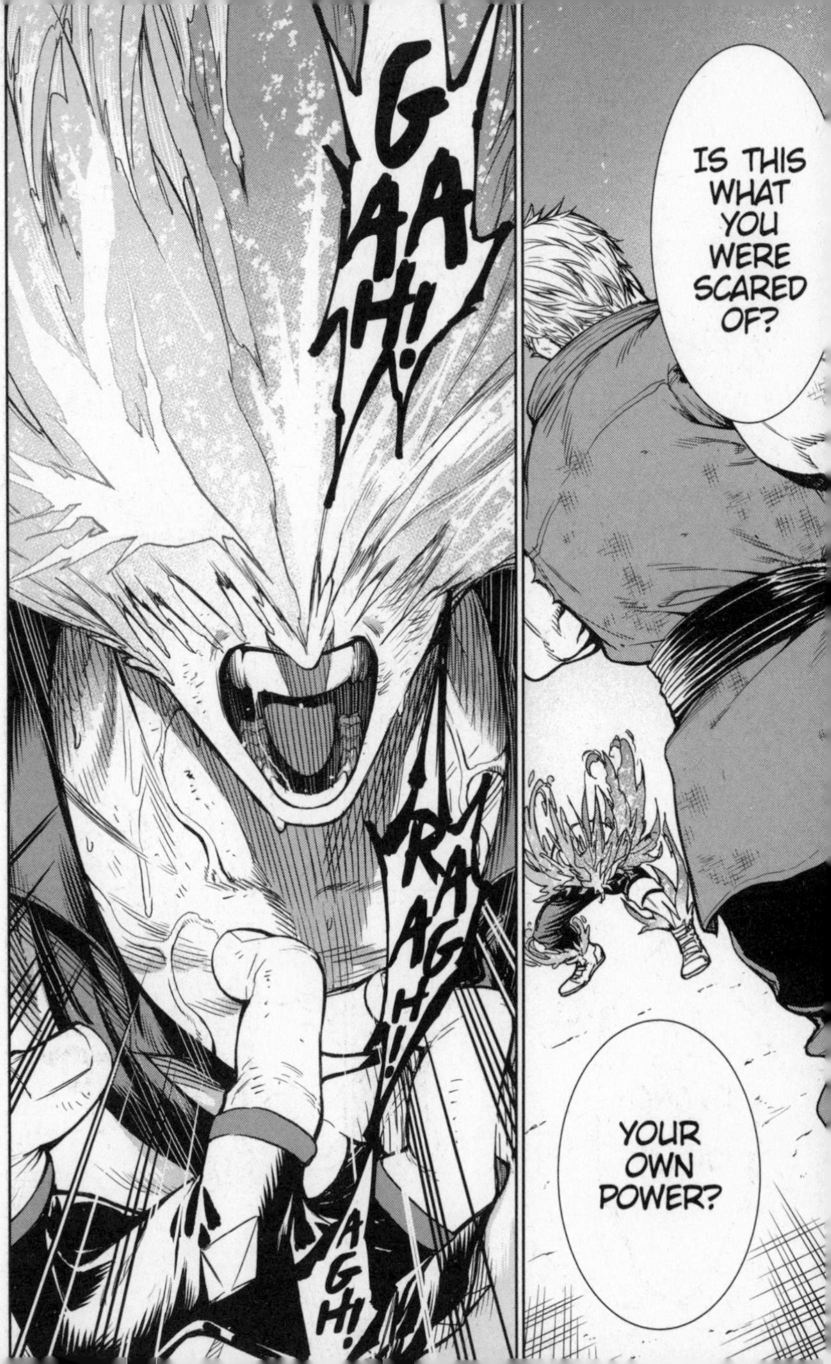
IS THIS WHAT YOU WERE SCARED OF?
YOUR OWN POWER?
GAAH!!
URAAGH!!
AGH!

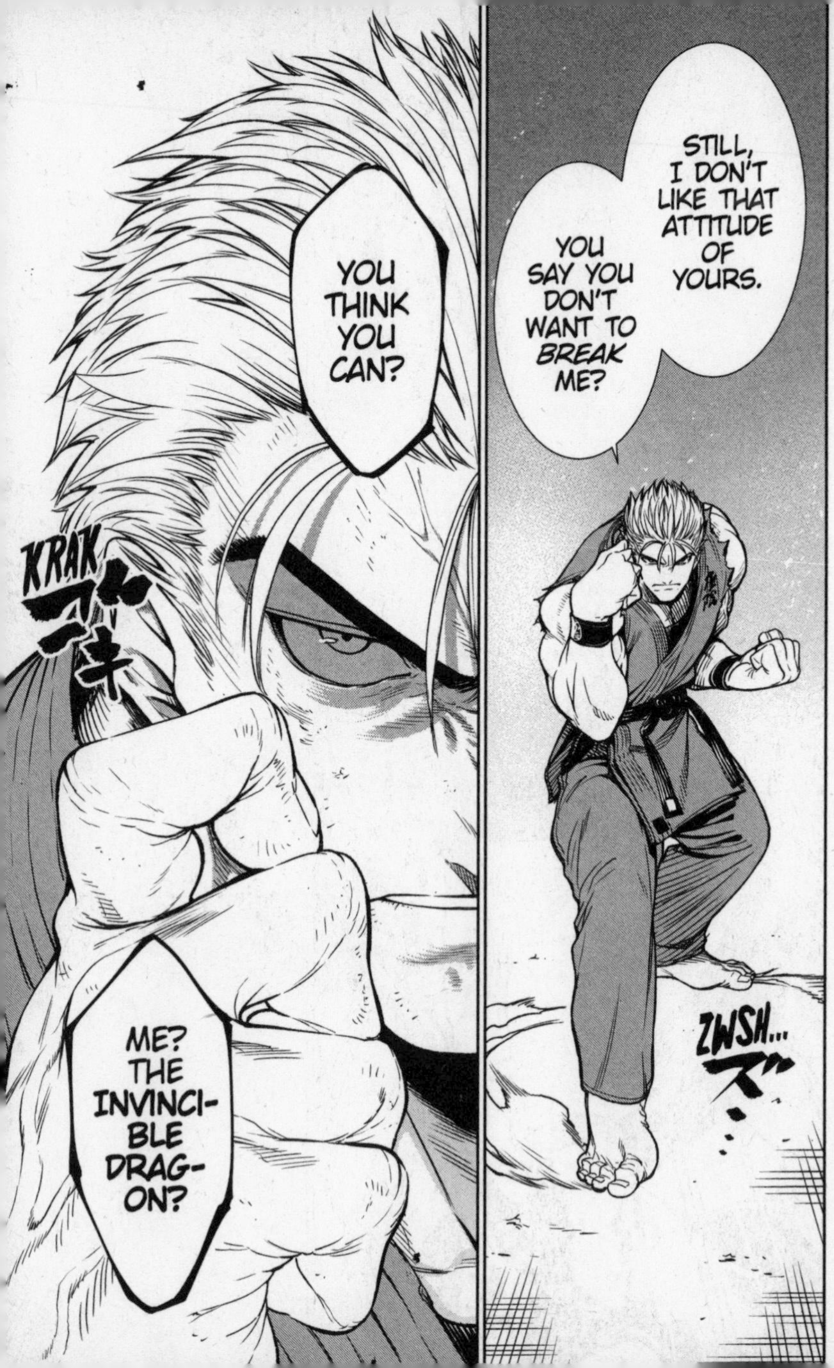

STILL, I DON'T LIKE THAT ATTITUDE OF YOURS.
YOU SAY YOU DON'T WANT TO *BREAK* ME?
ZWSH...
YOU THINK YOU CAN?
KRAK
ME? THE INVINCI-BLE DRAG-ON?

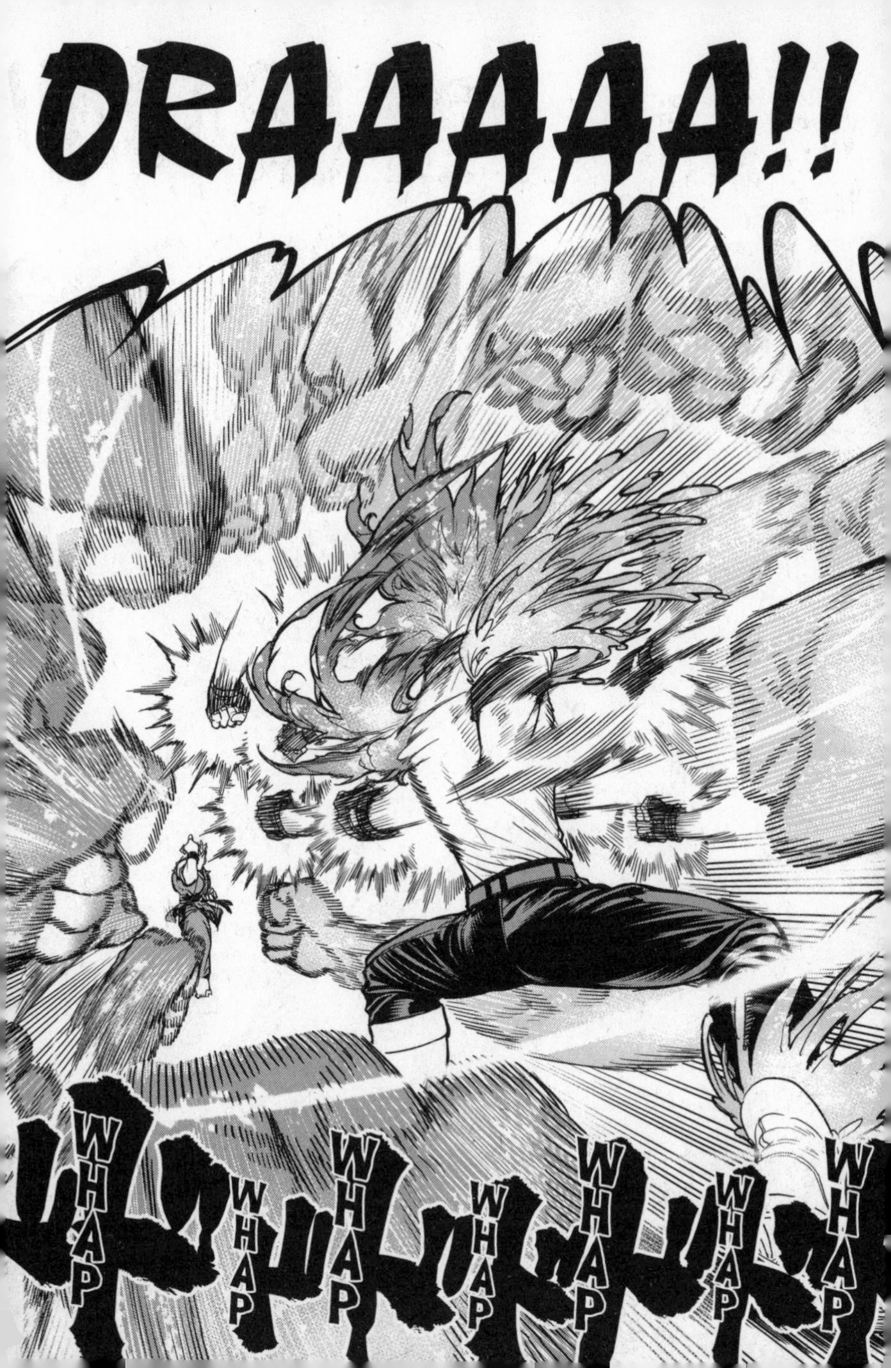
ORAAAAA!!
WHAP
WHAP
WHAP
WHAP
WHAP
WHAP
WHAP

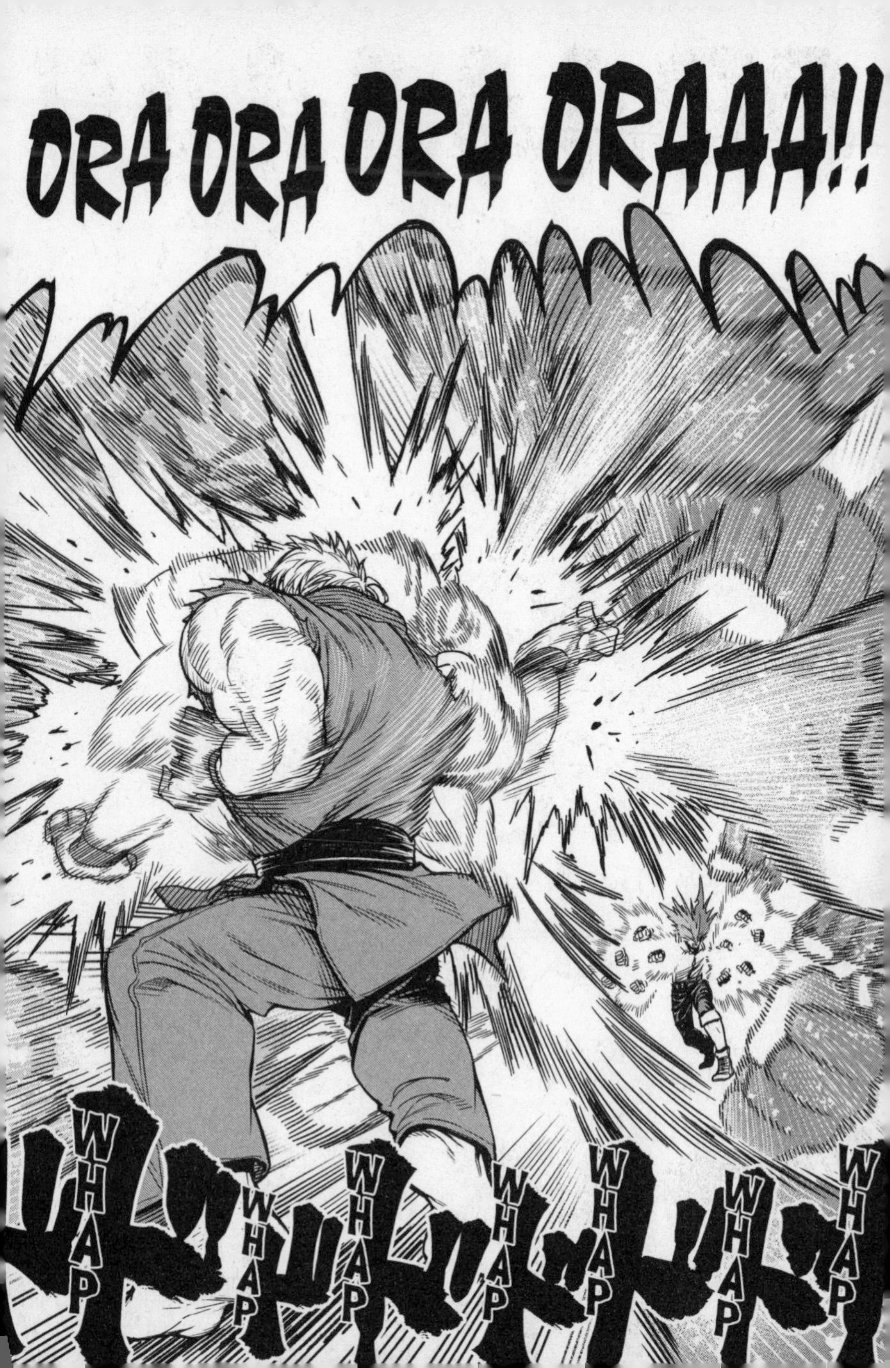
ORA ORA ORA ORAAA!!
WHAP
WHAP
WHAP
WHAP
WHAP
WHAP
WHAP

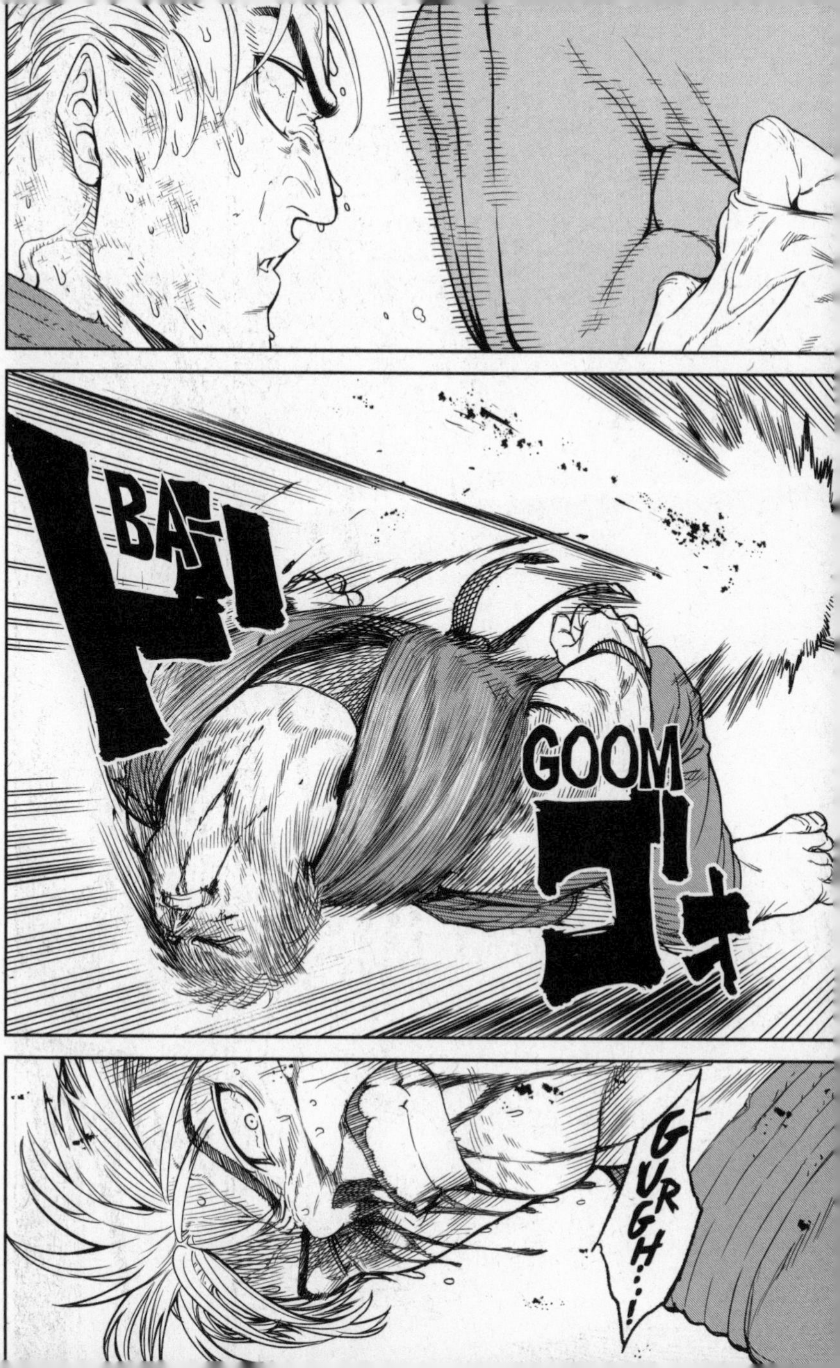
GOOM
BA-
GURGH...!

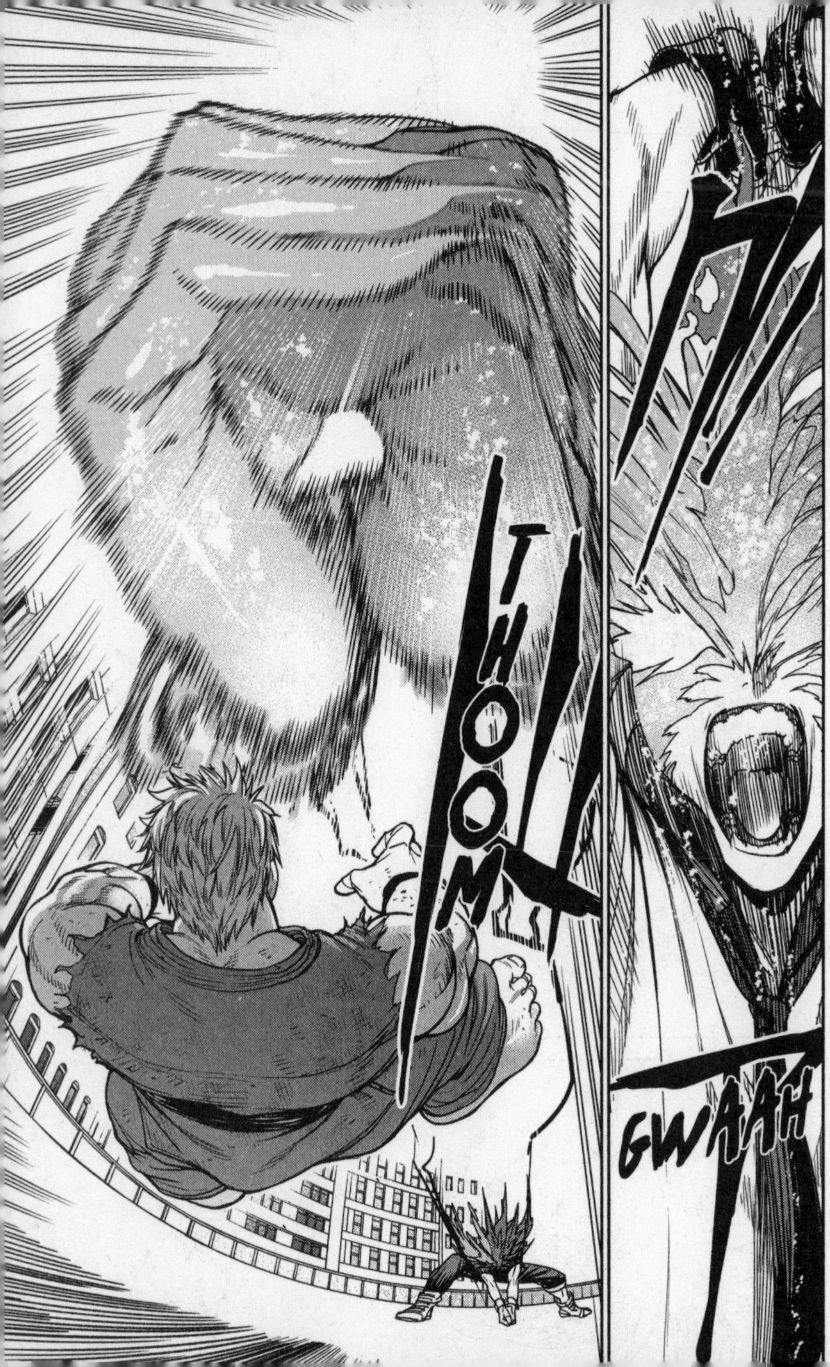
GWAAH
THOOOM

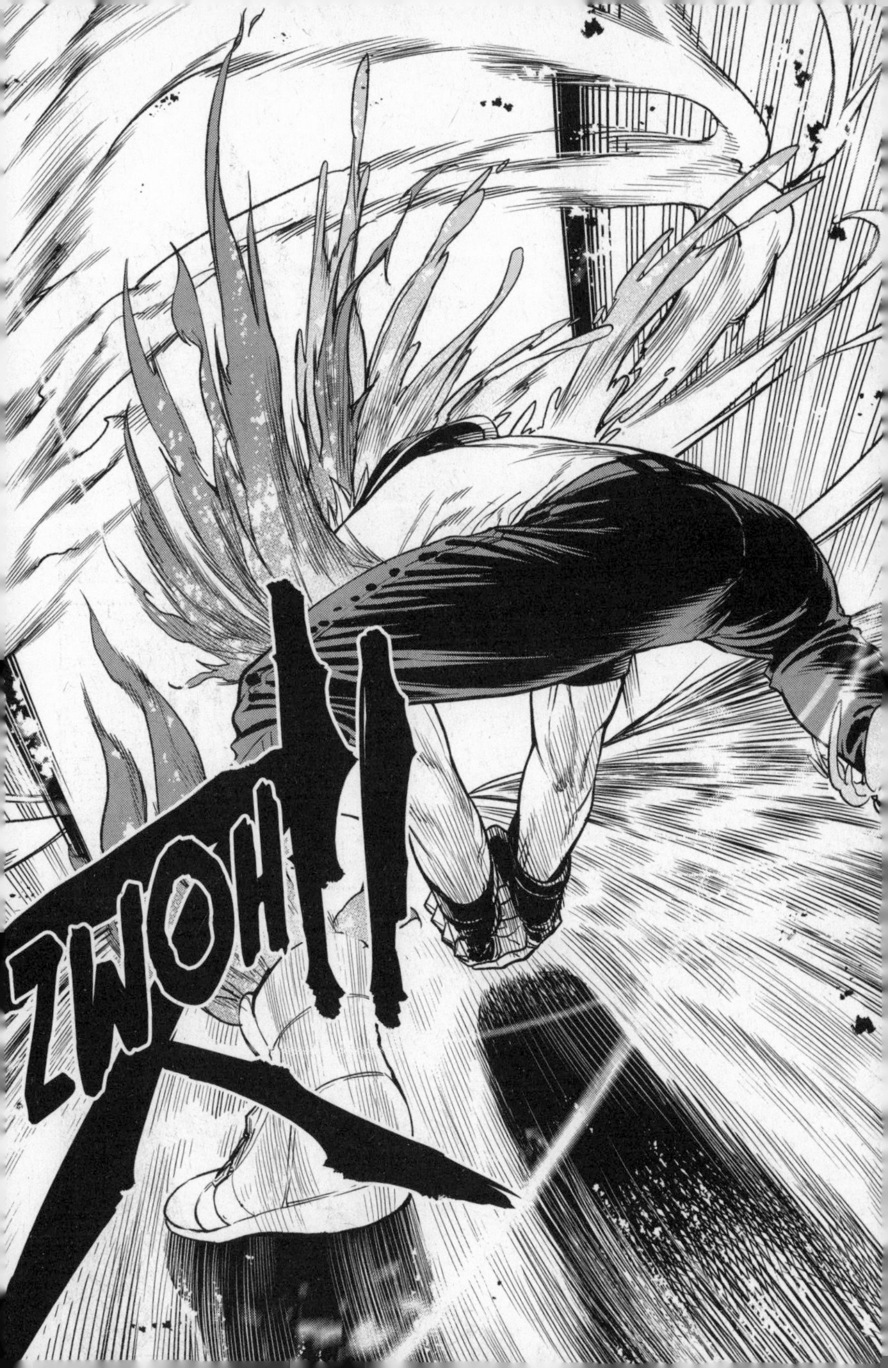
ZWOH!!

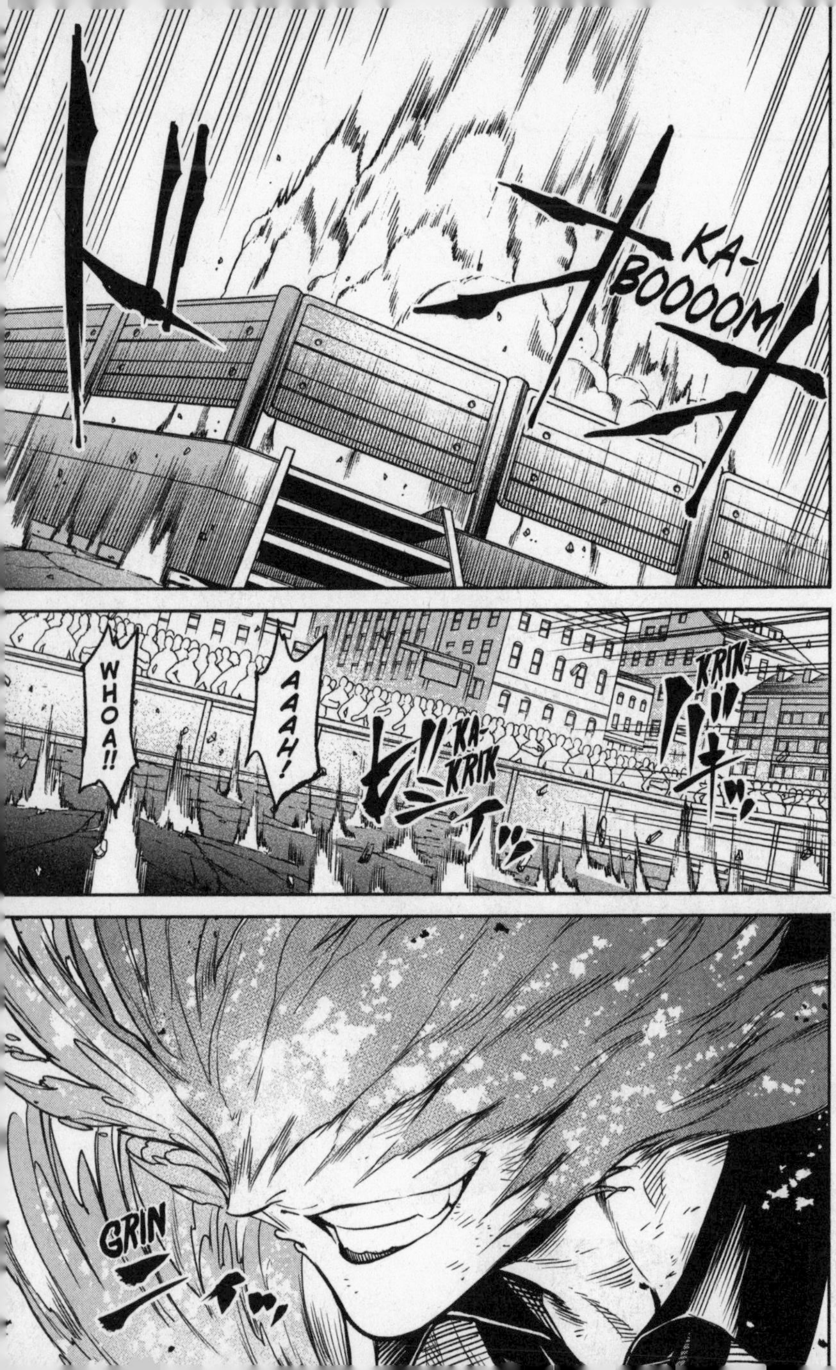
KA-BOOOOM
KRIK
KA-KRIK
AAAH!
WHOA!!
GRIN

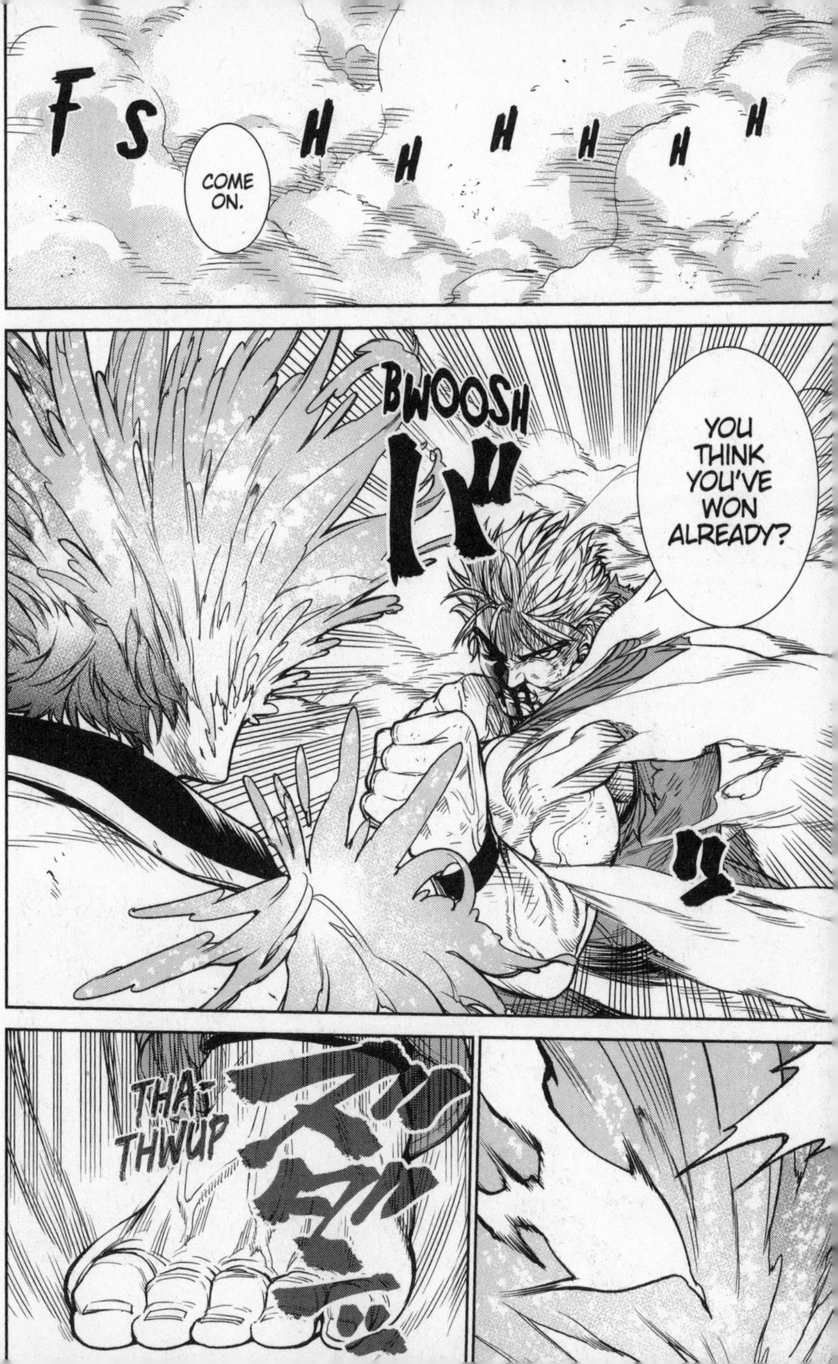
FSHHHHHH
COME ON.
YOU THINK YOU'VE WON ALREADY?
BWOOSH
THA-THWUP

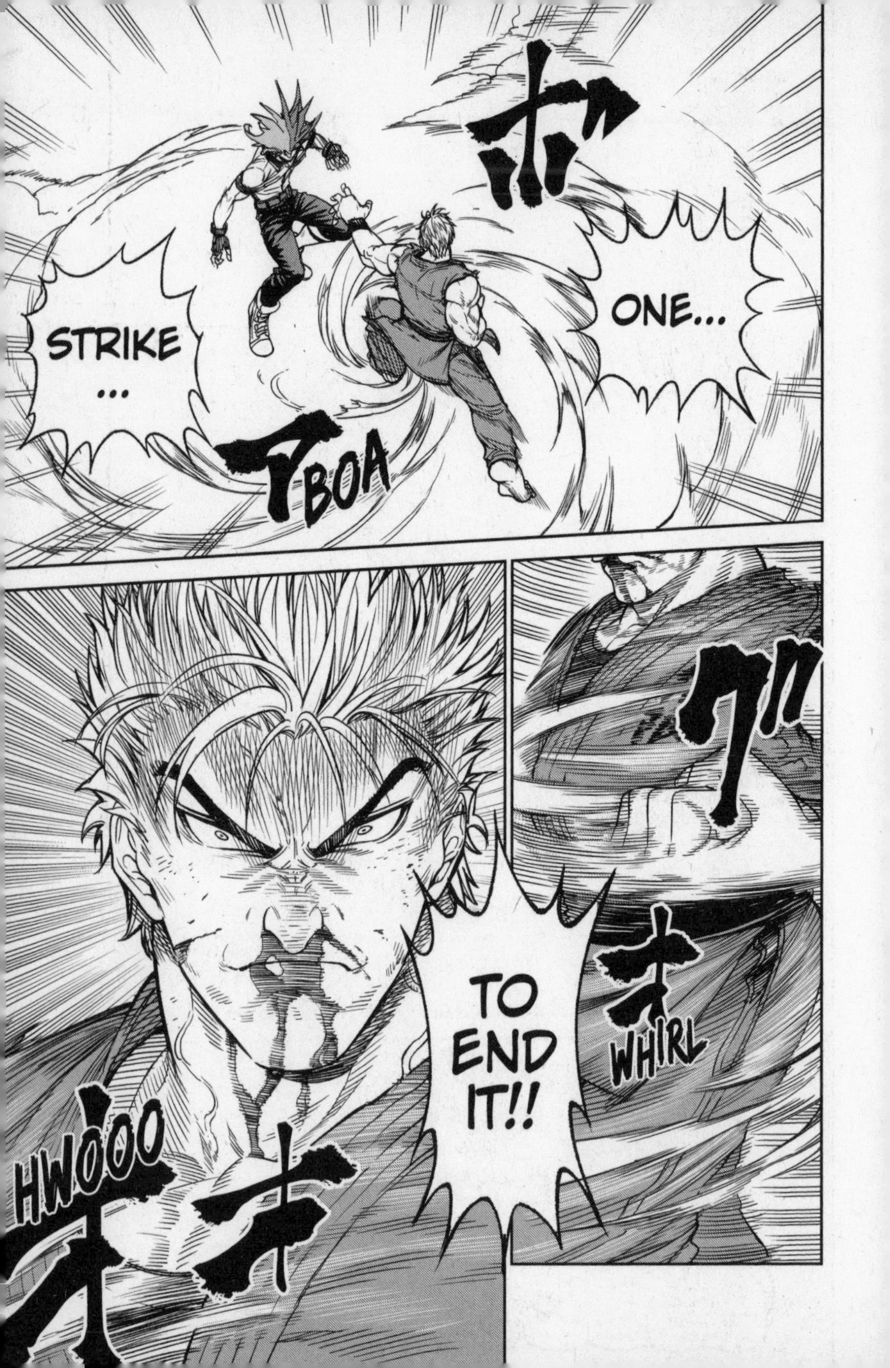
ONE...
STRIKE ...
BOA
WHIRL
TO END IT!!
HWOOO

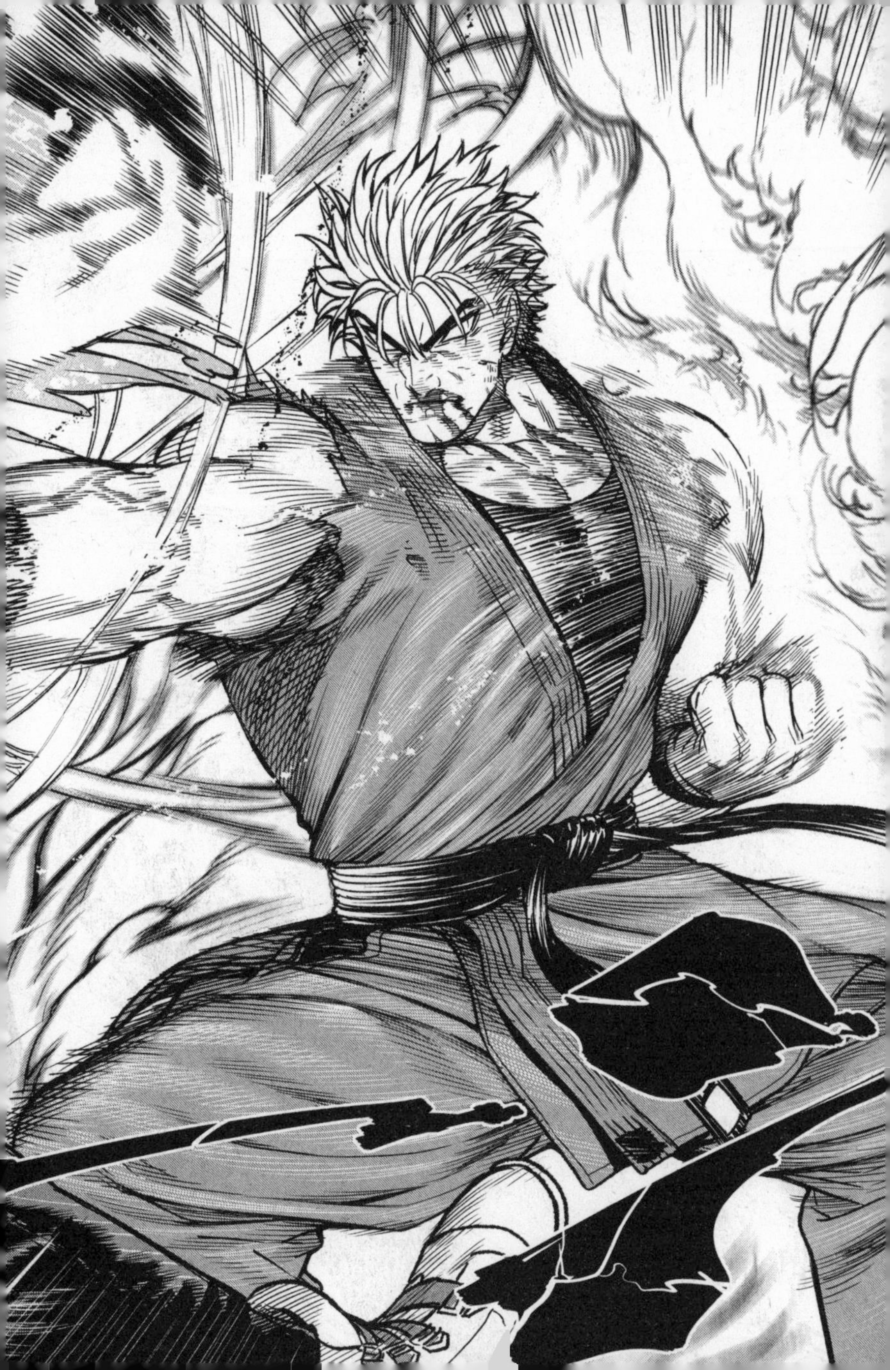

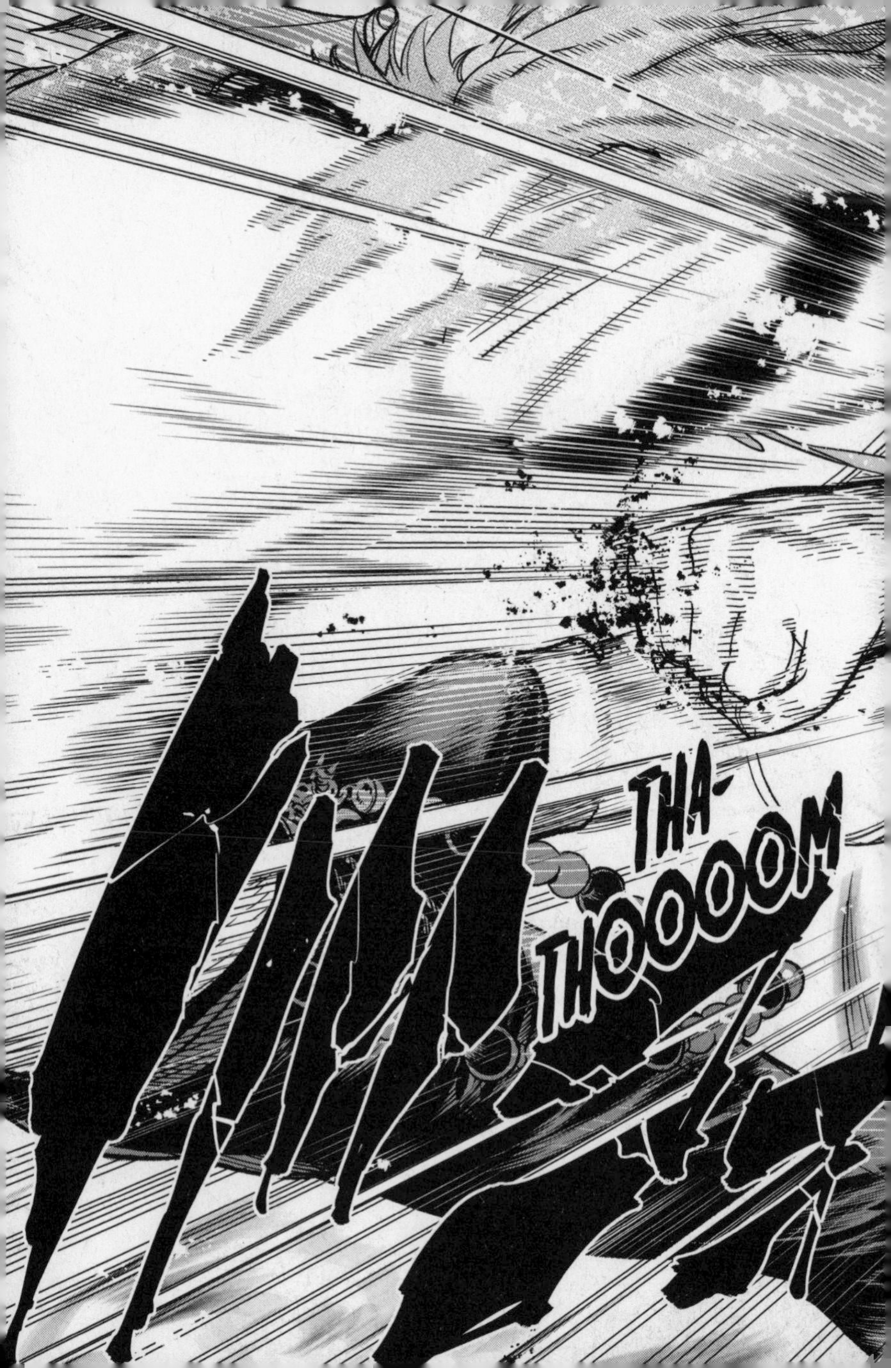
THA-
THOOOOM

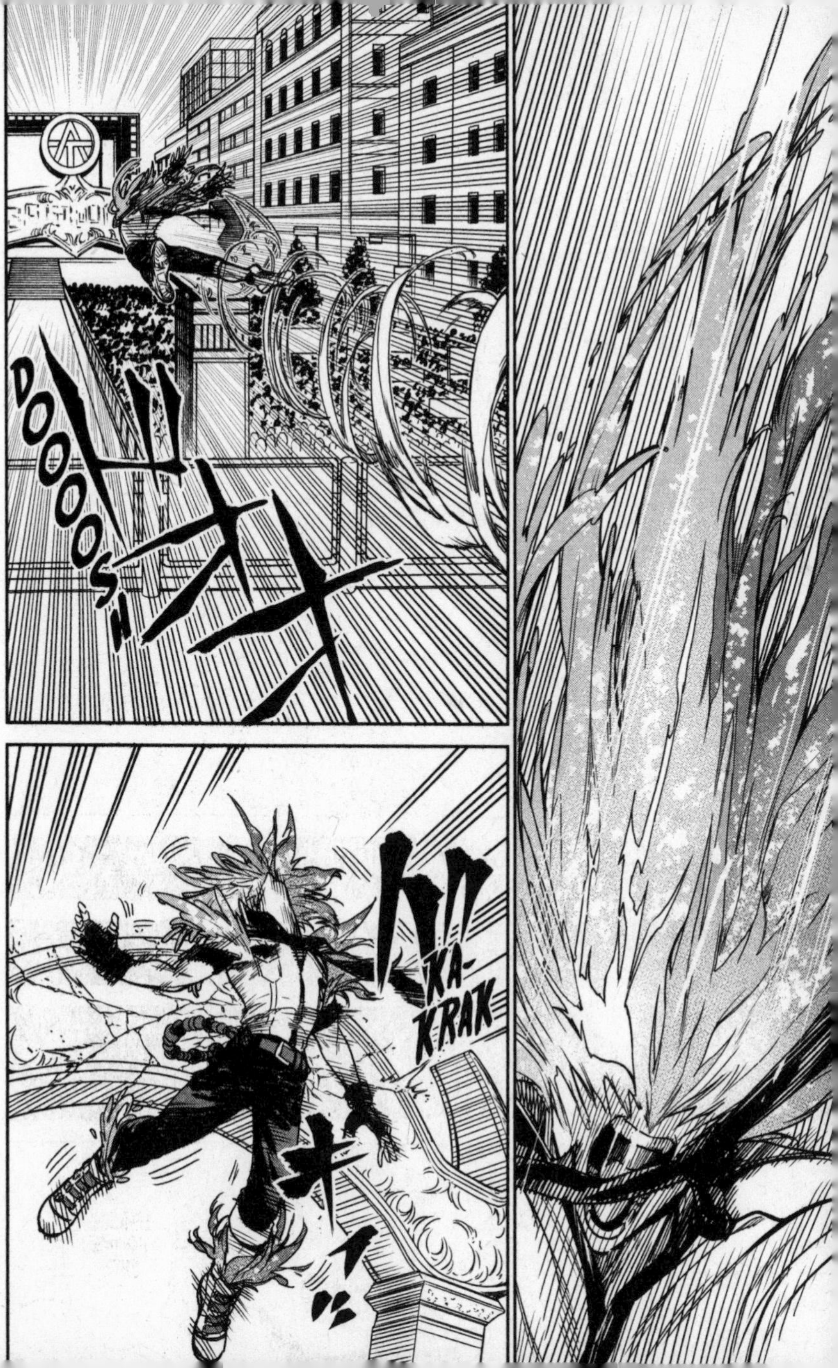
DOOOOSH
KA-KRAK

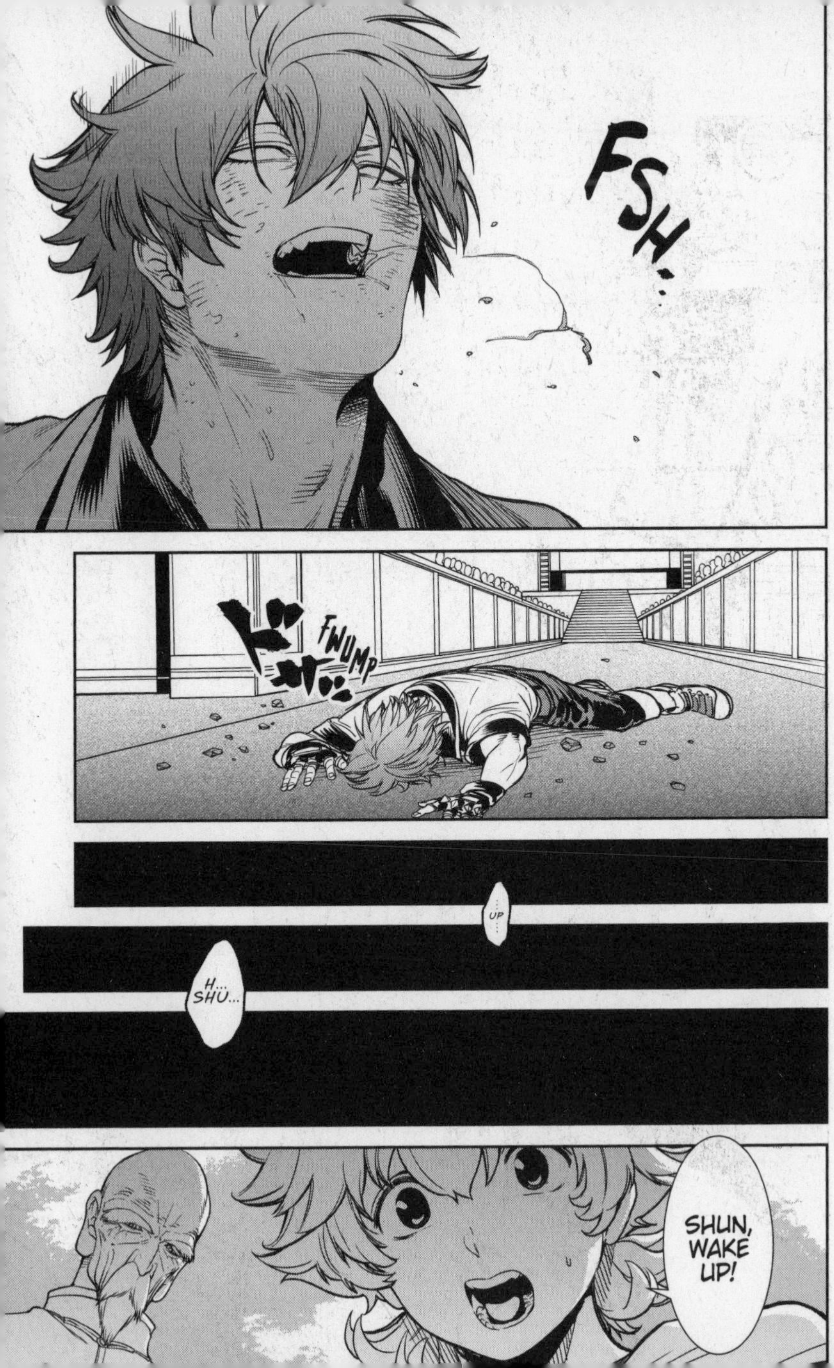
FSH
FWUMP
...UP...
H... SHU...
SHUN, WAKE UP!

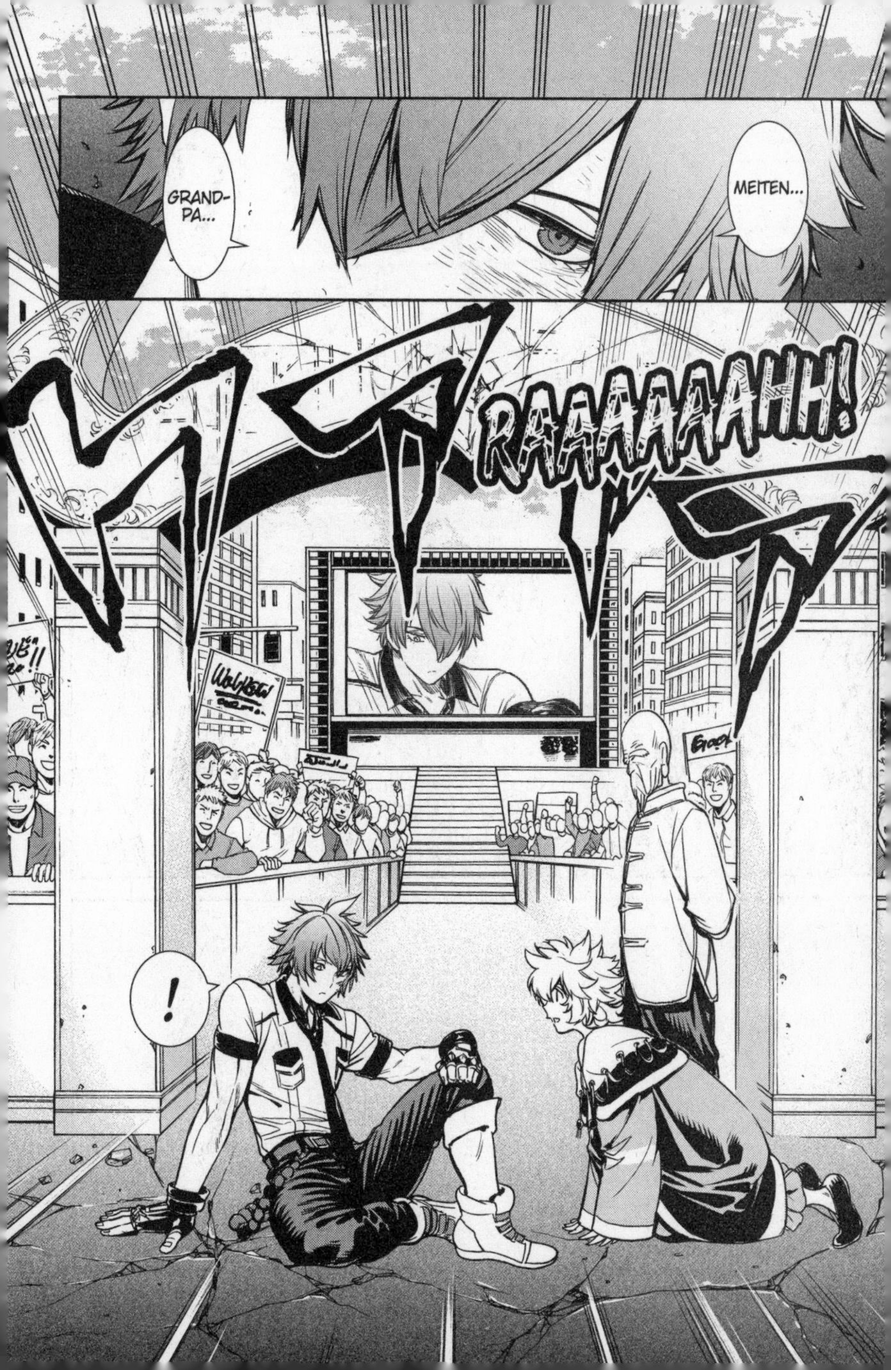
MEITEN...
GRAND-PA...
RAAAAAAHH!
!

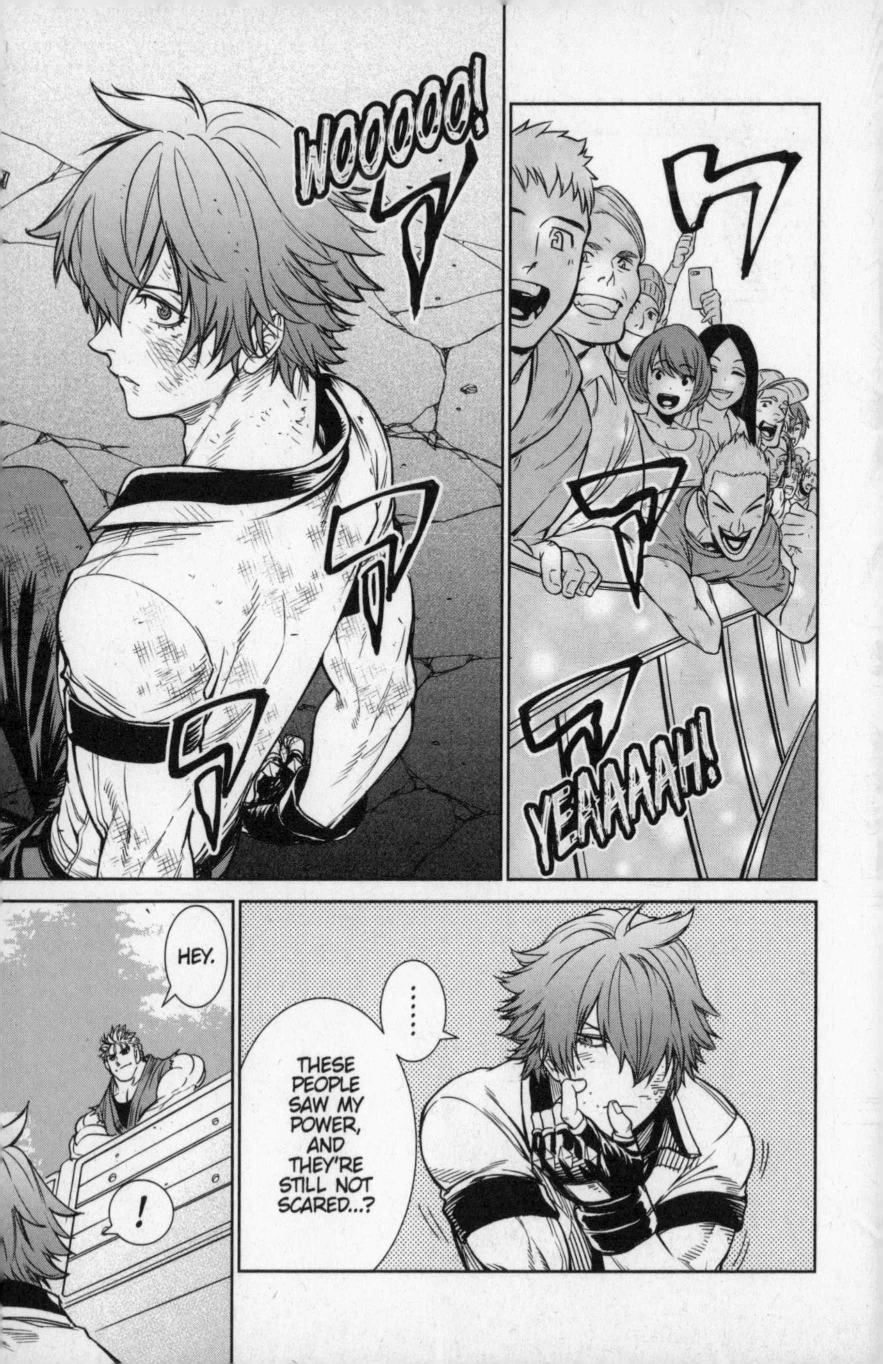
YEAAAAH!
WOOOOO!
……
THESE PEOPLE SAW MY POWER, AND THEY'RE STILL NOT SCARED...?
HEY.
!

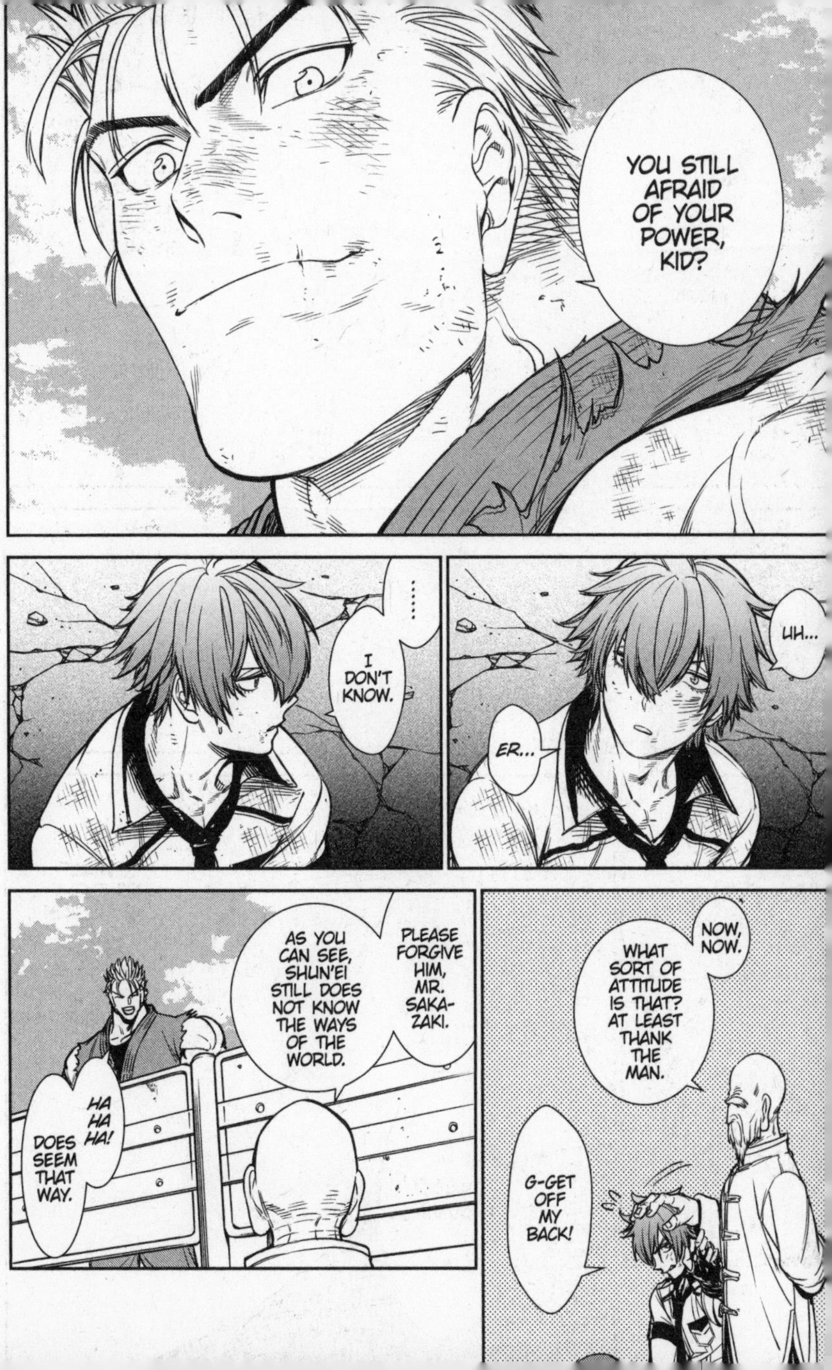

YOU STILL AFRAID OF YOUR POWER, KID?
UH...
ER...
......
I DON'T KNOW.
NOW, NOW.
WHAT SORT OF ATTITUDE IS THAT? AT LEAST THANK THE MAN.
G-GET OFF MY BACK!
PLEASE FORGIVE HIM, MR. SAKAZAKI.
AS YOU CAN SEE, SHUN'EI STILL DOES NOT KNOW THE WAYS OF THE WORLD.
HA HA HA!
DOES SEEM THAT WAY.

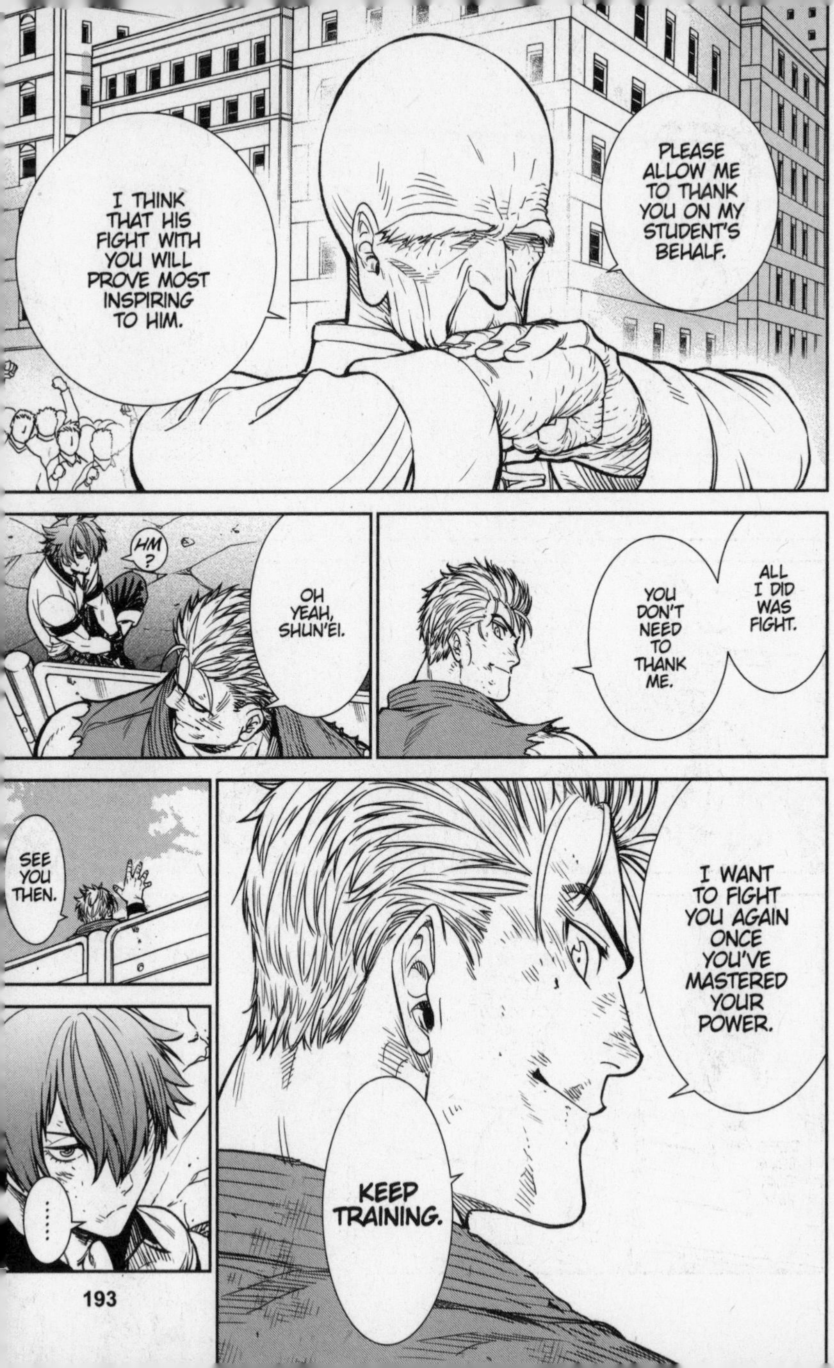
PLEASE ALLOW ME TO THANK YOU ON MY STUDENT'S BEHALF.
I THINK THAT HIS FIGHT WITH YOU WILL PROVE MOST INSPIRING TO HIM.
ALL I DID WAS FIGHT.
YOU DON'T NEED TO THANK ME.
OH YEAH, SHUN'EI.
HM?
I WANT TO FIGHT YOU AGAIN ONCE YOU'VE MASTERED YOUR POWER.
KEEP TRAINING.
SEE YOU THEN.
......

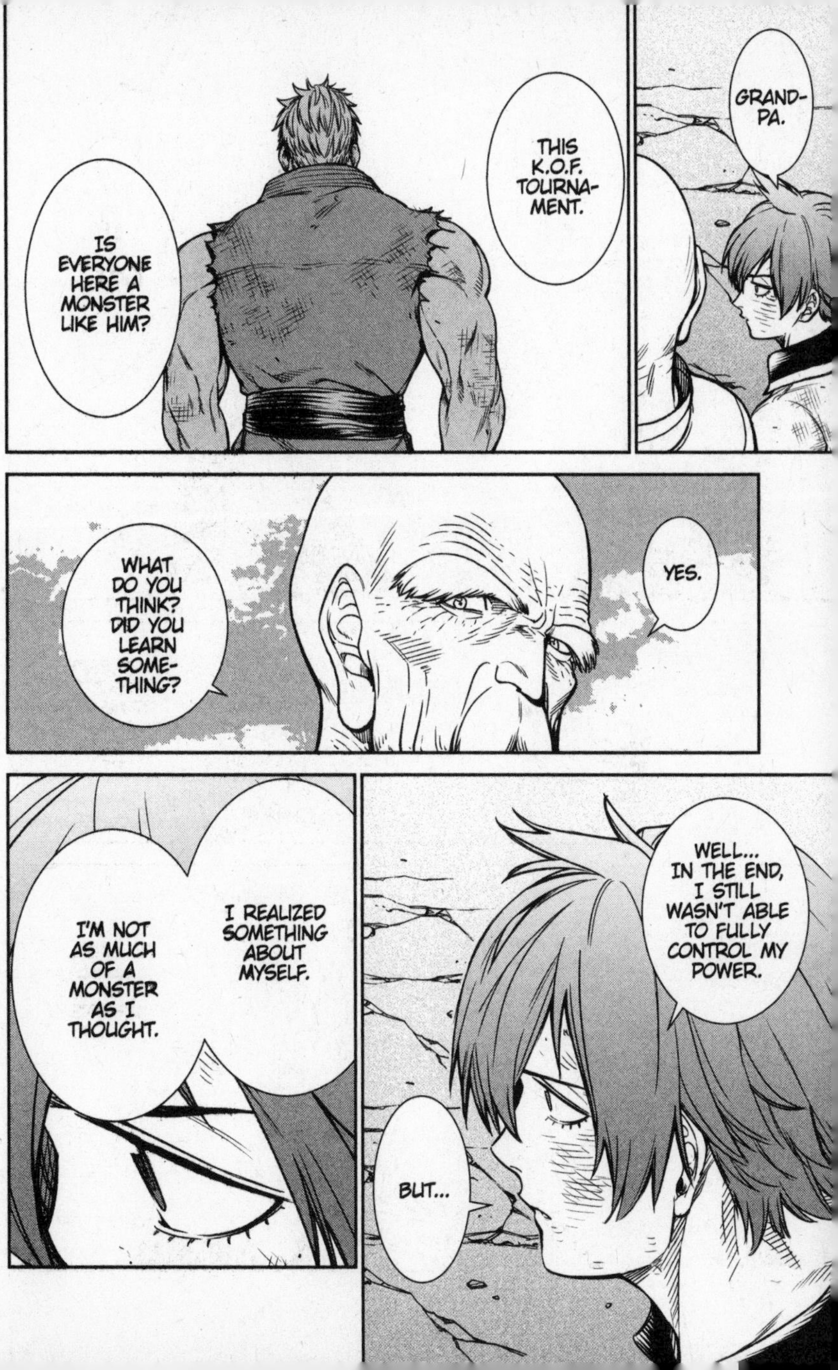
GRAND-PA.
THIS K.O.F. TOURNA-MENT.
IS EVERYONE HERE A MONSTER LIKE HIM?
YES.
WHAT DO YOU THINK? DID YOU LEARN SOME-THING?
WELL... IN THE END, I STILL WASN'T ABLE TO FULLY CONTROL MY POWER.
BUT...
I REALIZED SOMETHING ABOUT MYSELF.
I'M NOT AS MUCH OF A MONSTER AS I THOUGHT.

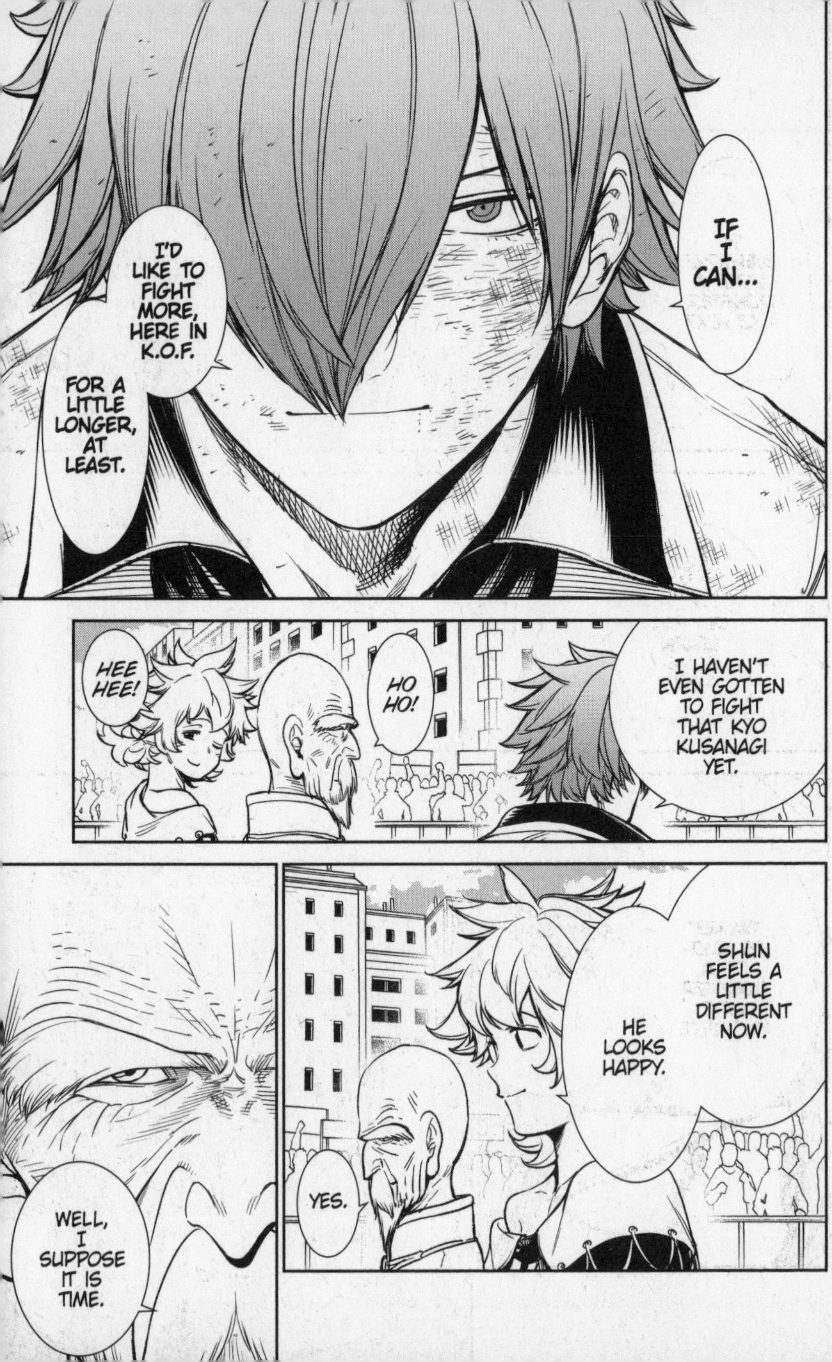
IF I CAN...
I'D LIKE TO FIGHT MORE, HERE IN K.O.F.
FOR A LITTLE LONGER, AT LEAST.
I HAVEN'T EVEN GOTTEN TO FIGHT THAT KYO KUSANAGI YET.
HO HO!
HEE HEE!
SHUN FEELS A LITTLE DIFFERENT NOW.
HE LOOKS HAPPY.
YES.
WELL, I SUPPOSE IT IS TIME.

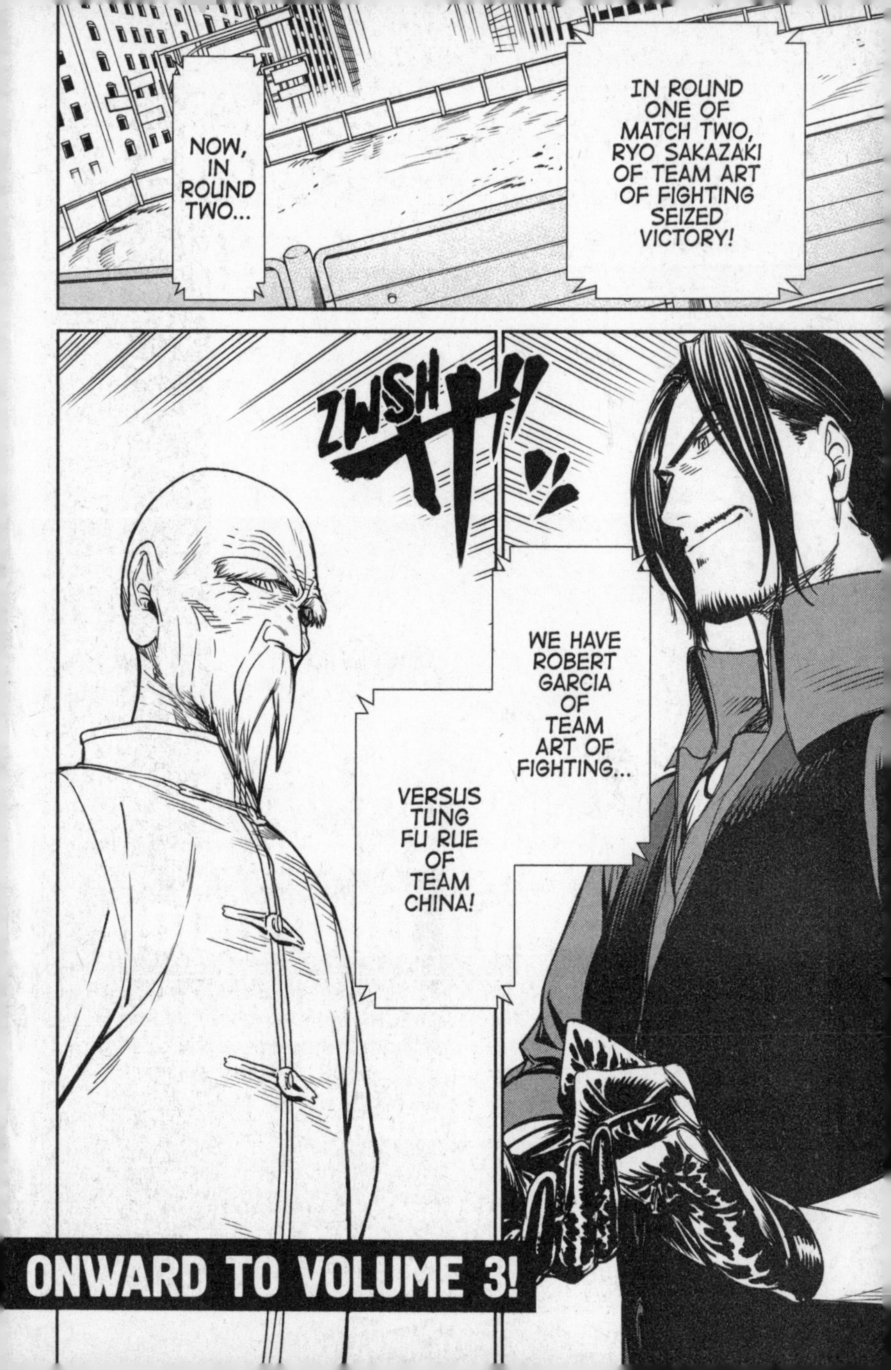
IN ROUND ONE OF MATCH TWO, RYO SAKAZAKI OF TEAM ART OF FIGHTING SEIZED VICTORY!
NOW, IN ROUND TWO...
ZWSH
WE HAVE ROBERT GARCIA OF TEAM ART OF FIGHTING...
VERSUS TUNG FU RUE OF TEAM CHINA!
ONWARD TO VOLUME 3!

MOVE LIST

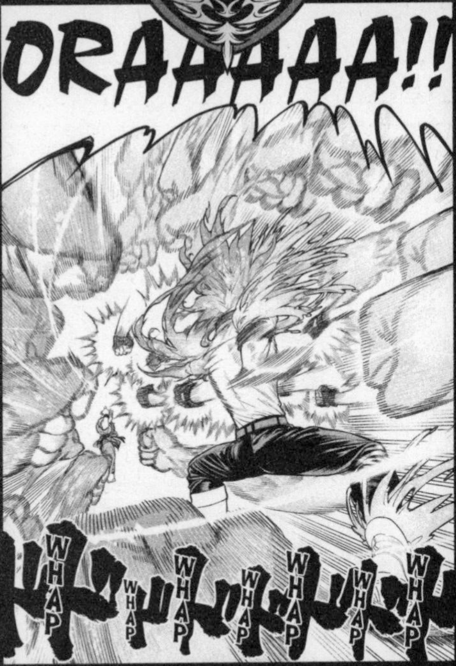
ORAAAAA!!
WHAP
WHAP
WHAP
WHAP
WHAP
WHAP
WHAP

Demolition Dimension

A finisher that pounds the opponent with a barrage of illusory fists. Here, Shun'ei is in a state of materialized illusion, so he is performing the move more recklessly than he does normally.

User: Shun'ei

Command:

→↘↓↙←→↘↓↙←+ LP + HP

MOVE LIST

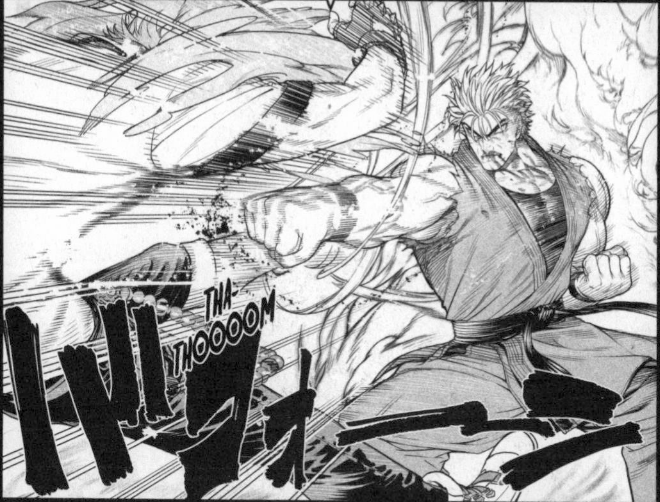
THA-THOOOOM

Shin • Tenchi Haoh Ken

A single, devastating straight punch. It has the power to break through the opponent's guard and take the most massive of adversaries off their feet. Ryo's ultimate arcane distillation of the Kyokugen style.

User: Ryo Sakazaki

Command:
↓↘→↓↘→ + LP + HP

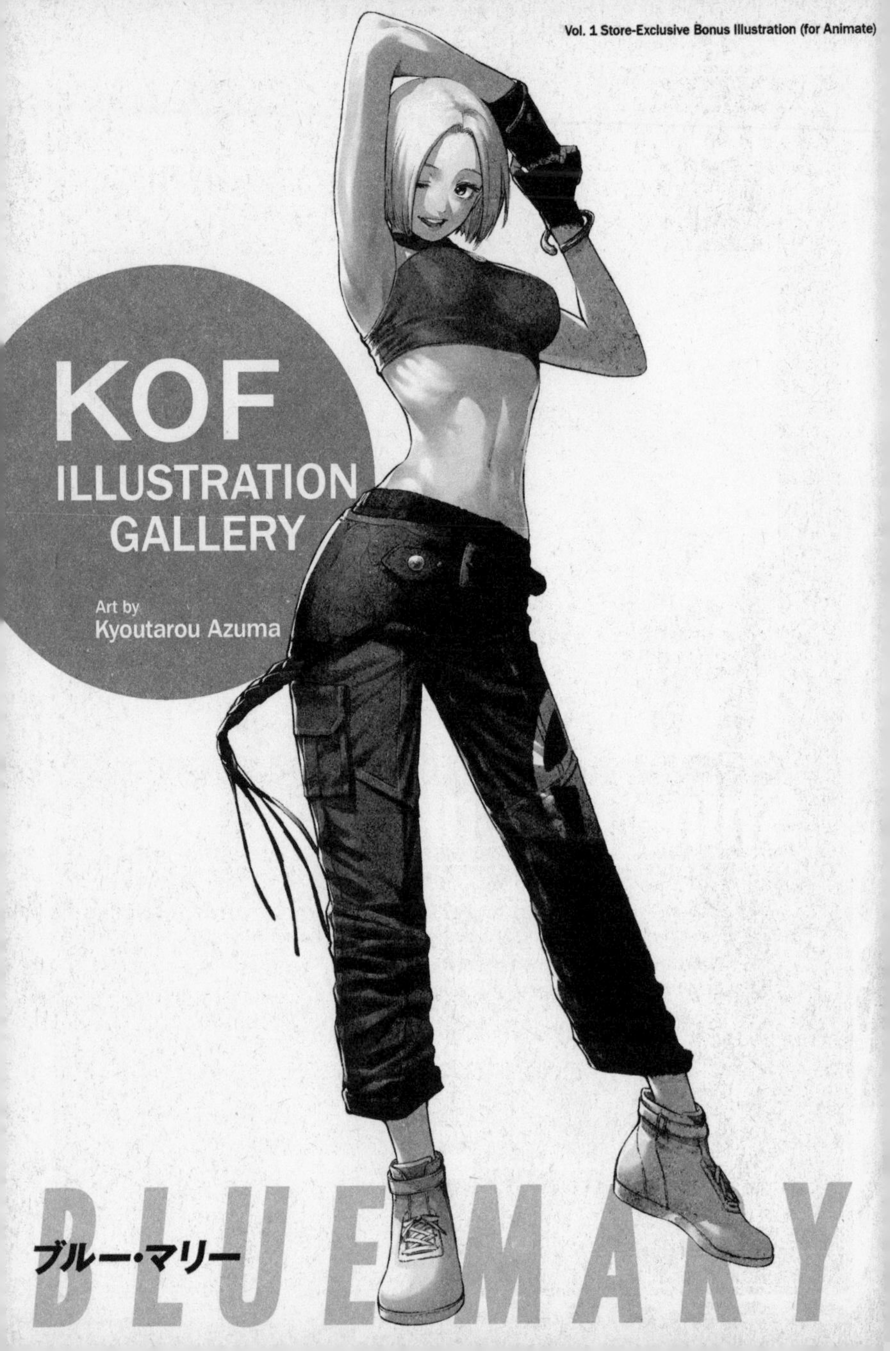
Vol. 1 Store-Exclusive Bonus Illustration (for Animate)
KOF
ILLUSTRATION
GALLERY
Art by
Kyoutarou Azuma
ブルー・マリー
BLUE MARY

Vol. 1 Store-Exclusive Bonus Illustration (for Melonbooks)

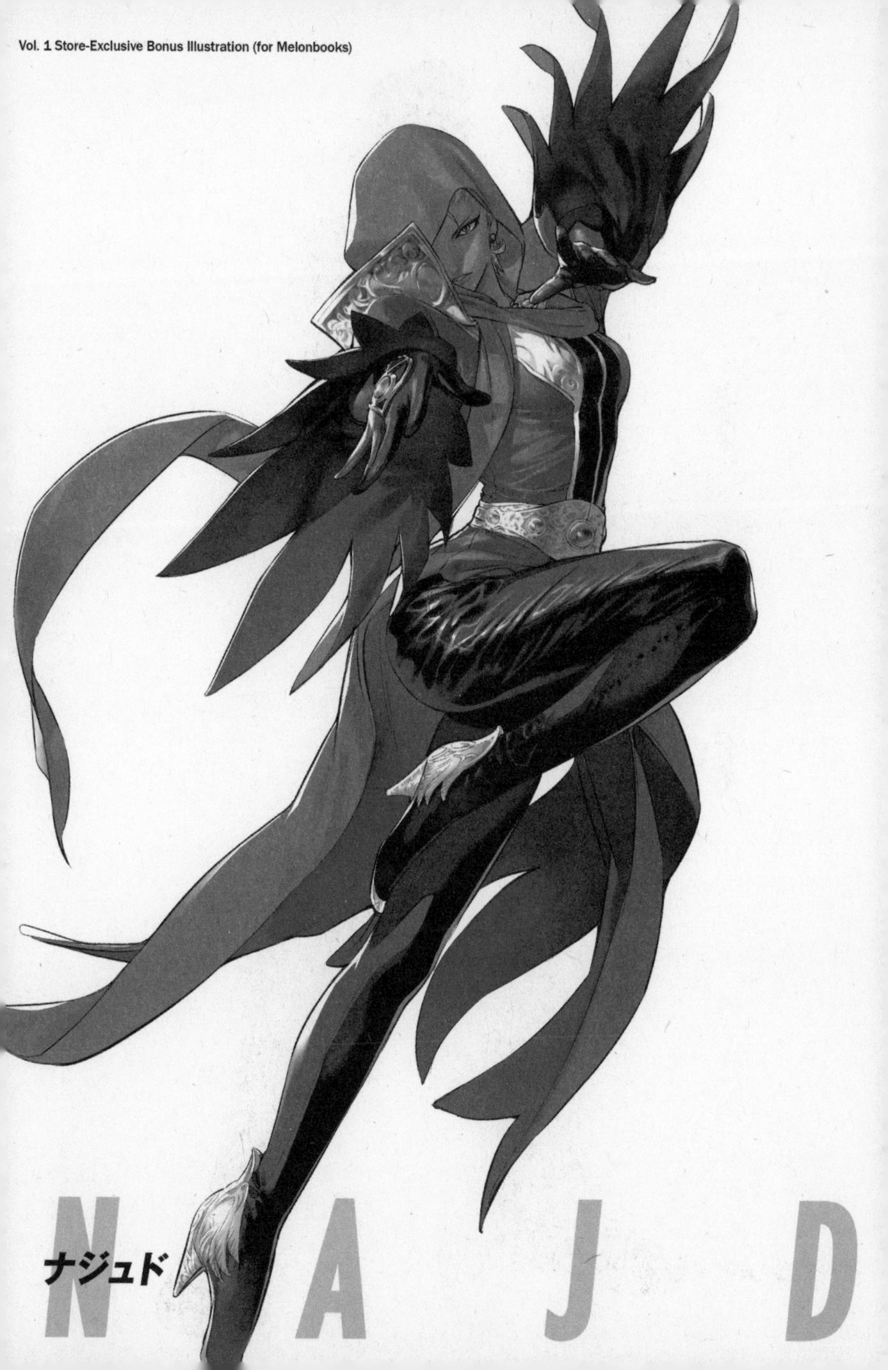
NAJD
ナジュド

Vol. 1 Store-Exclusive Bonus Illustration (for WonderGoo)

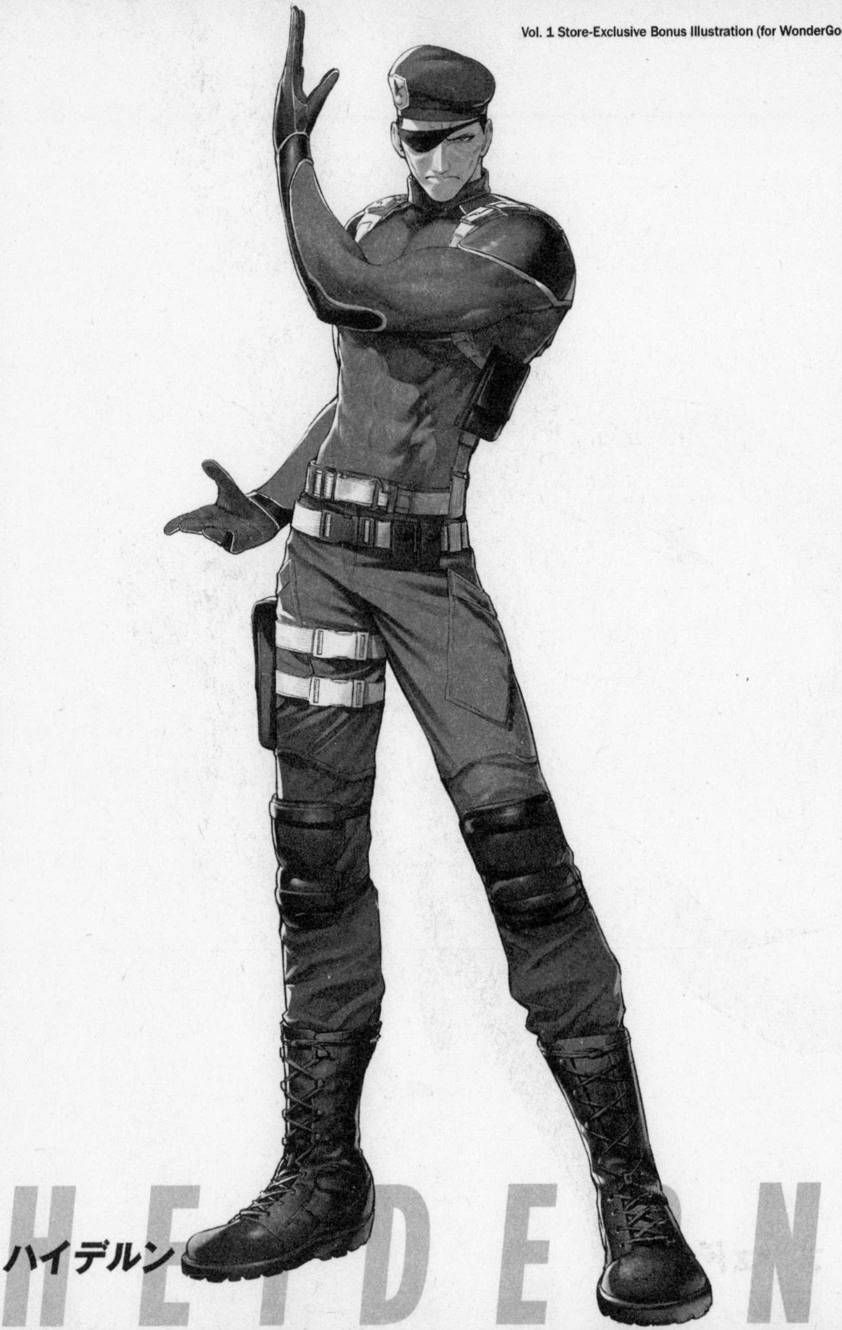
HEIDERN
ハイデルン

SNK Heroines Store-Exclusive Bonus Illustration (for Rakuten Books)

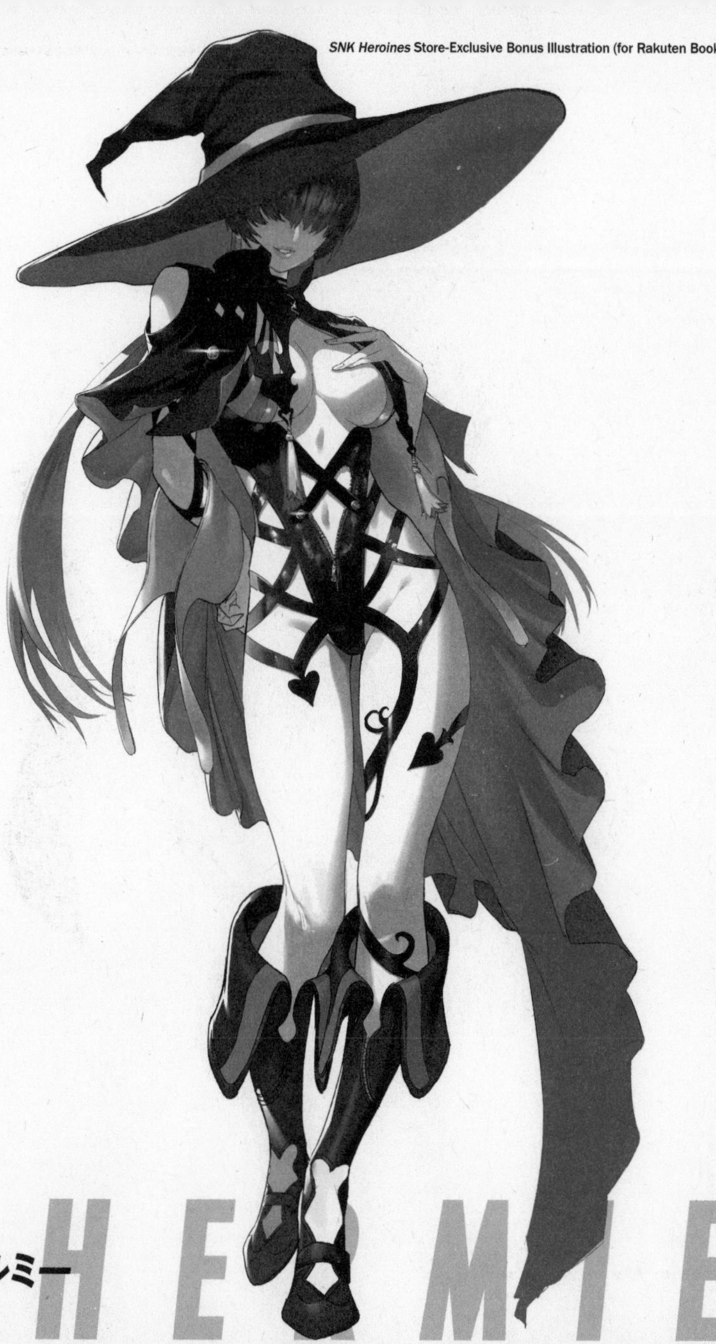

SHERMIE

シェルミー

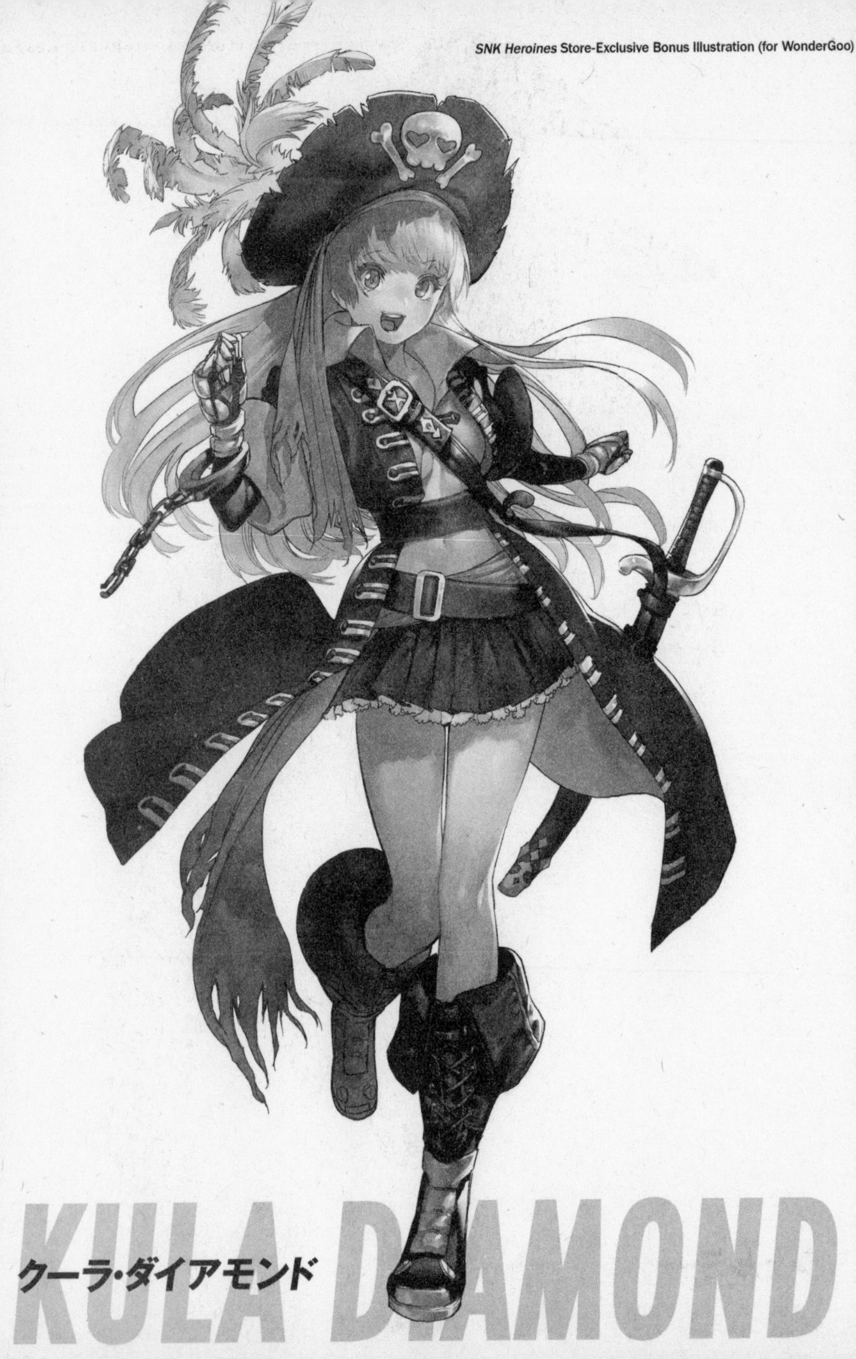
クーラ・ダイアモンド
KULA DIAMOND

SNK Heroines Store-Exclusive Bonus Illustration (for WonderGoo)

SNK Heroines Store-Exclusive Bonus Illustration (for Animate)

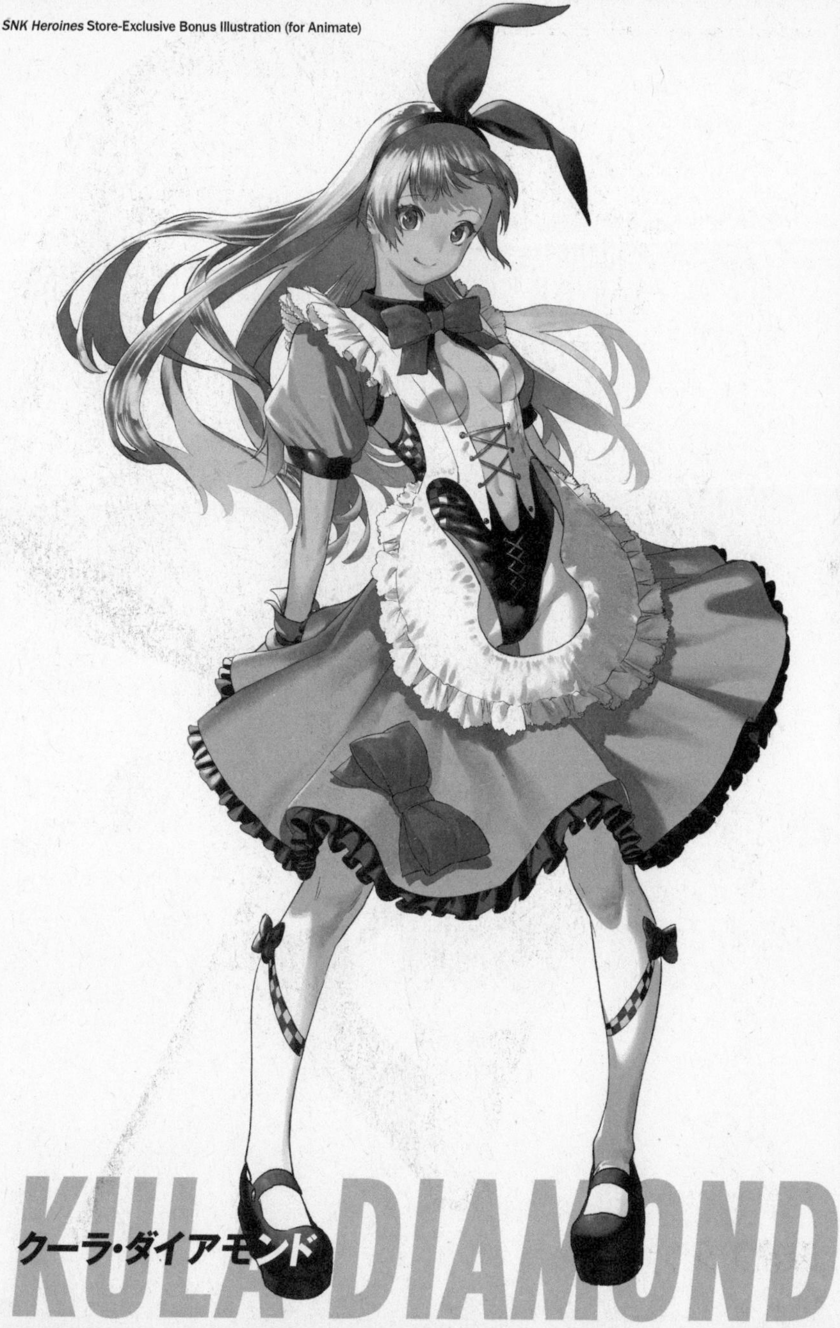
KULA DIAMOND
クーラ・ダイアモンド

SNK Heroines Store-Exclusive Bonus Illustration (for Sofmap)

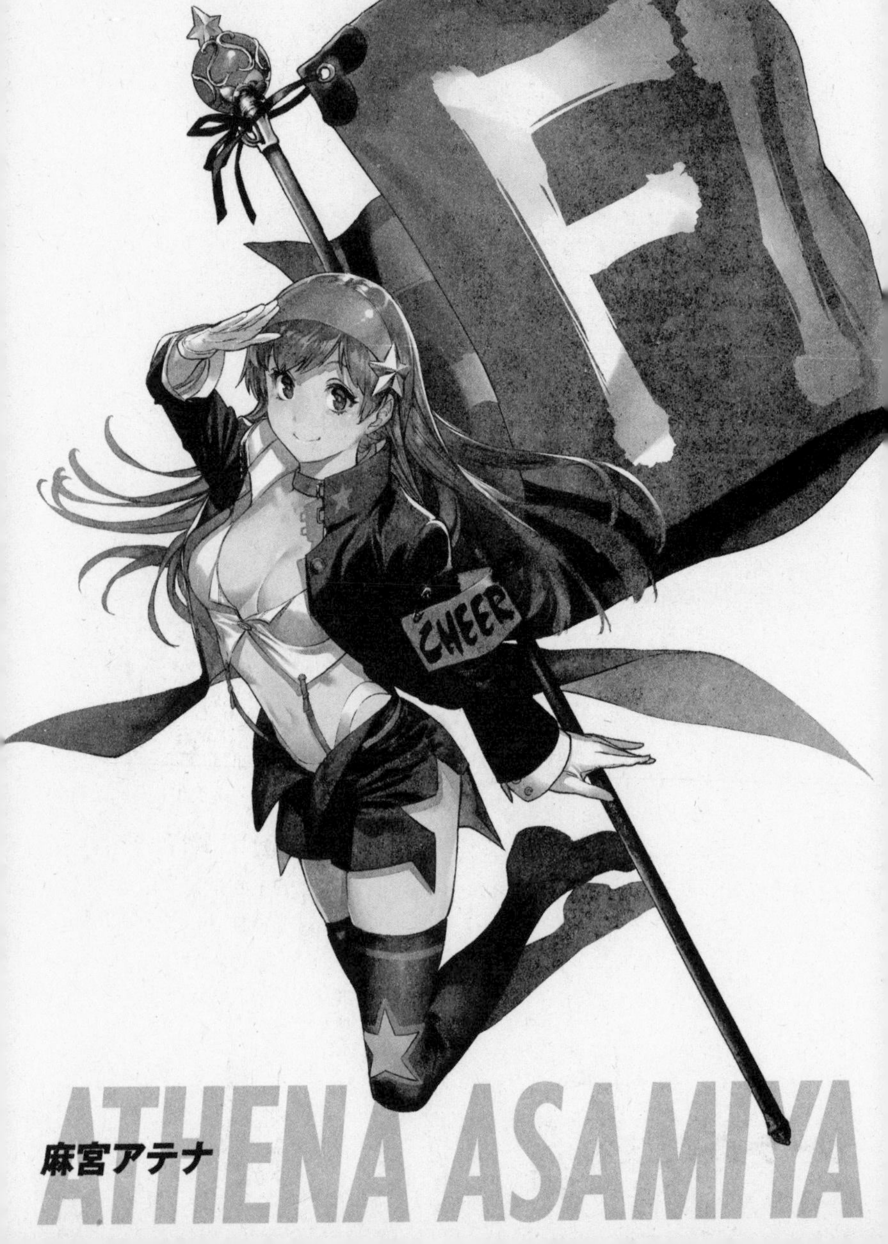
CHEER
ATHENA ASAMIYA
麻宮アテナ

SNK Heroines Store-Exclusive Bonus Illustration (for Geo)

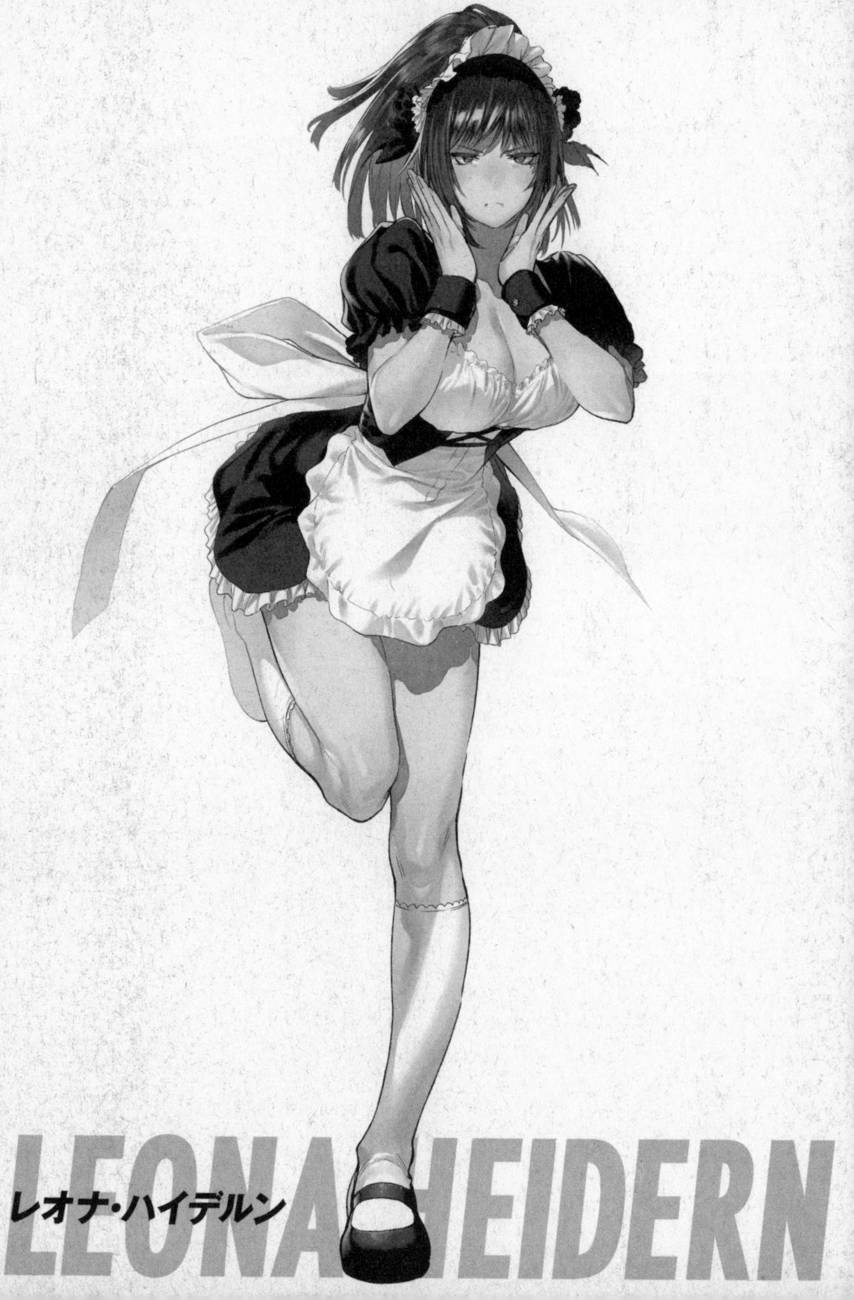
LEONA HEIDERN
レオナ・ハイデルン

THE KING OF FIGHTERS
A NEW BEGINNING

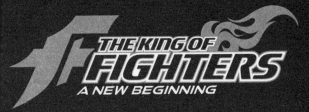

SEVEN SEAS ENTERTAINMENT PRESENTS

THE KING O RS

D0628219

story by **SNK CORPORATION**   art   2

TRANSLATION
Daniel Komen

LETTERING AND RETOUCH
Roland Amago
Bambi Eloriaga-Amago

COVER DESIGN
Nicky Lim

PROOFREADER
Brett Hallahan

EDITOR
J.P. Sullivan

PREPRESS TECHNICIAN
Rhiannon Rasmussen-Silverstein

PRODUCTION MANAGER
Lissa Pattillo

MANAGING EDITOR
Julie Davis

ASSOCIATE PUBLISHER
Adam Arnold

PUBLISHER
Jason DeAngelis

THE KING OF FIGHTERS ~A NEW BEGINNING~ VOLUME 2
© 2019 Kyoutarou Azuma • SNK CORPORATION.
All rights reserved.
First published in Japan in 2019 by Kodansha Ltd., Tokyo.
Publication rights for this English edition arranged through Kodansha Ltd., Tokyo.

Seven Seas press and purchase enquiries can be sent to Marketing Manager
Lianne Sentar at press@gomanga.com. Information regarding the distribution
and purchase of digital editions is available from Digital Manager CK Russell
at digital@gomanga.com.

Seven Seas and the Seven Seas logo are trademarks of
Seven Seas Entertainment. All rights reserved.

ISBN: 978-1-64505-184-8

Printed in Canada

First Printing: April 2020

10 9 8 7 6 5 4 3 2 1

FOLLOW US ONLINE: *www.sevenseasentertainment.com*

READING DIRECTIONS

This book reads from ***right to left***, Japanese style.
If this is your first time reading manga, you start
reading from the top right panel on each page and
take it from there. If you get lost, just follow the
numbered diagram here. It may seem backwards at
first, but you'll get the hang of it! Have fun!!

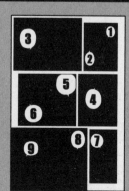